THE TRIALS OF ANTHONY BURNS

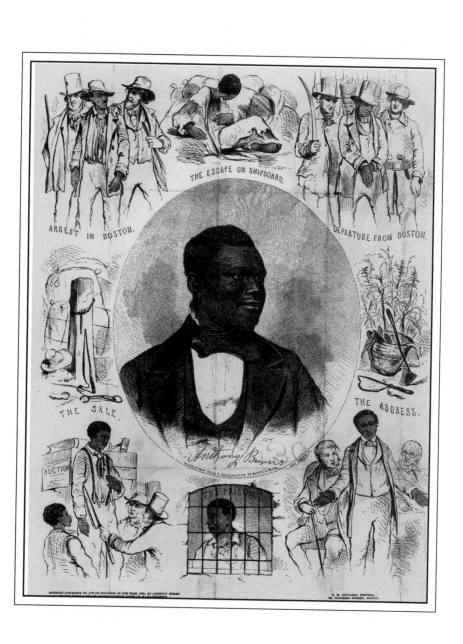

ARREST IN BOSTON.

THE ESCAPE ON SHIPBOARD.

DEPARTURE FROM BOSTON.

THE SALE.

THE ADDRESS.

AUCTION

THE PRISON.

Anthony Burns

ENTERED ACCORDING TO ACT OF CONGRESS, IN THE YEAR 1855, BY ANTHONY BURNS

R. M. EDWARDS, PRINTER,
156 CONGRESS STREET, BOSTON.

THE TRIALS OF ANTHONY BURNS

FREEDOM AND SLAVERY
IN EMERSON'S BOSTON

ALBERT J. VON FRANK

HARVARD UNIVERSITY PRESS
Cambridge, Massachusetts, and London, England

Copyright © 1998 by the President and Fellows
   of Harvard College
All rights reserved
Printed in the United States of America
Second printing, 1999

First Harvard University Press paperback edition, 1999

Library of Congress Cataloging-in-Publication Data

Von Frank, Albert J.
   The trials of Anthony Burns   :   freedom and slavery
in Emerson's Boston / Albert J. von Frank.
      p.   cm.
Includes bibliographical references and index.
ISBN 0-674-03954-8 (cloth)
ISBN 0-674-90850-3 (pbk.)
1. Burns, Anthony, 1834–1862—Trials, litigation, etc.
2. Fugitive slaves—Legal status, laws, etc.—
   Massachusetts—Boston.
3. Antislavery movements—Massachusetts—Boston.
4. Emerson, Ralph Waldo, 1803–1882.
5. Boston (Mass.)—Race relations.   I. Title.
E450.B93V66   1998
973.6'6'092—dc21   97-41957

Designed by Gwen Nefsky Frankfeldt

FOR RICHARD A. HOCKS

CONTENTS

🔥 *ILLUSTRATIONS*

Frontispiece:

Anthony Burns. Broadside. Boston: R. M. Edwards, 1855. Courtesy of the Library of Congress, Department of Prints and Photographs.

Following page 160:

Cover, *The Boston Slave Riot*. Boston: Fetridge and Company, 1854. Courtesy of the Huntington Library.

Ralph Waldo Emerson, 1854. From Emerson, *Complete Works*, vol. 9.

Henry David Thoreau, 1854. Crayon drawing by Samuel Worcester Rowse. Courtesy of Concord Free Public Library, Concord, Mass.

Walt Whitman, July 1854. Engraving by Samuel Hollyer. Frontispiece, *Leaves of Grass* (1855).

Henry Wadsworth Longfellow, June 1854. Crayon drawing by Samuel Lawrence. Courtesy of the National Park Service, Longfellow National Historic Site.

Theodore Parker, 1853. From John Weiss, *Life and Correspondence of Parker*, vol. 1.

Thomas Wentworth Higginson, 1857. From Mary Thatcher Higginson, *Thomas Wentworth Higginson*.

Lewis Hayden. Courtesy of the Boston Athenaeum.

John Greenleaf Whittier, ca. 1855. From Whittier, *Writings*, vol. 3.

Edward Greely Loring. From Warren, *History of Harvard Law School,* vol. 2.

Leonard A. Grimes. From Simmons, *Men of Mark*.

Richard Henry Dana Jr., ca. 1849. From Edward Emerson, *Early Years of the Saturday Club*.

Jerome Van Crowninshield Smith, 1854. From the *Boston Almanac for 1855*.

Map of downtown Boston, ca. 1854. From the *Boston Almanac for 1855*.

Marshal's posse with Burns. From Stevens, *Anthony Burns* (1856).

"Americans to the Rescue!" Broadside. Boston, 1854. Courtesy of the Massachusetts Historical Society.

Twelfth Baptist Church, Southac Street. From Stevens, *Anthony Burns* (1856).

Check for the purchase of Anthony Burns. Courtesy of the Massachusetts Historical Society (Barry Papers).

Anthony Burns, 1855. Courtesy of Oberlin College Archives.

❧ PREFACE

Paradoxical as it may sound, it was in fact under the impact of the Revolution that the revolutionary spirit in this country began to wither away, and it was the Constitution itself, this greatest achievement of the American people, which eventually cheated them of their proudest possession.

—HANNAH ARENDT

The framers of the Constitution meant, with an instrument, to "secure the blessings of liberty," then so recently won, and literally to preserve the spirit of the Revolution in the letter of the law. And yet the creation of a new institutional authority, needful as the expedient clearly was, could not be made entirely consistent with the central idea of the revolutionary document, the Declaration of Independence, that authority rested not in institutions or in charters, but in the people themselves—people who were "created equal."

During the early nineteenth century, even as the American legal system drew power and standing to itself from the Constitution, it reciprocally conferred power on the Constitution, and eminent lawyers like Daniel Webster came to be identified in heroic manner with the towering prestige of that document. It is significant that at what ought to have been the height of his public career (1850–1852), Webster was occupied in a desperate attempt to charge with treason citizens who, in fugitive slave cases, had set the revolutionary principles of the Declaration above the duties imposed by the Constitution. Webster never quite succeeded in formally defining these antislavery protesters as traitors, but a class of men was surely emerging who looked upon the Constitution, with its radical commitment to slavery, as a charter of despotism. A new revolution was opening.

In researching the Anthony Burns fugitive slave case, I was slow—

and, I think, cautious—in coming to the conclusion that the event and its sequel were revolutionary in a strict sense. I was inclined to discount the specific assertions of many of the participants that they were engaged in a revolution, since such claims are, perhaps in most instances, merely self-dramatizing and rhetorical. Then, too, it was hard to credit the existence of a revolution that American historians had never mentioned. It was generally understood that the 1850s were a period of rising sectional tension, political instability, and re-alignment dominated by the slavery issue, but if there was a crisis at this time, it involved the passage of the Kansas-Nebraska Act in 1854, rather than any one slave case or even all of them together.

Still, if one looks away from the national context and examines the Burns case, which set Boston on its ear in the spring of 1854 and made slavery at last unpopular there, what one sees is nothing less than a pocket revolution, operating most dramatically in the context of state politics, yet resonating largely and nationally because Massachusetts was not just any state, but arguably the home of antislavery and the capital of the culture of the North. If the definitional acuity of agitators in the heat of battle is not to be trusted, we can rely more confidently on the insights of a thoughtful historian like Hannah Arendt, whose *On Revolution* offers a cogent and particularized characterization of its subject. In Arendt's view, a revolution occurs when governmental policies are identified not just as despotic, but as simultaneously despotic and unnecessary or revisable. In its initial phase a revolution justifies itself as a return to a preferred older state of things, yet "only where change occurs in the sense of a new beginning, where violence is used to constitute an altogether different form of government, to bring about the formation of a new body politic, where the liberation from oppression aims at least at the constitution of freedom can we speak of revolution." Making allowances for the scale of this revolution in Massachusetts, there is little in Arendt's extended definition that is not pertinent, from the prior "weakening of institutionalized religious beliefs" to the important position of the *"hommes de lettres,"* from the function of property rights as a guarantor of liberty to the belief that political freedom is "the right 'to be a participator in government.'" Above all, as Arendt observes in quoting Condorcet, "the word 'revolutionary' can be applied only to revolutions whose aim is freedom." In proportion as slavery came to be felt as an encroaching form and philosophy of government (as it did most acutely in the Burns case), this liberationist motive was clarified and strengthened. My examination of the evidence convinces me that the Fugitive Slave Law, brought vividly home in a series of cases, was a far greater impetus to revolutionary protest, at least in Massachusetts, than was Kansas-Nebraska—that this was true not only because the slave cases played out before the astonished public gaze, and not only because it gave human faces to good and evil, but because the act for returning "fugitives from labor" became a trope for the tyranny of the legal system and revealed an intolerable stain in the Constitution itself.

The Burns case was at the heart of a revolution that had its own particular Bastille and riot, that toppled a government in Massachusetts, destroyed certain political parties, and extemporized others. This "pocket revolution," as I have called it, owes its qualities of drama and spectacle to its locale, but it demands to be seen as participating in a broader revolutionary impulse that was bent on sacrificing the Constitution to achieve its antislavery aims, and that required in the end a civil war, a series of constitutional amendments, and the reconstruction of the American body politic fully to work its will.

My original motives for examining the Burns case had little enough to do with the conclusions just sketched. Mainly I wanted to know, in as profound and intimate a way as possible, how the liberal, emancipatory ideas I admired in Emerson and his associates comported with or struggled against the social and political fact of chattel slavery. There has been for some time a tendency in academic circles to discount or deplore the social, moral, and ideological implications of Transcendentalism, and to regard Emerson himself as uncommitted to reform or as dissuaded from action by unattractive, privately held racial views. Without trying to shore up Emerson's personal reputation, I wanted to see whether ideas that I thought valuable had in fact any significant social utility when brought to bear on what was without doubt the great moral issue of the American nineteenth century.

I supposed that the best way to arrive at some answers was to linger, for once, over the historical moment, and to understand in such depth and detail as a novelist might command the crisis that brought these ideas to the test. The case of Anthony Burns was self-sufficiently dramatic. I have not had to help it along with inventions or embellishments of my own, but have merely tried to recover the reasons why, in 1854, it held the attention of so many Americans, and at the same time to understand what influences shaped the behavior it evoked. Having read many brief and superficial accounts of slave renditions—hardly more than passing references in the historical literature—I wanted to spend time with such a case, to see how the issues laid themselves out, what kinds of moral demands they made on spectators and principals, and how men and women justified to themselves their connivance with the Fugitive Slave Law or their opposition to it. I had ideas, to be sure, on all these points, but I realized they were entirely secondhand and traditional: none rested on any information I could regard as authentic.

My interest in the slave question as a test of Emersonian Transcendentalism had, I thought, a deeper justification in the bearing each independently had on freedom as a cultural theme. Freedom would inevitably mean different things to Ralph Waldo Emerson and to Frederick Douglass; yet if each failed to see his own position reflected in the statements of the other, some kind of blindness or hypocrisy would have to be involved. Thus there is a mutuality in the subject of this book that I am concerned to work out: if I think that Transcendentalism has been important to our national self-image in certain ways still not fully understood, so equally have race and slavery been. Black and white alike, we are accustomed to think of the African-American presence as that which troubles the dream of whiteness or as "a disrupting darkness," as Toni Morrison put it in *Playing in the Dark*. But it is not mere deconstructive legerdemain to insist that it has at times (and perhaps permanently) been the opposite of this as well, that what is marginalized is always secretly at the center, as when the figure of the fugitive slave—even Anthony Burns—comes into an ironic yet preeminent possession of the core idea of America and complexly represents to the nation the freedom it affirms most noisily and insistently, with flags and rockets and Fourths of July.

Anthony Burns was not a stereotypical slave: he never worked the tobacco fields, and indeed never did any kind of agricultural work. Apart from the fact that his wages seemed always to end up in his master's pocket, the most distinctive feature of his labor history was that it had annually a new chapter. Once he worked in a lumber mill and once in a flour mill, but most often he was a clerk or stock boy in a store in some town or city in eastern Virginia. His last slave job before his escape was one he found for himself, as a stevedore in Richmond. Although he was certainly and continuously exploited, there is no suggestion that he was worked unusually hard. If he was ever beaten, no serious allegation to that effect survives.

Southern apologists might have pointed to the conditions under which Anthony Burns lived and worked as exemplary of one of the milder forms of the peculiar institution. They would surely have gone on to compare his condition with that of a northern laborer, who had no master to see to it that he did not starve and die.

When Burns came to the attention of the abolitionists of Boston, they did not inquire into the conditions of his servitude. They did not propose to make judgments based on degrees of outrageousness, but considered that there was simply no form of slavery they were prepared to see a human being returned to. It was, for them, quite enough that Anthony Burns had been designedly kept poor and ignorant, that he had been systematically deprived of free will and self-determination, and that he now expressed a desire not to be controlled by the man who claimed to own him. Beyond that the details just didn't matter.

There may well be a problem in the abolitionists' indifference to the details, but it is not, I believe, just exactly the problem that Stanley Elkins made out in his 1959 *Slavery*. The great foible of the abolitionists, in Elkins' view, was the unmeasured quality of their response, the moral absolutism that sank the details of every particular case in the abstract, a priori righteousness of antislavery. The problem of abstraction in this context is that it involves one immediately in hard, nonnegotiable positions, invites thunderous Garrisonian ultimatums or intractable regional side-takings of the kind that makes politics and cultural institutions moot and leads in the short run to a destructive intolerance and in the long run to civil war. Elkins' formidable argument centers on the interesting but hypothetical possibility that the "tragedy" of the Civil War might have been avoided if the democratizing impulses of the age of Jackson, abetted by the Transcendentalists, had not subverted the people's faith in practical, coherent, time-honored institutional modes of problem-solving.

And yet the great service rendered by this party of iconoclasts was to show not that institutions should be done away with, but rather that institutions, as they found them in place, were infinitely more apt to establish injustice than justice. A reformer may *look* like an anarchist in some proportion to the corruption of the times. If the people had had a perfect and unshaken faith in their institutions (if the Transcendentalists had never convinced anyone of the value of self-reliance), if they had believed implicitly in the authority of the church, the inerrancy of the Constitution, the Solomonic wisdom of the leader class, what then? Why, then, hypothetically, they would have had slavery forever. It is a remarkable show of faith in institutions on Elkins' part to suppose that the very institutions that supported slavery could in any way be relied on to abolish it. The very best that party politics had ever been able to do with slavery was ineffectually to manage it. Elkins takes it for granted that institutions are a society's only channels of power; because this view leaves no room for genuine writers and intellectuals to operate, he cannot imagine how they *could* function relevantly.

The autobiographers of the antislavery struggle had it essentially right: the corruption of the institutional life could be exposed, condemned, and cured only from a vantage point outside and above it, which is to say from the direction of the ideal and the abstract. Another way to express the point is to say that motives to action had to be found with reference to the "higher law," not the lower. It is nearly impossible to give this proposition the kind of serious hearing I think it deserves against the almost unanimous assertion by historians of an intrinsic connection between idealism and irresponsibility— as though to affirm such a connection were not in itself intrinsically an anti-intellectual gesture. Emerson, for example, is repeatedly faulted by the historians (most prominently Schlesinger, Fredrickson, Elkins, and Rose) for not becoming actively involved in the organized opposition to slavery, with the implication that thinking and writing and speaking must be fraudulent or un-American if the author is unwilling to become embroiled in the associated life of politics. Apart from the usual misunderstanding of the force of ideas and of the power of literature implied in this judgment, there is an underestimated authority in the unmeant, nonpejorative supplement to the "irresponsible" position. Who, after all, sees an evil more clearly—the one responsible for it or the irresponsible one? It is specifically irresponsible to call for the dissolution of the Union merely because the Union is predicated on a foundational agreement to overlook kidnapping. And yet if a reformer does not begin his career this way as a marginal or ridiculous figure, he must remake himself into one. Jesus and Socrates were models here—very outside, very irresponsible.

Historians have been uncannily attuned to the ridiculous in Emerson, rarely, for example, passing up the chance to represent him as advocating "the perfectibility of man." The implication here is that Emerson will petulantly insist on the abolition of slavery because his standards for us are very high. It's not just Emerson with whom otherwise serious scholars will have their fun: Bronson Alcott invariably figures as the lovable visionary who can't tie his shoes, Margaret Fuller as the frustrated American virgin fulfilled in Italy, Thoreau as the crotchety hermit holding off the state with a sprig of huckleberries. The further one moves from the center of Transcendentalism, the less ludicrous and bemused the minor figures get, until at last James Freeman Clarke seems almost normal. It's a very good gauge of how alien and unreadable we still find any form of idealism, however secretly significant our own idealisms, acknowledged or otherwise, may be to us.

Historians keep coming back to the Transcendentalists, however, because they acknowledge that this group, for all its antic quirkiness, was "the closest thing to an intellectual community in the United States" and must therefore have some kind of importance. How to make out that importance, which is felt even by its detractors? In the limited context of the antislavery movement, one might begin by noting the contrast between modern historical assessments of the fatuousness of Transcendental reform and the high estimation in which Emerson was held at the time by abolitionist leaders, and then look a little less at what Emerson said and a little more at the evidence of his influence on the culture of antislavery. One may make a careful survey of Emerson's opinions on the subject and never come close to what it was in his thought that made a difference in the struggle. It can't seriously matter to anyone now living what Emerson's private views were, whether he was a racist or not (the success of antislavery did not depend on the prevalence of modern racial enlightenment), whether he vacillated in his opinions or was consistent, whether he spoke at a certain historic moment or kept his counsel; but we do all have a stake in understanding whether ideas make a difference, whether they have a transactional as distinct from an intrinsic value.

If Emerson is the subject of this book, Anthony Burns is its object. I have tried to express Emerson as plural by finding him in numerous influenced proxies, whom I call, somewhat loosely, "disciples." In representing Anthony Burns as singular, the effort is to resist the temptation, invariably felt by those around him, to see him as a symbol of slaves in general. Whatever was not fantasy in this tendency was fiction. On the contrary, his loneliness and isolation are facts to be respected. The culture was such as to allow Emerson to be almost infinitely reduplicated in others, to live and act through men and women, whom he may, in a sense, be said to have colonized. Not so with Anthony Burns, whose drama was a struggle of unity against nullity. To his enemies, including his owner, he was property; to his friends and defenders (with, I think, only one exception) he was a cause.

Burns's friends were a good deal more right than his enemies, but both their positions were defined in part by accidents of timing. On May 24, 1854, on the very evening that Burns was arrested, Democrats had streamed out of the Custom House, dragged cannons onto Boston Common, and fired off a crashing salute to the Kansas-Nebraska Act, passed that day in Congress. The event in Washington was taken to mean that the Democrats were firmly in control of national policy and that the West would soon be opened to slavery. As nearly as the newspapers can fix the time, both the arrest and the cannonading happened at eight o'clock, so that when the hand of deputy U.S. marshal Asa O. Butman fell from behind on the shoulder of Anthony Burns as he walked home along Brattle Street, a startling noise may have been heard by both men. A sound as of war in the city.

&

I wish to acknowledge the assistance I received while researching this book from the courteous and helpful librarians of the American Antiquarian Society, the Boston Public Library, the Houghton Library of Harvard University, the Library of Congress, the Lloyd House Library in Alexandria, Virginia, the Massachusetts Historical Society, and the Oberlin College Archives, as well as of the Holland Library at Washington State University. Manuscripts owned by the American Antiquarian Society, the Boston Public Library, the Houghton Library of Harvard University, and the Massachusetts Historical Society are quoted here by permission.

I am especially grateful to the American Antiquarian Society and its officers, Ellen S. Dunlap and John B. Hench, for awarding me a

Kate B. and Hall J. Peterson Fellowship and for the six weeks I was thereby enabled to spend with their superb collection of nineteenth-century newspapers and pamphlets. Conversations I had at this time with visiting scholar Barry O'Connell are reflected at various points in this book.

The manuscript, in different degrees of completeness, was read by Alice Randall, Anton Mueller, and Barbara Packer, whom I thank for their helpful criticisms and timely encouragement. I no longer do anything, it seems, without incurring a debt to Joel Myerson, which I trust says as much about his prolific, long-standing generosity as about my tendency to take advantage. Thanks also to Gary Collison and Dean Grodzins for their willingness to answer questions.

The book is very much better than it would otherwise have been for the careful and intelligent reading it got in all its stages from my wife, Jane.

No person held to service or labor in one State, under the laws thereof, escaping into another, shall, in consequence of any law or regulation therein, be discharged from such service or labor; but shall be delivered up on claim of the party, to whom such service or labor may be due.

—U.S. CONSTITUTION, ARTICLE 4, SECTION 2, PARAGRAPH 3

In free society none but the selfish virtues are in repute, because none other help a man in the race of competition.

—GEORGE FITZHUGH, *SOCIOLOGY FOR THE SOUTH* (1854)

✹ THURSDAY, MAY 25, 1854

In the name of the President of the United States of America, you are hereby commanded forthwith to apprehend Anthony Burns, a negro man . . .

WARRANT ISSUED BY E. G. LORING, May 24, 1854

On the north slope of Beacon Hill, in his house at 28 Grove Street, the Reverend Leonard Grimes was up early, with every expectation that the day would be a glorious one. Years of hard work and miraculous fund-raising were to culminate this day in the dedication of his trim new church around the corner on Southac Street. But shortly after 7:30 A.M., someone—probably his deacon, Coffin Pitts—arrived with the news that young Anthony Burns, a new member of the flock, had been arrested as a fugitive slave and was being held at the Court House. Getting as much information as quickly as he could from this messenger, Grimes sent him off to alert the Vigilance Committee, perhaps directing him first to the home of its leader, Theodore Parker. Grimes himself left immediately for Court Square. His first stop was the marshal's office, on the first floor of the austere four-story granite Court House. U.S. Marshal Watson Freeman was annoyed at this sign that knowledge of the case was spreading, but he confirmed that Burns was indeed in custody and that the hearing before Commissioner Loring was about to begin. He gave Grimes, whom he knew, a written permit to enter the courtroom.

Upstairs, Grimes displayed his pass and made his way through a milling crowd of armed guards, locating Burns seated between two deputies toward the front of the room. The high-backed judge's seat was empty. Grimes recognized, off to one side, lawyer Seth J. Thomas, who had made himself notorious in the Sims case in 1851, and before that in the abortive attempt to capture William and Ellen Craft. Clearly, he was determined to be the slave-catcher's lawyer of choice. Among the men seated around Thomas, Grimes noticed one in particular, a large, beefy man with a wispy Van Dyke beard whose clothing and general appearance were to his practiced eye unmistakably Virginian. But the minister's business, as usual, was with the slave, not with the master. He walked directly up to Burns, who turned slightly toward him and smiled wanly in grateful recognition. Grimes saw the heavy iron manacles that bound Anthony's good hand to his broken one, and tried to speak, but the guards interposed. Looking around, Grimes found among the crowd of deputies a man whom he knew and who knew him: the prisoner and his pastor were given leave to speak together, though there was no privacy. Their talk was in a double sense guarded.[1]

Outside the Court House, Richard Henry Dana was walking toward his law office at 32 Court Street. He was approached by a gentleman who told him an escaped slave was then in custody and about to be tried. The news was stunning. No fugitive had seen the inside of a Boston courtroom since 1851, and it had begun to look as though the Fugitive Slave Law might never again be tested there. In a single moment a three-year's growth of confidence in the immunity of Boston was shattered, and Dana, the most prominent lawyer on the Vigilance Committee, knew he would have to act.

He entered the United States courtroom about 8:30, while Grimes and Burns were conferring. He "saw a negro, sitting in the usual place for prisoners, guarded by a large corps of officers." Probably he spoke to Grimes, but his several accounts of the morning's events make no mention of the clergyman. He spoke to Burns but found the prisoner's responses disturbingly unsatisfactory, from both a legal and a personal point of view. Nothing he could gather from the stunned and frightened Burns offered any inkling of a line of defense; indeed, Dana's principal conclusion was that Burns did not want a defense at all, fearful that if he opposed his own rendition it would surely go hard for him back in Alexandria. Dana's personal impression of the prisoner was likewise unfavorable: "He is a piteous object, rather weak in mind and body, with a large scar on his cheek, which looks much like a brand, a broken hand, from which a large piece of bone projects, and another scar on his other hand. He seemed completely cowed and dispirited."[2]

Judge Edward Greely Loring's entrance now required that decisions be made. Dana had just offered to act as attorney for Burns, who had replied forlornly that it was "of no use." "They will swear to me and get me back," he had said; "and if they do, I shall fare worse if I resist." Dana could not have liked to see a defense declined out of a fear of retribution, yet he could not rationally hold out hope of a successful outcome, nor could he, as he felt, further press the matter on a man unwilling to be his client. Yet there was Ned Loring, a familiar figure as Suffolk Country judge of probate, ready to act in his other capacity as U.S. commissioner under the Fugitive Slave Law. Whatever was to be done had to be done now.[3]

What Dana did was strange and uncharacteristic: he went up to Loring and spoke to him privately, urging him not to act hastily and pointing out the prisoner's mental and emotional incapacity. Having apparently received some sort of assurance from Loring, Dana left the courtroom and proceeded to his own office across the street. Before the day was out, he was ashamed enough of this retreat to omit mentioning it in his daily journal, which in fact reads rather heroically. By 8:50 A.M., he had convinced himself that a quiet return of the slave to his owner was the best outcome this bad situation allowed. He knew that the Fugitive Slave Law made no provision for a legal defense, which in any event could not be foisted on an unwilling client. He would have to trust that Edward G. Loring was gentleman enough to administer this intrinsically unjust law with fairness to the hapless fugitive. By 8:55 Dana was pacing and sweating and thinking. Should he have been more insistent? If Burns had made a better personal impression—seemed less childishly cowed and confused—Dana might have found some opening. Perhaps the claimant's papers were not in order (he had mentioned this possibility to Burns). How, Dana asked himself, how could he have left him there defenseless?

Theodore Parker had been alerted at his home at One Essex Place and had set out not for the Court House but for Dana's office, which he reached just before 9:00. He found the lawyer striding back and forth in front of his desk "in considerable agitation."

"What is to become of the man?" asked Parker.

"I suppose he will be sent back as Sims was."

"Where is he?"

"In the courthouse. I just saw him."

"Who is his counsel?"

"He has none."[4]

Dana did not require much argument from Parker to get him

back into the courtroom. They arrived together a few minutes past 9:00. The proceedings had begun. Attorneys Charles M. Ellis and Robert Morris, both members of the Vigilance Committee, were now also among the spectators, having been kept away from the prisoner by the guards. Edward Griffin Parker, the younger of the claimant's two lawyers, was reading some documents into the record—the complaint, the warrant and return, and the record of the Virginia court, which asserted that on May 16 Charles F. Suttle "made satisfactory proof . . . that Anthony Burns was held to service and labor by him, the said Suttle . . . and that the said Anthony has escaped."[5]

By this time Dana had found a seat and was grimly observing the proceedings, while Ellis and Parker were frantic to get the hearing stopped. Alternately they pleaded with Dana to intervene and with Burns to allow a defense. The strategy of the Vigilance Committee had always been to throw every possible obstacle in the claimant's way in order to make slave-catching as expensive and vexatious as possible. Dana calmly explained to Wendell Phillips, who had also arrived, that he had not been formally retained, and that even if his assistance had been asked for, his interference was far more apt to cause pain and suffering to poor Burns than to win a favorable verdict and freedom.[6]

Theodore Parker had heard enough. He went over to Burns and explained that he was, by appointment of the citizens of Boston, minister at large on behalf of fugitive slaves, and asked him if he wanted counsel. Asa Butman, the arresting officer, leaned over across Burns's lap and said, "You may ask him as many times as you are a mind to; you will never get him to have counsel or to make any defence." "Well, Mr. Parker," said the guard on the near side, "it will do no harm to try; and I hope he will." Nevertheless, to Parker's question Burns replied simply that he had already been identified by his owner. "If I must go back, I want to go back as easy as I can."

"But surely, it can do you no harm to make a defence."

"Well," said Burns, uneasy with this pressure, "you may do as you have a mind about it."

Parker conveyed this slender authorization to Dana and urged him on the strength of it to stand as Burns's counsel with Ellis to help. But Dana was still unwilling. Ellis, full of anxiety, felt for his part that he could not act when Dana, a much more distinguished lawyer, held back. In frustration and disgust Parker then said to them both, "If no one else will be his counsel, I will myself."[7]

Meanwhile claimant's counsel had got through the documents and had called their first witness, William Brent, who had come from Virginia with Suttle for the purpose of identifying Burns. He testified for some minutes, indicating that he was a merchant of Richmond; that Suttle, residing in Alexandria, was also a merchant; that he had himself hired Burns from Suttle in 1846, 1847, and 1848; that he now saw Anthony Burns at the bar, and that the slave was missing from Richmond "on or about the 24th day of March last." Brent was about to launch into testimony about a conversation "last night" between the incarcerated slave and his master, when suddenly Dana jumped to his feet and interrupted:

> May it please your Honor: I arise to address the court as *amicus curiae,* for I cannot say that I am regularly of counsel for the person at the bar. Indeed, from the few words I have been enabled to hold with him, and from what I learn from others who have talked with him, I am satisfied that he is not in a condition to determine whether he will have counsel or not, or whether or not and how he shall appear for his defence. He declines to say whether or not any one shall appear for him, or whether he will defend or not.
>
> Under these circumstances, I submit to your Honor's judgment that time should be allowed to the prisoner to recover himself from the stupefaction of his sudden arrest, and his novel and distressing situation, and have opportunity to consult with friends and members of the bar, and determine what course he will pursue.[8]

Dana later said that his strategy was to hear the claimant's prima facie case, relying the while on Loring's privately stated intention not to rule without exploring the question of the prisoner's defense. Theodore Parker emphatically asserted that no such promise existed; that if it had, Dana would surely have mentioned the fact to him during these tense few minutes or during the many hours over the next week that they were together. However that may have been, Dana had recognized, while Brent was speaking, that improper and prejudicial hearsay testimony was about to be introduced and that there was no one to prevent it but himself.[9]

Edward Parker spoke in opposition to Dana's motion, noting that Suttle had come a long way at much expense and was entitled under the law to a speedy disposition of the case. The fugitive, moreover, did not want a defense. "The only object of delay is to try to induce him to resist the just claim which he is now ready to acknowledge." As to the prisoner's state of mind, if Dana meant to suggest that the prisoner was insane and would shortly recover, then Parker would withdraw the objection. "As it is, we do object."[10]

Dana replied to Parker at some length and with his usual tactical shrewdness, insisting in the first place that Burns was not in a state of mind to know what he wanted to do. "Indeed, he has said that he wishes a trial. But I am not willing to act on such a statement as that. He does not know what he is saying." Dana thought in his conversation with Burns that the man's confusion and alarm were signs of a feeble mind and a weak spirit. He was clearly disgusted with the prisoner's inability to bear up under the circumstances, and made no allowance for what the culture of slavery might have done to him. It is possible that in approaching this unknown black man, Dana had in mind—as others surely did—a rather romantic and idealized notion that fugitive slaves were the most enterprising and courageous of the race, that small upper fraction who could value freedom to the point of risking life and limb to obtain it. If such was Dana's thought, Burns fell a good deal short of the mark. Here was no heroic Frederick Douglass, no fighter, nothing but a young, very vulnerable black man half paralyzed by fear. Yet if liabilities of character and want of courage and decision prevented Burns from mounting a defense, these same discouraging traits could at least be used to gain time.

Proceeding with his reply, Dana insinuated that to go on with the hearing would be tantamount to accepting a guilty plea without so much as inquiring into the prisoner's capacity to plead. Referring to a murder case that was then in progress in the Supreme Judicial Court before Chief Justice Lemuel Shaw, Dana noted:

> It is but yesterday that the Court at the other end of the building refused to receive a plea of guilty from a prisoner. The Court never will receive this plea in a capital case, without the fullest proof that the prisoner makes it deliberately, and understands its meaning and his own situation, and has consulted with his friends. In a case involving freedom or slavery, this Court will not do less.[11]

The argument disguised the fact that in proceedings under the Fugitive Slave Law there was no such thing as a "plea" on the part of the prisoner, who indeed was not charged with any crime. From a technical point of view, the commissioner was presiding at a hearing for the recovery of personal property, and the property in question was not obliged to enter a plea—was in fact debarred from addressing the court at all. Thus the considerable force of Dana's argument was rhetorical, arising from the analogy with a criminal proceeding. The argument seemed to humanize the property in controversy; it sought to give to the prisoner a whole array of rights, remedies, and legal protections traditional in criminal trials but utterly unenvisioned in the Fugitive Slave Law. Already what was "meant" to be an action for recovery of property was turning into a contest between the fiction that Burns was a citizen of Massachusetts and the fiction that he was something owned by a man from Virginia. Both fictions had their problems, as events would show.

Commissioner Loring, evidently following Dana's earlier hint, called Burns up to the bench and, as Dana recalled it, "told him what his rights were, and asked him if he wished for time to consider what he would do. The man made no reply and looked round bewildered, like a child." Loring then asked him to whom, if to anyone, he had spoken since his arrest; Burns, flustered, answered that he had been allowed to speak to no one but "my master" and to one other. Dana, who did not record this exchange, noted that Loring once more "asked him if he would like to have a day or two and then see him there again." Burns's reply, hovering between thought and speech, was inaudibly soft.

"I understand you to say you do." The sentence was pronounced loudly by the judge, who, though addressing Burns three feet in front of him, had to talk past him to the entire room.

"I do," said the prisoner.

"You shall have it," declared the commissioner, who then ordered a delay until Saturday.

Before Loring could adjourn, however, Marshal Freeman approached the bench and whispered something to the judge. Loring answered him audibly: "No, Sir, he must have the time necessary." More whispering from Freeman. "I can't help that, Sir, he shall have the proper time."[12]

But for Loring's commitment to lecture to his class at Harvard Law School on Friday, the delay might well have been shorter. But for Dana's motion, as Phillips, Parker, and Ellis all were convinced, Burns would have been remanded into Suttle's custody before the midday meal.

✺ GRAPPLING

If Anthony Burns escaped for want of handcuffs, distinguished men would be mortified.

JOHN WEISS

It was cool and damp under an overcast sky when the commissioner's court adjourned. Burns was handcuffed again and led upstairs to the spare, unfurnished jury room where he had been held and which he would share now, round the clock, with no fewer than four of Freeman's "specials." Theodore Parker remained in the courtroom to count the guard that had been assembled: he made it sixty-five. Before he finished the tally Loring had left the bench and headed across the hall to the law library. There, in casual conversation with a professional acquaintance, he was asked why he had granted the continuance. He answered that he had done it solely to mollify Dana and Ellis. The only question they could possibly raise was that of Burns's identity, and such a tactic seemed fruitless against conclusive evidence. Loring had no doubt but that he should be obliged to send the man back. The conversation was overheard by a man named Edward Avery, who repeated it a year later before a committee of the state legislature.[1]

It rained most of that afternoon. Members of the Vigilance Committee had been gathering since early in the morning as they were individually notified or as they accidentally heard of the case. There had been no news of it in the morning papers. Dr. Henry I. Bowditch was informed early and joined the meeting at the office of the New England Antislavery Society at 21 Cornhill, the same building that housed Garrison's *Liberator*. "The committee," he recalled, "kept in permanent session during the day." The meeting was disorganized by the stream of late arrivals and by the absence at court of key members of the Executive Committee; what was known about the case was rehearsed over and over again among small knots of men who talked and plotted among themselves.

After Parker and Phillips arrived, the Executive Committee met apart. They were generally agreed that the case of Thomas Sims in 1851 had shown that legal stratagems might provide delay but not deliverance. That Loring would in the end remand Burns was a virtual certainty, and so it seemed inevitable that they should discuss a rescue. This, then, would be a main topic when the committee of the whole met in the afternoon. Only a few preliminary measures were agreed upon at once: that they would convene in the more spacious Meionaon Hall at Tremont Temple; that a petition would be drawn up to secure Faneuil Hall for a mass indignation meeting on Friday night, and that handbills would be printed and distributed to alert and stir the public.[2]

Bronson Alcott, who was then living at 20 Pinckney Street, Boston, rather than in Concord, was present at this morning meeting, trying to get all the information he could, knowing that he had to travel that afternoon to Worcester to give one of his "Conversations." While there he would spread the news of the Boston slave case, and particularly inform the man who had arranged for his talk, Thomas Wentworth Higginson, one of the few members of the Boston Vigilance Committee not resident in the city. A number of Committee members were anxious to have Higginson informed. Samuel May Jr., Boston merchant and kinsman of Alcott's wife, wrote to Higginson that morning from the meeting. Alcott carried the letter with him to Worcester:

> 21 Cornhill, Boston
> Thursday May 25th
>
> Dear Mr. Higginson,—Last night a man was arrested here as a fugitive Slave. Master is here from Virginia. Case bro't before Commissioner Loring this morng. at 9 o'clock, and by him adjourned to *Saturday* at 9 o'clock.
>
> We have called a public meeting at Faneuil Hall for tomorrow (Friday) evening, at which we want to see Worcester well represented. Give all the notice you can. The friends here are wide awake and unanimous. Vigilance Committee meet this afternoon. The country must back the city, and, if necessary, lead it. We shall summon all the country friends.
>
> Bowditch says you'll come if your health allows. Come strong.
>
> It is thought the City Government will not act,—any way.
>
> 'Tis said, the man in private expressed willingness to go back, but not in public. In haste, Yours
>
> S. May, Jr.

Wendell Phillips also wrote to Higginson, saying, "you'll *come* of course," signing it, "in no hope."[3]

Phillips may have had no hope, but he was certainly a leader in planning the Faneuil Hall meeting, at which he would be one of the principal speakers. He and Parker headed the 158 signers of the hurriedly prepared petition for the use of the hall, and it was he who presented it that afternoon to a regularly scheduled meeting of the City Council. Alderman George F. Williams, noting "the gross outrage committed in this city last evening," moved for unanimous consent. That the motion passed so easily gave the petitioners reason to believe that city officials—and Mayor J. V. C. Smith in particular—were sympathetic. In fact, while certain of the aldermen were strongly opposed to the Fugitive Slave Law, there were equivocators and doughfaces among them, including the mayor.[4]

Requests for the use of Faneuil Hall were not always granted, though the city usually paid a heavy political price for refusing. In 1837 it had denied access to citizens wishing to protest the murder in Alton, Illinois, of the abolitionist editor Elijah P. Lovejoy. At that time the great Unitarian preacher William Ellery Channing rose up to make the government feel the force of his moral authority. The city backed down, and Wendell Phillips' speech in the meeting that followed launched his career as an antislavery orator. More recently the hall had been denied to Daniel Webster, who had sought its use to explain and defend his stunning Seventh of March speech, in which he had embraced the Compromise of 1850 and endorsed the Fugitive Slave Law. Shortly thereafter, during a Boston reception for Millard Fillmore, the aggrieved senator ostentatiously failed to recognize the mayor and his party of city officials, who never did get to meet the president.[5]

The first of the Vigilance Committee handbills was printed, making no mention as yet of Friday's meeting.

KIDNAPPING
AGAIN!!
A MAN WAS STOLEN LAST NIGHT BY THE
Fugitive Slave Bill COMMISSIONER!
HE WILL HAVE HIS
MOCK TRIAL
ON SATURDAY, MAY 27, AT 9 O'CLOCK,
In the Kidnapper's 'Court,' before the Hon. Slave Bill Commissioner,
AT THE COURT HOUSE, IN COURT SQUARE.
SHALL BOSTON STEAL ANOTHER MAN?

Thursday, May 25, 1854.[6]

Another handbill, undoubtedly produced the same day, links the Burns case to the passage of the Nebraska Bill:

CITIZENS OF BOSTON!
A Free Citizen of Massachusetts—Free by Massachusetts Laws until his liberty is declared to be forfeited by a Massachusetts Jury—is
NOW IMPRISONED
IN A
MASSACHUSETTS TEMPLE OF JUSTICE!
The Compromises, trampled upon by the Slave Power when in the path of Slavery, are to be crammed down the Throat of the North.
THE KIDNAPPERS ARE HERE!
Men of Boston! Sons of Otis, and Hancock, and the "Brace of Adamses"!
See to it that Massachusetts Laws are not outraged with your consent.
See to it that no Free Citizen of Massachusetts is dragged into Slavery,
WITHOUT TRIAL BY JURY! '76![7]

Samuel Gridley Howe, coming in from his Massachusetts Asylum for the Blind in South Boston, arrived late at the morning meeting; by the time he was brought up to speed, Parker and the rest of the Executive Committee had left. Howe had been active in antislavery since 1845 and the controversy over Texas annexation; in 1846, spurred by a fugitive slave case, he had presided over the forty members of the first Boston Vigilance Committee. Now fifty-three years old, he was still living up to the swashbuckling reputation he had given himself in his youth when he and Lord Byron had fought against the Turks for Greek independence. Today, as ever, Howe was eager for action, impatient with half-measures, impatient with talking. Concerned that a large demonstration such as the Faneuil Hall meeting would put the marshal and his men on alert and make a rescue more difficult, he went to Parker's home with a quickly extemporized plan. Failing to find Parker, he left a note:

My dear P.: I have come to see you:—no public meeting I think, but a band of fifty, to say the man shall not go out into slavery, but over our bodies:—of the fifty one is

S. G. H.[8]

The afternoon session was held at the Meionaon, the smaller of two assembly halls at Tremont Temple. Captain Austin Bearse, the Committee's doorkeeper, checked off names as members and a few vouched-for guests arrived through the drizzle and chill. Such precautions were necessary because all the activities of the Committee were proscribed by the Fugitive Slave Law and members were liable to heavy fines and imprisonment. Daniel Webster had been sure that such activity was treasonous, though his view of the matter (still perhaps a majority opinion in Boston) had as yet to be sustained in a court of law.

Howe contended for his plan that afternoon against those who preferred a night attack on the Court House, against those who wanted a mass assault, and against those who rejected violent means altogether. His idea was that a group of forty or fifty men would go to the marshal in broad daylight and demand that Burns be turned over to them; they were to be prepared, in the event of a refusal, then and there to rescue the fugitive at all hazards. Among those who volunteered to go with him was Albert Gallatin Browne, erstwhile mayor of Salem and member of the Governor's Council during the administration of Democrat George S. Boutwell.[9]

But Howe's plan was voted down. The majority preferred to await Loring's decision, and then, if it was adverse, to block the rendition with large crowds of determined bodies and to hurry Burns off in the confusion. The fact that this plan, though favored by the majority, was not adopted either only demonstrated the difficulty with which a committee of more than 200 is brought into agreement on anything. Howe desperately longed for the efficiency of the lean old Committee of 1846. Under the circumstances, the only course of action generally supported was simply to watch and wait as events developed, and particularly to see how the Committee might (or might not) be supported by the public at tomorrow's Faneuil Hall meeting.

One immediate concern was that Loring might decide that Burns was not after all entitled to a defense, hold a secret nighttime session, and deliver him up without opposition. This fear was well grounded, since that is precisely what had happened in the case that had occurred just the night before in New York City, where three Maryland slaves—the brother and two nephews of the Rev. James W. C. Pennington, himself a celebrated fugitive slave—had been remanded in a late-night judicial end run. It was therefore determined that the Boston Court House would be kept under continual surveillance.

That job was given to a group of black volunteers who were not members of the Committee.[10]

Harriet Beecher Stowe and her husband had come to Boston from their home in Andover to attend a number of the religious meetings scheduled for this anniversary week. Curiously (and some people remarked on the curiosity of it), Mrs. Stowe offered no comment on the case of Anthony Burns, then or later. Having made herself preeminently the voice of conscience in regard to slavery by means of her spectacular *Uncle Tom's Cabin* (1852) and her polemical *Key to Uncle Tom's Cabin* (1853), still she was uncomfortable with her public role and reluctant to forgo the privileges and immunities of a guarded domesticity. She was (and knew it) a brilliant parvenu, moving ill-equipped and uneasily among the antislavery vanguard, and so she chose as much as possible to work behind the scenes in more familiar contexts. Yet the power conferred on her by her celebrity was formidable, and it pressed her, often against her will, into the public sphere. She was, for example, directly responsible for what both senators from Massachusetts were doing this Thursday, May 25, 1854.

In February, as debate on the Nebraska Bill began in Congress, Mrs. Stowe swung into action, composing her "Appeal to the Women of the Free States." On February 23, the same day her essay was published in the New York *Independent,* she wrote to Charles Sumner to say that she had organized a petition drive among the New England clergy, opposing the bill. She was in fact devoting part of her *Uncle Tom* income to this effort. She hoped the petition would be ready for presentation to the Senate "by the 7th of March," the potently symbolic anniversary of Webster's defection.[11] Eventually 3,050 ministers signed the protest:

To the Honorable the Senate and House of Representatives,
in Congress assembled:
   The undersigned, clergymen of different religious denominations in New England, hereby, in the name of Almighty God, and in His presence, do solemnly protest against the passage of what is known as the Nebraska Bill, or any repeal or modification of the existing legal prohibitions of slavery in that part of our national domain which it is proposed to organize into the territories of Nebraska and Kansas. We protest against it as a great moral wrong, as a breach of faith eminently unjust to the moral principles of the community, and subversive of all confidence in national engagements; as a measure full of danger to the

peace and even the existence of our beloved Union, and exposing us to the righteous judgments of the Almighty: and your protestants, as in duty bound, will ever pray

Boston, Massachusetts, March 1, 1854[12]

The petition—all 200 feet of it—arrived in Washington on March 14, ten days after the initial vote in the Senate approving the Nebraska Bill. For tactical reasons it was introduced by men not closely identified with the antislavery struggle—that is, not by Sumner in the Senate, but by his colleague, Edward Everett, and by William Appleton, a Cotton Whig, in the House. Everett's handling of the matter was, to put the best construction on it, hurried and perfunctory; some would suggest that it was stunningly naive. He was, in any event, entirely unprepared for the furious outburst that followed from partisans of the bill, and especially from Stephen Douglas, who did not care to have matters of state commented on by a horde of meddling "political preachers." Dazed by this unexpected result, and by the vituperation unloaded on the clergy of his native region, Everett virtually apologized for having brought the matter up at all, noting that he had scarcely had a chance to read the petition.[13]

Everett was already under a terrific cloud for having missed the vote on the Nebraska Bill on the morning of March 4, pleading indisposition on that occasion and saying that had he been there he would have voted against it, as he had earlier voted against it in committee. Such statements made little headway against the loud denunciations and charges of cowardice and time-serving that filled the antislavery press. The matter of the petition was yet another fiasco, another indication of personal weakness that laid him open to a second wave of withering criticism. Dana supposed that Everett was paralyzed by a desire to avoid offense. It was said on the streets of Boston that the senator "did not have the backbone to be a deacon in a church." Quiet and scholarly by nature, hating contention, and painfully sensitive about his collapsing reputation, Everett resigned his seat on May 12 and returned home to Boston, physically and emotionally spent. His own political incompetence gave him a character that he probably did not deserve. Emerson, who years earlier had idolized him for his oratory, said now that though he "is ornamental with liberty & dying Demosthenes . . . when he acts, he comes with the planter's whip in his buttonhole."[14]

On May 25, when Anthony Burns was arraigned, Everett was at his home on Summer Street immersed in Victor Cousin's translation of Plato's *Republic.* The papers that day speculated about the choice of his successor.[15]

In Washington, Mrs. Stowe's petition had not been lost sight of. Sumner, angered and embarrassed by Everett's performance, seized on some lately added names as a pretext to reintroduce it. The petition formed the nominal basis for the speech delivered on May 25 and published as his *Final Protest for Himself and the Clergy of New England against Slavery in Kansas and Nebraska.* He more than suggested that Senator Andrew P. Butler of South Carolina, Senator James M. Mason of Virginia, and Senator Douglas of Illinois could profitably be instructed in manners, morals, and wisdom by the free-state clergy. The infamous Nebraska Bill, he went on to say, conceding its final approval, had one thing to recommend it: that by repealing the Missouri Compromise, it "makes all future compromises impossible. Thus it puts Freedom and Slavery face to face, and bids them grapple. Who can doubt the result?"[16]

Harriet Beecher Stowe, together with circumstances she might have only dimly foreseen, had in effect put Northern ministers face to face with Southern politicians. Neither group was inclined to retreat, but the repeal of a fundamental sectional agreement in the Missouri Compromise had withdrawn a basis for mutual action and understanding. Much that had been regarded as settled—and well settled, and settled for thirty-four years—was now suddenly up in the air. Everything had to be reexamined apart from the old premises, and grappling was to be the order of the day.

🌿 FRIDAY, MAY 26

Slave. 1. A person who is wholly subject to the will of another. 2. One who has lost the power of resistance; or one who surrenders himself to any power whatever. 3. A mean person; one in the lowest state of life. 4. A drudge; one who labors like a slave.

NOAH WEBSTER, *AN AMERICAN DICTIONARY OF THE ENGLISH LANGUAGE* (1847)

Apparently no one made an effort to see Burns in his place of confinement after the abbreviated hearing on Thursday morning. Phillips and Parker were busy with the Vigilance Committee, while Dana was trying to be unobtrusive. If anyone sought out the prisoner it would have been Leonard Grimes, but the marshal had decided that until Burns had an attorney, no one but Dana had any right of access.

On Friday morning, however, the Reverend Grimes, Deacon Pitts, and Wendell Phillips came to the Court House to learn whether Burns would consent to have a defense. Freeman, obviously worried about an escape, was in a truculent mood and would allow no one to talk to the prisoner. Not even an order from Judge Loring, he said, would get them in. The three men left immediately to consult with Dana, who felt certain the judge would issue the order; he advised them to apply for it and test the marshal's resolve. Probably he thought that Freeman was simply bluffing, but the more intriguing possibility was that the marshal had determined to serve the interests of Franklin Pierce, who had appointed him, rather than take orders from a slave-law commissioner, whose position in the structure of the federal judiciary was admittedly a little vague.[1]

It was determined that Phillips would pursue Loring to Cambridge to get the order; he carried a note from Dana explaining why it was impossible that he (Dana) should see the prisoner.

Loring was teaching his regular Friday class at the Law School, where for the past two years he had held a lectureship at an annual salary of $1,000. His appointment to that post, newly created in February 1852, had excited much surprise at the time, especially as an effort to increase his salary as Suffolk County probate judge had failed a short time before. The public was inclined to suppose that all Lorings were in the natural course of things comfortably situated, yet at age fifty-two, with seven children to support, this particular Loring would pay conspicuous attention to his income. The fact that his wife came from a wealthy family did not lessen his expenses.[2]

If the manner of his getting the Harvard lectureship raised eyebrows, Loring had temporarily succeeded in beating down any suspicion of unfitness by becoming popular with his students and, yet more pertinently, with his colleagues, Joel Parker and Theophilus Parsons, who together made up the entire Law School faculty. At the instigation of Parker and Parsons, the Harvard Corporation voted in December 1853 to create a third Professorship of Law at a salary of $2,500 and to appoint Edward Greely Loring to fill it. This maneuver, however, was blocked by Harvard's Board of Overseers on the basis of an adverse internal report prepared in March 1854 by Francis Bassett, a recently retired justice of the Supreme Judicial Court. Bassett's report made much of the heavy work load of a probate judge, noting that 4,000 deaths occurred annually in Suffolk County and that assets worth $7–10 million went each year through his court. Yet beneath the obvious concern about the time Loring would have to devote to his Harvard duties there were discreetly muted suggestions that he was simply not a good enough lawyer. The report conceded, for example, that Joseph Story had held two jobs: "but Judge Story was an extraordinary man." Political motives were also at work: although Loring's responsibilities as a commissioner under the Fugitive Slave Law went unmentioned, Bassett must have been aware that Loring had written a series of articles in the *Daily Advertiser* defending that law at the time of its passage. The report did allude, however, to the fact that "the judge of probate has jurisdiction of questions deeply affecting personal liberty," principally in guardianship matters. The implication was that no one who had professional charge of other people's personal liberties ought to be distracted by the demands of a regular Harvard professorship.[3]

And yet that responsibility seemed to rest lightly enough as Edward G. Loring entered the lecture hall on the morning of May 26—rested lightly, perhaps, for the last time, for he was unexpectedly greeted "with a storm of hisses, and other marks of disapprobation" from a roomful of normally genial and placid young lawyers-in-training. The demonstration became more raucous still when the Southern students—always a large contingent at the Law School—countered with cheers.[4]

Phillips found Loring in his second-floor office. The judge, expressing some doubts about his authority to compel the marshal, wrote out a note to Freeman requesting, as though it were a personal favor to himself, that the prisoner be allowed visitors. No sooner had he finished, however, than he tore up the note and recast it in the form of an order. Handing the document across his desk, Loring said, in a confiding and helpful tone, "Mr. Phillips, the case is so clear that I do not think you will be justified in placing any obstacles in the way of this man's going back, as he probably will."[5]

On his way out of the building, Phillips met an acquaintance, Charles Grafton, who was anxious to know what the chances were that Burns would be discharged. He answered that it was unlikely, as the judge had just told him that the evidence, in his opinion, was irresistible. Phillips seems to have received Loring's statement at first as an all too realistic assessment of the probabilities—one that he himself shared; but by the time he arrived back in Boston he had decided that the remark was disturbing, perhaps outrageous—evidence of flagrant bias and prejudgment.[6]

While Phillips discussed the case with Dana (not forgetting to comment at length on Loring's advice), Grimes and Pitts, who had been waiting at Dana's office for Phillips' return, went over to the Court House and were admitted before noon to the converted jury room. What Grimes saw appalled him: there was Burns engaged in writing a letter at the dictation of one of the guards—a letter addressed to Suttle. Its purpose, from a certain point of view, was conciliatory. It was meant to assure Suttle that he, Burns, had never said that Suttle was a hard master—that if such a rumor had got around, as the guards told him it had, he was not the source of it. But Grimes saw its purpose from another point of view and told the guard, simply: "You know better than that." He directed Burns to get the letter back and destroy it, which, with some difficulty, and perhaps with some mortification and amazement, he did. He tore it up. Small bits of paper fluttered down from the barred window high on the west side of the fortresslike building. The pieces fell among the granite cobbles of the street under the routine work-week traffic of Court Square in the very center of the capital of Massachusetts, 400 miles, it was supposed, from any place where a slave addressed words to his master.[7]

Then Wendell Phillips arrived, and after a brief interview Burns gave a power of attorney, authorizing his friends, in the words of the defense's first press release, "to do everything in [their] power to save him from going back to slavery."[8]

"Back to slavery?"

The first statement issued by the authorized agents of "the alleged fugitive" (as he was now carefully called) incautiously implied that he had been a slave at some time in the past. His "identity" was the only legal issue in the commissioner's purview, the only thing the claimant had to prove, and here was the defense fashioning an identity for public consumption predicated on a slave history. This statement, prepared for publication by Wendell Phillips (signed also by Pitts), branded as "A LIE!" the claim of Suttle's lawyers that Burns "wished, or is willing to return to slavery." Whatever admissions Burns may have been tricked into making to Suttle and Brent on the night of the arrest—whatever he may have been tricked into writing in a letter this morning—it was now and henceforth his position that he had not offered to "return," quietly or otherwise. The scotching of this rumor, of course, was necessary to establish that Burns was the uncoerced author of his own defense—that the contest that was unfolding was not the creature of ideologically interested Northern meddlers. Yet in the very language of this denial Wendell Phillips had made a decision that Burns would figure in the public arena, before the million-eyed spectator-nation that America was even then becoming, in the role of Charles F. Suttle's self-emancipated slave.

Had it been the controlling aim of the defense team to get Anthony Burns out of danger, they might not have been so quick to concede that he had ever been a slave. The Vigilance Committee, without fanfare or the least desire to make ideological headway with the public, and without even convening as a body, had aided hundreds of anonymous fugitives. But in legally contested cases arising under the Fugitive Slave Law, the abolitionists—white abolitionists especially, who had better access to the court system—routinely felt obliged to look beyond the fate of particular victims to larger antislavery goals. Victory could consist only in blocking the return of an actually escaped slave; if all they accomplished was to extricate a man by showing he had been threatened by mistake, the case would have little political significance. If, here, they maintained that Burns was not in fact a slave, they might save him, but at the cost of affirming and even strengthening the very law they meant to destroy. The Committee was by no means averse to saving individuals: it did so regularly and very efficiently when it could work unseen. But as soon as Burns fell into the hands of the federal authorities, conditions of privacy no longer obtained; he had to be defended not against the plots of particular slave-catchers, but against the power of abstract entities, directly against the law and the government itself. And just as the government's moves in the impending trial were scripted in advance by law and politics, so the opposing force had to meet them on public and symbolic ground.[9]

Burns's escape from Virginia might be construed as an effort by Burns to overcome the oppression of the symbolic realm and to create a proper life on a foundation of privacy. For several weeks the effort had been an entire success. He had found work and lodging (he both lived with and worked for Deacon Pitts), received pay for work, and walked about the city at liberty without papers or a pass. But at and by the moment of his arrest, in the very instant he fell into the hands of Asa Butman, he was restored to the symbolic realm as "the slave." Even those who thereafter took it upon themselves to oppose his rendition were forced to regard him in this symbolic light. The dispute that now broke over his head immediately took the form of an argument about his "identity," in which the contending parties, hoping to reduce the intolerable oxymoron of "fugitive slave," were at bottom more agreed than they ever suspected or could afford to admit: it was a feature of the government's Fugitive Slave Law to amplify the voice of the claimant's position that Burns's identity was that of a slave; the defense, ironically, was left to offer as an identity nothing but the role of victim, a term that could scarcely be distinguished, even in their own minds, from "slave."

No one seems to have appreciated how unslavish it was of Burns to have authorized a defense at all.

In the morning, while Phillips was negotiating with Loring, Thomas Wentworth Higginson and Bronson Alcott were traveling "by early train" the forty miles from Worcester to Boston and the scene of action. Alcott had, the evening before, delivered his scheduled discourse on "The State"—with what topical references one can only surmise. The discussion had taken place before a select audience of the friends of reform at the Worcester home of Thoreau's utterly devoted disciple, Harrison Gray Otis Blake. Alcott, Blake, Higginson, and others of that circle stayed up late in Blake's parlor discussing what Alcott in his journal coolly referred to as "the matter of rescue."[10]

No direct evidence survives of what was said at this meeting, but Alcott's idea of a rescue would have drawn heavily on the example of the famous "Jerry rescue," successfully carried out in Syracuse in 1851 under the leadership of Alcott's brother-in-law Samuel J. May. As it happened, there was among Higginson's parishioners a man who had taken part in that rescue: Martin Stowell, now Higginson's closest ally in an aggressive local temperance crusade. In all likelihood Stowell was present at the meeting at Blake's house, because by the time Higginson and Alcott left for Boston early the next morning, Stowell was rounding up Worcester volunteers pledged to act that day for freedom.

❧ THE JERRY RESCUE

It is treason! treason! TREASON! and nothing else.

DANIEL WEBSTER, SPEECH AT SYRACUSE, MAY 26, 1851

In Syracuse, as in Boston, the people—or rather, some few of them—had responded to the Compromise of 1850 by forming a Vigilance Committee. The purpose of the organization was to protect the local black population from federally sponsored "kidnappers" and in general to render the Fugitive Slave Law inoperative in upstate New York. The Syracuse Committee was established on October 4, just a few weeks after the fugitive bill was signed into law. Among those present at the organizational meeting were the Reverend Samuel J. May (a veteran antislavery worker, called "God's chore-boy" by Emerson), the wealthy abolitionist and Liberty party stalwart Gerrit Smith, and two notable escaped slaves, newspaper editor Samuel Ringgold Ward and orator and activist Jermain W. Loguen.[1]

In Syracuse, as in Boston, conservative forces had organized a Union meeting to swear allegiance to the law of the land, to support the Compromise, and to discourage unsettling agitation on the slavery issue. Addressing this meeting on May 26, 1851, Daniel Webster attacked the radicals for their "higher law" position: "We hear of persons assembling in Massachusetts and New York who set up themselves over the Constitution—above the law—and above the decisions of the highest tribunals—and who say that this law shall not be carried into effect. You have heard it here, have you not? Has it not been said in the County of Onondaga? And have they not pledged their lives, their fortunes and their sacred honor to defeat its execution? Pledged their lives, their fortunes and their sacred honor! For what! For the violation of the law—for the committal of treason to the country—for it is treason and nothing else."[2]

The overt act of treason came five months later. At about noon on October 1, 1851, an escaped mulatto slave named William Henry (known as "Jerry"), while working at his trade as a cooper, was arrested and confined in the Syracuse Police Office by deputy U.S. Marshal Henry W. Allen on behalf of the slave's owner, John McReynolds of Hannibal, Missouri. A crowd quickly gathered at the commissioner's hearing, which began within an hour of the arrest. The crowd soon pressed into the courtroom, and in the confusion the prisoner managed to slip away, leading several deputies and civilian volunteers on a brief footrace before being recaptured.[3]

At the Vigilance Committee meeting that evening, Gerrit Smith urged them to action: "It is not unlikely the Commissioner will release Jerry if the examination is suffered to proceed," he advised them, "but the moral effect of such an acquittal will be as nothing to a bold and forcible rescue. A forcible rescue will demonstrate the strength of public opinion against the possible legality of slavery, and this Fugitive Slave Law in particular. It will honor Syracuse and be a powerful example everywhere."[4]

Samuel J. May later recalled the plans:

> At a given signal the doors and windows of the police office were to be demolished at once, and the rescuers rush in and fill the room, press around and upon the officers, overwhelming them by their numbers, not by blows, and so soon as they were confined and powerless by the pressure of bodies about them, several men were to take up Jerry and to bear him to the buggy aforesaid. Strict injunctions were given and it was agreed not intentionally to injure the policemen. Gerrit Smith and several others pressed this caution very urgently upon those who were gathered in Dr. [Hiram] Hoyt's office. And the last thing I said as we were coming away was, "If any one is injured in this fray, I hope it may be one of our own party."

All this time, Jerry was in his cell, "yelling like a mad man" and swearing that he "would tear out his master's guts if he could but lay his hands on him."[5]

At 8:30 a file of men, black and white, armed with clubs, axes, and iron rods, proceeded down Salina Street to take the jail by force. Other men, including Loguen, carried on boards between them a stout wooden beam to serve as a battering ram. Dousing the street light, they overwhelmed the guards in darkness. Jerry was clearly underdefended. Marshal Fitch of Rochester got off a couple of shots around the edge of the battered and unhinged door of the jail, wounding one assailant, before vacating the premises through the window, breaking his own arm in falling ignominiously into the Erie Canal. Hiding for five days in various safe houses, Jerry recovered from the beatings he had received from the police and at last made his way to safety in Kingston, Canada West.

Millard Fillmore and his secretary of state, Daniel Webster, were determined to make an example of the rescuers and directed the U.S. attorney for New York, James R. Lawrence, a retired judge, to bring treason charges. Although Lawrence had a number of people arrested, he found it insurmountably difficult to gather evidence to support so grave a charge. Twenty-six men were indicted for rioting, including Ward and Loguen, who avoided prosecution by following Jerry to Canada. Only four of the rescuers actually stood trial: three white defendants were acquitted, while the lone black defendant, Enoch Reed, was convicted under the Fugitive Slave Act of 1793, thus utterly defeating the political aim of vindicating the law of 1850.[6]

Thereafter, for ten years, the abolitionists of Syracuse celebrated "Jerry Rescue Day" on October 1, annually bringing in such speakers as Frederick Douglass, William Lloyd Garrison, Lucretia Mott, and Lucy Stone. Details of the rescue were well known in antislavery circles throughout the North. And because the rescue was the proudest moment in the life of Samuel J. May, his brother-in-law, Bronson Alcott, cherished the memory as well. And Martin Stowell had been there.

❧ MARTIN STOWELL

Whenever a mind is simple, and receives a divine wisdom, old things pass away,—means, teachers, texts, temples fall; it lives now and absorbs past and future into the present hour.

RALPH WALDO EMERSON, "SELF-RELIANCE"

Stowell was in many respects a typical footsoldier of American romantic reform, though time and chance would thrust him momentarily into a position of leadership. Born January 20, 1824, he was the youngest of the ten children of Jonathan and Eliza Ann Stowell, members of the Congregational church in Wales, a small village in south central Massachusetts. By the age of twenty-three he had moved a few miles north to the town of Warren, on the coach line between Springfield and Worcester, where he followed his father's trade of shoemaking. He was already an avid reader of the *Liberator*.[1]

One day in the fall of 1847 Stowell read in the *Liberator* that William Wells Brown, an escaped slave and ally of Garrison, might be available to lecture in Warren on his way back to Boston from Springfield. Brown had just published a very popular narrative of his life and was then, as later, in considerable demand as a speaker. Excited at the prospect of hearing an authentic, firsthand account of slavery, Stowell applied to the deacon of his church to rent the vestry for a lecture hall. The deacon's flat refusal came with the all-sufficient explanation, "You know, Mr. Stowell, that Garrison is an Infidel." The Universalists also turned him down. By the time a room was found (above a sawmill two miles from the village), Brown, and the opportunity to hear him, had passed by.[2]

The incident was an opening wedge to separate Stowell from the church. In the following Sunday's sermon, he noticed that the minister's elaborate vindication of his sect as a true church consisted entirely of exaggerated professions with no allusion to its action—no mention of "the fruits," as Stowell put it, "by which Christ's church will be known." A few weeks later, in the midst of this growing controversy with the Congregationalists, Stowell married twenty-three-year-old Eliza Ann Ward, an exceptionally outspoken and fervid reformer and a member, like Stowell, of the Warren church. She, too, was interested in hearing William Wells Brown and, with the help of a handful of local sympathizers, managed to get the speaker—"the convincing and soul-stirring fugitive slave," as Stowell called him—before a local audience at Seminary Hall on May 13, 1848. "To say that there was no small stir among the scribes and Pharisees, would be saying comparatively nothing," he subsequently wrote, "for it is evident to all thinking minds that there had been a plan laid by the churches to keep the Garrisonians or abolitionists from propagating their principles in this place." But "the spirit of freedom," he was glad to report, had been advancing in Warren, so that now

Even the priests and Levites begin to tremble for the gods they have set up. They have succeeded until this time in stopping, to a great extent, the mouths of those who would speak. Notwithstanding they have succeeded in staying its course for a while, it has at last burst its bands, and not only has, but is now, like a mighty avalanche, destroying the sectarians and politicians from one end of the town to the other ... Permit me to say, that there are not a few who have hitherto been with the church, who are indignant at the action of those who opposed the opening of the Seminary for these lectures.

These restrictions of the church are arousing the honest portions of this community to a sense of the hypocrisy of the church, and must sooner or later bring upon it certain destruction.[3]

The following January, in what was surely a continuation of this dispute, Stowell's wife brought charges against the church "for sustaining War, Slavery, and Capital Punishment." She requested a public hearing of her allegations. At the time appointed for the meeting, the minister "disgraced himself by giving that lone female a reprimand for bringing charges of so sweeping a nature against old hoary-headed men, who had been church members for nearly thirty years." When the parish made no overtures of repentance and indeed by vote sustained the minister in his rebuke, Eliza Ann Stowell rose from her seat "and in a calm, distinct voice, said, 'Then I do hereby declare my brothers and sisters of the Congregational Church in Warren and throughout the country, expelled from my communion.'" In recounting this episode, her husband approvingly explained that she had recently been reading William Goodell's *Come-outism; The Duty of Secession from a Corrupt Church* (1845).[4]

In 1850 the Stowells moved to the more congenial political climate of the fast-growing, newly industrialized city of Worcester, just then filling up with "intelligent mechanics" who voted the Freesoil ticket. That party had had its birth in Worcester two years before when the Whigs and the Democrats, in nominating Zachary Taylor and Lewis Cass, turned their backs on the Wilmot Proviso and in the view of the radicals truckled to the Slave Power. In Worcester the new party had been announced with the ringing declaration that "Massachusetts goes now, and will ever go, for free soil and for free men, for free lips and a free press, for a free land and a free world." For the time being, however, they meant to contain slavery, quarantine it in the South, and preserve the greater part of America for a race that knew what to do with freedom. In Worcester the Stowells were among the most faithful attenders at antislavery and temperance gatherings, but in the main withheld themselves, as other Garrisonians did, from organized politics.[5]

The Jerry Rescue of the following year developed too quickly for Stowell's involvement to have been anything but an accident. Presumably he was in Syracuse to attend the antislavery convention called by Gerrit Smith and S. J. May in a vain attempt to resuscitate the Liberty party, which, even at its height in the 1840s, had been a weak vehicle for political abolitionists. Smith and May had reasonable grounds for the belief they later expressed that Jerry's arrest had been arranged for political effect to coincide with their meeting. However that may have been, Stowell was probably in the East Genesee Street Congregational Church listening to Gerrit Smith when news of the arrest was announced. The meeting broke up at once, and Stowell simply followed the crowd to the police station. He was glad to help. He returned to Worcester immediately after the event, and there, a few days later, received a letter from one of his colleagues in the rescue:

> The fugitive, Jerry, is safe in Canada. His honor the President, Millard Fillmore, has received a nice box, by express, containing Jerry's shackles. At the time of the arrest of our citizens for aiding in the rescue, the alarm bell was sounded, and in five minutes the Congregational church was filled to overflowing. We took sweet counsel together, and pledged our lives, our fortunes, and our sacred honor, in defence of the men arrested, and [of] our glorious principles . . . Judge Lawrence, who was so officious in kidnapping Jerry, and who bailed the *southern* kidnapper, has been presented, by *the ladies of Syracuse,* with 30 pieces of silver,—(3 cent pieces)—the price of betraying innocent blood.[6]

The rash of fugitive slave cases in 1850 and 1851, including especially the rescue of Frederick "Shadrach" Minkins and the rendition of Thomas Sims, both at Boston, further electrified the Worcester comeouters. By May of 1852 they had coalesced into a recognizable activist group, a "Free Church," and settled on the Reverend Thomas Wentworth Higginson as their leader. The letter inviting Higginson to Worcester was signed by Martin Stowell.[7]

There was much in Higginson's record at this time to recommend him to the Worcester radicals. In 1848, to the annoyance of his conservative Newburyport congregation, he allowed himself to be coaxed into open support for the new Freesoil party by a surprisingly effective political operative by the name of John Greenleaf Whittier. Higginson's biographer calls this a "turning point" in his public career, mostly because it led in 1850 to his departure from the regular Unitarian ministry, but also because it weakened the restraints on his conduct imposed by a commitment to Garrisonian moral suasion. In 1850, shortly after he had been ousted from his pulpit, Higginson was put forward (by Whittier) as the Freesoil candidate for Congress from the third district; the Essex convention nominated him, and he ran an uncompromising "higher law" campaign. Of the Fugitive Slave Law, Higginson said at that time simply: "DISOBEY IT . . . and show our good citizenship by taking the legal consequences!"

In October, while this election campaign was under way, the first of the Boston slave cases arose; slavehunters were in the city looking for William and Ellen Craft, who had escaped overland from Georgia in 1848. The light-skinned Ellen had disguised herself as a white gentleman planter, sickly and therefore muffled and goggled, traveling by train with a black servant, in fact her husband, William. For two years they quietly enjoyed their freedom in Boston, William working as a cabinetmaker, Ellen as a seamstress. Now, with arrest warrants out against them, they were being feloniously sheltered by Theodore Parker, their minister, and by Lewis Hayden and Dr. Henry Bowditch of the Vigilance Committee. Higginson urged that the Crafts stand their ground and allow the law and the resolve of antislavery Boston to be tested once and for all. But Parker located the claimant's agents at the Revere House and singlehandedly bluffed them all the way back to Georgia. Only then did he send William and Ellen Craft to a safe haven in England. In his journal, Parker wrote that he would probably "have to go to gaol this winter."[8]

Higginson lost the election to his Whig opponent but was necessarily drawn into the machinations of the Freesoil-Democratic coalition of that year in engineering the election of Charles Sumner to the Senate. Though still living in Newburyport, Higginson was becoming more deeply involved in the fugitive slave cases in Boston. He praised the action of the black rescuers of Shadrach in February 1851, exulting simultaneously in the deliverance of the man, the thwarting of the iniquitous law, and the success of nonviolent though forcible tactics. When twenty-three-year-old Thomas Sims was arrested by Asa Butman on the night of April 3, Higginson was summoned by messenger to join in the deliberations of the Vigilance Committee.[9]

When he arrived at the meeting at the *Liberator* office, it appeared that only he and two black men—Leonard Grimes (not listed as a member of the Committee) and Lewis Hayden, the architect of the Shadrach rescue—were in favor of forcible intervention. Half the Committee were Garrisonian nonresistants, while the other half, the Freesoil members, were unwilling to do anything that would place them "outside the pale of good citizenship." To a friend, Higginson wrote: "It is worth coming to Boston occasionally to see that there are places worse than Newburyport; there is neither organization, resolution, plan nor popular sentiment—the Negroes are cowed and the abolitionists irresolute and hopeless, with nothing better to do on Saturday than to send off circulars to clergymen!"[10]

The Vigilance Committee applied for the use of Faneuil Hall to get up a demonstration, but the mayor had already billeted a company of militia there, intending to deploy them against expected rioters. The Committee then applied for the use of the lawn in front of the State House, but the legislature refused by a vote of 147 to 113 to allow it. The Committee finally gathered on Boston Common, with nobody's permission, and there 1,000 people heard Wendell Phillips say how much better and more prudent it would be to destroy the steamboats and railroads of Boston than for Massachusetts to send a man into slavery. Public opinion, however, sided with the newspapers that called Phillips and his colleagues "an imbecile faction."[11]

Over the next several days Higginson attended the proceedings in the federal courtroom before Commissioner George Ticknor Curtis, the same man who had presided—briefly—over Shadrach's case. To get into the Court House, Higginson, like all the others, including an outraged state judiciary, had to stoop to pass under the chains with which City Marshal Francis Tukey had encircled the building. Inside, Higginson listened to the arguments of the claimant's lawyer, Seth J. Thomas, and of defense counsel Charles G. Loring and Robert Rantoul, while Dana, Sumner, and Samuel Sewall ineffectually pursued writs of replevin and habeas corpus in state and federal courts. On April 7 Lemuel Shaw denied the writ of habeas corpus and delivered the unanimous opinion of the Supreme Judicial Court that the Fugitive Slave Law was constitutional. At that point it was clear that Sims was doomed. "What a moment was lost," Emerson wrote in his journal, "when Judge Shaw declined to affirm the unconstitutionality of the Fugitive Slave Law!"[12]

The next day, April 8, the Vigilance Committee called a mass meeting at Tremont Temple, which was then a Baptist church under the ministry of Committee member Nathaniel Colver. Chosen to preside was Congressman Horace Mann, the Conscience Whig whose loud opposition to the Fugitive Slave Law had so nettled Daniel Webster. Speeches were made by Samuel Gridley Howe, director of the Massachusetts School for the Blind and one of the projectors of the *Commonwealth*, the new Freesoil paper; by John Gorham Palfrey, Unitarian minister turned Freesoil politician; Anson Burlingame, a rising young orator; Henry Wilson, the "Natick cobbler," architect of the coalition between the Freesoilers and the Democrats; Samuel Hoar of Concord, Emerson's neighbor, who had been famously ejected from Charleston, South Carolina, in 1844, for daring to investigate the illegal jailing of Northern black sailors; Elizur Wright, an editor at the *Commonwealth*, currently under indictment for treason in connection with the Shadrach rescue; William Henry Channing, Unitarian minister, at work just then with Emerson on the *Memoirs of Margaret Fuller;* Wendell Phillips; and Thomas Wentworth Higginson. Most of the speakers were content to denounce Webster, Shaw, and the Fugitive Slave Law—but Higginson went further and insisted on the moral duty to rescue the yet unremanded Sims. Howe, always dramatic and mercurial, commended Higginson for "bringing the community to the verge of revolution." But the passion and the rhetoric went for naught when Charles Mayo Ellis (Dana's junior counsel in the Burns case) gave a dampening speech against lawless action.[13]

Thus the meeting failed to endorse a rescue, and it was left to Higginson, Grimes, and Hayden—at last as at first—to act on their own. The plan was to have Sims jump from his third-floor window, land on a few mattresses to be supplied moments before, and then escape in a waiting buggy. Grimes got in to see Sims the next day, and the prisoner agreed to the plan. Mattresses were stowed in the Court Square law office of William Bowditch, but when the time came for the escape, Higginson saw to his dismay that workers were installing iron bars over the outside of the small jury-room window.

Despite some further plotting by the Vigilance Committee for a rescue at sea, Sims was in fact returned without further incident to Savannah, Georgia, where on April 19 he received a nearly fatal public whipping.

The bars on the window remained in place for many years thereafter. Anthony Burns would come to know them well.

Higginson, for his part, found he had a relish for cloak and dagger work: "In fact," he wrote, "I walked in a dream all that week. It is strange to find one's self outside of established institutions; to be obliged to lower one's voice and conceal one's purpose; to see law and order, police and military, on the wrong side, and find good citizenship a sin and bad citizenship a duty." He discovered the intoxication of taking risks for freedom. The world, he thought, looked a little larger than it had a while ago—as though, somehow, he were a kind of fugitive slave himself.[14]

This was altogether the sort of man whom the come-outers wanted for their Free Church in Worcester, a church like Theodore Parker's in Boston, where Christianity was enacted and not merely professed— where the people might actually and immediately taste "the fruits by which Christ's church will be known."

❦ STRATEGIES

A MAN KIDNAPPED.—A Public Meeting will be held at Faneuil Hall this (Friday) evening, May 26, at 7 o'clock, to secure justice for a man claimed as a slave by a Virginia kidnapper, and imprisoned in Boston Court House, in defiance of the laws of Massachusetts. Shall he be plunged into the hell of Virginia slavery by a Massachusetts Judge of Probate?

HANDBILL, MAY 26, 1854

On Friday morning Stowell was rounding up a large contingent to take to Boston. Among those whom he enlisted the leaders were Dr. Oramel Martin, head of the Worcester Freedom Club; Thomas Drew, editor of the Worcester *Spy;* Jerry Valentine, president of the local Know-Nothing lodge; and Freesoiler Adin Ballou Thayer, later Judge Thayer, "the greatest organizer of righteousness in his generation."[1]

Meanwhile Higginson and Alcott arrived together at the Vigilance Committee meeting at Meionaon Hall, perhaps stopping on their way in from the Fitchburg Depot to pick up a copy of the *Commonwealth.* The morning's papers carried the first reports of the case, together with announcements of the Faneuil Hall meeting. The *Commonwealth,* with close ties to the BVC, had borrowed the language of the Committee's handbills: "The slave power," it said, "crams the infamous swindle of a Nebraska bill down our throats, and then piles an outrage upon an insult, and undertakes to steal a MAN! Leave your fields, your work-shops, your stores, your homes—leave any occupation, duty, and pleasure, and swarm to Boston!" This address to the countryside was predicated on the common belief that antislavery flourished among the farms and villages of Berkshire, Hampshire, and

Essex Counties, and in Freesoil strongholds like Worcester, while it starved and fainted in wealthy Boston.[2]

That morning in Amesbury, Whittier took in the news with his breakfast and dashed off a letter to a friend in Boston, Committee member Dr. Henry I. Bowditch:

> That man must not be sent out of Boston as a slave. Anything but that! The whole people must be called out, the country must precipitate itself upon the city—an avalanche of freemen! Where are your circulars and your expresses? In the name of God, let the people be summoned! Send out the fiery cross without further delay! Tell us what you want and what we can do! Thousands are waiting for the word from you.
>
> Is it not possible to keep the matter open until next week? If so, will not some of the Anti-Nebraska pulpits speak out? . . . If you want the country into Boston, say so at once. If another man is to be sacrificed to Moloch, let the whole people witness it.

While this letter was being written, Bowditch was at the Committee meeting, where, as he later noted, "sundry discussions took place . . . about resorting to violence, but coming together anew after a three years' separation, each man wanted to talk, and no man entirely trusted his neighbor or himself apparently. This was the bane of everything. No leader, no head, and consequently anarchy was the result."[3]

Higginson was likewise disappointed to find that "there was not only no plan of action, but no set purpose of united action." It felt, in fact, like an adjourned meeting from the Sims case, every bit as bad as it had been in 1851, when he had cause to bemoan the Emersonian self-reliance of his colleagues: "The Vigilance Committee meetings," he then told Samuel May Jr., "were a disorderly convention, each man having his own plan or theory, perhaps even stopping for anecdote or disquisition, when the occasion required the utmost promptness of decision and the most unflinching unity in action." In 1851 Higginson had "the strongest impressions of the great want of preparation on our part for this revolutionary work . . . Especially this is true among reformers, who are not accustomed to act according to fixed rules and observances, but to strive to do what seems to themselves best without reference to others." Three years later he found nothing changed.[4]

But the besetting sin of independence among reformers was now of less concern to Higginson than their increasingly ludicrous nonresistance. The morning meeting actually broke up when it was reported that Suttle and Brent were passing by in the street and half the Committee took the chance to go out and "point the finger of scorn" at the enemy. Higginson welcomed this defection of the nonresistants, for it left him an audience, he supposed, willing to act more forcibly. The rump meeting of thirty men chose Higginson as their chairman; he in turn called on Dr. Howe to speak, who "gave some general advice, very good and very spirited." The problem of leadership was the first issue addressed. Higginson urged the selection of a single person to direct the rescue operations, but the group would accept no fewer than six to serve as an Executive Committee. These were Higginson, Phillips, Parker, and Howe (all members of the leadership of the general Committee) as well as two individuals of proven physical courage who had been active in previous interventions: Henry Kemp, described by Higginson as "an energetic Irishman"; and Captain Austin Bearse, admiral of the antislavery navy. Knowing that Stowell was bringing a body of men from Worcester, Higginson added him as a seventh member. A night attack on the Court House was proposed and generally agreed to. This seemed like progress, yet the rescue committee could not immediately find even twenty individuals willing to be commanded.[5]

All who have experience with committees will understand what happened next. In the afternoon session everything fixed upon at the morning meeting was up for reexamination. Albert G. Browne of Salem reintroduced Howe's plan—the group of forty who would call on the marshal and demand the prisoner's release. The returning non-resistants were particularly unhappy with what had been decided and freely challenged the morality as well as the practicality of forcible tactics. Bowditch's own concerns centered on the tactical question and were colored by jealousy over the issue of leadership. "I felt all the while as T. W. Higginson, in his calm but enthusiastic manner, talked of his 200 good and true men from the heart of the Commonwealth, that he was but little aware of the toughness of the head of the old Bay State. It is easy to do anything when all are agreed, but for a small minority, as Abolitionists of Boston are, to attempt to break stone walls is another matter." There was resentment at the implied slur on Boston's courage. Was it up to the provinces, then, to do what the capital would not? Such parochial chauvinism made agreement difficult, though by late that afternoon a general and vaguely settled feeling emerged that the rescue—if there was to be a rescue—should follow the Shadrach model, not the Jerry model, and that it should take place Saturday morning, while the trial was under way. Then a great crowd gathered outside would flow irresistibly into the courtroom and carry off the victim of the law.[6]

Yet in fact nothing was decided. With the Faneuil Hall meeting just two hours off, the Committee could come to no definite decision about any course of action, and Higginson, no doubt disgusted, left—around 5:30—to meet Stowell at the train station. His feeling, as he recollected it, was that "something must be done; better a failure than to acquiesce tamely as before."[7]

Something *was* being done. However inefficient and chaotic the Committee proved to be when caught thus unprepared, individual members, acting with varying degrees of independence, kept up pressure on the slavehunters. At 5:00, Suttle and Brent were·arrested at their hotel, the Revere House, on a charge of conspiring to kidnap. The complaint had been sworn out by Lewis Hayden, the most militant of Boston's black abolitionists, with the assistance of lawyer Seth Webb Jr., both Committee members. Bail of $10,000 was forthwith posted for the Virginians by Watson Freeman and Henry Hallett, the latter the slave commissioner son of Benjamin F. Hallett, the U.S. district attorney. Suttle and Brent were released, though for the duration of their stay in the city they remained under an intentionally conspicuous surveillance by black volunteers, directed by Hayden and the Vigilance Committee.[8]

Having been authorized around noon to act for Burns, Dana moved to prepare a writ of personal replevin, a tactic that had been used without success in all the previous fugitive cases. The purpose of the writ, as of the better-known writ of habeas corpus, was to gain a legal hearing to determine whether a given detainee was or was not lawfully held, though it was designed to be served on private individuals rather than on officers of the court. Thus in theory it would be more effective against a slaveholder sojourning in Massachusetts with a slave attendant than against a U.S. marshal holding a suspected fugitive on a warrant. Even in the latter case, however (and this, of course, was the point), a jury might find the warrant illegal or the detention unconscionable and so free the fugitive. It was the distinctive advantage of the writ of personal replevin that it secured a jury trial rather than a hearing before a judge, as would a writ of habeas corpus. It was resorted to, in other words, in order to appeal from a narrow construction of the law to the wider latitudes of the social conscience, or more pertinently, perhaps, from the social conscience of the class of men who sat as judges to that of the class of men who labored with their hands. It had been a notoriously antidemocratic feature of the Fugitive Slave Law—troublesome even to Daniel Webster—that it made no provision for a trial by jury, even though, as the law's opponents never ceased to point out, the Constitution affirmed the right to such trial in all disputes involving assets of at least twenty dollars value. Dana's strategy, like that of the opponents of the Fugitive Slave Law in general, was to champion trial by jury, on the premise that juries were less friendly to slavery and less subject to both legal precedent and political discipline than judges were.[9]

Now obsolete, the writ *de homine replegiando* was anciently recognized in English common law, and while it had been adopted early into the statutes of Massachusetts, it had fallen into disuse during the Federalist period and was abolished in the 1836 revision of the state code. Alert to its potential usefulness, however, antislavery lawyers, led by Robert Rantoul, restored it in 1837 as part of a general personal liberty law, and it remained on the books thereafter. It stated: "If any person is imprisoned . . . unless it be in the custody of some public officer of the law, by force of a lawful warrant . . . he shall be entitled, as of right, to a writ of personal replevin."[10]

The revived writ was first used in 1842 against Nathaniel Coolidge, the officer in charge of Boston's Leverett Street Jail, where George Latimer, a fugitive slave, was being held not by force of law, but at the request and by the authority of his supposed owner, James B. Gray, of Norfolk, Virginia. Judge Joseph Story had ordered Gray to detain Latimer while he, Gray, secured evidence of ownership from Virginia. When Samuel E. Sewall served a writ of replevin on Coolidge, the jailer simply ignored it. It took a writ of habeas corpus to get Coolidge before Chief Justice Lemuel Shaw to show cause why he had defied the writ of replevin. In this action, Shaw held that the overriding consideration was the effective cooperation of the state in the federally mandated return of "persons held to service and labor." No state or local process, in his view, could be allowed to interfere with or nullify the operation of the fugitive slave clause of the Constitution. Shaw agreed with the expressed belief of Judge Story in the recent Supreme Court case of *Prigg v. Pennsylvania* that the Union could not have been formed in the first place without this compromise of the founding fathers in regard to property in slaves. Therefore, in Shaw's mind, as in the minds of other Northern Constitutional Unionists, slavery was inseparable from the very idea and existence of the nation. In *Prigg* (1842) Story had affirmed the constitutionality of the 1793 Fugitive Slave Act, but asserted that enforcement was a federal, not a state, affair. States could not interfere with the operation of this act, but neither did they have to cooperate in its working in order to meet their obligations under the federal contract. Still, it was among the first legal consequences of Story's decision that Shaw would proclaim it the imperative if unpleasant duty of Northerners to overlook certain breaches of traditional freedoms and to weigh the advantages of Union against the distrained liberty of George Latimer, held in a Boston jail without warrant and without evidence of his status as a slave. This gutting of the Personal Liberty Law of 1837, together with the impact of Story's decision in *Prigg,* prompted the antislavery faction in Massachusetts to compose the so-called Latimer Law, authored by Charles Francis Adams, which forbade any kind of state aid in the capture or rendition of fugitive slaves.[11]

In the case of Thomas Sims in 1851, Sewall, apparently with Dana's help, had a writ of personal replevin sworn out and served by the sheriff on U.S. Marshal Charles Devens, requiring that Sims be set at liberty under a bond of $3,000 and that Devens himself appear in court to answer for his actions. When Devens was served, he refused to comply and told the sheriff that if an attempt were made to take the prisoner, it would be resisted by force.[12]

By 1854, if not earlier, it was clear that the writ of personal replevin was a weak instrument and of doubtful application, particularly when directed against federal authorities. The existence and purpose of the writ were not widely understood, yet it was easy to procure—and weak for both those reasons. In principle, it did not have to issue from a court at all, but could issue by right of common law. Preprinted forms existed pre-endorsed with the facsimile signature of Roger B. Taney; they could be filled out by any lawyer or indeed by any friend of the prisoner and served at will. But in fugitive slave cases the writ required, as a practical matter, some extraordinary supplemental authority (such as a federal judge) to compel the attention of federal officers to its requirements. It was undoubtedly for this reason that Dana chose to involve the U.S. District Court in the issuance of the writ, which he and Sewall prepared on the afternoon of May 26. Judge Peleg Sprague, however,

> replied that it was not a writ known to the U.S. Courts, one never issued, to his knowledge by those Courts, & as he understood it, not issuable at the Common law when the party was held under legal process. We [Dana and Sewall] replied that it did not appear in the writ that [Burns] was held under legal process, & that it was, on the face of the proceedings, a writ of right. But the Judge refused the writ, after stating many other reasons, on the ground of its not being a writ known to that Court. He added that if the writ was issued it would contain the clause that it was not to be served if the party was held by legal process, & could do us no good.

Sprague, sixty-one years old and totally blind, was known to be an exceptionally acute lawyer. Here he was finding plausible reasons for not sustaining Dana's writ, which he implied was a matter not for a federal court to consider but for the state courts, since the state had seen fit to embrace the writ. Furthermore, he was comfortable in assuming the legality of the process under which Burns was held—just the point that the writ was meant to test. Sprague's opposition was forced on him not by the law, but by his own political views. It was long remembered against him that in 1835, while serving as U.S. senator from Massachusetts, he had invoked the figure of Jesus Christ as an example of the toleration of slavery. Jesus, according to Peleg Sprague, was no abolitionist and "would not interfere with the administration of the laws, or abrogate their authority."[13]

The writ was denied at 6:00 P.M.

Unbeknownst to Dana, Seth Webb Jr. (having procured the arrest of Suttle and his witness Brent) succeeded in getting a writ of personal replevin, though it was issued by Judge Daniel Wells of the Court of Common Pleas, an inferior state court. The writ was given to Boston coroner Charles Smith, known to be sympathetic to the antislavery cause, who was thereby directed to "replevin the body of Anthony Burns from the custody of Watson Freeman." Marshal Freeman should be prepared to answer for his actions "on the 7th day of June next." Smith served the writ, and Freeman refused to comply.[14]

Webb's activities in the kidnapping complaint and in the writ of replevin appear to have been undertaken on a completely different track from that pursued by Dana, whose accounts of the case make no mention of Webb. The evidence suggests that the Vigilance Committee constructed no overarching legal strategy, but confided the trial to Dana and Ellis and allowed an equally free hand to its other lawyers. Webb's connection with Hayden may indicate that he was working for the black faction of the BVC or perhaps for concerned black citizens determined in the first flush of the excitement to operate outside the structure of the Committee. In any event, his efforts in court were suspended at this point, as though in deference to Dana's emergent control of the legal campaign. Like Hayden, Webb would now turn to violent confrontation.

 BLACK BOSTON

I came from old Verginny here,
　My stocking in my hat,
And so I went to State Street
　To see what folks were at.

"JIM CROW, AS SUNG AT THE WARREN THEATRE, BOSTON," CA. 1850

It has been estimated that during the year 1850, when the Fugitive Slave Law was passed, 1,000 slaves escaped to the North. Even at the most conservative valuation it is evident that more than $500,000 of Southern assets were walking off each year. Enough of these fugitives reached Boston that under the provisions of the new law as much as a fifth of the city's black population was subject to being reclaimed as property. The immediate reaction among Boston's black residents— in the Sixth Ward, along the north slope of Beacon Hill, and in the North End slums—amounted almost to panic. The African Methodist Episcopal Church lost 85 of its members to Canada. Leonard Grimes's Twelfth Baptist church, long favored by the fugitives, lost more than a third of its membership in the few months before Sims was arrested. According to Hayden, this evacuation of Boston took out of the community a good many of those who would have fought most strenuously against the execution of the law. Of those who remained the great majority were day laborers, seamen and stevedores, waiters and hotel workers, barbers, and small tradesmen.

As a labor force they were unskilled, largely illiterate, often unemployed, and too small to operate politically even if they had been organized. If under the provocation of the Fugitive Slave Law they made little noise, it was because their attention centered on rudimentary economic survival. Most had been born in New England and felt less threatened in their persons by the new law than by the ever-increasing tide of Irish immigration, which was inexorably pushing them out of traditional occupations. Their sympathy for the fugitives ran high in 1850, but other concerns were more permanent.[1]

From 1830 to 1850 the small black community of Boston had been remarkably stable, rising only from about 1,800 to 2,000, though as a percentage of the growing urban population as a whole they had declined from 3.1 percent to 1.5 percent. At midcentury 138,788 people were living in Boston, including 46,000 Irish. Nearly half of the city's residents—and more than half of the schoolchildren—were foreign born. Eighty-seven percent of Boston's laboring jobs were held by European immigrants. Between 1850 and 1855 the number of Boston's Irish increased 200 percent, while the American-born population rose a mere 15 percent.[2]

These were among the reasons why the agenda pursued by the core of black activists in Boston differed somewhat and in general from that of the white Freesoilers and Garrisonians, whose efforts were devoted mainly to countering the Fugitive Slave Law and keeping the territories free on the one hand and, on the other, to bringing the nation to mortification and final repentance over the sin of slavery. Black reformers and white worked together as opportunity presented itself (most notably in high-profile fugitive cases), but otherwise they had developed separate methodologies adapted to separate concerns. Not surprisingly, the degree of their cooperation began to be examined as a political question, particularly as Frederick Douglass' influence came at this time into open conflict with Garrison's. The perception that moral suasion was not producing results turned out to be a great recruiter for Douglass, whose optimistic reading of the Constitution as a fundamentally antislavery document pointed the way to a more pragmatic and politically engaged alternative. The response of black Boston to the Burns case was to be conditioned by separate circumstances and a unique history.

By 1854 the city's black activist community had defined itself in campaigns against segregation and for equal civil rights. Interestingly, at a historical moment when the conditions of labor were at the forefront of political attention, labor issues were not being directly agitated among the blacks themselves, except through an acknowledgment of the need for education and training to improve their position in the labor marketplace. Within the community the most talked-about item on the reform agenda, eclipsing even the Fugitive Slave Law, was Douglass' industrial trade school, an old idea revived under the new pressure of Irish labor. Douglass—and indeed many of his generation—felt that the future of the race lay in self-improvement, and not in a head-to-head competition with European immigrants for low-paying unskilled jobs. Rising economically was simply the next logical step in a total process of emancipation, a rise blocked principally by a subtler version of the same force that held Southern blacks in thrall: race prejudice. This prejudice was to be overcome by rising, through education, to standards of social usefulness supposed by many whites to be unattainable or undesired by a race overwhelmingly identified with the degradation of enslavement. As William J. Watkins, a black Garrisonian, wrote in 1851, "we must . . . study to show ourselves approved workmen, that need not to be ashamed."[3]

The fugitive slave cases did not belong to this agenda. Indeed, from an ideological point of view, these episodes presented the black man as on his knees before white power, in the position iconographically caught in the famous antislavery medallion, with manacled hands uplifted in supplicatory prayer. Though it may well be true that the beleaguered fugitive's most dependable allies were to be found in the Northern black community, that community had inevitably to contend with various subtle and not-so-subtle ideological resentments at the public display of black helplessness and dependence.

For white audiences fugitive slave cases were undeniably dramatic—in part because they were rare (most fugitives were never pursued), in part because, like the formal published slave narratives, they exercised the emotions in service to a moral lesson and allowed people to "feel right" (as Mrs. Stowe had put it) on the great question. The public always seemed taken by these cases unawares, by the buzz and stir, the sudden excitement, the emergence into consciousness, as threatened, of the otherwise repressed black body. While these cases won many emotional white converts to antislavery, alignments based on local indignations often proved as superficial and ephemeral as the events that converted them. And of course many were converted in the other direction, taught by events to adhere more strongly to law and order. The fact that the cases presented these options of self-definition was precisely what made them seem important public rituals, not much different, in many respects, from a political election. The elements of publicity, theatricality, and melodrama in the fugitive cases were part of what prevented some radical reformers from getting very deeply involved in them. "A great deal is said . . . in regard to the Fugitive Slave Law," Garrison pointed out in 1852. "Many persons glory in their hostility to it, and upon this capital they set up an antislavery reputation. But opposition to that law is no proof in itself of anti-slavery fidelity. That law is merely incidental to slavery . . . Our warfare is not against slave-hunting alone, but against the existence of slavery." The pitch and quality of one's protest signaled how deeply one thought the evil ran, whether in the shallows of public conduct or in the abysses of human depravity. But who had got to the bottom of this business?[4]

Free Northern blacks, for their part, were also concerned with "the little lower layer," with matters that did not come and go—not so much with the power of Virginia slaveholders (a point of white fascination), but already with the next evolutionary step, emerging from the quasi-slavery of their own Northern identity. The progressive separation of black and white abolitionists—or the increasing independence of the former over the decade of the 1850s—is marked by a shift in their attention from the slave's plight to their own, by coming to focus on the continuities between black slavery and white prejudice. One clear indication of this advancing recognition may be seen in the call issued by William J. Wilson of New York on May 10, 1855, for a "National Convention of Colored Americans":

> Years of well-intended effort have been expended for the especial freedom of the slave, while the elevation of the free colored man as an inseparable priority to the same, has been entirely overlooked. But to every true friend of freedom it must now be too obvious, that the whole process of operation against the huge and diabolical system of oppression and wrong, has been shorn of more than half its strength and efficacy, because of this neglect of the interests of the Free People of Color—interests so vital that we dare not longer permit them to remain in a state of neglect. If nothing else, then, these years of experi-

ence have taught every true friend of Liberty, that the elevation of the free man is inseparable from, and lies at the very threshold of the great work of the slave's restoration to freedom, and equally essential to the highest well-being of our own common country.[5]

The statement reflects a widespread despair in 1855 over the feck-lessness of abolitionism. The fact that a quarter-century of agitation had produced no tangible result caused many people (including Daniel Webster in 1850) to lose faith in its moral cogency. Wilson's statement, however, proposed to give force and power to black reform, to change the equation by abandoning abolitionism as a proxy move-ment, or an "argument on behalf." Garrison's main positions, from his attack on colonization to his advocacy of nonresistance, from his re-liance on moral suasion to his insistence on absolute and immediate emancipation, were developed to address slavery, and to address it on a national scale; they were not well adapted to militancy on the Northern front, and although Garrison was personally emphatic in his condemnation of race prejudice and although he was a sympathetic ally in reform causes in Boston (as the black community long and af-fectionately remembered), still it is clear that these took second place, logically and tactically, in his scheme. Garrison might lead the assault on slavery, having virtually defined that endeavor, but the need for black leadership in confronting Northern conditions was becoming more and more evident: thus as Douglass' role was clarified, the Boston community was polarized, and Garrison necessarily lost some of his followers.[6]

The schools, whether trade schools or grammar schools, were the main site of adjustment for anxieties over the position of free blacks in Northern society.

In the late 1840s, following the integration of the schools in Nan-tucket and Salem, Boston's remained the only segregated system in the state. The Smith School in the Sixth Ward, founded in 1812 through a bequest from philanthropist Abiel Smith, was where the city's black children, wherever they might live, had to go. Long neglected by the city, the building was run-down and its operation underfunded. A number of academic subjects taught at the white schools were regarded as unnecessary here. As early as 1845, John Telemachus Hilton, a hair-dresser, Jonas W. Clark, a clothing dealer, and William Cooper Nell, a black protégé of Garrison's who had been trained in the law, joined in organizing a boycott of the Smith School. City officials tried to head off the protest by offering to make repairs and to appoint a black headmaster, a solution that strongly appealed to a minority of outspoken cultural separatists among the protesters. But the integrationist position, with Garrison's support, prevailed at every step, and the boycott went forward. Eventually a lawsuit was brought against the city by one of the protesters, Benjamin F. Roberts, a printer, on behalf of his daughter Sarah, who had been denied access to several white schools located closer to her home. This suit was argued by the state's first black attorney, Robert Morris, and, on appeal before Chief Justice Lemuel Shaw, by Charles Sumner with assistance from Morris.[7]

Sumner eloquently argued that the state constitution recognized no racial distinctions and that the Boston School Committee had exceeded its authority when it created a racial criterion for admission. Separate schools should be abolished both as intrinsically unequal and as a standing endorsement of white racial prejudice. History gives Sumner the credit for this argument, but much of it originated with Morris, just as the agitation against the "caste schools" arose first in the black community. Still, Shaw's decision in *Roberts v. Boston* (1849) affirmed the separate-but-equal doctrine advanced by Sumner's opposing counsel, Peleg Chandler, and the Boston school system remained officially segregated.

The campaign to integrate the schools was itself a school for politics, and from it a number of black activists graduated into local prominence, including Robert Morris, who was just twenty-five years old when he first entered a courtroom on Sarah Roberts' behalf. Grandson of the slave Cumono, who had been stolen out of Africa as a child and transported to Ipswich, Massachusetts, before the Revolution, Morris grew up in Hawthorne's Salem, where he was first employed as a "table boy" in the home of Essex Institute curator Henry F. King. There he was noticed by King's friend, the abolitionist Ellis Gray Loring, who in 1837 put him to work in his Boston law office. He proved to be a favorite among Loring's large circle of abolitionist friends, including Lydia Maria Child, who made one day memorable for young Robert by giving him a copy of Olaudah Equiano's slave narrative. Morris progressed rapidly from messenger to copyist to law clerk, and at last, in February 1847, he was admitted to practice in the state. Though successful as an attorney and well regarded for his talents in the courtroom, he was placed on the BVC Finance Committee rather than its Legal Committee, perhaps for his talents as a fundraiser among the black community. In 1854 he seems to have been forced aside by Dana and Ellis when the matter of Burns's legal representation was settled. Morris had offered his services and was mentioned in the first newspaper reports as a member of the defense team, but it may have been that his involvement in the Shadrach rescue of 1851—for which he had been tried and acquitted—made him unsuitably controversial. It may also have been supposed that Morris' feelings were too deeply engaged in the case, but in fact he had already had considerable experience, in his trial work, keeping his passions and resentments to himself. As a professional man, he was noted for meeting racism with wit and geniality. The tactic worked well with juries.[8]

Morris' life was an odd blend of radical activism and establishment conformity, an incoherence undoubtedly aggravated on the one hand by a profession that distanced him from the working-class black community and on the other by a consciousness of himself as a leader and role model. In 1844, a year after the Massachusetts law against miscegenation was repealed, he married a white Catholic girl, Catherine Mason. He worked steadily on school desegregation, despite the setback of *Roberts,* representing Edward Pindall in an almost identical case in 1853—with, however, no better results. He supervised the Sunday school at the AME church and belonged to the Boston Lyceum, as well as the Prince Hall Grand Masonic Lodge, the latter a sort of headquarters for radical black activism. He was a leader in integrating public accommodations, especially the theaters and lecture rooms. In the 1850s he converted to his wife's Catholicism and, as many white professionals were also doing, moved out to the suburbs. His heroes were Denmark Vesey and Nat Turner, "whose very names were a terror to oppressors."[9]

Apart from the integration of the schools, the most hotly agitated question among Boston's black community (or at least among the younger male members of the community) was their exclusion from the militia. The U.S. Constitution had accepted the British colonial system of local militias, and gave Congress the power to "provide for calling forth the Militia to execute the Laws of the Union, suppress Insurrections and repel Invasions." The practice of excluding blacks from the various state militias—of keeping them unarmed—was founded not in any provision of the Constitution but in the enabling legislation passed by Congress in 1792 and in the state laws that followed. This exclusion was widely regarded as prudent, on the assumption that blacks had fewer motives to law and order than did the governing white population. Then, too, the "Insurrections" most feared were slave revolts. One of the first major sectional contentions, aggravated by Nat Turner's Rebellion, was whether free-state militias could be counted on to quell revolts in the slave states. This issue was underscored as early as 1826, when, in his first speech in Congress, Edward Everett reassured his Southern colleagues by offering to strap on a knapsack and undertake the job himself.[10]

The climate was a little different in the early 1850s. Volunteer militia companies had proliferated and become a more symbolic and visible part of the nation's civic life; originally designed for defense of frontier settlers against the Indians, by 1850 they were to the various communities that sponsored them more or less what professional sports franchises are to cities now. They served the public's need for spectacle and diversion by means of the musters and the training, and by the snappy uniforms and the plumed helmets favored by "old boys" of eighteen.

Militia companies, to be sure, had also a deeper ritual significance. They were a way of endorsing America's heritage of militarism, which in the years following the Mexican War was in full bloom. The national government, to all appearances, was in the hands of a coterie of Mexican War generals. Honor and preferment, under this martial regime and its expansionist ideology, followed the flag. The Fourth of July was then—much more obviously than at present—a military holiday, an occasion to remind everyone that citizenship and its privileges—the very right to call oneself an American—derived immediately from the military operations of their grandfathers in 1776. If Americans had misgivings about the potentially despotic uses of a standing army (and therefore kept theirs small), they had no such doubts about the home-town democratic feel of the militia. If any segment of the populace needed to show itself as American, to offer itself as a legitimate part of the body politic, it would, in 1850, get a charter to form a militia company— just as, indeed, the Irish immigrants in Boston had promptly done.

The leaders of the movement for a black militia unit in 1852 and 1853 (Morris, William C. Nell, and William J. Watkins) were the same individuals who had led the school campaign. The arguments

advanced in this cause, like those put forth in the struggle to deseg-
regate the schools, were critically important because they had to do
with fundamental issues of black social identity and recognition—
precisely the question on which, both in the largest philosophical
sense and in the narrowest legal sense, the case of Anthony Burns
would also turn.

The right of able-bodied males of a certain age to participate in the
general defense was a constitutionally recognized right of citizenship;
the exclusion of blacks therefore raised questions about their status as
citizens, and about the equal legal protections such a status implied.
In renewing a petition for a charter in 1853, Robert Morris reminded
a legislative committee that a company of naturalized Irish immigrants had recently been authorized: "We do not want a step-mother,"
he said, "who will butter the bread for one, and sand it for another.
We hunger and thirst for prosperity and advancement, and, so far as
in your power lies, we wish you to do all you can to aid us in our en-
deavors. We wish you to make us feel that we are of some use and advantage, in this our day and generation." In Morris' mind the militia
company had a value in securing an honorable place for African-
Americans in the larger community; what a group thus organized
could "feel" was the essential consequence.[11]

In arguing for the petition, Morris was assisted by William J.
Watkins, another young veteran of the school protest. Born in 1828 to
free parents in Baltimore, he left home in 1849 for the more tolerant atmosphere and greater opportunities of Boston, where he was received
and helped along by his father's old friend, William Lloyd Garrison.
The first act of young Watkins' career as a reformer was to oppose
Thomas Paul Smith and the separatist faction in the school controversy.
In articles in the *Liberator* in 1851 and 1852, he complained of the willingness of the black community to take shelter in its own separate institutions, not hesitating even to attack the black churches:

> Were we compelled, on account of our complexion, to occupy the
> higher seat in the synagogue, or hide ourselves in some remote corner,
> and catch the crumbs as they fall from the white man's table; then there
> would be extenuating circumstances sufficient to justify us in wor-
> shipping God exclusively under our own vine and fig tree. But no such
> mitigating circumstances present themselves. Churches in which we
> can unite and worship God as men and brethren are thrown wide open
> for our reception, but few of us wend our way thither.

Watkins' argument against the delusive safety of the old black institutions belonged to an agenda by which rights would be actively claimed and a people encouraged to compete in a marketplace made progressively more equitable by reform agitation. The argument displays the typical impatience of the reformer with old institutions, but there is no reason to suppose that Watkins misunderstood the contribution that the black churches had made—and continued to make—to the community's sense of identity. He was simply prepared to reject that identity.[12]

Watkins' simultaneous advocacy of a black militia unit sustained rather than contradicted this logic. There were, in 1853, no militia equivalents to Theodore Parker's integrated Twenty-eighth Congregational Society or to Nathaniel Colver's Baptist Church at Tremont Temple. The idea in the militia campaign was not to create a new black institution but to assume a place, symbolically, within the core notion of American citizenship and at the same time to refashion the identity of the free black population.

The argument that Watkins made before the legislative committee on February 24, 1853, on behalf of "sixty-five colored petitioners" was a conscious attempt to reorder white perceptions. Speaking for the community of the petitioners, he said: "while I stand up to represent those with whom I am proud to be identified, I respectfully solicit you, gentlemen, to regard us not as obsequious suppliants for favor, but as men, proud of, and conscious of the inherent dignity of manhood; as men, who, knowing our rights, dare, at all hazards, to maintain them." To be excluded from the military was in a sense to be emasculated, but to seem to be asking, as suppliants, to have an identity conferred on them by those who powerfully withheld it (as in Morris' image of the "step-mother") was also feminizing. Watkins was careful to frame the matter as he undoubtedly saw it, as the claiming of a right unlawfully denied—which helps to explain both Watkins' occasionally bellicose tone and the attraction that the petitioners felt toward the masculine military persona. A main theme in Douglass' *Narrative* had been the revelation of identity in the connection between asserting one's manhood and procuring freedom. The important fact about the abolitionist slogan, "Am I not a man and a brother?" had always been its presentation as a question.[13]

Who are the petitioners? Watkins asked. His answer: "they are among the most respectable men in the community. They are law-abiding, tax-paying, liberty-loving, NATIVE-BORN, AMERICAN CITIZENS; men who love their country, despite its heinous iniquities; iniquities piled up in dreadful agony to the heavens." One has to pause and admire Watkins' rhetoric. In the culture of his auditors "the most respectable men in the community" did not—could not—refer to sixty-five obscure colored men, but rather to the likes of George Ticknor, Edward Everett, William Appleton, Samuel A. Eliot, Edward G. Loring, George T. and Benjamin R. Curtis, Ezra Stiles Gannett, and Lemuel Shaw—in short, to the whole class of Boston-area Hunker Whigs who would soon be allied against Anthony Burns. But in the sentence that follows Watkins opened up the presumptively closed and decided question of what "respectable" might legitimately mean in republican America. It did not have to mean powerful and illustrious; it might also mean behaving in a way that commanded respect in the context of liberal, Jeffersonian values. Watkins' language forced his hearers to confront their own hypocrisy.[14]

That second sentence, in a manner similar to the first, assumed something not obviously in evidence: the claim that the petitioners were American citizens was clearly at the heart of the whole dispute. If there had not been some doubt on that point, the process to which Watkins' address belonged would not have been contentious—would not, perhaps, have been necessary at all. Young black men could not have been excluded from the military in the first place unless someone had decided that they were, at best, quasi-citizens, possessing some but not all the rights of citizens. This indeed was the prevailing view, comfortable so long as assumed and unspoken, patently outrageous when formally announced as national policy in *Dred Scott* (1857). Little wonder that proslavery forces had for twenty years taken their stand on the characteristic position that slavery and free speech were permanently incompatible.

The statement that the petitioners "love their country, despite its heinous iniquities" was certainly no gratuitous introduction of the slavery issue, but a direct acknowledgement and confrontation of white fears that an armed body of black citizens in their midst would be disrupters, not defenders, of the public peace. Watkins understood that these fears were the main obstacle to justice and argued that black patriotism—the authorizing certificate of a still unalienated citizenship—should remove all cause for alarm. Watkins further implied that these white Whigs and Democrats had a chance not to add to the high-piled iniquities, a chance now not to offend heaven or to give just cause to peaceable citizens—engaged in the lawful and respectful process of legislative petition—to take up positions outside the system and become revolutionaries.

The specter of revolution hovers over the whole of Watkins' performance, not generally as a threat, but as a consequence of a series of vivid and explicit reminders that the American Revolution (which, as it gave the country to the people, became at once the actual and symbolic predicate of citizenship) was not to be regarded historically as a model for white exclusivity. Blacks had fought. The name of Crispus Attucks is remembered. Large segments of Watkins' address are given over to quotations from a recently published pamphlet by William Cooper Nell titled *Services of Colored Americans, in the Wars of 1776 and 1812,* the first work of black American historiography. The exclusion from the military of the sons and grandsons of black patriots is not only a shameful stroke of ingratitude but an aggressive move in a covert and unequal struggle for cultural ownership of the war for national independence, beyond doubt the most potent political signifier in America and *the* event, as everyone acknowledged, from which all subsequent political power and benefit derived.[15]

When the hearing was over the committee gave the petitioners "leave to withdraw" and voted to take no action in the matter. Watkins' address was published as a pamphlet by Benjamin F. Roberts, the complainant in the school case, and distributed in the black community. William Cooper Nell revised and expanded his pamphlet into a book, *Colored Patriots of the American Revolution,* published in 1855 with an introduction by Harriet Beecher Stowe. But the language of black protest was in the main successfully suppressed by conservative power. Efforts to change the exclusionary state laws relating to the militia were made at the Massachusetts Constitutional Convention in 1853, under the sponsorship of Freesoiler Henry Wilson. The measure was opposed by the renowned Whig lawyer Rufus Choate and the Democratic machine politician Benjamin F. Hallett. Choate was of the opinion that nothing could be done for "this colored race, by putting them in one of the high places of the Commonwealth, with weapons in their hands, and allow[ing] our glorious banner to throw around them all the pomp and parade and condition of war; the color cleaves to them there, and on parade is only the more conspicuous." Hallett's position was that should a black militia company be called to duty outside the state, its power and authority would not be recognized. When another petition, headed by

Nell and Watkins, was offered to the convention, Hallett argued—successfully—that it should not be entered on the official record. "This final action," Nell wrote, "was highly discreditable to the Convention; for the petitioners, having been virtually excluded from the pale of American citizenship by that body, had a right at least to have their protest . . . placed on the records."[16]

It is not surprising that reform-minded blacks came at this time to focus their attention on their unequal treatment in regard to the militia, or that they were caught up in the militaristic and nationalistic rhetoric that then especially suffused the language of white discourse. But this particular reform campaign posed a special problem for Garrisonians like Watkins. Laying claim to the right to carry a gun in public and to associate formally with other public gun-toters ran counter to the interest most radical reformers felt in peace principles. When Watkins' address was published, its author felt compelled to add a preface:

> The Author is not a man of war. He thinks the Apostolic injunction, "Be at peace with all men," should elicit universal and implicit obedience. These pages are a vindication of our RIGHTS AS CITIZENS, not a discourse upon our DUTY AS CHRISTIANS. A military Hero is not his *beau ideal* of a Christian . . . The vocation of Beelzebub, is to "scatter, tear and slay;" that of Man, to "deal justly, love mercy, and walk humbly before God."

This conflict between peace principles, a bedrock of white as well as of black reform, and the whole system of establishing political rights through revolution, ritually affirmed every Fourth of July, would shortly find its most dramatic expression in the case of Anthony Burns.[17]

 ECLIPSE

An eclipse of the sun, precluded by clouds and falling rain, takes place today, and a shadow darker than the clouds and falling rain lies upon the hearts of all true and thoughtful men.

COMMONWEALTH, May 26, 1854

At 63 Mount Vernon Street, a stone's throw from the trim brick tenements of "Nigger Hill" in the Sixth Ward, Elizabeth Rogers Mason, the twenty-year-old daughter of a millionaire, put down the sentimental novel she was reading—*The Heir of Redclyffe*—and went to the window to watch the eclipse. It was late in the afternoon, and the sun was playing peekaboo with the rain clouds. No one was to have a good look at this veiled, once-in-a-lifetime show. To Elizabeth the western view over the city and the river beyond seemed "impressive . . . a bright darkness, if such contrary terms can be used together, as sometimes before a severe thunderstorm."[1]

Simultaneously, at his house on Summer Street, a sick and weary Edward Everett laid aside Layard's book on Nineveh to observe the eclipse. Having resigned his senatorship two weeks before, after the disgrace of missing the Nebraska vote and of bungling the presentation of the clerical petition, eclipses seemed to suit his mood. How recently he had been spoken of as the worthy inheritor of Webster's mantle—he, the Defender of the Union as Webster had been the Defender of the Constitution. There had been eager talk of his chances for the presidency, which only the temporary weakness of the Whig party prevented him from taking more seriously—that and his damnable habit of breaking under pressure. Only the year before he had told a friend that, yes, he stood a chance for the presidency—if he were younger . . . and if he were a Democrat . . . and if he owned 100 slaves. As he looked out from his scholar's library at the dimmed-down western sun, he knew he had reached and passed the apogee of his public career and would hereafter rest content to be, as Oliver Wendell Holmes without irony called him, "the yardstick by which men are measured in Boston."[2]

Caroline Barrett White of Roxbury looked at the sun, too, and, having a better view, could note that totality occurred at precisely 5:40. She forgot her recent displeasure at the high price of tickets for Anna Cora Mowatt's performances ("I think I have seen as good actresses before") and allowed herself to be dazzled by the moon's passing off the disk of the sun, when "a beautiful crescent was formed, white and silvery." It was a better show by far, she thought, than the dark, disturbing slave case, "which is raising quite an excitement." Her sympathies, however, were clear: "The passage of the Nebraska Bill has so fired the people with *indignation* against the South, that I hope they will show them in this case, that Boston is not the place to catch *men* and carry them back to bondage though it has been done once."[3]

In Cambridge during the eclipse Longfellow was working on a wistful, elegiac poem about the inevitable extinction of a despised and outcast race. Four days later he put "The Jewish Cemetery at Newport" in the mail to *Putnam's,* where it duly appeared in July. How, he wondered, had these refugees, forever alien and unassimilated, come to New England?

> What burst of Christian hate,
> What persecution, merciless and blind,
> Drove o'er the sea—that desert desolate—
> These Ishmaels and Hagars of mankind?

In the spring of 1854 Longfellow was a burned-out academic; his resignation from the Harvard faculty was already given in, and he was now about to deliver the last of his annual lectures on Dante's *Inferno.* His wife said he was looking forward to having time "for other things and to feel free," looking forward to years yet of poetry and the social life. The state of the country and the angry tone of politics depressed him, so he resolutely thought and spoke of "other things." He would praise the nobility and courageous self-sacrifice of his dear friend Charles Sumner, yet he would never feel called on to acknowledge the issues in any less romantic light. Nothing vulgar or disturbing but had its poetic, elegiac, or heroic side, and this he would seek out. In his journal he wrote: "Yesterday a fugitive slave was arrested in Boston! To-day there is an eclipse of the sun. 'Hung be the heavens in black!'"[4]

North of Boston the view was even more obscure. In Gloucester, seventeen-year-old Francis Bennett was clerking at a dry-goods store. "Today," he wrote in his diary, "was the great annular eclipse of the sun. Such an one will not be seen again during this century. It was a source of great disappointment." He had hoped that it would be the most exciting thing since the temperance mob earlier that month "tore the front . . . off of Moses Gilbert's building in Beach St., which was used for a rum shop by an Irishman."[5]

In Salem, young Charlotte Forten had arrived from Philadelphia, where no amount of money, it seemed, could get a black girl into a good school. Her family had had to send her away, as they could afford to do, and so hers was now the latest name on the rolls of the old Higginson Grammar School, so called for Francis Higginson, the Puritan minister who had guided the founding of Massachusetts' first town. The new student passed half this afternoon perched on the schoolhouse roof awaiting a revelation of celestial mechanics "in eager expectation." But "I saw nothing; heard since that the sun made his appearance for a minute or two, but I was not fortunate enough to catch even that momentary glimpse of him." She had spent the foregoing part of the afternoon discussing with her teacher, Mary Shepard, why it was that America's Christian churches supported slavery.[6]

In Boston, the lineal descendant of Francis Higginson was heading out of the chaos of the Vigilance Committee meeting. He had just scribbled a note to his wife back home in Worcester:

> Friday aft'n
> I don't think anything will be done tonight, but tomorrow, if at all. The prospects seem rather brighter than before, and there are *better leaders than I.*
>
> I stay with W[illiam] F[rancis] C[hanning] tonight and will write or telegraph tomorrow.

He put the note in his pocket and walked over to the Fitchburg Depot, which he must have entered in the "bright darkness" of totality, there to meet Martin Stowell and a band of men chosen for having a purpose at heart. Privately, Higginson was conceding that "All hopes now rested on Stowell."[7]

 FANEUIL HALL

I never saw a more earnest feeling.

ANNE WARREN WESTON

When Mr. Burns was kidnapped, a public meeting was called in Faneuil Hall. Who went there? Not one of the men who are accustomed to control public opinion in Boston.

THEODORE PARKER

When Judge Sprague denied the writ of personal replevin at 6:00 P.M., Dana went to visit his client, whom he had not seen since the proceedings on Thursday morning. In the third-floor jury room he found Burns with some six or eight guards whom Dana sized up as "of the rough, thief-catching order."

I withdrew to a window and talked quietly with the man. He appeared a very different man from what he was the day before. He seemed self-possessed, intelligent, and with considerable force both of mind and body. His hand had been broken, in a saw mill, he told me, and his face was scarred by a burn. He said that he had not lived with his master since he was seven years old, but had always been hired out by him. That his master had offered him for sale, and he knew very well that if he was delivered up, he would never see Alexandria again, but would be taken to the first block and sold for the New Orleans market. He said that there, he might be put to some new work he was not accustomed to, and be badly treated for not doing it well. He was in fear of his master, who, he said, was a malicious man if he was crossed.

After this interview Dana went home for supper rather than attend the Faneuil Hall meeting. He was surprised there was so much sentiment in favor of a rescue, but rather more surprised that "some of the Abolitionists talk quite freely about it." A conservative at heart, never quite counting himself among the abolitionists, he thought the natural climate of lawbreaking was secrecy.[1]

He got to his home in Cambridge in time to receive an unexpected visit from Amos A. Lawrence, prince of Boston's Cotton Whigs, a man shaken by the Nebraska Bill out of his long policy of appeasing the slave power. Lawrence told Dana he was prepared to spend whatever it might take to hire an eminent Whig lawyer to serve as co-counsel in the Burns case. The public must understand that it was not Freesoilers only who favored the cause of the slave. The "solid men of Boston" for whom he spoke—those who had supported Webster in 1850—now wanted to go on record on the side of freedom. Dana was stunned: this man, as they both no doubt recalled, had volunteered, in a letter to Marshal Devens, to join the posse in arresting the Shadrach rescuers just three years earlier. Of course Lawrence was not now proposing what the abolitionists were so freely talking about (the Cotton Whigs had not become revolutionaries), but the reversal of policy was astonishing nevertheless: he wanted the Webster Whigs to share in the credit for blocking the rendition, and the only way to have that public glory was to accept it on terms dictated by the Freesoil party! Nebraska had not accomplished this. Nebraska had not this evening brought Amos Lawrence round to Dana's door: Anthony Burns had.[2]

That very evening, while the meeting went on at Faneuil Hall, Dana went to call on the lawyers that Lawrence named. Judge Richard

Fletcher, recently retired from the state supreme court and an opponent of Shaw on school desegregation, was sympathetic but hopelessly tied up with a piece of writing for the *Monthly Law Reporter*. Rufus Choate, whom Dana both feared and worshipped, was ostensibly concerned that taking the case would be inconsistent with his earlier positions. Charles G. Loring was out of town. So, after all, he would have to show up in court tomorrow with only Freesoiler Ellis in tow.[3]

John L. Swift, Vigilance Committee member, estimated the crowd at Faneuil Hall that night at 5,000, the largest attendance anyone could remember. There were no seats on the floor of the large hall—only in the upper galleries—and the excited crowd stood, densely packed, from the stage to the double doors of the south entryway, filling every inch of space beneath the jutting crowded balconies. Parker and Phillips arrived early, escorting abolitionist friends Anne Weston and Phoebe Garnault. Weston, sister of the formidable Maria Weston Chapman, estimated that there were no more than 300 women scattered through the crowd: it was, she said, "a man's meeting." By prior arrangement, Phillips and Parker met the remainder of the rescue committee in the anteroom for some last-minute discussion. Higginson failed to arrive, and with others, not privy to their plans, stopping to talk to them, it became impossible in the mounting noise and bustle to firm up their strategy. Parker at last entered the hall in company with lawyer John Albion Andrew and joined the speakers on the bright, gas-lit stage.[4]

It was 7:00 P.M. The meeting was called to order by Samuel E. Sewall, who had spent the day helping Dana with the writ of replevin. Sewall's public career as a reformer, stretching back to 1836 and including his work on the Latimer case, seemed genealogically ordained, as though he could never forget that he descended from Judge Samuel Sewall, who had published *The Selling of Joseph,* America's first antislavery tract, in 1701. In fact most of the leading white abolitionists were the descendants of long-established Puritan families, so that the history of the Bay State figured for them as a version of family history, a familiar thing, to be cherished, affirmed, and extended. Sewall was also a cousin of Bronson Alcott's wife and a slightly more distant relation of Samuel J. May. By virtue of his years of devotion to antislavery, he was on good terms with all the most active abolitionists in the state. His law partner, George T. Angel, said that "he spent almost half his time in endeavoring to protect the weak and defenceless," and that his office was a place of frequent resort for Sumner, Wilson, Andrew, Garrison, and Phillips. Sewall gloried in the distinction of being the only one of that group to have been personally horsewhipped by a slaveholder. He was a member of the BVC Finance Committee, though as a nonresistant he had already determined to have nothing to do with a rescue.[5]

George R. Russell was chosen to preside at the meeting. He was one of the few wealthy merchants who jumped the Whig party in 1848. Born in 1800, he made his fortune in the China trade as a partner in the firm of Russell and Sturgis and was able to retire to politics and literature by the age of thirty-five. He was a founding member of the Boston Vigilance Committee and, as the treasurer's accounts show, always a dependable and munificent friend to it. When news arrived of the Burns case, his wife sent Wendell Phillips $100 with a note to say that "if more is wanted" he should call on her "for all I have or can command." Russell had recently served as mayor of West Roxbury; later in 1854 he would decline the Freesoil nomination for governor.[6]

Of those chosen vice presidents of the meeting a bare majority were BVC members: Samuel Gridley Howe, William B. Spooner, Francis Jackson, Timothy Gilbert, T. W. Higginson (though not present), and Samuel Downer Jr.—the last a merchant and longtime friend and confidant of Horace Mann. Five were not members: the Rev. Leonard A. Grimes, Samuel Wales Jr., Albert G. Browne of Salem, Gershom B. Weston of Duxbury, and Francis W. Bird of Walpole, chairman of the Free Soil State Central Committee. Lawyers Robert Morris and William I. Bowditch were the secretaries.[7]

Russell's brief opening address established the tone of the meeting by framing the Burns case as an instance of Southern aggression.

> When we get Cuba and Mexico as slave States—when the foreign slave trade is reestablished, with all the appalling horrors of the Middle Passage, and the Atlantic is again filled with the bodies of dead Africans, then we may think it time to waken to our duty! God grant that we may do so soon! The time will come when Slavery will pass away, and our children shall have only its hideous memory to make them wonder at the deeds of their fathers. For one I hope to die in a land of liberty—in a land which no slave hunter shall dare pollute with his presence.

The purpose of the meeting was the same as that which Thoreau announced in the book he was just then finishing: to wake his neighbors up. Nebraska had been a rude shock, but not even Nebraska had seemed at first to stir the North to a convincing sense of its danger. Had it done so, the organizers of the Faneuil Hall meeting would not have been as uncertain as they manifestly were about the popular response to the capture of Burns.[8]

In a more particular sense, the purpose of the meeting was to determine whether a crowd could be assembled at Court Square in the morning and in such a frame of mind as to back a rescue. This was the tenor of the resolutions offered by Howe and of the brief speech by the Freesoil leader, Frank Bird, which urged the crowd to forcible resistance. John L. Swift, the next speaker, insisted that the Nebraska Bill had effectively repealed the Compromise of 1850 and the Fugitive Slave Law with it, as perhaps also the notion of compromise itself. The very word—"compromise"—was an honorific term in every recognizable political context, but now it clashed hopelessly with the categorical imperatives of romantic and Transcendental morality. "This is a contest," said Swift, "between slavery and liberty, and for one I am now and forever on the side of liberty." He was also the first (of many) to exploit the religious symbolism of the event: "Tomorrow Burns will have been incarcerated . . . three days, and I hope tomorrow to witness in his release the resurrection of liberty."[9]

The longer and more effective speeches were the last two, delivered by Phillips and Parker, which are worth looking at as powerful rhetorical performances of a revolutionary character.

Phillips began by relaying the prosaic but crucial information that the city government was on the side of the reformers—that the police had been instructed not to assist "the kidnappers," as the state's Personal Liberty Law prohibited their involvement. He presented this information somewhat disingenuously as an implied leave to mount a rescue: "Tomorrow," he said, "is to determine whether we are ready to do the duty they have left us to do." A revolution does not require the permission of the constituted authorities, but it needs *someone's* permission, and Phillips understood well enough that the crowd would prefer to act—and would be more likely to act—with the blessing of the mayor than without it. The implication that they would not be arrested by the police took some of the terrors and perhaps even some of the illegality out of their prospective activity. But Phillips went further: "There is now no law in Massachusetts, and when law ceases the people may act in their own sovereignty." This is no doubt one of those sentences whose meaning and effect depend on the context of oral delivery. Perhaps he meant to support Swift's contention that the Fugitive Slave Law had become a dead letter, and to add to that the constructive absence of the police, suggesting that no Massachusetts law visibly stood in the way of seizing the moment's vividly real sense of justice. However that may be, he appealed to the crowd in their presumptive legal sovereignty, demanding of them whether they favored the precedent in the case of Shadrach or the precedent in the case of Sims. He was making judges of them, as possibly he thought they really were and of right ought to be. "Will you adhere to the case of Sims, and see this man carried down State street between two hundred men?" "No!" roared the crowd.

> See to it, every one of you, as you love the honor of Boston, that you watch this case so closely that you can look into that man's eyes. When he comes up for trial get a sight of him—and don't lose sight of him. There is nothing like the mute eloquence of a suffering man to urge to duty; be there, and I will trust the result. If Boston streets are to be so often desecrated by the sight of returning fugitives, let us be there, that we may tell our children that we saw it done. There is now no use for Faneuil Hall. Faneuil Hall is the purlieus of the Court House tomorrow morning, where the children of Adams and Hancock may prove that they are not bastards. Let us prove that we are worthy of liberty.[10]

The recent lesson of *Uncle Tom's Cabin*—that there is indeed nothing like the mute eloquence of a suffering man to urge to duty—had made for a large part of the dramatic difference between the public reaction to the Sims case in 1851 and to the Burns case in 1854. Sympathy of a very special sort was now fashionable and could, it turned out, be put to use. This very day there happened to be a Tom show at Worcester City Hall; another, put on by R. Sands & Company, a circus troupe, was touring the North Shore. These dramatic performances were as ubiquitous now as the novel had been a year ago, showing men like Phillips that the new faith came from seeing, not from hearing as in the old time. One of Mrs. Stowe's sympathetic "pictures" had been worth more than all the thousands of words of moralizing abstractions in the mountains of antislavery prose. The eye, which Emerson had called "the best of artists," was also the best of reformers; it took the measure of the real and was the point of essential contact between the world's cruelties and the human heart. Fix that on Anthony Burns, said Wendell Phillips, and the paralysis of cautious thinking will pass off like a dream. The scene of talking will be transformed into the scene of action: Faneuil Hall becomes the Court House. Conscience becomes judgment.[11]

The crowd was already frantic with excitement, then, when Parker rose to speak. He addressed them as men already defeated in a struggle they had scarcely noticed: "Fellow-subjects of Virginia!" he exclaimed. There were loud cries of "No, no," and "You must take that back!"[12]

"Fellow citizens of Boston, then.—I come to condole with you at this second disgrace which is heaped on the city made illustrious by *some* of those faces that were once so familiar to our eyes." His reference was to portraits of the city's revolutionary fathers, which had been removed from their usual conspicuous places in the hall. The emphasis on "some" was an allusion to Webster's portrait, which remained. Parker proceeded to insist that the guilt and shame of the present affair rested squarely with Massachusetts: "A deed which Virginia commands has been done in the city of John Hancock and the 'brace of Adamses.' It was done by a Boston hand. It was a Boston man who issued the warrant; it was a Boston Marshal who put it in execution; they are Boston men who are seeking to kidnap a citizen of Massachusetts, and send him into slavery for ever and ever. It is our fault that it is so."

The speech would make slender demands on Parker's expert knowledge of Massachusetts history: the barest sketching in of the Revolutionary context sufficed to place the present action under the sign of patriot courage and the defiance of foreign despotism. With great economy of reference he surveyed instances during the past eight years of Boston's ineffectual resistance to and outright support of federal provisions for returning fugitive slaves. "Had Faneuil Hall spoken then on the side of Truth and Freedom," he concluded, "we should not now be subjects of Virginia." Taunting them again for their servility before the slave power, Parker evoked renewed cries of protest. "I will take it back," he said, "when you show me that the fact is not so . . . I am not a young man [he was forty-three]; I have heard hurrahs and cheers for liberty many times; I have not seen a great many deeds done for liberty. I ask you, are we to have deeds as well as words?" He made it clear that shame and hypocrisy lay in easy words, valor in hard deeds. He made it clear that this was to be a struggle not for Anthony Burns, but for the soul of Massachusetts and for the manhood of every one of its citizens. Parker, who loathed revival preaching, could lay it on at will.

He presented his auditors with a choice between the "two great laws of this country"—describing first and at length the "law of slavery." This, he said, was the law of the president of the United States, the law of Commissioner Loring, and the law "of every Marshal, and of every meanest ruffian whom the Marshal hires to execute his behests." It had been declared a "finality." Yet it "tramples on the Constitution": "Once the Constitution was formed 'to establish justice, promote tranquillity, and secure the blessings of liberty to ourselves and our posterity.' *Now,* the Constitution is not to secure liberty; it is to extend slavery into Nebraska." But however often he brought Nebraska up, he returned the point immediately to Boston: the law of slavery "treads down State Rights":

> Where are the Rights of Massachusetts? A fugitive slave bill Commissioner has got them all in his pocket. Where is the trial by jury? Watson Freeman has it under his Marshal's staff. Where is the great writ of personal replevin, which our fathers wrested, several hundred years ago, from the tyrants who once lorded it over Great Britain? Judge Sprague trod it under his feet! Where is the sacred right of *habeas corpus?* Deputy Marshal Riley can crush it in his hands, and Boston does not say anything against it. Where are the laws of Massachusetts forbidding State edifices to be used as prisons for the incarceration of fugitives? They, too, are trampled under foot. "Slavery is a finality."

Nothing in the whole record of the Burns affair is more striking to a modern audience or at first more off-putting than the apparent incapacity of even the most committed of the radicals to express a direct, authentic outrage on Burns's personal behalf. Phillips' unelaborated reference to his "suffering" is as close as they come. The evil that Parker undertakes to agitate against is the threat to the civil liberties of Northern white men. There is an oddity about this argument even on the supposition that it consciously appeals to self-interest. No single item in Parker's bill of particulars, taken by itself, could reasonably be expected to alarm the most selfish white man who ever lived. The "great writ of personal replevin" could be utterly abolished—as in fact it has been—without perceptible anguish or injury. The omission of trial by jury in fugitive slave cases carries no implication that it will be any less available than it presently is to the free white population. And, for the audience in Faneuil Hall, no obvious jeopardy attaches to the use of state buildings as federal jails. The resonance of the argument comes from the conspiracy of an invasive foreign power that is made to appear in the pattern. The point about the particular curtailed liberties is not so much that the value of their several uses is lost, but that they are synecdoches for a generalized culture of liberty that is now uniquely Northern (if not specifically Bostonian) and the legacy of a revolutionary past. These "liberties," and liberty in general, are the only thing in the experience of the culture for which, as everyone believed, honorable men had actually fought and died. And if they are to be made to fight again, it must probably be for the same thing and not (at least in the first instance) for something new—as, for example, the right of another man than oneself to be free.

The second of the "two great laws of this country" is Parker's own construction of the meaning of American democracy, though in formulating it he elects to quote a popular Tennessean: "It is the Law of the People when they are sure they are right and determined to go ahead." His main illustration is the laudable conduct of the people of Massachusetts at the time of the Stamp Act, when they coerced the commissioner, the brother-in-law of the governor, into refusing to collect the tax. "That," said Parker, "was an instance of the people going behind a wicked law to enact Absolute Justice into their statute, and making it Common Law." In Parker's philosophical view, the ability of any society to "establish justice" is the ultimate—perhaps the exclusive—test of its legitimacy, and it therefore follows that all societies must have a profound, permanent, and unabridgeable right at any and all times actually to do it. The crucial act in the deed demanded is the supplanting of a lower law by a higher one: it is thus a movement toward more law, more perfect governance, not toward less. The goal is certainly not lawlessness, as Parker's enemies would soon be angrily charging.

Parker summed up: "Well, gentlemen, I say there is one law—slave law; it is everywhere. There is another law, which is also a finality; and that law, it is in your hands and your arms, and you can put it in execution, just when you see fit." He pointed out that he was a clergyman, a man of peace. "But there is a means, and there is an end; Liberty is the end, and sometimes peace is not the means towards it. Now, I want to ask you what you are going to do." From the excited crowd came excited voices: "*Shoot! shoot!*" Parker blanched and fumbled for a reply; he seemed stunned, uncertain. "There are ways of managing this matter without shooting anybody," he said, collecting himself. "Be sure that these men who have kidnapped a man in Boston, are cowards, every mother's son of them; and if we stand up there resolutely, and declare that this man shall not go out of the city of Boston, *without shooting a gun,* then he won't go back." Encouraged by the applause that greeted this remark, Parker asked for a show of hands from those who favored his proposal to adjourn to Court Square at 9:00 the next morning. Many raised their hands, but others loudly declared they would go to the Court House immediately; others proposed to "pay a visit to the slave-catchers at the Revere House." "Put that question," they yelled. Parker hesitated again: it was getting uncomfortably tumultuous and democratic. "It is not a vote," said Parker sternly. "We shall meet at Court Square, at nine o'clock tomorrow morning."

Sufficient order was restored to pass the formal resolutions of the meeting, but immediately again there were cries of angry determination to hunt the slavehunters. The crowd was very nearly out of control. Phillips jumped up from his seat and took the rostrum. He implored the crowd not to balk tomorrow's effort by premature demonstrations, which could only put the enemy on its guard. He tried to make them think well of tomorrow's plan by assuring them it had the sympathy of the moneyed interests of State Street and of the large body of anti-Nebraska Whigs. "The zeal that won't keep till tomorrow," he admonished, "will never free a slave."

At this moment, when Phillips' pleas seemed to have turned aside the wrath of the crowd, a solitary voice boomed out from near the door: "Mr. Chairman, I am just informed that a mob of negroes is in Court Square, attempting to rescue Burns! I move we adjourn to Court Square!"

No one waited for a vote.

THE BATTLE AT THE COURT HOUSE DOOR

Through a long succession of years, Boston has been distinguished for a love of order and good government; and for the honor of the age in which we live, may that fair fame be transmitted, unimpaired, to posterity, that all may exclaim in the fulness of hope,—*God save the Metropolis of Massachusetts.*

MAYOR J. V. C. SMITH, JANUARY 16, 1854

I cannot but think that forcible, revolutionary resistance was justifiable.

ALBERT G. BROWNE JR. TO THOMAS WENTWORTH HIGGINSON, JUNE 19, 1854

Both Phillips and Parker had made conspicuous reference to the mayor's position in the Burns matter—not to commend him for it, but in a vain effort to hold him to it. Dr. Jerome Van Crowninshield Smith, fifty-four years old, was a notoriously pliable man—of the sort then known as a "doughface"—eager as any politician has ever been to please whomever he happened to talk to. Nominally a Freesoiler, yet with strong ties to the proslavery Irish community, Smith owed his broad appeal to a talent for not taking positions, controversial or otherwise. He was best known as the longtime editor of the *Boston Medical and Surgical Journal,* the immediate predecessor of the *New England Journal of Medicine* and a bully pulpit from which he preached vaccination. More recently he had taken to writing pleasant little travel books: at the time of the Burns case his *Turkey and the Turks,* published in 1852, had arrived at its nineteenth printing. Sworn into office at the beginning of the year by Lemuel Shaw, he was, in Dana's words, "a physician of a timid, conceited, scatter-brained character, raised by accident to the Mayoralty."[1]

In one of the few concrete proposals offered in his January inaugural address, he had spoken of his discomfort at being, as mayor, in personal command of the police. This traditional line of authority might seem, he thought, to infringe on the political freedom of these city employees. "Besides it is unsafe . . . to place several hundred men . . . at the free disposal of the chief magistrate, who, under some unforeseen combination of circumstances, might insult and overawe those whom they were appointed to protect." He suggested the creation of a board of police commissioners, but by the end of May the enabling legislation was stalled, and the police remained the mayor's private army.[2]

Smith's concerns reflected a recent turbulence within the department. In 1851, at the time of the coalition between the Freesoilers and the Democrats, it had abandoned its long-standing policy of noninvolvement in city politics, with the result that many veteran officers lost their positions. Francis Tukey, the leading figure in the Shadrach and Sims cases, was appointed to the newly created post of chief of the Boston Watch and Police (vacating the abolished post of city marshal) and then was purged by Mayor Benjamin Seaver in favor of Gilbert Nurse, who was chief when Smith came to office. Permission from the state legislature for a complete reorganization of law enforcement in Boston was sought and granted in 1853, and in the following year the 229-year-old Watch and Police (independent systems of day and night patrols) went out of existence, to be succeeded by the Boston Police Department. Mayor Smith asked for the resignations of every constable and watchman and appointed a new force under Chief Robert Taylor. This change, coincidentally, occurred on May 26, 1854, at 6 P.M., one hour before the Faneuil Hall meeting, and at precisely the moment when Martin Stowell stepped off the train from Worcester and spotted Higginson waiting for him on the platform.[3]

When Higginson told his friend of the plan for the next day's rescue, Stowell said flat out that it wouldn't work. His opinion was that no band of liberators could succeed that offered to act in cold blood. The attempt to moderate passion out of some scruple about violence was a serious tactical mistake: it would set a disastrous upper limit on the courage and determination of the attacking party, and in the end all their effort would be so much force lost. What was needed, Stowell thought, was momentum, such momentum as would be generated at the Faneuil Hall meeting. Yet it would not do to attack the Court House after the meeting, since the marshal would certainly be looking for it and just as certainly be reinforced and ready.

A proper plan—Stowell's plan—took shape while the two men walked back from the depot down Haverhill street. Higginson later recalled it:

Could there not be an attack at the very height of the meeting . . . ? Let all be in readiness; let a picked body be distributed near the Court House and Square; then send some loud-voiced speaker, who should appear in the gallery of Faneuil Hall and announce that there was a mob of negroes already attacking the Court-House; let a speaker, previously warned,—Phillips, if possible,—accept the opportunity promptly, and send the whole meeting pell-mell to Court Square, ready to fall in behind the leaders and bring out the slave. The project struck me as an inspiration. I accepted it heartily.[4]

They stopped briefly at a dry-goods store, where Higginson bought half a dozen new axes nested together in a box, their blades wrapped protectively in brown paper. He told the store clerk his name was "Higgins." Stowell was then sent off to hide the axes in Court Square and to make preparations, while Higginson went on to Faneuil Hall, where the rescue committee was to have assembled before the general meeting. The group, however, never quite managed to get together, and Higginson had to buttonhole individuals as he found them. Bearse rejected the proposal: too much the old salt, Higginson thought, to warm to anything attempted on land. Howe and Parker, seen only in passing, "gave a hasty approval," but there had not been time to make them understand what they were agreeing to. Phillips could not be reached at all, the urgent messages sent out to him lost in the confusion. Kemp, the Irishman, opposed the plan and tried hard to talk Higginson out of it, but when he realized that the assault would go forward with or without him, he gave in. As Higginson summed up the equivocal endorsements, it was five in favor, one against, and one not voting. It was decided.

He got a pledge from John L. Swift, "a young man full of zeal, with a stentorian voice," to give the signal that would break up the meeting. It now remained only to assemble the shock troops, the nucleus of the attack. To ten of Stowell's closest confederates, brought from Worcester and by this time stationed in Court Square, would be added five white men recruited by Kemp, while Lewis Hayden would furnish ten blacks. When the meeting began at 7:00, Higginson was at the door, gazing over the immense crowd at the speakers on the platform. He saw Phillips, but there was no way to communicate with him, there being no open aisle between and no private entrance at the rear. The size of the crowd and its excitement were decidedly encouraging, but he had no way of knowing what the proportion was of curious spectators to ardent sympathizers. He left to take up his position at the Court House and wait.[5]

The light of this cloudy day was failing for a second time as the conspirators milled about the exterior of the building, passing quietly up and down the 200 feet of its eastern and western sides, glancing at City Hall across from its southern end, mixing with the sparse crowds or standing solitary, eyes fixed on the lighted windows that signified a murder trial in progress. Since the day before, when news of the captured fugitive had begun to spread, there had been in Court Square small knots of the somberly curious, hoping to get a sight of this innocent victim of a guilty law. Even to the unsympathetic it was an exotic spectacle, something rarely seen, like the eclipse.

There was a police station in Court Square known as the Center Watch House, but no officers were in sight. A number of them were, in fact, in the Court House, because the Supreme Court was still in session. Lemuel Shaw was presiding over the conclusion of a murder trial that evening. The jury was being charged. At 8:30, while Stowell and Higginson paced the pavement outside, the jury began deliberating the fate of James Wilson, an obviously insane inmate of the state prison, who had strangled William Adams, a guard. John Henry Clifford, prosecutor in the spectacular John White Webster murder case in 1849, Whig governor of Massachusetts in 1852, and now attorney general, appeared for the state.[6]

Suttle was also in the building, consulting with Marshal Freeman and District Attorney Hallett, perhaps airing concerns about a rescue attempt. Freeman had between forty and fifty men with him in the building, a posse of temporary deputies recruited mainly from among Custom House truckmen who owed their livelihood there to Colonel Peter Dunbar, a Democratic machine politician. Other members of the posse were out-of-work Boston policemen. Many of them also had criminal records.[7]

Higginson and the others might simply have walked into the building and taken up positions inside, but instead they awaited the crowd from Faneuil Hall. The delay seemed endless. At last, at about 9:30, Higginson caught sight of "a rush of running figures, like the sweep of a wave," coming up State Street from the direction of the hall. "I watched it," he later said, "with such breathless anxiety as I have experienced only twice or thrice in my life." As this first group came up, Higginson's heart sank within him: it contained no familiar faces, none of the leaders from Faneuil Hall, but instead "the froth and scum of the meeting." Someone emerged from the basement of the Court House near where Higginson was standing, looked him in the face for a moment, then retreated in alarm, shutting and locking the door behind him. Mingling in the crowd, Higginson quickly found Kemp, who advised him to wait until a stronger force arrived, predicting disaster if he moved too soon. But Stowell had already broken out the axes. Some of Stowell's men, as if in quotation of the Jerry Rescue, were bringing up a long wooden beam taken from a nearby construction site. At Stowell's direction it was brought to the door at the south end of the west side, which gave on to the stairway leading up to the jury room and the prisoner. Higginson grabbed the end of the beam across from a burly black man, and they and Lewis Hayden and the dozen other men who had hold of it took it up the few stone steps of the entryway and swung it hard against the panel of the oaken double doors.[8]

As the attack commenced, the crowd from Faneuil Hall continued to arrive in Court Square, though a good part of it dallied uselessly on the east side of the building. In fact, many fewer came than Higginson had expected. When Swift's announcement broke up the meeting, many in the audience suspected a trick. Since Parker and Phillips had made it clear that they thought an immediate assault on the Court House would be unwise—that it would jeopardize the morning's rescue—it seemed not implausible that this sudden news was an invention of enemies to betray the abolitionists into a calamitous—or ludicrous—course of action. Others, undoubtedly thinking of the Shadrach case, were only too glad to have the blacks rescue their own; perhaps, on second thought, attacking public buildings in the night was not, after all, the clear duty of a gentleman. But most critical in keeping down attendance at Court that night was the architecture of Faneuil Hall: with only a single exit for the whole assembly, its potential leaders and directors found themselves hopelessly trapped in the rear. By the time they got into the street a majority of the crowd had already elected in favor of home and hearth. "I never saw such enthusiasm," said Higginson of the Faneuil Hall meeting, "and (though warned that it would be so) I could not possibly believe that it would exhale so idly as it did in Court Square."[9]

Still, the crowd at the Court House now numbered 500 or more. The door, stout and resistant, was being rammed repeatedly, while the Court House responded with its bell in tones of seeming pain and panic. Watson Freeman gathered a squad of 15 in the besieged entryway; heads appeared at open windows on the third floor; pistol shots rang out. Most said the shooting came first from guards at the upper windows, though in fact all the damage from gunfire was in the building. Windows were shot out, including some in Lemuel Shaw's courtroom, but most were shattered by cobbles and brickbats.[10]

Report of a "noise in Court Square" brought Police Chief Robert Taylor out from the station house, the first officer to respond. In the space between the Court House and City Hall, he saw a man shinny up a lamppost and extinguish the gaslight. Taylor assisted another officer in arresting the man, John J. Roberts, a mechanic employed at the machine shop of the Boston and Worcester Railroad. Roberts had been at the Faneuil Hall meeting with his friend, Alonzo Colburn, to whom, just minutes before, he had confided the hope that there would be "no trouble or riot about the slave that night." Colburn said that it was bad business to attack the Court House, and Roberts agreed. But when they got there, it was Roberts who responded to the cry "Douse the lights!" He was taken by Taylor to the Williams Court lockup.[11]

The police were absurdly ineffective because they could arrest only one rioter at a time and then had to escort the offender to jail, putting themselves out of action for up to a quarter of an hour on each occasion. As a tactical matter, the rioters might as well have been arresting the police. When Taylor returned from Williams Court, he got his first good look along the west side of the building: the square was full, people were shooting at the Court House and throwing bricks, screaming "Take him out!" and "Rescue him!" and—indicative of the confusion of it all—"Where is he?" At the south end of the building Taylor saw several men striking the door with axes. He later testified: "When I got there they had a stick of timber; should judge there were from twelve to twenty men hold of the timber; think I cried out 'hold on'; I then went up to the steps and seized a man by the collar who had struck the door twice with an axe, and was in the attitude of striking again." This was the arrest of Martin Stowell. Taylor took him off to Williams Court. After that he made one more visit to Court Square and one more arrest—of Walter Phenix, a black man, for throwing a brick. The chief had personally made three of the nine arrests that evening.[12]

A great deal had happened, however, before Stowell was taken off. The party with the battering ram, including Higginson, Hayden, and the lawyer Seth Webb Jr., had managed at length to force the door. The marshal's guard within secured it, but a few moments later, with one of the lower panels broken though, a main hinge gave way, and the right-hand door swung slantingly open, giving just room enough for a man to enter. Higginson recalled: "I glanced instinctively at my black ally. He did not even look at me, but sprang in first, I following." Another black man, the third to enter, seems to have made it just barely past the threshold. The passageway, lit by a single gas lamp twelve feet back from the door, was defended by several rows of special deputies wielding billy clubs. Freeman was in the third row back, urging on his men, who were now slashing away with their clubs, aiming—to the extent that aiming was possible—for the head. In the front rank of deputies, Sullivan Cutting, otherwise employed as a watchman, had his left hand on the door when the beam came through. He cried out: "Boys, they are after us—come up here." James Batchelder, a twenty-four-year-old Irish-born Custom House truckman, placed himself on Cutting's right, squarely in the middle of the entry. He was there, his left hand bracing the door when, two poundings later, it crashed open and a burly six-foot black man was upon him.[13]

There was a brief, furious hand-to-hand scuffle before the attackers were beaten back. As they exited the passageway, Batchelder, facing the open door, suddenly staggered backward, exclaiming, "I am stabbed!" then collapsed sideways into the arms of friend and fellow Custom House worker Isaac Jones. Jones and another man carried him to the marshal's office, just off the corridor, and laid him out on the floor. Blood, oozing from his groin, pooled on the carpet. He died a few moments later without saying another word. Cutting, who had, with Batchelder, borne the brunt of the fighting, supposed (the dying exclamation notwithstanding) that his comrade had been shot. He and others reported hearing gunfire at the time, and saw a muzzle flash. At least two men—Martin Stowell and Lewis Hayden—had in fact fired pistols into the doorway to cover the retreat of Higginson and his fellows. Hayden was never apprehended. Stowell, arrested some moments later for hacking at the door with an ax (it had been shut again), spent the night in jail, the pistol still lying undiscovered in his pocket.[14]

When Higginson emerged, his face bloodied by a gash in the chin, he yelled out from the steps: "You cowards, will you desert us now?" The repulse of the attackers—rather than the death of Batchelder, which was yet unknown—took out what little starch was left in the mob. To Higginson it all seemed to come down to a matter of personal courage, an important matter—especially to those like him who, in their despair at the cheapness of much talking, supposed that the next step, that of revolution, was at hand. This is how he had read the excitement at Faneuil Hall—what he had read also in the eye of Samuel Gridley Howe, who had fired the BVC meeting at the Meionaon; who had promised to march at the head of 200 liberators on Saturday morning; who had written to Parker that "the man shall not go out into slavery, but over our bodies"; who had approved the late-developed plan of this evening's attack. What of Chevalier Howe? Where was he? In fact he had arrived on the spot late, like the other leaders, but in time to see the breaking in of the door. There he hesitated and thought of his wife, Julia Ward, at home all that day in bed, pregnant and sick with a fever, worn out with what she called, in a letter of the next day, her "habitual struggle against crying." Howe watched the son of the ex-mayor of Salem, a student in Ned Loring's Law School class, throw a brick at the deputies through the open door. Then he went home.[15]

And what of Dr. Bowditch, who had so resented Higginson's implied slur on the courage of the Boston men? When he left Faneuil Hall, he had only the vaguest idea of the new plan, and might have gone home, except that outside the hall he came across John L. Swift, who was trying to steer the crowd up the hill to the Court House. Remembering that Parker and Phillips had done what they could to restrain this self-same crowd, Bowditch felt an "indecision":

> I supposed that the attack was made by foolhardy individuals who had not calculated the cost. I, however, rushed towards Court Square. Mingling in the crowd in the darkness, I lost Swift. A large body was on the east side, but the persons seemed collected without any purpose. I was alone; I knew not whether they were police or friends of the slave. Soon I heard the crack of what seemed a pistol-shot on the west side, and immediately a loud pounding as if doors were being battered down. I ran round, but all was over, and the multitudes were flying, apparently from the very spot. Only two or three, apparently, had hold of a beam; but before I reached them it was dropped, and one or two had gone in, but the door was immediately closed from within. I walked near, and certainly I never had more mingled emotions of shame and horror. Was I called upon to rush in after and give myself up in a hopeless conflict, or should I pass out from the Square? I chose the latter alternative. I am now glad I did so. It could have done no good to do otherwise. I heard afterwards that Kemp and others of our best men were trying to check the too ardent and premature movements of Higginson and his party, for I suppose I do them no dishonor in thus writing the truth. It was noble on their part. Would to God we had more like them! When Massachusetts is filled with such, then slave hunting will be impossible. I felt I was really unworthy of them when I passed away.[16]

Wendell Phillips did not get even that close. When the meeting broke up he escorted his female houseguests home. There he looked in on his invalid bedridden wife, Ann, described on that day as "pale and suffering." Only then, with Edmund Quincy, did he venture out to see what was doing in Court Square. But by the time they arrived, the night's work was finished, and not until the next day did they learn what had happened.[17]

Samuel Sewall left the Faneuil Hall meeting long before it was finished, arriving at his estate in suburban Melrose by 10:00. He reported to his aunt, Hannah Robie, that the meeting had been enthusiastic and unanimous in its determination that the slave should not be carried off. He supposed there was danger of bloodshed in tomorrow's rescue and would not participate. Mrs. Robie thought "he is very willing it should be done, and I am sure I hope it will."[18]

Bronson Alcott, walking stick in hand, proceeded at his usual measured pace from Faneuil Hall to the Court House and arrived just after the killing of Batchelder. He approached Higginson, who stood in front of the Railroad Exchange across the street from the fatal door, tending to his wound. "Why are we not within?" asked Alcott. "Because these people," Higginson replied, motioning to the crowd, "will not stand by us." Without a further word, Alcott crossed the street, his walking stick swinging at his side, and, with a hundred eyes fixed on him, calmly mounted the steps and peered inside. Higginson later claimed that a revolver shot rang out at this moment from inside. If it happened, Alcott never mentioned it. In any event he turned and retreated, not varying even for a moment from his usual measured pace. Higginson ever after kept the grateful and astonished remembrance of this act of courage.[19]

AFTERMATH

Under the excitement that now pervades the city, you are respectfully requested to cooperate with the Municipal Authorities in the maintenance of peace and good order.

The laws must be obeyed, let the consequences be what they may.

MAYOR J. V. C. SMITH, MAY 27, 1854

The defenders of the Court House door had, with reason, been as frightened as the attacking party outside. The marshal later said that the surprise had been complete and that a slightly larger or more determined mob might have succeeded in taking Burns that night; this was also Higginson's opinion. Yet even if they had overcome the posse on the first floor, the attackers would have encountered difficulties at the door of Burns's cell, which was "barricaded by seven massive iron bars extending from top to bottom at intervals of not more than a foot," and with the half-dozen well-armed guards confined behind it with the prisoner. Freeman and the men below, not expecting an attack, had been armed only with billy clubs—or so they later swore. Higginson himself had seen no swords or sabers but always maintained he had been slashed by an edged weapon. Others, including Howe, who looked in from the street, claimed to have seen cutlasses. At the first lull in the attack, however, sidearms were distributed from the marshal's office, and the men then ranged themselves along the stairs of the entryway, a descending line of heads and pistols showing above the balustrade.[1]

Suttle had scuttled out the east door when the gunplay started, leaving Freeman to guard his property.[2]

Most of the jury in the Wilson murder trial at the far end of the building had kept their heads down during the fight, but a few peeked out the windows and were shot at for their curiosity. Clifford later commented on the shocking disorderly irony of a murder's interrupting a murder trial. "Judges, Jurors, Counsel & Culprit," he wrote, had been "exposed to the missiles of a mob which came crashing through the windows of the Court Room." The harried jury nevertheless did its duty, came out when the trouble ceased, and gave in a verdict of guilty at precisely 10:15. James Wilson would hang. Most of the radical abolitionists were also firm opponents of the death penalty, but if anyone cared about the fate of this man, that night or ever, the evidence of it has disappeared.[3]

Lemuel Shaw, ashen-faced and shaken (though not by the verdict), demanded a police escort home and got it. Clifford and the other judges, Theron Metcalf and George T. Bigelow, couldn't get out of the Court House fast enough. They made their way to the Tremont House, angry that police and city officials had been so conspicuous by their absence. They found Mayor Smith at the hotel—whether because they knew his whereabouts or by happenstance does not appear—and Clifford gave him a public dressing down. The first point of his lecture involved the stupidity of the policy whereby for a few dollars of rent the U.S. government became entitled to use Boston's Court House at will for a slave pen, making possible such riots as had just happened. The second point involved the suggestion that when the Court House was attacked by an armed mob, a responsible, self-respecting city government might be expected to make some show of objection. His Honor replied that the police were, in fact, on the ground, and that for his part he had done what he could to suppress the riot. Smith added that what had been said at Faneuil Hall about his sympathy for the slave was "utterly false."[4]

Probably in consequence of this galling interview, Smith determined to spend the night at City Hall and, in a move of questionable legality, called out two companies of state militia to stand guard. These were the forty-man Companies A and B, Fifth Regiment of Artillery, Massachusetts Volunteer Militia, known respectively as the Boston Artillery (Captain Thomas H. Evans), posted at City Hall, and the Columbian Artillery (Captain Thomas Cass), posted at the Court House. They appeared at midnight, and within half an hour Court Square was clear of civilians.[5]

Meanwhile Watson Freeman was making his own security provisions. Shortly after 10:00 he despatched his deputy, John H. Riley, to East Boston to charter the steamer *John Taylor* and with that ship to pick up a company of U.S. Marines at Fort Independence. These men, commanded by Major S. C. Ridgely, were quartered in the Court House by sunrise. They joined another force of Marines procured at the same time from the Charlestown Navy Yard by another deputy. Over the next several days Freeman recruited additional men for his personal guard, which eventually numbered 125.[6]

Early on Saturday morning, Freeman sent a telegram to President Franklin Pierce:

> In consequence of an attack upon the Court House last night, for the purpose of rescuing a fugitive slave under arrest, and in which one of my own guards was killed, I have availed myself of the resources of the United States, placed under my control by letter from the War and Navy Departments in 1851, and now have two companies of troops from Fort Independence stationed in the Court House. Every thing is now quiet. The attack was repulsed by my own guard.

Pierce wired back: "Your conduct is approved. The law must be executed."[7]

After the fight, when he was about to leave the scene, Higginson was reminded by a friend that he had left his umbrella on the railing by the Court House door; conceding that the forces of law and order had won the field, he picked up "this important bit of evidence" and went to spend the night at the home of his kinsman Dr. William F. Channing. There, while his wound was being tended to, he remembered the note, still in his pocket, that he had earlier scrawled to his wife. He added a few sentences: "There has been an attempt at rescue and failed. I am not hurt, except a scratch on the face which will probably prevent me from doing anything more about it, lest I be recognized. But I shall not come home till Monday morn."[8]

If he was expecting further forcible tactics over the weekend, he was to be disappointed, for by the time he awoke on Saturday morning, the Court House was impregnably defended. Soldiers kept the crowds from the building and off the sidewalks; in fact, much of the square had been cordoned off with ropes. Mercifully they had avoided the horrible symbolism of 1851, when the Court House had been encircled with heavy chains, obliging the judges, even the majestic Lemuel Shaw, to stoop on entering. But the visible reminders that Boston's Court House had become a federal fortress and slave pen were no less incendiary to the public. The identity of interests between the Southern slave power and the national government could not have been more vividly exemplified.

The Boston Vigilance Committee leadership met early that morning at Tremont Temple. Among the few nonmembers present was a young Harvard divinity student, Moncure Daniel Conway, who had come in from Cambridge to see Wendell Phillips. Born and raised in Falmouth, Virginia, Conway belonged to a well-to-do slaveholding family who were in fact distantly related to Brent and near neighbors of Suttle. In 1848 Suttle had been the Whig candidate from Stafford County for the Virginia House of Delegates, running against Conway's uncle, Richard Moncure. Then sixteen years old, Conway contributed an anonymous political squib to the local paper that made free with Suttle's corpulent person and shifty character and included a predictable pun on the candidate's name. Suttle lost the election that year, though he won in 1849 and 1850 against other opponents. While Suttle went to Richmond, Conway, still in his teens, became interested in universal free education as advocated by Horace Mann, a cause that in his own state he found tragically blocked by slavery. He began reading Horace Greeley's *Tribune* and was fascinated by the reform ideas he found there. He was increasingly drawn to the more progressive social schemes of the North as remedies for the defects, daily more evident to him, in the slave culture of his native region. Behind this attraction, as also behind his growing desire to reach and elevate the people of Virginia through a spiritual ministry, was the central and ever-widening influence of Emerson's writings. Without access to Emerson's Divinity School Address (he allowed that it would have made a difference) he chose, as by default, a familiar sort of evangelical Methodism as the vehicle for his New England–tinged gospel of self-culture. It proved, however, an unsatisfactory vehicle, and in a short time, on the recommendation of two Unitarian ministers who knew Emerson well—George Burnap and Orville Dewey, whom he met in Baltimore—Conway headed North to enroll in the Divinity School at Cambridge. It was from here that he began to cultivate the personal acquaintance of his hero in Concord and consciously to equip himself with new views on life.[9]

At the meeting at Tremont Temple Conway found "a small number of antislavery leaders." He noticed particularly the seated figure of Wentworth Higginson, "holding part of his cloak over his mouth." The cloak is an interesting detail, since overnight Higginson's identity had become as crucial a question for the authorities as that of Anthony Burns had been. The marshal's men could identify their attackers (including the presumptive murderer of Batchelder) only as two stout Negroes and a white man wearing a "shawl." The fashion of shawls for men was the inspiration of cotton mill owner Samuel Lawrence, whose invention of the popular "Bay State shawl" was credited with pulling the industry out of the doldrums. Thus, for the time being, the police who were investigating the murder could be on the lookout for an abolitionist wearing a product of slave labor.[10]

Higginson said nothing at the meeting. In fact the only one known to have spoken was Parker, whose theme was a bowing to the inevitable. He thought any forcible action this morning at the Court House would be impractical and fraught with danger. He would not participate and was unwilling to advise others to a risk he would not run himself. The fate of the slave he regarded as sealed. All this was said in tones of deep chagrin and exasperation, and was probably couched as a direct rebuke to Higginson.[11]

He knew—they all knew—that there was nothing to be hoped for in the legal proceedings that were about to begin. The lawyers had found no flaw in the record of the Virginia court. As Dana said:

The legal questions respecting the admissibility of such a record had been fully presented by Mr. Charles G. Loring and Mr. Rantoul, in the case of Sims, and had been over-ruled. We had little doubt that Judge Loring would follow that precedent. The Supreme Court of Massachusetts, and the Circuit Court of this Circuit had pronounced the law constitutional, and sustained the jurisdiction of the Commissioner. On the point of identity, there was no hope of a defence. Col. Suttle and Mr. Brent were present, who had known him from a boy, and the latter was a competent witness. Burns had admitted the facts in the presence of Brent and the officers, and he had answered in open Court to the name in the Record. We had no reasonable hope of a successful defence.

The universal expectation was that Burns would be remanded to Suttle's custody this morning. Thus the urgency of the still percolating plans of rescue.[12]

Charles M. Ellis attended this meeting also, and must have confirmed to the group the hopelessness of Burns's legal position. He had earlier decided not to participate in the defense, partly out of a sense of its pointlessness, but more because of his current ill health, his continuing duties at the police court, and the wishes of his family that he not become involved. But learning of the previous night's failed rescue, he found his duty somehow altered, and "in view of what had happened," he got leave from the police court judge to absent himself and would now, he decided, stand with Dana against the government.[13]

As the meeting broke up, Parker prevailed on Higginson, in view of his "somewhat battered condition," to go home. He could do nothing more in Boston, and there was danger in his staying. Parker, Phillips, and Ellis then went together to Dana's office, where it was at last agreed that a legal defense would be mounted. Ellis' offer to assist was accepted, and the four men made their way across to the Court House, arriving shortly before 10:00. Burns had been brought in a little after 9:00, as the *Liberator* reported, "hand-cuffed and guarded by five desperate looking fellows, all of whom were armed with revolvers, the handles of which protruded from the pockets of their coats." The lawyers got in only by picking their way through the crowds of armed militiamen that lined the stairs and the Marine platoons with fixed bayonets that filled and blocked the passageways. Guns were everywhere; even Suttle's lawyers, nervous and presumably threatened, were carrying pistols. The defense attorneys made a point of going unarmed.[14]

The state courts found it impossible to conduct business in this swarm of soldiers. At the far end of the building this morning, Lemuel Shaw hurriedly sentenced James Wilson to be "confined to hard labor in the House of Correction for one year from the 26th of May, 1854, and then to be taken to the place of execution, and hanged by the neck until dead." He then as hurriedly left the building, shutting down the Supreme Judicial Court for the duration of the Burns affair. "Thus," Dana commented, "the Judiciary of Massachusetts has been a second time put under the feet of the lowest tribunal of the Federal Judiciary, in a proceeding under the Fugitive Slave Law."[15]

As the Burns hearing opened at 10:15, Ellis immediately moved for a delay, stating that since he and Dana had been retained only the previous evening, the defense had not had proper time to prepare a case. He thought that the overwhelming show of military force and the excitement that had produced it were not conducive to a judicial hearing, and sought a delay for that reason as well. Calm deliberation was especially necessary in a case that would determine, without the possibility of appeal, the question of a man's freedom or perpetual slavery.[16]

Edward G. Parker opposed the delay on the ground that no amount of time could produce a rational challenge to the documents in the case, which were decisive. He further took the position that the commissioner's decision was merely "preliminary"—would, that is, merely return the man to Virginia, rather than settle the relation of the parties: if Burns maintained that he was not a slave, that question would properly be determined by a court in his home state. Parker closed by suggesting that public excitement in Boston was a reason to expedite matters, not to delay them. Seth Thomas, in seconding these arguments, at one point expressed the hope that opposing counsel were not, as he feared they might be, among those who had Batchelder's blood on their hands. The facts in the present case admitted of no defense. No reason advanced for a continuance amounted to anything but an objection to the law itself: it was every bit as treasonous to seek this law's nullification as to "go to the other end of the courthouse and rescue the man who has been tried and found guilty of murder."[17]

Dana replied that indeed they might not have a defense, but they hadn't had time even to determine that. More time than they were now asking for had been granted in the Sims case. He went on to contradict Parker's assertion that a remanded fugitive could plead for his freedom in the state from which he had escaped: such a provision had been in Henry Clay's original bill, but it had been rejected, and the claimant might now take his recovered slave anywhere—even sell him to the New Orleans market, as Burns presently feared that Suttle would do—and not even the Supreme Court could prevent it. This was not an action for extradition, as the learned counsel asserted; it had not one feature of extradition, but was instead the restoration of a man to another man as private property, an entirely unique proceeding, which ought on that account alone to be conducted with utmost deliberation. "A suit on a note of hand for twenty-five dollars," Dana pointed out, "could not be tried except after two weeks' notice, and several days more for filing pleas or answers; and here a day's delay is objected to in a case which practically decides the freedom of a man forever."[18]

Judge Loring ruled that the request for a delay was reasonable and within the discretion of the court to grant—and adjourned the proceedings until Monday at 11:00.

Another legal proceeding was under way that morning in yet another part of the building: the arraignment of the nine Court House rioters. Thomas Drew, associate editor of the Worcester *Spy,* who had come into Boston with Stowell the day before, and Simon P. Hanscom, a Vigilance Committee member and a reporter for the *Commonwealth,* attended the session at Judge Thomas Russell's Police Court. When they arrived, the judge called Drew over and told him there was a man downstairs who wanted to see him. Descending into the "tombs"—the bank of brick-lined holding cells in the Court House basement—Drew was allowed a private interview with Stowell, who told him that he had slept the previous night in a particular cell in the Williams Court lockup and that he had hidden his pistol—the one Drew had given him in Worcester yesterday morning—under the mattress there. "I'm afraid, Tom," he said, "I did some mischief with that pistol, and if they find it, it will go hard with me. Can't you get hold of it?"

Drew and Hanscom left immediately for Williams Court, where they found the station guarded by a single constable dozing in a chair at the doorway. They struck up a conversation with him and at length invited him to "take something" at the Bell in Hand, a nearby saloon. "I don't mind going," the policeman replied, "but I can't leave this place alone." Hanscom resolved the difficulty by suggesting that his friend Tom would be happy to watch it for awhile. The officer got his drink, and Drew got his pistol.[19]

Meanwhile, at the Court House, Stowell and the other eight men were held on a rather indiscriminate charge of "having committed, with malice aforethought, a felonious assault, on the 26th day of May, 1854, upon the person of James Batchelder, with firearms loaded with powder and ball, and that they did kill and murder the said Batchelder." Charles G. Davis, acting as attorney for the whole group, expressed his opinion that the state simply wanted them all held on an unbailable charge while it figured out how to proceed. He thought the least they could do would be to exclude those who had been arrested before Batchelder was killed, but Judge Russell put off going into particulars until the following Tuesday.[20]

🌿 FOR SALE

And so the reliance on Property, including the reliance on governments which protect it, is the want of self-reliance.

EMERSON, "SELF-RELIANCE"

Dana had been more than usually brilliant that morning. Something in the nature of the case, now that he was past the embarrassing rocky start of it, was making him eloquent, even in procedural matters. "I . . . never spoke more to my satisfaction in my life," he wrote in his journal. The other lawyers, throughout the trial, would betray a constant guarded fear that decisions would go against them, and accordingly labored to give their arguments emotional and rhetorical weight; they affected outrage, indulged in hyperbole, and showed at every turn something of the pressure they felt. This was never Dana's way, who was always the least nervous, least contentious man in the courtroom. In the present contest, he thought young Parker, with his evident shamefacedness, and Thomas, with his "petty, mean voice and manner," were "the best foils I could have desired." There was more than a little arrogance in Dana's self-conscious and rather theatrical approach to the courtroom, but his poise and talent were undeniable. His lawyerly genius consisted in making his own sense of the issue seem to his audience (always principally the commissioner) noble, beautiful, sweetly reasonable, and at last inevitable. Does he wish a continuance? He begins at once to consider why the commissioner should *want* to grant one. Of course, he would imply, a gentleman would not be rushed to judgment by threats of violence. Surely the commissioner would wish to present a public face of independence and judiciousness when the presumption was universal that he loved the Fugitive Slave Law, and that he would do in office what those who appointed him expected. How would it look, after all, if he hurried the defense into a trial? A good lawyer does his job when he shows a judge a clear and alluring path to the desired end, be that end what it may. He must see for the judge, and the judge must see through his eyes.[1]

The other lawyers, including Ellis, were apt to get sidetracked onto issues having no useful effect on making the commissioner tractable. Ellis' hobbyhorse was the question of whether Burns was or was not handcuffed during the proceedings. His great fault as a lawyer was that he never missed a chance to feel outraged on his client's behalf. Opposing counsel chose to make a fetish of the law—a better tactic, as keeping the commissioner in mind of the position from which Dana was bent on prying him. But then the commissioner knew the law, or supposed he did, so that the reiteration of this approach by Suttle's attorneys was bound to become tiresome, even condescending. Their position was that a certain law having been enacted, the judiciary was bound to look on its operation as utterly routine and unremarkable. If Dana kept insisting that here was a weighty matter involving a man's freedom, Thomas and Parker were there to suggest that it was nothing more than an action to recover property. There were no moral questions beyond those sufficiently addressed by the law itself. At bottom, however, the reliance of Suttle's lawyers was not on the affirmative argument, but on a designedly intimidating display of the terrors of nullification, of what could be expected to follow from the lawlessness of any course but that of sending Anthony Burns to slavery in Virginia.

The main difficulty confronting Thomas and Parker—one already evident in Saturday's hearing—was that because Dana was so superlatively good at his job, they often found themselves in a reactive stance, probing his speeches for the vulnerable sentence, or his sentences for the vulnerable clause. This is what seemed to be happening when, from Dana's lengthy summation of the grounds for a continuance, Parker singled out for objection one of the very smallest points—the claim that Suttle, given custody of Burns, might well sell him in New Orleans. His whole reply to Dana's well-reasoned motion consisted of a denial that Suttle had any such intention—and of the logically subordinate assertion that his client would be willing to sell his man here and now. At that point Loring granted the motion for continuance, and Parker's bit of news hung unregarded in the air, its significance as a modest offering against the granting of the motion immediately deflated.

But in the audience Leonard Grimes was listening with a mind preoccupied with different concerns, and what others missed, he heard. When court was adjourned a few moments later, he approached Parker and Suttle and sounded them out about the offer to sell Burns. Parker, who had impressed Dana as "timid" and "ashamed of what he was doing," had in fact grown more and more unhappy about his role in the whole affair and fearful of what it might cost him professionally; that very morning he had urged his client to consider a sale. Suttle had consented, but without enthusiasm. He would ask $1,200, stipulating that the money had to be raised today, although the goods would not be delivered until the commissioner had rendered his decision. Suttle wasn't about to let the transaction be used, in bad faith, to delay or derail the hearing. That, in any event, seems to have been his position when Parker spoke of it in open court. Now, under the impact of Loring's grant of a delay, Suttle backed off more than a little and, in this face-to-face negotiation with Grimes in the courtroom, agreed to a sale that would legally preempt a decision.

Parker was anxious that the agreement should be concluded before Suttle changed his mind, and more than once he impressed on Grimes that "all must be done that day or never." Grimes, of course, did not have $1,200, but he thought he could raise it by subscription. The lawyer immediately wrote out a paper and handed it to the clergyman:

Boston May 27. 1854

It being understood that the person named Anthony Byrnes now & here claimed as a fugitive will be sold by his alleged master for a sum certain to wit $1200; we whose names are annexed promise to pay the sums annexed to their names for that purpose forthwith—[2]

Grimes was well suited to the task he assumed at that moment and to which he would devote all the remaining hours of the day. He had been raising funds since his arrival in Boston in November 1848, when, at a salary of only $100 a year, he became pastor of the homeless Twelfth Baptist Church and its twenty-three members. Since then his congregation had increased tenfold, and a tidy little stone church had been erected on Southac Street at a cost of $13,000—a sum already more than half paid off. Beyond that, money had constantly to be raised to meet the urgent needs of the many poor of the parish. A significant portion of his flock were escaped slaves, and the freedom of some of these had been bought with the help of church funds.

Grimes knew the ways of slavery a good deal better than the other clergymen of Boston. Born to free parents in Leesburg, Virginia, in 1815, he had assisted many fugitives while working as a hackney driver in Washington, D.C. Arrested and convicted for aiding in the escape of some Virginia slaves, he had served two years in a Richmond prison. There he had experienced a religious conversion and begun to preach. He returned to Washington and his work on the Underground Railroad, but his calling to a religious life soon took him to his first regular pastorate, in New Bedford, Massachusetts, the Quaker port city that a few years before had so surprised Frederick Douglass with its wealth and refinement. Leaving for Boston two years later, Grimes became a highly regarded spokesman for and defender of the interests of the black community. It was said of him that he was not an eloquent speaker—his education had been rudimentary at best—"but as a pastor he had no equals, and was powerful in prayer."[3]

Grimes would have to make his appeal where the money was, in the white community. He first contacted Hamilton Willis, a Boston merchant and stockbroker who had retired from business in 1853, having made his fortune. Willis' aunt was Abigail May, wife of Bronson Alcott; his uncle was the prominent abolitionist Samuel J. May.[4]

Willis entered into the project immediately, contributed twenty-five dollars, and offered to advance the full amount against the secured pledges. He seems to have disliked the form that Parker had written out, perhaps objecting to a bill of sale that on the face of it called attention to Suttle's ambiguous right of ownership. Willis wrote out a new instrument, reproducing Parker's misspelling of Burns's name:

> Boston, May 27, 1854.
>
> We, the undersigned, agree to pay to Anthony Byrnes, or order, the sum set against our respective names, for the purpose of enabling him to obtain his freedom from the United States Government, in the hands of whose officers he is now held as a slave.

Willis promised to be present at the meeting that evening at Loring's office, where the sale was to be concluded. Grimes took the paper and left. The first and most munificent donations were from Hunker Whigs, Thomas B. and Charles P. Curtis, whose availability for this purpose had been intimated to Grimes by lawyer Parker. At 4:00 Grimes was at the Court House, soliciting a donation from Benjamin F. Hallett, the U.S. district attorney, who had in fact been busily discouraging potential subscribers. Hallett told him that the sale would not be allowed—that the law, as obnoxious to him as to anybody, could not be trampled under foot. When Grimes persisted, he said he would not give anything now, but that if the man were sent back, then perhaps he would pay $100. Grimes said that he wanted the money now or never.[5]

When Dana saw Grimes early that evening, he was in the company of Boston merchant J. M. S. Williams, who had pledged $50. They informed Dana that they had raised nearly $700 and had contingent offers for more. Inevitably there was some talk about the steepness of the price demanded. Dana's main impression was of the strangeness of it all. He remembered that Burns had told him that Suttle took out an $800 insurance policy on him when he was in Richmond, from which fact Burns deduced that he was probably not worth more than $1,000. "It was a new language," Dana concluded, "to hear a man estimating his own value by the rate at which his owners insured him."[6]

By this time, around 8:00, Suttle's lawyers were out in the streets trolling for millionaires. Shortly before 8:30, Parker—or Thomas—stopped at the Mt. Vernon Street home of William Powell Mason, whose daughter, twenty-year-old Elizabeth, could not decide "whether to think [the purchase] wise or not—on some accounts it is certainly bad." (*Uncle Tom's Cabin* had not made it easier for scrupulous white people to jump into the slave-buying business.) Although the two lawyers finally succeeded in raising $400, it was clear that many people—Garrison and Theodore Parker most prominent among them—shared Elizabeth's scruples about lining the pockets of slave-holders. To Grimes, however, it was just money. He had other things to care about than who ended up, at the end of the day, with a little more or a little less of white men's cash.[7]

By 11:00 all the money was secured: one check for $800 signed by Hamilton Willis and another for $400 signed by E. G. Parker. Grimes had met Parker and Thomas at the Revere House, where a final approval was obtained from Suttle. The clergyman and the two lawyers went from there to Loring's office at 16 Court Street, where they joined Loring and Willis. The commissioner wrote out a document:

> Know all men in these Presents—That I, Charles F. Suttle, of Alexandria, in Virginia, in consideration of twelve hundred dollars, to me paid, do hereby release and discharge, quitclaim and convey to Antony Byrnes, his liberty; and I hereby manumit and release him from all claims and services to me for ever, hereby giving him his liberty to all intents and effects for ever.
>
> In testimony whereof, I have hereto set my hand and seal, this twenty-seventh day of May, in the year of our Lord, eighteen hundred and fifty-four.

Suttle, who was not present at the meeting, had presumably authorized his lawyers to sign for him. Loring then sent a messenger to summon the marshal from his office in the Court House. When Freeman returned answer that he could not come, Judge Loring suggested they all go over to the marshal's office. They found Freeman at his desk, Hallett standing over him, talking. Loring sat down at another desk, and a few minutes later Freeman and Hallett engaged him in a discussion of the legality of the sale. Hallett's main objection was that if Burns were sold, the law would be evaded, and if the law were evaded, the expenses already incurred would not be paid by the federal government. Loring took up a copy of the Fugitive Slave Law and explained its provisions in a way that seemed to satisfy Hallett on this point. But he had other objections: there was, for example, a state law forbidding the sale of slaves. Grimes jumped in, offering to take responsibility and to be arrested under that law. "I will take the penalty."[8]

Hallett said nothing for a moment, looking somber, like a man who has used up all the reasons he dares to express, while hanging on to a yet deeper one. He glanced about the room and his eye settled on the clock. "It is Sabbath day now, and it will not be legal to do it any how."[9]

🔥 ANTHONY BURNS

Oh, the Baptists go by water, and the Methodists go by land.
S. SKYLAR AND D. WATSON, "YOU MUST COME IN AT THE DOOR"

When, earlier in the month, Suttle had offered a Virginia judge a legal description of the human property he meant to reclaim, he had described Anthony Burns as "a man of dark complexion, about six feet high, with a scar on one of his cheeks, and also a scar on the back of his right hand, and about twenty-three or four years of age." Estimates of Burns's age given by Boston newspapers at the time of the trial ranged upward to thirty years. It is evident that no one really knew how old he was, perhaps not even Burns himself. Moncure Conway, who had known him in Virginia, guessed that he was "about twenty"—which is to say, just two years younger than himself. As it happens, that agrees with the probably supposititious date of birth— May 31, 1834—inscribed on Burns's tombstone and reported at the time of his death.[1]

"Tony," as all the Virginians called him, was the youngest of his mother's thirteen children. His mother, who worked as cook in the master's household, and her third husband, who labored in a stone quarry—and of course all the children—had earlier been owned by John and Catherine Suttle of Stafford Court House, a village of eighty or ninety houses that served as the seat for Stafford County. When Charles Dickens toured the area in 1842, he thought it had a distinctly unprosperous look, the soil worn out by the improvident methods of cultivation by slaves. It was a point that American Freesoilers would make over and over again—that slavery was unkind to the land, as of course it was. But unlike the Fitzhughs or the Brents, whose slaves had been killing the soil of Stafford County for two centuries, the Suttles were not farmers. John and Catherine had household servants and others who quarried an inferior sandstone from which the U.S. Capitol and the White House had been built—stone that, after a while, seemed to melt in the rain. The Suttles had more than enough slaves for this purpose; indeed, they had difficulty finding places to hire out the surplus. In 1843 one of their female slaves was living as the otherwise unemployed wife of a free black man; Catherine had to remind her that she was still a slave—her labor might be called on at any time.[2]

John Suttle died shortly afterward and the family's finances suffered, forcing Catherine to sell off a number of slaves, including five of Anthony's siblings. To economize further, she moved the family a few miles north to the sleepy hamlet of Aquia Creek, held in local tradition to be the site of the first European settlement in Virginia: it was said that a Spanish Jesuit encampment there had been wiped out by Indians in 1571. Forty years later John Smith, coming north from Jamestown, explored the same area, but it wasn't permanently settled until the middle of the seventeenth century, when Giles Brent brought his Piscataway Indian wife, Kittamaquad, to the shore of Aquia Creek and named their home "Peace." Aquia, well remembered by Conway for the haunted ruins of its ancient Catholic church, would in time become the site of the first battle between Union and Confederate troops—on May 31, 1861, seven weeks before Bull Run. Perhaps Anthony Burns, ignorant of the date of his own birth, counted himself "born" on that day.[3]

The move to Aquia Creek did not, in any event, solve Mrs. Suttle's problems, so Anthony's mother was hired out to a "distant city," separating her from the remaining children, including Anthony, for two years. During this interval Mrs. Suttle died, and her eldest son, Charles Francis, paid off the debts of the estate by mortgaging the slaves. It appears that all the Suttle slaves would remain mortgaged, off and on, for many years to come. Anthony was now of an age to be hired out and would never again live with Master Charles, who now kept a dry-goods store in Falmouth. In his spare time Suttle became a deputy sheriff, then high sheriff of Stafford County, a colonel in the state militia, and at last, in 1849 and 1850, a representative in the Virginia legislature.[4]

Probably in 1843, when he was seven, Anthony lived with his married sister, who had been hired to a distant plantation; he was assigned to watch her infant child while she labored in the fields. The plantation owner's sister, a certain Miss Horton, was then engaged in teaching some neighboring white children, from one of whom Anthony obtained a primer and was covertly launched on the mystery of letters.

In 1844 he was himself hired out for the year "to three maiden ladies" to run errands. The fifteen dollars this brought in was the first money Suttle got from owning Anthony.

All that is known of Burns's whereabouts during 1845 and 1846 is that he was at a place "some miles distant" from Stafford Court House.

In 1847 and again in 1848 William Brent, a longtime crony of Suttle's, hired Burns for fifty dollars a year to work in his grocery store in Falmouth. Conway undoubtedly saw him there, if he didn't know him earlier. Brent testified in Boston that he had hired Burns for three years, but Burns himself said that he had refused the third year, and because he backed up his refusal with a threat to escape ("The *woods* is big enough for me"), Suttle allowed him to have his way. Brent was said to have married well: the Falmouth "mansion," the money, and the family slaves had been hers. Burns recalled that she had been good to him, but he hadn't cared at all for William Brent, who spent most of his time eating, drinking, and hunting.[5]

In 1849 Anthony was hired by a man named Foote, a transplanted Yankee who ran a sawmill near the Culpeper County line. One day that spring, Foote started up the machinery when Burns, standing nearby, wasn't expecting it. His hand severely mangled, he traveled back to Suttle's (at Falmouth, where he was sheriff) for two months to mend. If the injury was treated at all, it certainly was not treated correctly, since ever afterward nearly an inch of bone stuck up through the skin of Anthony Burns's right wrist. This was the "scar" that Suttle mentioned to the judge. Recovered as far as he ever would be, Anthony returned to serve out his year with Foote.

In 1850 he was hired to a new master in Falmouth, who turned out to have little for him to do and so sublet him for the second half of the year to a local wholesale merchant.

In 1851 he was hired out to a tavern-keeper in Fredericksburg—and the next year, in the same town, to an apothecary. In 1852 Suttle moved from Stafford County to Alexandria.

In January 1853, at the time of the annual hiring-out, Burns, now much trusted by his owner, was ordered to take a coffle of Suttle's slaves to Richmond and to report there to Brent. When informed that he would be working for Brent's brother-in-law, Burns again refused, hiring himself out instead at a flour mill where his own brother—of uncertain ownership—also worked. No one interfered with this independent selection.

When hiring time came round again at the beginning of 1854, Burns, only very loosely under the direction of Brent as Suttle's agent, found a place with a Richmond druggist named Millspaugh. As had happened before, this man hadn't enough work to keep a slave busy, but instead of turning over the labor contract to someone else, he suggested that Burns go out every day and pick up what work he could find until the $125 due to Suttle was paid off, then, after a deduction for Burns's food and clothing, they would divide his surplus earnings between them. Millspaugh surely knew that the laws of Virginia frowned on this practice; but it was common enough, and Burns, who had been dreaming of escape for years, commended the idea, encouraging Millspaugh with expectations of a handsome return.[6]

Burns made a point of seeking work along the docks, and in spite of his crippled hand he managed to find remunerative day labor. The income, however, was spotty at first, and the daily settling of accounts with Millspaugh was suspended, at Burns's suggestion, in favor of a fortnightly meeting. But when Anthony brought twenty-five dollars to the first of these settlements, Millspaugh was alarmed that his slave should be going about with so much cash. Over Burns's protests he reimposed the daily reckoning. By this time Burns had picked out his ship and was ready; the thought that the druggist would miss him so soon as the next evening filled him with dread—but in the end he decided that Millspaugh would probably credit his nonappearance to mere sullenness over the new demands.

Wearing all the clothes he had, he left his room before dawn and made his way to the wharves, where, with the help of a friendly Northern sailor whom he had met only days before, he stowed away among the cargo in the hold of a ship bound for Boston. The ship headed down the James River and put in for most of a day at Norfolk before making its way into open ocean. The voyage North normally took seven to ten days, but bad weather kept the ship back and Anthony in the hold for upwards of three spectacularly uncomfortable weeks in February. It is not known precisely when he disembarked in Boston, but he later said that the docks were deserted that morning; the evidence points, then, to a Sunday—probably February 19. Burns rested for a week recovering from the cold, hunger, and cramp of his ordeal, then spent a week as cook on a mud scow before being fired for not being able to make the bread rise. On March 4, it seems certain, he was cleaning windows at the Mattapan Iron Works.

Religion played a very important role in Burns's life. His mother's piety had made an early impression, but she was evidently not a strong or persistent presence. As a young boy, Anthony, together with the whole surrounding region, was swept up in the Millerite frenzy of 1843, which, coinciding in northern Virginia with a plague of scarlet fever and the appearance of a comet, seemed to make everyone giddy and grave at once. The mystic susceptibilities raised at that time came back strongly when his accident at the sawmill nearly killed him. It was then that he began to reason with himself in all seriousness: "Here have I been praying to Jesus, whom I have never served, and have never thought of praying to the Devil, whom I have always served." It struck him, he later recalled, as a kind of revelation, how unreasonable it had been to expect help from one whose service he had not entered. He asked Suttle's permission to be baptized. Permission was denied, Suttle giving as his reason his fear that if Anthony joined the church, he would soon be drinking and "following the women." Later, however, the master relented, and Anthony was received into the Baptist church at Falmouth. Suttle, according to Burns's statement, belonged to no church at all, but, had he wished, he might have belonged to this one, where black and white, slave and free, were separated only by a partition of pine boards.[7]

Within two years, Anthony applied to his church for an informal approbation of his desire and ability to preach. Just barely literate, he had plowed a painful and erratic course through the scriptures, but would rely in his exhorting more on the oral culture and emotive style of the camp meeting. Without a regular ordination, he would henceforth be a folk evangelist. He was called on to perform slave marriages and to bury the dead. But most of all he preached to small illegal gatherings in the slave quarters or in the back room of the absent master's house, assemblies likely at any moment to be broken up (with serious consequences) by officious whites. Within the real constraints of his own abilities he taught other slaves to read and write.

One effect of conspicuous piety in young people is to make them elaborate reasoners in moral questions. In Burns's case, his whole hankering to escape had now to be squared with Baptist scruples.

Slaves in the Bible who escaped were regularly remanded by high authority to their masters. Of several such instances, Burns liked best the story of Onesimus, who, though sent back, was commanded to be received as a brother and not as a guilty slave. He liked least the story of Hagar, who was sent back to be instructed in submissiveness. On the whole, the New Testament seemed to him more to the point than the Old: he thought he could detect in it a spirit of equality under God—who had "made of one blood all the nations of the earth"—a spirit surely inconsistent with the pretensions of slaveholders to property in men.

At the same time and only a few miles away, another young man, just two years older, was struggling with the same questions, framed in the context of Methodist scruples. Conway, himself a preacher, was likewise meditating an escape to the North, and the question of slavery was oddly at the center of *his* crisis of faith. Methodists had split into factions on the question, but at the core of the creed as one found it in Virginia there seemed a strong connection between a conviction of the innate corruption of every heart on the one hand and the endorsement of slavery as a social system on the other, which had to do, in the end, with a profound and permanent human need for government. Conway had been instructed in all this from infancy. His father was one of those old-school slaveholders who professed to dislike slavery on purely rational grounds or "in the abstract," but who found it suited, after all, to his creedal sense of the human condition. As his son, reading Emerson and mixing with Quakers, wavered toward abolitionism, the father threatened him with disinheritance.[8]

Conway's attitude toward slavery was at the mercy of his religious ideas, rather than the reverse. His reading of Emerson had weakened his attachment to the darker doctrines of Methodism—and to creeds in general—but he was only gradually coming to appreciate the bearing of the Transcendental gospel on slavery. In a chance meeting with the writer Grace Greenwood in 1851, he said to her that the slaves in Stafford County were well treated and did not suffer. Her reply was to recommend that he read a story by a certain Mrs. Stowe just then appearing in installments in the *National Era*. He didn't do so, however, until the next year, when simply everyone was reading *Uncle Tom's Cabin*. For now, in the throes of a private crisis of faith, he could not read fiction. He turned instead (in his loneliness, as he later recalled) to the man who seemed to be the source of his changes. He wrote his first letter to Emerson:

> About a year ago I commenced reading your writings. I have read them all and studied them sentence by sentence. I have shed many burning tears over them; because you gain my assent to Laws which, when I see how they would act on the affairs of life, I have not the courage to practise. By the Law sin revives and I die. I sometimes feel as if you made for me a second Fall from which there is no redemption by any atonement.[9]

In the North in 1854, these two fugitives, haunted by their separate Southern histories, pressing forward—as each distinctly understood—to new and freer worlds of the imagination, were received and sheltered by separate religious establishments, neither of which proved strong enough to preserve its inmate against the revolution now at hand. Conway's time at the Divinity School saw the beginning and end of his affiliation with orthodox Unitarianism; the Burns case—and the manner in which Emerson's still-growing influence prepared him for it—remade him into a committed abolitionist and "the most thoroughgoing white male radical produced by the antebellum South." Burns himself—homeless and unemployed after finishing his stint of window-washing at the Iron Works—was received into the Baptist Church on Southac Street. Its deacon gave him a job and a place to live, and its minister gave him untiring assistance at the crisis of his life when a nation watched to see if freedom or slavery would triumph in Boston.[10]

 ## SATURDAY, MAY 27

All day about Court Square, in Court, in counsel with the Vigilance Committee; the crowd very large and much excitement prevails in all classes.

BRONSON ALCOTT, JOURNAL, MAY 27, 1854

While Leonard Grimes was hurrying around town with his subscription paper, his parishioner, Anthony Burns, spent his time in the confinement of the jury room watching his guards play poker and three-card monte. The marshal's men had got over the death of their comrade at least to the extent of being slightly nettled that Burns would not join in their games. Sims, they told him, had had no objection to playing. They didn't mention that Sims was a man seriously addicted to his pleasures, a drinker and habitué of the Ann Street bordellos. He had been something of a hard case: he carried a knife, and when arrested had cut Asa Butman pretty severely in the leg. All of this had been known at the time of his trial, and it had put such a damper on Boston sympathies that when he was finally taken off it would have been hard to find a respectable white man—besides Vigilance Committee members—who cared very much at all. The abolitionists put it out that Sims had died from the whipping he got when he arrived back in Savannah that spring of 1851. But it wasn't true.[1]

Apparently Sims had also entertained his guards by singing. Burns was asked to do the same, but reportedly declined, saying that he feared his singing days were over. He kept his spirits up by smoking cigars given him by the deputies and by watching the crowd for many hours at a stretch, posting himself at the window, his upper body cushioned against the jutting sill with a pillow. The milling crowd, including reporters, took to yelling questions at him, to which, as time wore on, he sometimes replied.

One evening Peter Dunbar the younger, son of the Custom House boss and himself captain of the guard at the entry, shouted up, "Anthony, why didn't you go out to ride with me this afternoon, as I invited you?"

"Oh," came the prisoner's answering shout, "they could not spare us both at one time; if I went, you would have to remain."

Dunbar was pleased with the reply. "Sensible to the last," he said.[2]

For more than two hours that afternoon a mysterious, well-dressed young woman without an escort tried to talk her way past Dunbar and the guards to get in to see the prisoner. Charming at first, more vehement toward the end, she proved entirely undissuadable and was at last arrested for her marathon of concern. "It was the most remarkable case of feminine curiosity" that police officer J. C. Warren had ever seen. They took her off to the Center Watch House but released her a few hours later, exasperated beyond measure that she would not stop singing "liberty songs." Her name was Caroline Hinckley. Presumably they did not know or care that she was the mistress of Vigilance Committee member John M. Spear, once a Universalist minister, long an abolitionist ally of Garrison, and now the head of a spiritualist free-love commune in Lynn, Massachusetts, which was collectively engaged in perfecting "the new mola," a huge perpetual-motion machine that would "revolutionize the world" by harnessing the energies of the General Assembly of Spirits.[3]

❦ AUTOPSY

Last night there was a meeting in Faneuil Hall, and afterward an attempt at rescue, which, I am sorry to say, failed. I am sick and sorrowful with this infamous business. Ah, Webster, Webster, you have much to answer for!

HENRY WADSWORTH LONGFELLOW, JOURNAL, MAY 27, 1854

Longfellow was no revolutionaire.

WALT WHITMAN

James Batchelder's corpse had lain overnight, face up, on the floor of the marshal's office. Saturday morning it was put in a coffin, carried out to a hearse (a show that quieted the crowd for a while), and carted off to Charlestown, where Batchelder had lived, and where coroner Charles Smith proposed to have the body examined. Despite the exclamation of the dying man that he had been stabbed, it was universally assumed that his death was the result of a gunshot wound. The indictment of the Court House rioters at 2:00 that afternoon, before the results of the postmortem could be known, specified that the murderers had used "firearms loaded with powder and ball." The marshal's men who had been toward the front in the fight were convinced that their comrade had been shot, and they testified that they had heard the reports of pistols and seen muzzle flashes in the murky darkness beyond the door. In fact one bullet, fired by Lewis Hayden, barely missed Watson Freeman, passing between his arm and torso and slamming into the wall behind. News of this event had wrung from Theodore Parker the anguished exclamation, "Why did he not hit him?"[1]

The Saturday morning papers were already developing divergent theories to account for what all were agreed was a death by gunshot. According to the Freesoil *Commonwealth,* no guns had been fired from outside (a patent falsehood), so the fatal ball "seems to have been fired by one of [Batchelder's] companions, who handled his pistol carelessly." The *Post,* a Democratic sheet closely allied with District Attorney Hallett, reported that Batchelder had been "shot through the bowels, dying almost instantly." The paper did not hesitate to hold the speakers at Faneuil Hall responsible.

The official records of the Boston coroner's office for this period are missing, and contemporaneous newspaper accounts differ somewhat, both from one another and from the later recollections of interested parties. It is clear, however, that before Batchelder's lightly attended funeral in Charlestown on Sunday afternoon, several doctors saw the body. According to a report published in the *Commonwealth* on June 5, Dr. Charles H. Stedman, another of Boston's eight coroners, performed a postmortem examination with the assistance of Dr. F. S. Ainsworth. They cut away the dead man's pantaloons and shirt, which "were still wet and clotted with blood," and found that "in the region of the groin three inches to the left of the front bone was a smooth, clean incision, which measured an inch in length." The wound, they said, was six and a half inches deep, "made in an inward and backward direction," and had "nearly divided" the femoral artery. They also found a bruise on the forehead and four wounds to the scalp, one of which seemed to have been made by "a sharp instrument." The blunt-force trauma to the head suggested to the doctors a blow that "would have knocked a man down," but their conclusion was that Batchelder "came to his death from the sudden loss of blood following the division of the femoral artery, and that the wound was inflicted with a long narrow and sharp instrument."

This report provided the basis for a formal coroner's inquest, which concluded on June 1, six days after Batchelder's funeral. The jury's verdict in the inquest was reported in the *Post* on June 2:

That James Batchelder, on the 26th ult., at about 9 3/4 o'clock, P.M. while employed with others, by Watson Freeman, Esq., United States marshal, as an assistant in defending the west entrance of the court house, in Boston, from the assaults of a mob, received a wound in the left groin, severing the femoral artery, which caused his death. And the said wound was inflicted by a long, narrow, and sharp instrument in the hands of some one of the persons engaged in the said assault, to the jurors unknown. And the jurors further find that Samuel Proudman alias John J. Roberts, Martin Stowell, Walter Phenix (colored), John C. Cluer, Albert J. Brown[e], Jr., John Wesley (colored), Wesley alias Walter Bishop (colored), Thomas Jackson (colored), Henry Stowe [that is, Howe], John Thompson, and John Morrison were identified as engaged in a greater or less degree in said riotous attack.

(Signed) Charles Smith, Coroner; Francis D. Stedman, foreman; Geo. H. Munroe, Horace Smith, E. Sewall Price, Richard Williamson, John Wilson, jurors.

The fact that Batchelder's clothes were undisturbed at the time of the Saturday postmortem shows that Smith never personally examined the body; if he saw it at all, it could only have been at the marshal's office, in the same building as his own office. Probably only two men—Stedman and Ainsworth—participated in the medical examination, though years after the fact Higginson claimed that another doctor, Charles T. Jackson, Emerson's brother-in-law, "was one of the surgical examiners." Like his sister, Lidian Emerson, Dr. Jackson embraced abolitionist views, though he was not notably active in reform. The jury at the inquest, of course, never saw the body, but depended on Stedman's report, together with the testimony of several witnesses.[2]

Concerning these witnesses nothing is known with certainty. The only published allusion to them occurs in an anonymous article written for the Boston *Daily Advertiser* more than thirty years later, which argued that the inquest had been compromised by political pressures, resulting in a failure to detect Stowell as the gunman. The article contains some intriguing reminiscences, combining rumor, fact, and clear error in about equal proportion:

> At the coroner's inquest one of the jurymen was an abolitionist. A witness of the riot came forward and swore that he saw, in the crowd around the court house door, a man who appeared to be an Italian, and who carried a round dirk. In the opinion of the Garrisonian juryman, the wound on the body of the deceased bore unmistakable evidence of having been inflicted by the dirk. Accordingly no postmortem examination was ever made, [Stowell's] pistol was never found, the bullet was not discovered, and the coroner's verdict was to the effect that Batchelder came to his death by violence at the hands of some party unknown.

Clearly, some sort of forensic examination *had* occurred. The figure of the knife-wielding Italian—a flagrant stereotype—is not to be credited, but is nevertheless interesting for its connection to the rampant ethnic prejudice of the period and for its suggestion that someone may have wanted to mislead the investigators. The hint that some abolitionists might have been tempted to cover for other abolitionists cannot be dismissed as easily as the immigrant scapegoat. Whatever respect and sympathy the rough-and-tumble Irish truckman elicited—such as collects around any victim of violence—could not prevail in all minds against the feeling that here was a death well and justly earned. Some such thought was evidently rattling about in Parker's brain when he made his uncharacteristically bloodthirsty remark about Hayden's faulty aim. It stands to reason that whatever passion and sense of justice brought the gun *into* Court Square could as easily have taken it *out* of the inquest.[3]

Coincidentally—or otherwise—suspicion very soon fell on a man with a knife. Late on Saturday afternoon the police had "a stalwart colored man named Nelson Hopewell" under surveillance when the suspect got into a heated argument with lawyer William C. Fay in the large crowd at the Court House. Hopewell assaulted Fay and was arrested. How long he had been under surveillance is unclear, but later testimony would identify him as having been among the attackers on Friday night. On that evening, moments after Batchelder's death, he was allegedly overheard to say to a group of fifteen or twenty men that "they have got the blood out of one of the kidnappers, and if they had not been such cowards, [they] could have got more." At the time of his arrest—5:30 P.M. on Saturday—he had pulled a knife on officer William B. Tarleton. This weapon was said to be "an African knife, called a *creese,* the blade of which is some ten inches long, curved and slender, and bore upon it distinct stains of blood." Properly, a creese is a Malay or Javanese dirk, not African, but this exotic immigrant detail, finding its way into the Queen's English of a Boston police report, has a nice ethnological ring to it, and produces the calculated shiver. As in the case of the Italian and his stiletto, Hopewell and his creese link the likelihood of murder with the foreign races.[4]

In several newspapers the account of Hopewell's arrest was followed, in the next paragraph, by news of the postmortem results, and although it is reasonably clear that the arrest took place at 5:30 (some indeterminate time after he became a person of interest to the police), the issuance of Dr. Stedman's report is said more vaguely to have occurred during the evening.

Setting aside the real possibility that Dr. Stedman's talents as a forensic pathologist had their limits—that he might not have been able infallibly to distinguish a small-caliber bullet wound from a knife wound—the remaining possibilities are interesting. Hopewell, to be sure, may have been the culprit, in which case Stowell's shot missed. Possibly neither one was responsible. The theory that Higginson publicly maintained for years afterward—that Batchelder had been done in by the carelessness or private malice of his own co-workers—might be right, despite the stout avowals of the marshal and his men that they were armed with nothing but billy clubs. If, however, Stowell was the killer (as Stowell himself believed), some-one must have prevailed on Stedman to make the case more rather than less puzzling by obscuring the evidence—much, indeed, as Thomas Drew and Simon Hanscom had already done. The suborning of official misconduct, one supposes, would have seemed an act of greater desperation and culpability than the secreting of evidence not yet in police hands, and yet, under the exceptional circumstances that prevailed, it is not inconceivable. Whether any such conspiracy is credible depends not at all on the likelihood that Stowell's friends would defy the law (clearly they were ready for that), but on the scope and extent of abolitionist lawlessness. The pertinence of that subject goes well beyond the relatively minor question of how far the conspiracy to save Martin Stowell actually went.[5]

LAW

Ask not, Is it constitutional? Ask, Is it right?

EMERSON, JOURNAL, CA. JUNE 1854

Properly speaking, the immediate abolitionists were only a single group—one of several—in the antislavery ranks; indeed, the half-decade with which we are concerned—the "American Renaissance" of 1850–1855—was the period of maximum faction in the agitation of the slavery question. The Garrisonian abolitionists looked on slavery as a sin and demanded that it be renounced immediately, utterly, and universally; they could not be content with half-measures like those advocated by their sometime colleagues the Freesoilers, who wanted to keep slave labor out of the Western territories. Geographic containment involved a constitutional squeamishness about disturbing slavery "where it already exists," but such a policy could not be, in the view of the abolitionists, a competent response to sin. Garrison had long since led the abolitionists to the conclusion that the U.S.

Constitution was a proslavery document—a "covenant with death and an agreement with hell"—whose authority he and they would therefore refuse to acknowledge. This meant, among other things, that abolitionists could not conscientiously vote or have normal dealings with the government. Having in effect seceded from the United States, this group of antislavery reformers consciously deprived themselves of any direct political power and rested their argument, and the whole power of their strategy, on a moral and religious appeal—that is, on the evident superiority of the laws of God to the laws of men.[1]

While it belongs to the logic of abolitionism that it should reject compromise, and while Garrison owed his fame and influence to precisely this unwillingness to bargain with the devil, the abolitionists were actually less isolated than their defiant posture would imply. Individually and collectively, they were constantly going into and out of coalitions with other antislavery elements that had not shorn themselves of political influence. Indeed, they would cooperate with just about anyone whose principles were unfavorable to slavery. They could be critical, for example, of Sumner's occasional restraint in the Senate and the Freesoil policies he supported, but they applauded his speeches and votes. Garrison himself was a member of the Vigilance Committee, where he encountered a spectrum of opinion wide almost to chaos.

The intellectual and emotional traffic between the abolitionists and the allies that opportunity kept finding for them made the antislavery crusade enormously dynamic. In considering the stance adopted by the abolitionists toward law, it is tempting to concentrate on all that esoterically follows from their attitude toward the Constitution, but that approach would give a false picture of their ideological purity and reinscribe them again in a caricature of isolation. What is most remarkable about their sense of law is not how distinctive it was, but how much, at bottom, it had in common with that of the Transcendentalists, how open, as romantic reformers, they lay on that side to the influence of Emerson and Thoreau. It also helps to explain why in 1854 the antislavery revolution virtually fell into the hands of the followers of Emerson.

Emerson's career as a thinker and writer was arguably about the need for permanent revolution. "I unsettle all things," he said. All evil and difficulty—all that he ever wrote against—were the manifold forms of impedance thrown up in the way of the natural, progressive unfolding and refinement of human power and self-realization. Evolution, change, development, coming-to-be—that, for Emerson, was the direction of history and the moral of its lesson. All-sufficient reasons for hope were woven into the fabric of the universe. Genesis would have its triumph—was indeed having its triumph at every moment—because each forward step in the moral universe was ground permanently gained. Opposing this process was a less deeply authorized power that Emerson sometimes—as in his essay "Compensation"—called "Nemesis," a power intrinsically and permanently incompetent to hold its ground and therefore constantly being overcome by progressive forces. Its style was coagulation. It "settled all things." Conservatism was less deeply authorized because, as Emerson believed, growth and not stasis was the naturally empowered order of things. History found its forward movement in the perpetual breaking of this conservative impedance by works of genius and heroism, life ever leading on to more and fuller life by acts of death-defiance.[2]

Although Emerson drew on the widest variety of writers and thinkers, his main source for these ideas was the development of his own powers, or his own perception of "the growth of the poet's mind." Truth to self was at once doctrine and method, though his own case was not different, he felt, from that of others: "To believe your own thought, to believe that what is true for you in your private heart is true for all men,—that is genius." It was genius because it was the courageous, progressive, and therefore revolutionary reversal of the prevailing conservative mode, which was simply, as in a bad school, to accept as true for oneself what the generality of others had agreed to regard as valid and estimable. The private road to truth had some advantages over the rutted public way, including the possibility that the future would be different from the past, that the world would be inhabited by free individuals and not merely by those who amiably took direction from the dead. This election of the private sphere as offering the best stance from which to oppose the conservative principle meant that the revolution that would change the world would be a matter not of pistols and barricades, but of individual secessions into self-reliance. Reference in Emerson is invariably to what is going on in the interior of the simple separate person. Because he trusts that outward consequences cannot long mismatch motives, he often professes a disregard of the social, political, or public sphere. When he writes about public affairs, as in his various neighbor-induced pronouncements on slavery, he is self-conscious and apologetic, feeling that circumstances have betrayed him into approaching the question from the wrong end.[3]

In the Emersonian scheme, then, revolutions go best when they are conducted in private—especially because in that site they can and should be chronic rather than acute. The sharp collisions of a public revolution testify to an earlier inactivity in the private sphere, as a result of which, in effect and for a time, too much power has been ceded to the conservative settlement. Power always exists and will flow toward whatever user is momentarily active. For Emerson, as for Thoreau, it is only in the sleep of reason that evil acquires its strength. That erring power becomes consolidated in the form of a barrier to further progress—in the form, say, of a Fugitive Slave Law—eliciting and requiring a proportionate further power to overcome it.

The government's proslavery measures—particularly the Compromise of 1850—were in Emerson's terms a virtual caricature of conservatism in their avowed purpose of putting a stop to antislavery agitation, of ensuring the perpetuation of human bondage where it already existed, and of imposing a specific limit on the conscience of all those who sympathized with slaves. It was inevitable that Emerson would oppose this law, even had he not, somewhat belatedly, decided that slavery was "the greatest calamity in the Universe." Of the Fugitive Slave Law, that "filthy enactment," he said: "I will not obey it, by God." Emerson's "by God" is at once swearing and not swearing.[4]

One of Daniel Webster's most careful defenses of the 1850 measures, and of the Fugitive Slave Law in particular, was addressed in a public letter to the citizens of Newburyport, to precisely that audience which had embraced Webster's conservatism and rejected Higginson's Emersonian gospel. In that letter, Webster identified the minority who opposed him as those who are "borne away, by the puffs of a transcendental philosophy, into an atmosphere flickering between light and darkness." Indeed, the widespread circle of Emersonians had been on him from the start. In the weeks before the Seventh of March speech, one idealistic voice of conscience—one only—had come to Webster, warning him off the course he would adopt: William Henry Furness, Emerson's lifelong friend, seems to have been alone in suspecting Webster's imminent defection, and alone in urging him to adopt a heroic pro-freedom stance on Clay's Compromise. Yet in the attack on Transcendentalism in the Newburyport letter, it was probably not Emerson or Higginson or Furness that Webster had mainly in mind, but Theodore Parker, whose sermons he had been used to hearing at the Melodeon, and who, long since disowned by Boston's Unitarian establishment, now thundered denunciations of wickedness in high places. The Fugitive Slave Law would have no more active and voluble opponent than the best, most appreciative reader of Emerson in Boston—unless, perhaps, it was Furness, Emerson's best reader in Philadelphia.[5]

Webster may also have had in mind the troublesome argument of New York Senator William Henry Seward, who was first to attack the Compromise provision on fugitive slaves as a violation of the "higher law." Webster tried repeatedly to laugh this off—much to Emerson's disgust—but the notion that a law had to square itself with abstract justice, and not merely with the Constitution, would be core doctrine to Webster's opponents, whether Emersonian or abolitionist.

The idea of a "higher law" superseding and governing human enactments had a long and honorable history, but it had not been routinely a part of senatorial debate, so that its deployment by Seward in opposition to a particular bill turned out to be more surprising than effective. The term itself proved a clever satire on the secular nature of politics, and was resented, as the clerical petition would be resented four years later, for its embarrassing redefinition of the business of legislation. The discourse that it emphatically *did* belong to was that of New England Transcendentalism—rather more than to the often biblical and prophetic discourse of abolitionism. In Emerson's writings the concept had always had the greatest vitality, resonance, and plausibility. In order to recover it from Webster's levity, Emerson had only to surround it with his own attention:

> I am surprised that lawyers can be so blind as to suffer the principles of law to be discredited. A few months ago, in my dismay at hearing that the Higher Law was reckoned a good joke in the courts, I took pains to look into a few law-books. I had often heard that the Bible constituted a part of every technical law-library, and that it was a principle in law that immoral laws are void.

He went on to survey such authorities as had weight with the legal fraternity—Cicero, Grotius, Coke, Blackstone, Montesquieu, Burke, and Jefferson among them—finding it repeatedly affirmed, as he expected, that no human laws are of any validity if contrary to the law of nature. Or, as Blackstone had simply said, "if any human law should allow or enjoin us to commit a crime, we are bound to transgress that human law."[6]

Encouragement to "transgress that human law" on the authority of the private conscience had been more than implicit in Emerson's earlier writings. Before the looming monstrosity of the Fugitive Slave bill "forced us all into politics," Emerson had extended his general argument into the realm of the law. In "The Young American" (1844), he said: "I conceive that the office of statute law should be to express and not to impede the mind of mankind." The law, in other words, is objectionable when it serves the interest of stasis or conservatism or when it comes to be regarded as a finality; it is always properly an instrument, a subordinate means to an essentially revolutionary end, and must be judged according to its fitness for that purpose. But the radical inference is not that law may on this occasion be a help and on that a hindrance, but that its relevance is permanently in question—in light of the always superseding relevance of the onward development of the "mind of mankind." Thus a sort of proto-Nietzschean hero is implied who finds himself not so much "above the law" as level with the "higher law." According to Emerson, "It will never make any difference to a hero what the laws are. His greatness will shine and accomplish itself unto the end, whether [the laws] second him or not."[7]

It is a delicate amusement (if a somewhat self-indulgent one) to spend the day in explanation of Emerson's artful meanings; yet there is a sense in which "his" meanings may come to assume an aspect of conservative hurtfulness unless we decide they have a more operative life in the constructions of those who read him, heard him, or were influenced by him and who built therefrom their own worlds. It may be more pertinent—if no easier—to consider what Martin Stowell or Wentworth Higginson or Moncure Conway might have made of such talk as this of Emerson's than to be concerned exclusively with authorial intent. What these men show themselves as responding to, in statement and in action, is the liberating, progressive quality of Emerson's thought, the way its opposition to conservative formalism in particular seems to remove proscriptions on (and so to authorize) a bolder, more lively engagement with the world, opening up for them a further range of novel and authentic action. They see in Emerson that objective law *in general* has come to be a false god, worshipped by men who believe—as in Webster's own misplaced transcendentalism—that it defers to nothing, is sponsored by nothing, that nothing lies behind it. In the essay "Politics," Emerson deconstructs law in its pretension to be taken for a transcendental signifier:

> In dealing with the State, we ought to remember that its institutions are not aboriginal, though they existed before we were born: that they are not superior to the citizen: that every one of them was once the act of a single man: every law and usage was a man's expedient to meet a particular case: that they are all imitable, all alterable; we may make as good; we may make better.[8]

Emerson's intention in this passage may have been, for all we can surely know, to encourage voting. Better, perhaps, to historicize and ask how such a statement might be received by the relatively small class of readers already well disposed to the idea of revolution or radical reform. Such readers would perhaps respond to the reminder that, even as the great federal documents declared, political authority rests with the people. This had once been revolutionary doctrine; Emerson alarms the reader with the possibility of its having dwindled to the dimensions of a service contract. His sentence might look to radical readers like an invitation to take possession of a power actually confided to them but which has long lain dormant. It might also suggest acting in the present "to meet a particular case." But a deeper and more thoughtful response would have involved seeing Emerson's general point about the tendency of law to become reified and inflexible—a conservative shibboleth—and about the implied better case, in which it remains open and fluid, impressible by that will which it ought always and properly to express. Whose interests are served by regarding the law as rigid and closed? What benefits flow from a living code of justice? Here as elsewhere in Emerson the effect is to present the reader with a choice—whether law is to be a popular and democratic self-government or a tyranny of the past over the present. A man is, legally speaking, either slave or free, either the subject of an external code or by nature and conscience a lawgiver. If the former, then, potentially, a revolutionary insurgent. If the latter, then also, at will, a repealer of laws.[9]

"That government is best which governs not at all," said Thoreau, placing behavior under the aegis of the "higher law" and rendering irrelevant the "lower law" of external restraint. As both Emerson and Thoreau supposed, if one listened to the voice of God in the conscience and sternly followed that, one could dispense with the statute books without fear that any just law would ever be violated. Conscience, it was agreed, *would* impel a man into open opposition to the Fugitive Slave Law, a human enactment that defied the eternal law by which freedom had precedence over (more natural power than) slavery, and which defied the law of God by compelling men to turn kidnapper and do the devil's work. Conscience would bless the opposing effort and strengthen the actor's resolve to vindicate the ways of God to man. Such conscience might be supposed to hesitate before taking the proffered loaded pistol from Thomas Drew in Worcester—but such felt magnitude in the stake, such sense of election, finds a way of accepting.[10]

We don't know what Stowell might have read, besides the ongoing antislavery martyrology of the *Liberator,* but it begins to look as though there are no political motives to action that are not also, first, literary. It is merely a rhetorical strategy to insist that the Fugitive Slave Law intrinsically creates the opposition it meets; the public has to be taught to suspend its law-abidingness; to recognize an emergent occasion; to see justice where authority sees crime, and vice versa. Thus to rush voluntarily into physical danger needs a devotion to abstract principle such as literature and culture alone can provide and which they do routinely provide. Rhetoric, the politically active element in literature, might be defined from one point of view as the textual importation and exportation of permission, and the weight of it, collectively, in several coinciding discourses, may be supposed to be decisive over time. Effective antislavery rhetoric at this historical moment was such as designedly created heroes—which, it so happens, had been Emerson's business all along: "whoso is heroic," he once declared, "will always find crises to try his edge."[11]

We know more about Higginson's reading than about Stowell's, though one looks in such cases not for a single radicalizing text but more generally for indicators of attraction and repulsion, a susceptibility to certain rhetorical styles. Higginson, an early and enthusiastic reader of Emerson, also knew Thoreau's writings well—was one of the few unrepentant purchasers of the *Week on the Concord and Merrimack Rivers,* had made a memorable visit to Thoreau in Concord in 1850, and had helped to arrange his lectures in Newburyport and Worcester. If we credit Higginson's own statements, what he mainly liked about Thoreau was his embodiment of Emerson—not just his Emersonianism, but the process of its representation or "acting out." Thoreau seemed to offer clues to something that Conway, for another example, had been desperately curious about, as in his first letter to Emerson: what an Emersonian style of behaving in the world would look like. While the modern image of Thoreau stresses his autonomy, he was for his contemporaries (both the disconcerted and the appreciative ones) often a sort of "applied" version of his mentor.[12]

Thoreau was Emerson's rebellious "protester." Unwilling that "his money or his life" should further the interests of militant slavery, he had once famously withheld his tax and been led off to Concord jail, a prisoner of conscience. Emerson privately disavowed the act, declaring it to be in "bad taste," but there was a necessary ambivalence in his judgment because, as Richard Lebeaux stresses, the act was consonant both with Emerson's general views on self-reliance and with his particular opinion that "The abolitionists ought to resist and go to prison in multitudes on their known and described disagreements from the state." No misgivings that Emerson may have derived from the culture of his class—no falling back on the unrepresented portion of himself—could prevent others from seeing in this legal drama anything but the upshot of Emerson's own views.[13]

In "Resistance to Civil Government," surely the finest antislavery tract ever written, Thoreau had said: "Under a government which imprisons any unjustly, the true place for a just man is also in a prison." That is to say, a man is just, and (a separately important issue) knows himself to be just, precisely to the extent that he is willing to act (and not merely to speak) on the side of justice, even as such conformity brings him into collision with the unjust laws of the government. One of the most important ways in which "Civil Disobedience" (as the essay is more familiarly known) seems to depart from the Emersonian mode is in its introduction of a division between speaking and acting. If Emerson characteristically makes the reader feel that words *are* actions (as he said), no reader of "Civil Disobedience" has ever received the words except as a subordinate gloss on a central significance-endowing action. The point is not just that this effect corroborates the "applied" persona, but also that it signals the opening factional split between what might be called the party of the word and the party of the deed, and the crisis faced by the former in light of the advancing power of the latter. If Emerson, the writer/lecturer, is taken to represent Transcendentalism and if Garrison, the nonresistant, is taken to represent abolitionism, one sees their homologous relationship in a strenuous mutual privileging of language—at a time, moreover, when language was under enormous political stress. Thoreau's "bad taste" is a defection as notable and blameworthy in the context of literary transcendentalism as Frederick Douglass' was in the context of apolitical abolitionism.[14]

Another, perhaps less interesting way of putting the same point is that Emerson covertly appealed to that advancing hunger for heroism to which Thoreau, in "Civil Disobedience," catered openly and dramatically. If heroism may be supposed to occur when an individual's love of justice exceeds his fear of unrighteous punishment, then heroism may be manufactured (as "Civil Disobedience" attempts to do) by bolstering that love or, equally, by allaying that fear. One way in which Thoreau evades the Emersonian style is by attending more directly to the negative case. The high comedy of his essay comes from seeing "jail" as an absurdly aggrandized signifier, a tawdry bogeyman of the slave power. Here, then, is another way for rhetoric to convey permission. The revolutionary sign in "Civil Disobedience" is not in the novelty of its ideas, but in Thoreau's recognition of the need, just then, to manufacture heroes by insinuating the inauthenticity or insufficiency of language in competition with action.

The new hero is a breaker of laws:

> If the injustice is part of the necessary friction of the machine of government, let it go, let it go: perchance it will wear smooth,— . . . but if it is of such a nature that it requires you to be the agent of injustice to another, then, I say, break the law. Let your life be a counter-friction to stop the machine.[15]

Martin Stowell, sitting in the tombs beneath the Boston Court House this day, might have quoted Thoreau's imperative to justify the actions he undertook out of his unwillingness that the official injustice of enslaving Anthony Burns should go forward, and especially that it should go forward in the name of Massachusetts and her citizens. This was no internal governmental dispute that he could "let go," nor a private matter between two individuals. The moment the law recognized the conflict between Anthony Burns and Charles Suttle—and the conflict was fitted to the law—it expanded to the dimensions of America, and the president dropped what he was doing and took an interest in it. The recovery of Anthony Burns was a political device to make Massachusetts and all her citizens individually and collectively complicit in the Fugitive Slave Law and compliant to its workings. It was hatched in the hell of slavery (as Garrison might have said) to prevent individuals in all these free states from supposing they stood or could stand passively aloof from the law. It now requires you, Martin Stowell, "to be an agent of injustice to another." What better incitement to bold action and heroic protest can there be?

But Stowell did not conclude, for all the justice of his motives, that his place was in prison. Perhaps he was not a Thoreauvian. For that matter, Thoreau, who was not in prison at this time, was also not going out of his way to get in. This fine Saturday, the end of a cool and rainy week, he had taken a tour of inspection to Saw Mill Brook, and would maintain in his journals for a few days more the accustomed springtime silence of the Concord and Acton woods. At last, however, on Monday, while the issue still hung in the balance, Thoreau erupted in his journal: "Rather than thus consent to establish hell upon earth,—to be a party to this establishment,—I would touch a match to blow up earth and hell together. As I love life, I would side with the Light and let the Dark Earth roll from under me, calling my mother and my brother to follow me." But surely he knew that he *had* called his brother to follow him. Perhaps he did not know as yet (as he did a week later) that his brother had responded—in the person of Martin Stowell, who was encouraged to think independently about the justice of the laws, to suppose that there were options about obeying them, to regard the demands of his private conscience as imperative, even sacred, and to act out of uncompromising principle on behalf of truth and justice. If Stowell had not been thus directly encouraged by Thoreau (whose works he may not have read, whose lectures he may not have attended), then he was surely encouraged by that progressive climate of opinion of which a fracturing Transcendentalism still formed the active, articulate core.[16]

EXTEMPORIZED SCRIPTURE

The frank blue eyes [of Theodore Parker] caught a steely gleam, as of bayonets levelled to clear the hall, to sweep the great iniquity out by the doors. An undeniable glitter as of steel, seen in that hall more than once, menacing in the name of the real commonwealth of the people, the Massachusetts of freedom. How little seemed the Fugitive Slave Bill that day! "Take away that bauble!" was the virtual speech, with steel in the eyes of the speaker, now at length become steel in the hands of the doers.

JOHN WEISS

On the way to church this morning, Ascension Sunday, thousands saw the placards on the lampposts:

THE MAN IS NOT BOUGHT!
HE IS STILL IN THE SLAVE-PEN, IN THE COURT-HOUSE!

The Kidnapper agreed, both publicly and in writing, to sell him for 1200 dollars. The sum was raised by eminent Boston Citizens and offered him. He then claimed more. The bargain was broken. The Kidnapper breaks his agreement, though the United States Commissioner advised him to keep it.

BE ON YOUR GUARD AGAINST ALL LIES!
WATCH THE SLAVE-PEN!
LET EVERY MAN ATTEND THE TRIAL!

A good many Bostonians had thought the sale would surely go through and the whole disgraceful business be peaceably concluded. This short-lived expectation had had a wonderfully calming effect after the riot of Friday night, keeping down the crowds at the Court House and perhaps preventing more violent displays. Possibly that was all that Suttle had ever meant to accomplish by his offer, but more likely there had been a genuine change of mind, the agreement first extorted by fear, then withdrawn under strongly worded advice from partisans of the law.[1]

Death threats had been made against Suttle and Brent, who would trade their first-floor rooms at the Revere House for more defensible quarters in the hotel's garret; there they stayed with a volunteer guard of Southern students from Harvard. Conway had been asked to join this group, but he declined.[2]

The fear of personal violence was general among the actors in the drama. District Attorney B. F. Hallett and his son, Henry, on leaving the Court House around 12:30 this morning, noticed they were being followed by two black men, probably agents of the Vigilance Committee. One of them, James Palm, was arrested. Joshua B. Smith, an escaped slave from North Carolina, now a successful Boston caterer, had declared his readiness, even at the cost of his own life, to kill Watson Freeman—if only Smith's wife and children might be taken care of. He compromised: his waiters would refuse to serve the military personnel dining at the downtown hotels.[3]

Death threats had been made against the Faneuil Hall speakers as well. Wendell Phillips came home Saturday evening to tell his wife of the rumors—which he didn't believe—that they were to be mobbed that night by Peter Dunbar's truckmen. So much did he disbelieve the threat that he actually left the house again, still at work on the Burns case. About 9:00 Theodore Parker arrived, telling Ann Phillips that the house would be sacked within the next ten minutes and that she had to leave immediately. Badly frightened, Mrs. Phillips nevertheless decided to wait for her husband's return. Shortly thereafter a group of men from the Vigilance Committee—Francis Jackson, Henry Kemp, Samuel J. May, and Bronson Alcott, among others—arrived, each with a pistol, and stood watch in the parlor through the night. Wendell's brother Tom went to the mayor, who assured him that the police knew about the threats and had the house under surveillance. Later, letters published in the newspapers would charge Wendell Phillips with cowardice and hypocrisy—not for leaving his wife undefended, but for calling on Mayor Smith and the police for protection.[4]

Parker's own house close by had also been threatened, making it impossible for him to fulfill the expectation of his audience at church for an entire sermon on the Burns case. Instead, he would deliver what he had written, a discourse on the outbreak of the Crimean War (noting at the end that war was here in Boston, too), and replace his usual prefatory scripture reading, or "Lesson for the Day," with an extemporaneous denunciation of Commissioner Loring.

As he walked down Winter Street to the Music Hall, home to his Twenty-eighth Congregational Society, he recognized his own prose in the posted handbills.

The Music Hall could accommodate almost as many listeners as Faneuil Hall itself. Parker's audience, the largest by far of any Boston minister's, came mostly from the working class, the mechanics, artisans, and shopkeepers. It was generally understood that money and power worshipped elsewhere. Some went to Federal Street to hear Ezra Gannett, others to Brattle Street or the Old South for the proslavery ministrations of Hubbard Winslow or G. W. Blagden. Edward Everett, worn out and disgusted by politics, would this day attend the Park Street Church and hear the Reverend George Ellis discourse on the eclipse. Rufus Choate, who had once said, "I go to my pew as I go to my bed—for repose!" most often went to the church of his friend and counsellor the Reverend Nehemiah Adams—though Adams happened this day to be in Port Royal, South Carolina, whence he would return with material for his *South-Side View of Slavery,* a soothing bedtime story for Hunkers, offered as a rejoinder to *Uncle Tom's Cabin.*[5]

Parker's audience, on the other hand, were such as wanted to keep awake, and included, every Sunday, a large supplement of irregulars eager to hear what piquancies the outlaw minister might deliver. Longfellow was there this morning, as were Conway and Alcott—as, indeed, were 4,000 others.

"Since we last came together," said Parker, "there has been a man stolen in this city of our fathers." The historical and patrimonial note was inevitable with him; his farmer grandfather had led the American minutemen at Lexington in 1775, and this sense of proprietorship in the Revolution (he kept his grandfather's gun as a relic in his study) gave a permanent historical coloring to his feeling for Boston, his adoptive city. The attitude, generally speaking, was not uncommon: many of those listening to him this day could remember from their childhood close relatives who had fought in the war. Characteristically, Parker addressed himself to a native Anglo-American population: not to an audience of immigrants, not to an audience whose values he didn't confidently know.[6]

From the pulpit he gave the latest news: Anthony Burns, he said,

is now in the great slave pen in the city of Boston.

He is there against the law of the Commonwealth, which, if I am rightly informed, in such cases prohibits the use of State edifices as United States jails . . . Any forcible attempt to take him from that barracoon of Boston, would be wholly without use. For besides the holiday soldiers who belong to the city of Boston, and are ready to shoot down their brothers in a just or an unjust cause, any day when the city government gives them its command and its liquor, I understand that there are one hundred and eighty-four United States marines lodged in the court-house, every man of them furnished with a musket and a bayonet, with his side arms, and twenty-four ball cartridges.

The despotism of martial law, he implied, had as yet a small geographic range—the dimensions of a single building—but it had already taken from the public its own courts of justice. The will of the people, in which justice lives, was overawed and thwarted by an army of occupation, and slavery had built a colony in the heart of Boston. All hope of a rescue gone, the personal fate of Anthony Burns was to be looked upon as settled. A sort of rhetorical autopsy would now follow.

Parker's explanation of how this result could have occurred and by whose hand it had been brought to pass launched him on a long and absorbing exercise in scapegoating, in which he was to be joined by a great many others. In one sense, the complex distribution of blame—more complex as time passed—looks like a meaningless gesture of frustration by a party out of power, a nearly random displacement of anger onto targets of convenience. But in fact the ensuing recrimination became in itself an imaginative, boldly stylized revolutionary art form, a process, however erring, clumsy, and passionate at times, whereby the moral landscape was enduringly reconfigured by new allocations of social and political value. Through its whole extent, this indecorous festival of blame-laying proved a bright engine of social change. What the Burns case most gave to a Northern public lukewarm in its mild, abstract antislavery was a set of local demons, neighbors with their manacles and bullwhips showing and drunken Irish bullies roving about in pretentious uniforms and with loaded guns. The slave, the erstwhile invisible man, the public had seen: thousands literally had their eyes on him, as Phillips had urged, only to sink him immediately into a sentimental archetype of beset manhood. But, as Garrison knew and as Parker seems also to have known, a movement in the masculine mode is energized less by future righteousness than by present enemies. The public was now made to see the avuncular mayor, the affable judge of probate, the protective policeman on the corner, in a strange new light. The state had teeth, it turned out, and no conscience or honor.

Parker noted that Mayor Smith, "who, the other day 'regretted the arrest' of our brother, Anthony Burns, and declared that his sympathies were wholly with the alleged fugitive—and of course wholly against the claimant and the marshal—" had chosen at last to keep the peace at the cost of becoming "corporal of the guard for kidnappers from Virginia." And this he had done "over the graves, the unmonumented graves, of John Hancock and Samuel Adams." Modern readers, long accustomed to the wavering ways of politicians, are apt to find Parker's indignation naive, and the reference to Hancock and Adams a mere pious irrelevance. To his own audience, however, who shared the minister's heroic vision of history, the indictment resonated. The mayor's conduct was both the form and result of the dishonor in which Boston's Revolutionary past was officially held.

Parker next turned to the question of how another Bostonian, more recently dead, would be remembered.

> A man has been killed by violence. Some say he was killed by his own coadjutors: I can easily believe it; there is evidence enough that they were greatly frightened. They were not United States soldiers, but volunteers from the streets of Boston, who, for their pay, went into the court-house to assist in kidnapping a brother man. They were so cowardly that they could not use the simple cutlasses they had in their hands, but smote right and left, like ignorant and frightened ruffians as they are. They may have slain their brother or not—I cannot tell. It is said by some that they killed him. Another story is, that he was killed by a hostile hand from without. Some say by a bullet, some by an ax, and others still by a knife. As yet nobody knows the facts. But a man has been killed. He was a volunteer in this service. He liked the business of enslaving a man, and has gone to render an account to God for his gratuitous wickedness.

It is an odd and salient feature of the Burns case that the marshal's men came in for such extravagant verbal abuse. The fact that they were predominantly working-class Catholic immigrants from Ireland and Italy, quite a few of them with criminal records, made them an easy target for pent-up class anxieties. As a class, they had not previously entered into the moral reckoning; they ranged themselves outside of public affairs in an "underworld" of domestic employment, manual labor, poverty, and vice, altogether separated from the visible superstructure of Anglo-American institutional power. Despite their large and growing numbers, they had been substantially invisible and undiscussable—until they put their bodies in the way of a rescue, with the effect that they would now be seen, with all resentment, as defined in that act. Parker regarded them as moving in a moral universe of free choices, reaping where they sowed. That they were "volunteers" lay at the heart of the moral-rhetorical case against them. It would be wholly beside the point to suggest that a more complex notion of voluntarism might render their behavior more comprehensible and less monstrous. The effort in the sermon was wholly in the other direction. According to Parker's rules of moral engagement, which alone make his pronouncements intelligible, the actions of the guard had to be weighed and found wanting by other and higher standards than those presumed to have operated in the motive—those inhering in precisely that freedom and autonomy which the guilty actors lacked and which Parker was this morning concerned to cultivate in the native-born audience he addressed.

Parker does not "reach out" to his enemies or try to understand them or sympathize with them in their difficulties. If such is an emphasis in modern Christianity, it was not a notable feature of American Protestantism circa 1854; it was not this quickness to accuse that had made the breach between Parker and his fellow ministers, but rather his postulate of a connection between free will and moral behavior. That freedom which the Calvinists were busy denying he held, much as Emerson held, to be the indispensable ground of virtue. He further maintained that its eclipse in every avoidable consent to be manipulated, as in the actions of the un-self-relying Irish guard, was the root reason why now one man was kidnapped and another lay murdered.

In an effort not so much to understand as to indicate Boston's guilt in the matter of slavery, Parker went on to review the recent history of the city's compliant love of compromise, finding that it had, not with mere docility but with positive eagerness, accepted the leadings of a man who repudiated the higher law. Webster had sarcastically asked the Union meeting in 1850, "Will you have the 'higher law of God,' to rule over you?" The meeting, Parker recalled, "howled down the higher law of God!" In the face of such blasphemy, "Boston was non-resistant." It forgot its Revolutionary commitment to freedom, as Parker supposed, and submitted to slavery at the behest of "the greatest man in all the North." Less than a year later it offered 1,500 "gentlemen of property and standing" as volunteers to aid in the reenslavement of Thomas Sims.

What had been at stake then and now was not the lives of particular slaves, hard as Parker had worked to save them, but the freedom, and thus the moral power, of the North. Those men who were guided not by themselves, not by the voice of the higher law in the conscience, but by Daniel Webster and his posthumous legacy bore the responsibility for the passage of the Nebraska Bill. "To every demand of the slave power, Massachusetts has said, 'Yes, yes!—we grant it all!' 'Agitation must cease!' 'Save the Union!'" What Emerson had earlier said about individual self-reliance, Parker now said about sectional self-reliance: that unless you take your own proper values for the informing of your character, we cannot know you—we shall see only that overmastering, overshadowing power which signifies for you. "Southern slavery," said Parker, "is an institution which is in earnest. Northern freedom is an institution that is not in earnest. It was in earnest in '76 and '83. It has not been much in earnest since." As Parker would have it, a lack of earnestness or a weakness of will is an invitation to become colonized and irresponsible. Then language becomes what Emerson called a "rotten diction," and slavery ("the only finality") lays hands on all meanings.

As if to display his own earnestness, Parker devoted his final paragraphs to an ecclesiastical judgment of the judge as that party of all others who, in taking up the matter, had acted in fullest consciousness and information. With every facility for moral behavior, this man had freely chosen to advance the cause of slavery, and so in his fall from honor and estimation he bore the greatest guilt. In his peroration, then, Parker took the alienated law back into his own hands and issued a criminal indictment of the commissioner.

> Edward Greely Loring, Judge of Probate for the county of Suffolk, in the State of Massachusetts, Fugitive Slave Bill Commissioner of the United States, before these citizens of Boston, on Ascension Sunday, assembled to worship God, I charge you with the death of that man who was killed on last Friday night. He was your fellow-servant in kidnapping. He dies at your hand. You fired the shot which makes his wife a widow . . . I charge you with the peril of twelve men, arrested for murder, and on trial for their lives. I charge you with filling the courthouse with one hundred and eighty-four hired ruffians of the United States, and alarming not only this city for her liberties that are in peril, but stirring up the whole Commonwealth of Massachusetts with indignation, which no man knows how to stop—which no man can stop. You have done it all!

The audience in the Music Hall was not disappointed.

With the rights of [fugitive slaves] I firmly believe Massachusetts has nothing to do. It is enough for us that they have no right to be *here* . . . Whatever natural rights they have—and I admit these natural rights to their fullest extent—*this* is not the soil on which to vindicate them. This is *our* soil, sacred to *our* peace, on which we intend to perform *our* promises, and work out, for the benefit of ourselves and our posterity and the world, the destiny which our Creator has assigned to *us*.

BENJAMIN R. CURTIS, NOVEMBER 26, 1850

The fact that Loring's activity to this point had consisted mainly of granting defense motions for continuance makes the severity of Parker's charge all the more notable. One could argue that the commissioner's responsibility for riot and murder—such as it was—had arisen most immediately from his willingness to accommodate the abolitionists. Batchelder would still be alive had Loring been more compliant on Thursday toward the demands of the claimant or less conscientious about Burns's right to a defense—a right nowhere stipulated in the Fugitive Slave Law. But the alleged guilt lay more generally in his comprehensive endorsement of the federal system of slave recapture and not, as yet, in any action that was bound to follow from that choice. The gathering multitude of Loring's detractors understood that he could afford to be responsive to procedural requests from the defense to the extent that the outcome of the process was certain. As New Englanders were likely to recall from their ancient *Primer*, "The Cat doth play, / And after slay."

The field of circumstance that conditions a moral declaration such as Parker's and that controls the style of its rhetoric need not be (and perhaps rarely is) the same as the field of circumstance that conditions the speaker's private motives in making it. It is unsafe to infer from an artful statement like Parker's that the speaker's mind is thereby fully or directly made known. The proposition that Loring is guilty of the murder of Batchelder is clearly not literally true, if "literally" is taken to imply that distinctive set of circumstances composed of guns, knives, hot blood, and the rules of the criminal statutes. Either the statement makes no sense at all or it is logically and coherently distanced from that literal in a way to make use of its structure while superseding its meanings. To attribute guilt to a judge is, for a minister, to appear in the role of a prophet, one who sees in the corruption of the laws a destructive parody of divine government. "Guilt" has literal meanings outside the courtroom, as Parker reminded his auditors while at the same time invoking the text/context question of the precedency of the higher or lower law: which is to be received as literal and which as metaphor? Parker's position was little different, finally, from that of the psalmist who prayed that "judgment shall return unto righteousness" and who denounced the man who "frameth mischief by a law." The lawyer who presumes to hold the veto on an innocent man's God-given right to liberty transgresses (or crosses a line, as Emerson tells us) in a more literal sense than Parker, who in effect transgressed back, issuing a ministerial indictment in legal form. The effect of the religious allegory (rhetorically tied to "Ascension Sunday") was to prompt the audience to see the statute law not as the self-contained and self-referential system that some would make of it, but as lying open to the realm of the symbolic and ideational. So long as the law did not lie open in this manner, it became a vehicle without a tenor, a letter without a spirit, and could not be a signifier of justice. Statute law, in losing its connection to natural law, separates "judgment" from "righteousness"; in effect it loses its "soul" and becomes little more than a machine, altogether as rigorous and as predictable as the fate of Anthony Burns now seemed to be. As long as the outcome of the proceedings was certain, Parker could not afford to be generous. His desire to "unsettle" the law was completely Emersonian.

But Parker's principles were one thing and his passions were another. His best biographer maintains that he never embarked on a course of hard words without regret, that he did not love controversy, and that for him the rebuke of sin was ever a painful duty. There is much testimony to the effect that he lacked personal vindictiveness and could forgive and forget with the best of them, but he had always been notably fearless, energetic, specific, and unrelenting when attacking enemies for cause. At a time in America when conservatives were trying desperately to modulate the tone of public discourse, when the main objection to the abolitionists was the vulgar excess of their language, there was not a sharper or more talented controversialist to be found than Theodore Parker. And on this Sunday he was excited.[1]

He was bound to see this particular controversy as a defining moment in the history of Boston's Whig oligarchy, since, as he knew,

Loring was related by ties of blood and friendship to Parker's old enemies, the Curtis clan, the most prominent and powerful of the conservators of Webster's legacy. George Ticknor Curtis was Webster's executor, the author of the great man's last will and testament, his editor and biographer, and the finisher-up of certain uncompleted works of legal scholarship. He was often looked upon as the shadow of a departed substance. To Curtis' everlasting mortification, Edmund Quincy had hung on him the sobriquet "the Little Expounder." He was furthermore a slave law commissioner and was responsible for having issued the arrest warrants in the cases of William and Ellen Craft in 1850 and of Shadrach in 1851, and for having presided over the return of Thomas Sims to Georgia in 1851. In the Burns case, Suttle might have preferred to make use of Curtis rather than of Loring, but at the moment Curtis was fully occupied with the writing of his two-volume *History of the Formation and Adoption of the Constitution of the United States*—and with representing Father Edward Farrelly in a libel suit against the Boston *Bee,* which had accused the priest of having kidnapped the children of a man named Cassin.[2]

George's brother, Benjamin Robbins Curtis, had been known for many years as a protégé of Joseph Story and, after Story's death, as a prominent lawyer specializing in civil cases. He, too, belonged to Webster's inner circle and had helped to organize the Boston reception for the senator following the Seventh of March speech. The next year, after serving as the attorney for the marshal in the Sims case, he was appointed to the U.S. Supreme Court on Webster's recommendation. The position carried with it responsibilities for the New England circuit. Thus, in November 1851, after Curtis' presidential appointment but before his confirmation by the Senate, he presided at the jury trial of Robert Morris for his alleged involvement in the Shadrach rescue. Webster and the federal government were eager to have Morris prosecuted for treason, but the grand jury's indictment had been for a misdemeanor only. Morris was defended before Judge Curtis by New Hampshire Senator John P. Hale, an ardent Freesoiler, who argued that if the jury conscientiously believed the Fugitive Slave Law to be unconstitutional, it should acquit his client. This strategy, with which Hale was closely identified and which lay at the heart of abolitionist interest in the right of trial by jury, had actually been developed as an antislavery tactic by Vigilance Committee member Lysander Spooner, the movement's brilliant and eccentric legal theoretician. Curtis, however, specifically instructed Hale to make no such argument, declaring in his charge to the jury that judges alone were competent to form opinions about the law; juries in criminal cases were to be strictly triers of fact. There was much precedent against Curtis' position, which Parker and the abolitionists roundly denounced as judicial tyranny and fearsomely antidemocratic.[3]

Before his elevation to the Supreme Court, Benjamin Curtis had been the junior partner in the prestigious law firm headed by a distant cousin, Charles Pelham Curtis, who specialized in commercial law and managed the affairs of many of Boston's wealthiest merchants. In 1846 B. R. Curtis married the daughter of C. P. Curtis. Edward G. Loring, the commissioner, was the step-brother of C. P. Curtis and of C. P.'s brother, Thomas B. Thomas B. Curtis, a very successful merchant and importer, was mainly responsible, in 1850, for getting 900 Boston signatures on a letter commending Webster for supporting the Fugitive Slave Law. He also presided at the Union meeting in Boston on November 26, 1850, at which Benjamin R. Curtis, in a speech to the convention, denounced Parker for advocating jury nullification, which, in Curtis' view, involved perjury and the suborning of perjury.[4]

The family's association with fugitive slave cases extended back to 1832, when Charles P. Curtis had arranged the surrender of a minor child, who was then taken by his owner to Cuba. He and Benjamin R. Curtis (in one of the latter's first trials) appeared for the claimants in the celebrated case of the slave "Med," argued before Lemuel Shaw in 1836. Since 1850 three members of this one family had served as federal fugitive slave commissioners. In 1855—by which time, as we shall see, there was further cause for complaint against this plague of lawyers—Parker would identify the Curtis family as an ongoing criminal conspiracy, defenders of "the principles of despotism," and abettors, in a strict sense, of kidnapping.[5]

So while issues of judgment and righteousness had their eternal and sacred aspects and threw all men back on theory, they had also a life in time and personality. Had these Massachusetts men not been related, had they not been continually in league and consultation, and had they not been immediately tied to Webster, it would have been a great deal more difficult to make out the mortal shape of the wickedness Parker despised.

◖ LEWIS HAYDEN

I regard all violence as evil and self-destructive.

JOHN GREENLEAF WHITTIER, BOSTON *DAILY TIMES*, May 30, 1854

When the service was over at the Music Hall, Parker was approached by William F. Channing, Higginson's cousin, with the news that Lewis Hayden was in trouble. It seems that Asa Butman, the marshal's deputy, had warned Hayden—one Freemason to another—that he had been recognized on Friday night and would probably soon be arrested for the murder. Hayden, who knew he had fired his pistol at Freeman, thought it altogether possible that he had killed Batchelder by mistake. Oddly, his response to this warning was a profuse apology to Butman for trying to assassinate the marshal. Parker's response to hearing this story from Channing was a lament for Freeman's unscathed condition: "Why didn't he hit him!" the minister moaned. "Why didn't he hit him!" Channing and Parker concluded it would be best to get Hayden out of town, and that afternoon he was driven to Dr. Bowditch's Brookline home in a carriage with the curtains down.[1]

The number of people who had killed the Irishman was steadily increasing.

That evening, in his Brookline exile, Hayden led a secret assembly of angry black men. A series of resolutions was passed to liberate Burns "at all events." Bowditch, who was also present, read the letter he had received from Whittier, with its hasty declaration that Burns "must not be sent out of Boston as a slave. Anything but that!" A garbled report of this meeting appeared the next morning in the Boston *Times,* absurdly suggesting that the nonresistant Quaker poet had offered "any aid, by money or muscle," in support of a violent rescue.[2]

◖ NOT FOR SALE

Boston is a great city, in many respects the first in the Union; it is the seat of learning and of science; she has sent out to the South and West many a noble son, and her daughters are now the mothers of Southern children. Shall a few misguided men make odious the whole of this great city? No, never.

H. W. ALLEN, BOSTON *POST,* June 3, 1854

The previous midnight, when arrangements for the purchase of Anthony Burns had hung fire, the parties agreed that since the money had been raised and presented in good faith, the bargain might go through on Monday morning. Loring had told Grimes to be at his office at 8:00, cash in hand, and all would be taken care of. E. G. Parker was concerned that Suttle might need some persuading, since he had been so very clear in setting out the terms and timing. But the anxious and restive Parker resolved to argue hard.[1]

The handbills that went up on Sunday proclaiming that "The Man Is Not Bought" led many to the premature conclusion that all hope for a sale was ended. Rumors sprouted that Suttle had been getting urgent telegraphic messages from Washington and points beyond the Potomac, where in fact the case was being closely followed in the papers. Whatever Suttle may have been hearing from a distance, he was probably influenced as much by a closer source. Henry Watkins Allen, of Louisiana, a thirty-four-year-old slave-owning sugar planter, had just arrived in the city to enroll as a law student at Harvard. Allen had made Suttle's acquaintance at the Revere House, where both were staying, and had been consulted on Friday, as a young man of some experience, in appraising the slave's market value. It was he who had determined that Anthony Burns was worth $1,200. On Sunday morning one of Allen's friends, "not a professional gentleman," produced a copy of the statutes of Massachusetts and drew his attention to a law making it a criminal offense, punishable by a fine of $1,000 and ten years in prison, to sell a slave in the Commonwealth. Although Allen may have had his doubts about the applicability of this law to the circumstances at hand (he had been a practicing lawyer for years), he advised Suttle about the possible jeopardy, pointing out that he was already under arrest for kidnapping a man described in the charge as a "free citizen of Massachusetts"—the very article he now proposed to sell. Whether exchanging Anthony Burns for $1,200 amounted to a sale or a manumission was an even nicer technical point than the question of Suttle's clear title and right to sell, especially where he could be sure that even the flimsiest pretext for legal harassment would be eagerly taken up. Allen was clearly delighted with the irony that Burns's deliverance was prevented by the abolitionist law of an abolitionist state.[2]

E. G. Parker had a different story to tell, with different yet congruent ironies. The main condition imposed on the sale had been that the whole purchase price be raised on Saturday. Although this had been accomplished, it turned out that the $400 pledged to Parker was revocable if the sale was not concluded on that day. Presumably the stipulation was simply an acknowledgment of the terms by which Parker had solicited the money, expecting the sale to go through when and as his client wished. And yet, on Sunday, nothing that Parker could say would persuade the donor to honor his pledge a moment longer. The money was withdrawn, and Suttle was by his own conditions absolved from further dealings. The fickle donor proved to be none other than Thomas Buckminster Curtis, who by this time had undoubtedly heard what Theodore Parker had said at the Music Hall that morning about his step-brother. As in Allen's narrative, it was the uncontrolled upshot of antislavery work that kept the chains on Anthony Burns.[3]

Perhaps the most pathetic side of all these developments was that no one bothered to tell the Reverend Grimes that the deal was off. Through the day, as he heard vague rumors that pressure was being applied to Suttle not to sell, he got more and more anxious about his Monday morning meeting. By the time the Sunday evening service at the Twelfth Church was finished he could stand it no longer, and at 11:00 he went to pay a call on Loring at home, looking for assurance that the commissioner still meant to enforce the agreement. He told Loring that he had heard of "despatches from Washington" and was greatly worried that the agreement was being interfered with.

Loring hoped that such was not the case.

"I said I feared that they would not take the money; that there had been telegraphic despatches that the man must be sent back."

Loring replied that he hoped they would take the money; he thought they would.

And if they didn't, Grimes wanted to know, what then?

If they didn't take the money, and there was a doubt that could be raised in Burns's behalf, then he should have it, and he should walk out of the Court House a free man.

Grimes explained to the commissioner "what would be the happy feelings of his friends" if that should be the result, and then explained "what would be the awful state of things" should Burns be sent back. In that event, Grimes said, "there would be murder and bloodshed." The two men parted after midnight on the understanding that they would meet at Loring's office in the morning.[4]

During this interview between the minister and the judge there was a letter, perhaps lying open on Loring's desk, that he had received that day from John Gorham Palfrey, leader of the Massachusetts Freesoilers. Its purpose was to follow up on a conversation Palfrey had had with Loring on Saturday morning. He wanted to make sure the judge had taken his meaning precisely. Much could be said about whether the duties of a slave law commissioner were fit or unfit to be done by anyone, but there were special reasons why Loring in particular should not perform them—why, indeed, he should rather resign his place. Palfrey explained that as "an officer of Harvard College and of the Judiciary of Massachusetts," Loring had a "peculiar share of responsibility for the credit and safety of both those institutions."[5]

In regard to the judiciary, Palfrey indicated its special vulnerability at this time by alluding to the strong public sentiment in favor of the election of judges and the limitation of their terms of office, measures contained in the constitutional revision narrowly defeated by the voters just a year earlier. These measures, less radical than others proposed during the 1853 state constitutional convention, were anathema to conservatives (including most notably Richard Henry Dana), who took their stand squarely for the independence of the judiciary. Palfrey's immediate concern was that if Loring outraged public opinion by remanding Burns to slavery, he stood an excellent chance of being removed from his probate judgeship—and not by impeachment (since his offense would not be impeachable), but by the only other method available: popular address to the two houses of the state legislature. And once a judge was removed for political motives, Palfrey reasoned, the independence of the judiciary would be lost for good.

The argument in regard to Harvard College was more oblique and obscure, but Palfrey seemed to allude to the widely *unknown* fact that Loring had recently been denied a professorship on the particular ground that he adhered to the Fugitive Slave Law. Evidently that fact had been kept a closely guarded secret so that the College might continue to enroll the many Southern students on whose fees it largely depended. If Loring were to become politically obnoxious, these facts would come out, to Harvard's manifest hurt.

Palfrey concluded by putting himself in Loring's place: if he were conscientiously convinced that the work of the commissioner was "fit to be done, and that it was fit for me to do it rather than some other official equally competent, and that therefore I ought not to extricate myself by resigning that place, I should unquestionably forthwith adopt the alternative of vacating my offices under the University, & the Commonwealth, so as not to impair vast interests by my actions in the other office."

Loring must have wondered if this pressure was aimed more at obtaining his resignation or at procuring a favorable decision in the case before him. If Suttle was being strongarmed, so was the commissioner, who, if he did not understand it before this, now knew that the Burns case could result in nothing but disaster for himself.

Another, very different sort of letter was at the same time on the desk of Samuel May Jr., sent to him by Higginson, who was rapt in a moral giddiness not unlike that out of which Theodore Parker had spoken. There had been no abatement of enthusiasm or indignation at Worcester over the weekend; Higginson had seen to that. On Saturday night, with his face bandaged and his arm in a sling, he had addressed a raucous pro-Burns crowd, 1,000 strong, at City Hall. Speeches by Thomas Drew of the *Spy,* Stephen S. Foster, and Dr. Oramel Martin concluded in a unanimous determination to "lay aside business, on Monday, and proceed to Boston, en masse, there to meet friends of freedom and humanity from other sections of the State, and to take counsel together upon the emergencies of the times." In the near delirium of finding his own will so thoroughly reflected back from a huge and clamorous parish, Higginson wrote to May the next morning:

> Dear Sir,—The excitement in this city is tremendous; entirely beyond any imagination; tenfold what it was on Friday morning. The wildest things are proposed, and by persons whom I have considered very "hunkerish." For instance they talk of arming 500 men to go to Boston. But it would be *perfectly* practicable to arm and organize 100 if desirable. Shall we do it, and with what immediate object?

Higginson wanted the Vigilance Committee to understand that if it needed an army, he knew where to find one. But in fact he was doubtful that such a force was needed, "for I think that either the Kidnappers will be killed first; or else that Boston men will buy [Burns] to save the peace of the city." If neither result occurred and the slave was taken South through Providence, "we shall rescue him *to a certainty.* Any number could be sent from this place by an extra train."[6]

Higginson went on to suggest that if a great show of inland protest emerged in Boston on Monday—as he supposed it would—it might then be well "for a committee of such gentlemen as Deacon [Timothy]

Gilbert etc. to wait upon the Mayor, represent to him the impossibility of Burns's delivery without a riot and bloodshed, and also the *great danger to the lives of Suttle and Brent if they persist in the claim,* and urge him to advise the Kidnappers to relinquish their claim and leave town. This would be a virtual victory, if successful, and would at any rate increase the panic, and look well in the papers." The credibility of violence as a bargaining chip had been Higginson's contribution: he didn't wish to see it frittered away.[7]

The repulse at the Court House door on Friday night, which instantaneously put Anthony Burns into unreachable depths of federal guardianship, was after all a great and virtual success, even if Theodore Parker, in the chagrin of the morning after, could not see it. The wild crowd at Worcester City Hall could see it, and Higginson's own doubts had melted before that crowd's flashing determination to be the police of the higher law. "Send for me if you want me again," he wrote to May. "I am *thankful* for what has been done—it is the greatest step in Anti-Slavery which Massachusetts has ever taken. I am ready to do my share over again."[8]

🔥 MONDAY, MAY 29

Once I wished I might rehearse
Freedom's paean in my verse,
That the slave who caught the strain
Should throb until he snapped his chain.
But the Spirit said, "Not so;
Speak it not, or speak it low:
Name not lightly to be said,
Gift too precious to be prayed

. . .

Freedom's secret wilt thou know?—
Right thou feelest, rush to do."

EMERSON, "FREEDOM"

On Monday morning, while Whittier was reading in the papers that he was a fomenter of riots, the Reverend Grimes was on his way to Judge Loring's office, prepared to lay out hard cash to buy a slave, a member of his own church. The commissioner was not in his office at 8:00, nor did he appear during the hour that Grimes patiently waited.

At 9:00 he went to the Revere House, hoping to find Suttle. Unsuccessful there, he went to Seth Thomas' office at 46 Court Street, then back to Loring's office, then to the Probate Court. He could find no one at all. Finally, at the marshal's office he discovered Suttle, Brent, and Thomas in conference with Freeman and Hallett. Grimes reminded them of the eight o'clock appointment at Judge Loring's office and declared that he was ready to execute his part of the contract and deliver the money. Suttle, a large, beefy man said to resemble Senator Lewis Cass, turned toward Grimes and removed a cigar from his mouth in order to say that, because the sale had not been closed on Saturday night, he was no longer obliged to sell.

"And I shall not do it," said Suttle. "When I get him back to Virginia, then you can buy him."

Grimes protested, but the slaveholder merely repeated himself.

"Yes," said Hallett, "when he gets back to Virginia. Then you can purchase him, and I will give my hundred dollars."[1]

While this interview was going on in the marshal's office, Whittier, at his home in Amesbury, was writing to Dr. Bowditch, who had misapplied his earlier letter of alarm to arouse the wrong people. "I wish the demonstration of feeling to be deep and serious," the poet wrote in hopeful clarification, "but earnestly pray that there may be no resort to force. Cannot the man be *bought?*" Here was a wonderful, difficult economy of the passion for justice. Men all over Massachusetts were being urged in the most explicit terms to make a "demonstration of feeling" about a situation in which, as they were also told, the fate of an innocent man was to be sealed by tyrants— and yet the "demonstration" was not to consist in the use of force. A vast machinery had been deployed to make placid and law-abiding men angry enough to drop their Monday occupations and come in numbers to Boston—to do what? Were they supposed to write poems?[2]

Well, yes, in a manner of speaking. The party of the word were deeply attracted both to symbolic demonstrations and to the spiritual example of forbearance under temptation. The key to both these responses was the admirable "feeling" they bespoke, and the eventual winner in the contest was the party whose feelings were the most attractive. As in the sentimental literature of the period, feeling was becoming an end in itself, increasingly divorced from action and set in competition with it. Purchase of the slave would be desirable not because, as Whittier now wrote, Burns "must be saved if possible," but because ransom signified outwardly the right feeling and moral health of the community, as riot and bloodshed certainly could not. To the extent that feeling had been disconnected from action, it became available as gendered political space, offered to women by Harriet Beecher Stowe—and by the antislavery movement in general—as an appropriate mode of access for the disfranchised to questions of policy. *All* abolitionists, particularly in the wake of the Nebraska Bill, now looked upon themselves as disfranchised, but women especially were routinely urged to make "demonstrations of feeling," which would have, like poems, specific rhetorical effects.

But in the present case, purchase, like the nonresistance it conformed to, had for many the problematic look of a culturally feminized alternative, a weak poem whose hypersubtle signifying gave too much latitude for misconstruction. Who, after all, supported purchase? Mainly effete wealthy Hunkers, whose deployment of capital had always acknowledged Southern rights of ownership. But also, of course, Leonard Grimes, who seems exceptionally isolated in his personal concern for Anthony Burns, and for whom the purchase was no poem, no "statement," at all. And who could read the oddly correlative poem that nonresistance made and say for certain that it did not signify a feminine squeamishness about the contentions of the public sphere? Or that it signified high principle and not cowardice or acquiescence or defeat? If the party of the word lost control of its one weapon, there would be men enough, perhaps, to construct strong, muscular poems—revolutionary poems—whose meanings could not be mistaken.

The party of the word was having unprecedented difficulties commanding the meanings of its expressions, as may be seen in the continuation of Whittier's letter to Bowditch:

I regret the use of my letter to thee at a meeting of our colored friends. Surely no one who knows me could suppose that I wish to have any violent measures adopted. Pray see to it that no such impression was left in the minds of our colored friends. Oh, let them beware of violence! Let them not injure a holy cause by wrong action. God reigns, and if we are true to his laws we shall do more for liberty than by the use of the devil's weapons, of brute force. Nothing but great illness prevents me from coming down to use my influence on the side of freedom and peace. Dear

Doctor, act for me, then, and tide back all as far as possible from anything like violence. Beg our colored friends to bear and forbear.

In reading this letter one almost feels the violation of the doctor-patient privilege. The man of action (who is even at this moment, for all he knows, an accessory after the fact to murder) has the proxy for action of the laid-up, sidelined man of words. Alarmed in the first letter about Burns's impending loss of freedom, Whittier is now concerned about an excess of freedom and independence in his own meanings. He adds a reiterative postscript:

> P.S. Be good enough to obtain possession of my letter to thee and keep it. It was written in haste, and should not have been used by others, as I see it was by a paragraph in the "Times." I wished only that the people of Massachusetts could be witnesses of this awful sacrifice, in the hope that the peaceful, moral demonstration might be of service, if not to the poor victim, yet to the cause of freedom. God bless thee, my dear friend, and give thee wisdom and strength for the occasion.

Having called back and reinscribed his own "demonstration of feeling," having squelched the "life of its own" which it had taken on, Whittier sent off another letter of clarification and retraction—to the *Times*. That letter was published on Tuesday. On Wednesday, Hallett's newspaper, the *Post,* copied portions of it, praising Whittier as an abolitionist who has "come out in favor of the law."[3]

It was to be a week of just such contested and preempted meanings, in the courtroom, in the daily papers, and in the churches and public forums. What was said was likely, as never before, to be contrasted to what was done: chasms opened up between professions of concern and the incentives to do nothing. There was to be more loose talk in Boston this week than for whole ages past. Rumors, threats, broken promises, erroneous reporting, formal pieties, and posturing of all sorts would make the violent look at last like solid and committed men. The city was filling up for Anniversary Week, the annual convocation of the churches and the time appointed for meetings of reformers and politicians of all shades of purpose and conviction. It was the regularly scheduled, historically sanctioned week of talk in Boston. Most of the religious denominations were holding meetings, so that a substantial fraction of the whole clergy of New England would be in town closely observing the trial. Abolitionists, Unitarians, Congregationalists, Freesoilers, and the advocates of rights for women were the largest groups to schedule sessions, but among the smaller organizations forgathering this Monday—most dominated by ministers—were the Prison Discipline Society, the American Education Society, the Massachusetts Bible Society, the American Peace Society, and the Seaman's Friend Society. Thus the trial of Anthony Burns had fallen into the "festival of the Churches."

❧ MONDAY SESSION

About Court Square, and with Vigilance Committee at Tremont Temple: The trial proceeds and the crowd is large and clamorous for the issue of the case.

BRONSON ALCOTT, JOURNAL, MAY 29, 1854

When the trial began at 11:00, Ellis objected immediately to the show of force in and around the courtroom. He was reluctant to proceed, he said, while opposing counsel appeared with pistols and bowie knives, while the prisoner remained shackled, and while the courtroom itself, at the marshal's direction, was packed with armed hooligans. He further objected to the officious and belligerent military guard that blocked up the corridors, challenging public and counsel alike in their passage. In sum, the government was trying to intimidate the defense, and the commissioner needed to exercise control over his courtroom. The atmosphere, he said, was far removed from "the benignity that ought to be shed from a tribunal of justice"—and pressed for a delay until a semblance of decorum could be restored.

Ellis' remarks were briefly interrupted by a guard, who shouted that Burns was *not* manacled. Ellis had been unable to see his client, who was not seated at the defense table within the bar, but farther back in a group of the marshal's guard. That body now numbered over a hundred. It filled the otherwise unused jury box and most of the spectator seats. Indeed, the whole building and its environs looked more like a fortress or military camp than anything befitting a court of law. Every so often through the day the crowds in Court Square were flushed out by companies of marching troops or by cavalry sweeping through—yet the crowds reappeared again and again, like swirling water in a hole. All but one of the entrances to the Court House had been sealed off, and the one open door was guarded by the police and a platoon of Irish militiamen. It was said that Southerners could gain admittance here, but apart from the particular "friends of the prisoner" (Parker, Phillips, Grimes, and Morris), known abolitionists, even if members of the bar, could not.

In the courtroom, as Ellis spoke, one could catch the intermittent sounds of the workmen repairing last week's riot damage; but louder and more constantly came the shouts of the milling crowd outside, a din of the vox populi that (as a Southern student then sitting with Suttle afterward complained) made the nearer language of the lawyers hard to hear.[1]

Judge Loring indicated that the examination should proceed. He would consider Ellis' objections, "if necessary," at a later time.

B. F. Hallett, who had been muttering "shame, shame," throughout Ellis' remarks, rose unexpectedly from the court clerk's desk where he had been seated and fairly erupted with a defense of Freeman's conduct in providing security for the courtroom. He called the commissioner to task for accepting, without resentment, Ellis' malign and wrongheaded charges. Loring told Hallett that his comments were unnecessary, as the point had been decided, but the government's lawyer persisted, adding bitter comments against the seditious behavior of Ellis' friends, the Faneuil Hall speakers. He stated that he himself had summoned the federal troops as a *posse comitatus* under a certificate issued by Judge Sprague on Friday night in response to the riot.

"Mr. Hallett," replied the commissioner, "these remarks are irrelevant and entirely out of order."

Still Hallett pressed on, his anger rising. "The President of the United States has approved of this course," he said, "and the efficient aid which the marshal has, both armed and unarmed, to prevent further violence and murder, are here by the sanction of the President, and under a certificate of a judge of the United States courts; and therefore it is a proceeding, not only necessary, but such as the commissioner and all good citizens are bound to respect." Burns stared at the district attorney. Loring slumped back in his chair, waiting for Hallett to blow himself out. Dana interjected, saying to the court, "You will find it impossible to stop him if you do not commit him." Loring simply smiled at the idea, but Hallett at last sat down. The outburst was shocking in itself to onlookers, but more puzzling, to some, was Loring's passivity before it.[2]

There was no legal necessity for Hallett's presence in the courtroom: he was here, as was now obvious, simply because he had been for years a key figure in the Democratic party and meant to monitor—and affect to the extent he could—the unfolding of an immensely sensitive political trial. He wanted to be personally and conspicuously responsible for the rendition of a slave from Boston because such a victory for the policy of the Democrats would be deeply satisfactory to Hallett's fellow party member, Franklin Pierce. He was the president's man, and even Loring would treat him gingerly.

At the age of fifty-six, Hallett seemed to his contemporaries to have exchanged the fire of his youthful radicalism for the dubious securities of political advancement. Following his graduation from Brown in 1816 and his admission to the Rhode Island bar three years later, Hallett became a crusading Jacksonian populist, selecting cases in which he could argue for individual rights against the power of the government. The fact that his most celebrated case was a defense of Mashpee Indian property rights might suggest that he was a more consistent Jacksonian than Jackson himself. As an editor and journalist in Providence, he agitated for court reform and free suffrage. His advocacy of a wider franchise at that time—around 1840—belongs importantly to the background of the Dorr Rebellion in Rhode Island, a movement he eagerly supported and which he defended in a landmark case of constitutional law, *Luther v. Borden.* In 1831 he left Rhode Island to edit the *Boston Daily Advocate,* an anti-Masonic paper which he used to support Jackson's position on banks and monopolies. When the *Advocate* was merged with the *Post* in 1838, Hallett found himself at the helm of the major Democratic newspaper in New England and intimately associated with the paper's owner, Colonel Charles G. Greene, and with Greene's crony, David Henshaw, who together controlled patronage under Jackson, Van Buren, and Polk. As late as 1837 Hallett was still sympathetic to Garrison and the abolitionists, and participated prominently in the Boston meeting to protest the murder of Elijah Lovejoy. It was Hallett, ironically, who stenographically preserved Wendell Phillips' speech on that occasion, thus launching the career of his sharpest critic.

By the late 1840s, when Hallett was routinely chairing the Democratic party's Committee on Resolutions, his few contacts with the antislavery movement could only be construed as ploys for political advantage. In 1849, angry with Southern Democrats who had failed to support the party's nominee, Lewis Cass, he formed a coalition with the Freesoilers, hoping the combination would be formidable against the Whigs. To secure this coalition he had the Democrats adopt a resolution affirming that "We are opposed to slavery in every form and color, and in favor of freedom and free soil wherever man lives throughout God's heritage." But this ringing declaration merely bespoke the bankruptcy of political discourse, for immediately thereafter the Compromise of 1850 became policy for both major parties. Hallett's resolution and his flirtation with the Freesoilers had become a terrific embarrassment, one that might have cost him his political future had he meant what he said, but his apostasy was eventually forgiven in exchange for his stout and timely support for Franklin Pierce in 1852. In 1854 the district attorney for eastern Massachusetts owed more palpable debts of gratitude to General Pierce than did Nathaniel Hawthorne for his consular appointment.[3]

When Hallett finally sat down again, E. G. Parker asked whether evidence already entered had to be gone over. Loring didn't think so, but reversed himself when Dana pointed out that the defense had taken no notes on Thursday. Parker therefore reread the complaint, introduced again the warrant issued by Loring together with the marshal's return, and at 2:00 put Brent back on the stand.

Brent testified that he was a merchant residing in Richmond, Virginia. He had been born in Stafford County, three miles from the Suttle farm, and had known Suttle for as long as he could remember. He identified Anthony Burns as the prisoner at the bar, having known him for twelve or fifteen years. Burns, he said, was the slave of Colonel Suttle, who ordinarily hired him out, first in 1845 or 1846, the year before he (Brent) had hired him for three successive years beginning in either 1846 or 1847. For the past two years he had been Suttle's agent in hiring Burns to other parties in Richmond. He had leased Burns to one Millspaugh in March of 1853, Suttle receiving the wages. Burns had a scar on his right cheek and "a cut across his right hand"; he was about six feet tall. No, there was no other Anthony Burns about the places resorted to by Suttle. Brent had last seen Burns on Sunday, March 20; he was reported missing four days later.[4]

No one immediately noticed that March 20, 1854, was in fact a Monday; had they done so, it might have alerted them to other and more significant problems in Brent's testimony.

The examination had now reached the crucial point at which, in the first iteration of the proceedings on Thursday, testimony had been broken off in response to Dana's objection. Parker was about to have

Brent relate to the court damning admissions made by Burns while in custody on the night of his arrest. This time it was Ellis who objected, citing section 6 of the Fugitive Slave Law, which stipulated: "In no trial or hearing under this act shall the testimony of such alleged fugitive be admitted in evidence." Seth Thomas responded that admissions and confessions related by the party to whom they were made could not be construed as "testimony" from the alleged fugitive; of course Burns could not testify—he was a party in the suit, the defendant. At last Dana joined the argument, suggesting that it was cruel to the prisoner to take advantage of the only power he had under this law—that of speech—to his detriment, when the claimant had not only his own rights but, in these alleged confessions, a portion of the prisoner's as well.[5]

It seemed that the black man's very language could legally be colonized by his white owner. Brent and Suttle now had a sort of exclusive copyright on what Burns had spontaneously said on the night of his arrest. They could repeat it, they could use it; constructively they owned that language, which the slave, doubly cornered, doubly confronted, could not now disown. Had the words, he might have wondered, ever been properly his? The legal argument going on before the commissioner shaded into a psychological one about ventriloquism: it was urged that admissions made by a slave before his master were peculiarly apt to be coerced or misused and so open to influence as to be legally inadmissible. In advancing this argument, Ellis was not proposing that Burns actually *was* a slave: merely that statements cannot go to prove a fact that, if true, subverts the reliability of the statements that prove it. This elegant point seems to have been too abstruse for the moment. Thomas replied simply that when there was no proof of a threat or a promise having been made to a prisoner, spontaneous admissions were always accepted, and it should be no different in slave cases. Loring was inclined to agree with claimant's counsel but expressed an uncertainty, and so, out of fairness to the defendant, he concluded that Dana and Ellis would have the right to reopen the question later; for now he would accede to Parker's request that the testimony be admitted *de bene esse* (for what it's worth).

Brent first recounted what Burns had said about his departure from Virginia—that he had not intended to escape, but that while working on board a ship at dockside he had fallen asleep and the vessel had sailed without his knowledge. Brent then gave an account of the interview between Burns and Suttle on Wednesday evening shortly after the arrest. When Suttle entered the makeshift cell, Burns had greeted him in flustered surprise: "How do you do, Master Charles?" According to Brent, Suttle's first question had been "Did I ever whip you, Anthony?" Answer: No. "Did I ever hire you where you did not want to go?" No. "Did you ever ask me for money when it was not given you?" No. "Did I not, when you were sick, take my bed from my own house for you?" Yes. At this point Burns had recognized Brent. "How do you do, Master William?" he had said. He was asked if he was willing to go back. "I understood him to say, substantially, that he was," Brent said. "I do not know that he said so, but I understood him to signify that."[6]

As Burns listened to the testimony, he remembered the conversation quite differently. No words at all, he later maintained, had passed between himself and Brent, who had stood apart with the marshal, all the while silently observing. Neither had he replied to the gloating emphasis of Suttle's greeting, "How do you do, *Mr.* Burns?" But he had implicated himself by responding to Suttle's inquiry about why he had run away: the story of his falling asleep on board the ship had been accurately represented by Brent. And to the question about whether Suttle had made gifts of money, Burns recalled answering, "You have always given me twelve and a half cents once a year." When Brent testified that the slave had expressed a willingness to return to Virginia, courtroom spectators saw Burns shake his head in a vigorous mute denial.[7]

Brent's testimony continued. He knew that Suttle owned Anthony Burns because he could recall a time not long ago when Suttle had raised money for some transaction by mortgaging his property, "including this man Burns." A few questions about Burns's relatives were designed to show that they were all owned by Suttle. Brent indicated that Burns had a brother in Stafford County and a sister in Richmond, and that Burns's mother, then living on Suttle's farm, was also Suttle's slave.[8]

In one of the published trial transcripts there occurs at this point an interpolated editorial comment: "The witness here found difficulty in explaining the relation of Suttle's alleged property to him, from the fact that the Court said he must not state any person to be 'a slave' without corroborating legal evidence. Sundry questions bearing upon this point, were discussed at length by counsel." Loring's caution was evidently prompted by an objection from Dana or Ellis, who would have been anxious that the burden of proof not be lessened by casual statements about the status of Burns's mother. It was a well-known feature of Southern law that the child's status, free or slave, followed that of the mother; but federal law was written without reference to the internal workings of the slave code, which was therefore not available as a basis for proof here and now. The enactment known in common parlance as "the Fugitive Slave Law" itself pointedly avoided the term "slave." Because it affected to concern itself solely with "fugitives from service or labor," it was constrained by its own abstract fiction to consider only the matter of being bound to labor in the first place and the matter of escape in the second. All of this, of course, conveniently bracketed and disguised what was eminently nonfictional about the case: that it was to decide henceforth and forever whether Anthony Burns was to be a chattel or a man. Fittingly, a main purpose of the law, in respect to language, was suppression; it was designed to exclude the horror from the proceedings and to quarantine it firmly in the popular—in the shouts and the passions that government bayonets kept out (but which nevertheless came in at the windows), and in such ordinary and convenient terminology as the commissioner now ruled out of order.[9]

Not surprisingly, there was a concurrent linguistic dispute over the wording to be used in reference to Burns, the man (or thing) whose past and future status now lay open to official, enforceable determination. In one of the few personal papers that survive from the case, Dana wrote: "I notice that the counsel for the prosecution is a little at a loss to know what to call him. Sometimes he calls him the *person* at the bar. Where did he learn to call him a *person?* Not from his client, the claimant." In fact Thomas and Parker were laboring under the same semantic difficulty that embarrassed Brent: they could neither call Burns a slave, nor under the law could they treat him as a person. Dana solved the problem for himself: "I call him the prisoner."[10]

 ## CLAIMANT RESTS

The air is pestilential with this fugitive-slave case.
LONGFELLOW, JOURNAL, MAY 29, 1854

Ellis' cross-examination of Brent was probing but unfocused, showing that the defense had not yet devised a strategy. The first few questions elicited some personal information about Brent. He was thirty-five years old, engaged in the grocery commission business in Richmond. He owned several slaves. Some of these had come to him as the property of his wife, some were inherited from his father; he had not himself purchased or sold any for the past dozen years. He had met with Millspaugh after the escape and had given the news to Suttle by letter; Suttle had asked Brent to come North with him, which he had consented to do, without financial consideration, as a friend. They had arrived in Boston the previous Monday night and were rooming together.

Although he had said on direct examination that Millspaugh hired Burns in March of 1853, he now indicated that Burns's term of service under that contract ran from January 1, 1854. Asked for further details about the mortgage previously alluded to, Brent responded that the assignee was one John M. Tolson of Stafford County. Having heard Thomas say earlier that admissions were to be accepted in the absence of threats or promises, Brent now reported that Suttle had said to Burns on Wednesday night, "I make you no promises, and I make you no threats," which, if Suttle in fact said it, would suggest prior coaching from his lawyers. Following up with a few questions, Dana got Brent to admit that he hadn't reported all the conversation between Suttle and Burns—only what he'd been asked about—and that he had not reported even that verbatim, but "substantially, and as I recollect it." With that, Brent was excused from the witness stand.[1]

Next to testify was Caleb Page, a freelance truckman who lived in Somerville and was generally employed about Milk Street in Boston. On Wednesday evening he had been commandeered by Asa Butman to assist in the arrest and was one of the five who effected it. He had escorted the prisoner to the United States jury room and stayed there about three-quarters of an hour, during which time he had overheard snatches of the conversation between Suttle and Burns, and confirmed that questions had been asked about flogging, the giving of money, and the use of the bed when Burns was sick. The only reply that Page actually heard from the prisoner was a denial that he had come North, as Suttle supposed, in Captain Snow's vessel.

There is no indication that the defense interviewed any of the prosecution witnesses before they testified, nor were defense witnesses previously deposed by claimant's lawyers. One of the conditions of the hasty trial—which under the law was to have been a summary proceeding before the commissioner and not a trial at all—was that all who testified were in effect surprise witnesses. Though Page's corroborating testimony could not have been unexpected, it tells us something of the defense's tactics that Page was, later that day, privately interrogated by Edward Atkinson, a Vigilance Committeeman. This interview developed the information that, in participating in the arrest, Page had acted on Butman's assurance that Burns was being seized as a common thief, and that when Page discovered how matters really stood he had left the Court House in disgust. Atkinson informed Dana of this and suggested that the truckman might be useful as a defense witness—though in fact he was never recalled.[2]

Following Page's testimony, the claimant's lawyers closed their case by introducing the Revised Code of Virginia, "for the purpose of proving that slavery exists" in that state, and by reintroducing the Virginia court record, asserting that it was dispositive of the two points of owing service and of escape. They concluded their case by proposing that, in order to establish identity, the commissioner should examine the defendant to see if the marks on his body corresponded to those stipulated in the Virginia record. This Loring did by a slightly downward gaze from the bench; neither man stood; neither man approached the other, though Loring, who said he saw the scar on the cheek and the scar on the hand and estimated the man's height, asked the defense if they wished the prisoner brought up for a closer scrutiny. Ellis declined the offer.

The lawyers for the claimant thus rested their case. Ellis asked for a brief recess before the defense opened. It was now 2:50. Loring granted a recess until 3:30.[3]

The crowd outside, estimated at between 7,000 and 8,000, and drawn as much by curiosity as by sympathy, were not unanimously well disposed toward Burns, nor were they all clamoring for his release. Moncure Conway, who had tried without success to get into the courtroom that morning, was left to study the people in the street, including many who "held heavy sticks and appeared to be of the proslavery mob."[4]

Oliver Wendell Holmes was there as well, curious and observant, and if he held anything like a stick it was light and gold-tipped. Perhaps as he watched the crowd he remembered the slave his own grandfather had owned, the slave who had likewise been a watcher of crowds and who had seen Crispus Attucks fall at the Boston Massacre, just a block from where the slaveowner's grandson now stood.[5]

Holmes was patient and understanding when it came to slavery. He had been among the signers of the Boston letter in 1850 commending Webster's position on the Compromise, much to Emerson's annoyed surprise, who had thought that only old men would sign. And yet Holmes's support was understandable, for Webster's public position had been his own in private. He was more frightened by the prospect of civil conflict and disunion than he was opposed to slavery, about which he thought there was little, in any event, to be done. He deplored the raspy rhetoric of the "philo-melanic" abolitionists, and advised his fellow poets to steer clear of reform. "I shall always be better pleased to show what is beautiful in the life around me," he wrote to James Russell Lowell, "than to be pitching into giant vices, against which the acrid pulpit and the corrosive newspaper will always anticipate the gentle poet." And yet for all his considerable and eventually broadcast racism and for all his voting for the Whigs, he was philosophically a Freesoiler: "We can all agree," he said, "in saving every inch of American soil we fairly can for freedom, and reducing our involuntary participation in slavery to the minimum consistent with our existence as a united people. The question is, whether New England, bound up with a group of confederate sovereignties, cherishes the right temper and uses the right language to her slaveholding sister States." No one who cared—as he did—for the welfare of the inferior races could afford to rile their masters. "The white man must be the master in effect, whatever he is in name; and the only way to make him do right by the Indian, the African, the Chinese, is to make him better by example and loving counsel." At bottom, he felt that New England was confronted with a choice of alliances: either with an educable race of Southern whites, "which we can hope to raise to our own level," or "with the lower one which we never can." In any such choice it was natural that "our sympathies [would] go with our own color first." Here, then, was the choice that preserved the Union. So said Webster. So said Holmes's much-admired Harvard classmate, Benjamin Robbins Curtis.[6]

Thomas Sweney, publisher and proprietor of the *American Celt*, wrote to the editors of the Boston *Herald*:

At this time, when so much opprobrium is heaped on Adopted Citizens, it is astonishing to behold the alacrity with which papers heretofore *professing* to be *particularly* friendly to us, join in the hue and cry against us—take, for instance, the item in the Boston *Daily Times,* of this morning, in which it is stated that John C. Cluer, one of the alleged abolition rioters, is an Irishman. Now, it is known to the Citizens of Boston in general, and to the Reporter of the *Times* in particular, that John C. Cluer is a Scotchman. Since the passage of that questionable enactment, the Fugitive Slave Law, it has been openly and violently resisted, and violated in this city and elsewhere, by the descendants of the Puritans only—but in no instance have Irish Adopted Citizens cooperated with them. The Citizens of Boston, of Irish birth, have taken a solemn oath to sustain the Constitution and Laws of this glorious Union—and, to their honor be it spoken, they never have, and never will be found to act inconsistently with the proper observance of that solemn obligation.

Cluer was indeed from Scotland. He had been a mill operative in England, then a Chartist and a revolutionary. He had been a fundraiser for the Vigilance Committee and an agitator during the Sims case and for the ten-hour movement. More recently, he had served time in a New York prison for bigamy. Arrested on Saturday and charged with the murder of James Batchelder, he was currently languishing in jail with Martin Stowell.[7]

The tireless Reverend Grimes had not yet reached the limit of his resourcefulness. After the discouraging encounter in the marshal's office, he went back to Hamilton Willis for advice on how to proceed. Prompted by Grimes—and independently by false rumors that Suttle had raised the asking price to $4,000—Willis addressed a note to the slaveholder at court, reminding him how negotiations had stood at the point of suspension and saying that Grimes had a right to expect the agreement to be honored. He inquired also if more money was needed. Without leaving his seat in the courtroom, Suttle scribbled his reply: "The case is before the Court, and must await its decision." Willis determined to see Suttle in person the next morning.[8]

Thomas B. Curtis, having withdrawn his $400 on Sunday, thus scuttling the sale of Anthony Burns, drove out this mild, sunny spring day toward Cambridge. Crossing the Mill Dam, he lost control of his horse, and his carriage collided with an omnibus. He was thrown from his vehicle with such force as to break his leg just above the knee.[9]

The Worcester Freedom Club, including many black male residents of the city, descended on Boston at noon, 500 strong. Under the command of Dr. Oramel Martin they left the depot in a long file, two abreast, made their way up the middle of Washington Street, turned left at Court Street, and marched like Joshua's army round the fortified Court House. The *Liberator* said that their appearance "created some excitement" among the onlookers, "who cheered them with a will." They then retired to Meionaon Hall at Tremont Temple, and there heard speeches of varying degrees of encouragement from Dr. Martin, William Lloyd Garrison, Charles L. Remond, Simon P. Hanscom, and Stephen S. Foster. Garrison's speech was described as lukewarm: he had been engaged in the business so long, he said, that his zeal for martyrdom had become blunted, and he didn't feel like rushing toward it. The old man's nonresistance had certainly never been calculated to turn street theater into heroic confrontation, but Foster's nonresistance was made, rhetorically at least, of sterner stuff: he declared himself willing to "bare his breast to the bayonet," a phrase that lingered in the minds of the reporters if, perhaps, in no others. Hanscom asked for volunteers for a posse to assist the coroner in serving a new writ of replevin, which (as he didn't say), Samuel Sewall and Dr. Bowditch were even then trying to cajole from Governor Emory Washburn. But the Freedom Club voted instead to march around the Court House some more.[10]

Which they did, at 3:00, carrying their broad silk banner inscribed "Worcester Freedom Club" over the central figure of the goddess of Liberty and, below that, the legend "Warm Hearts and Fearless Souls—True to the Union and the Constitution." The police, who had been arresting miscellaneous street orators for the past two days, decided that this display was likewise incendiary and confiscated the banner after a brief, undignified tussle. Adin Ballou Thayer, of Worcester, who had participated in Friday's attack on the Court House, was chosen to negotiate with the authorities for its return. He was successful, but the gaudy banner was eventually torn to shreds by citizens who doubtless felt they were yet more true to the Union and the Constitution.

The effect of the Freedom Club as public spectacle was comically undercut when, on arriving at the Court House the second time, they discovered that they had been preceded a few minutes before by a band of twenty boys in folded paper hats, marching with tin drum and wooden swords around the building, "determined," they stoutly declared, "to rescue the fugitive."[11]

The failure of the operation on Friday and the subsequent reinforcement of the Court House led most people to give up on the idea of another rescue attempt. In fact the available repertoire of rescue strategies was exhausted, leaving the development of any future plans in the hands of those who weren't afraid to extemporize and who weren't deterred by wildness. Wendell Phillips got a letter from a "friend of the slave" in New York, suggesting that a force attacking the Court House might come in two waves: the vanguard would carry "ten pounds of chloroform," which would succeed in knocking out the watchmen as well as the attacking party, leaving those behind to finish up the rescue. This earnest tactician had sent the same letter to Theodore Parker.[12]

Parody comes in like a force of nature to chill the blood. The weirdness of its duplications literally diverts us, locating action and defining it by escorting us into the realms next adjacent: thus the Worcester Freedom Club is a parade; thus attackers always knock themselves silly and wake up arrested. But parody diverts in other ways as well. If it takes as a fundamental truth that action is always spectacle, always stylized "show," it nevertheless depends on the underlying seriousness it seems to deny. It mitigates real anxieties by transferring attention away from the authorizing issue. The parody of the Worcester Freedom Club would have been impossible had the public, as it watched, not been eager to suppress such information as the *Boston Evening Transcript* was reporting, that 1,000 pistols had recently been sold in Dock Square—many, presumably, to the nervous black men who worked there.[13]

THE DEFENSE OPENS

I now remark that this trial is political.

C. M. ELLIS, MAY 29, 1854

The hearing resumed sometime between 3:30 and 4:00, Ellis opening for the defense. His first care was to impress on Loring that the unusual nature of the case and the outrageous conditions under which it had to be argued made haste not only unseemly but substantially unjust. He pointed out that if the case had been one for the criminal or civil courts—had it involved only the defendant's coat rather than his freedom—"the wheels of justice could not be turned in months." Of the brief postponement already granted, "the Sabbath made part of the time"—when even lawyers were supposed to be in church. The case presented novel issues of law, yet the Court House law library had been locked up. Then, too, "precious as every instant is to one needing to use it to defend another's liberty, I have to-day lost much of the few minutes pause, forbidden to ascend the stairway, by soldiers with their bayonets at my breast."

Ellis knew that there would be no more delays and that the commissioner was powerless to affect conditions in his own courtroom. The point was not to gain more time, but to suggest to the commissioner that he needed hereafter to be specially indulgent to the defense, staggering as it did under this peculiar law's unequal burden.[1]

Ellis continued by suggesting that the claimant's case was too weak to prevail when (as "your Honor did well to remind counsel") the legal presumption had to be that the defendant was a free man. The contempt that Dana and Ellis felt for proceedings under the Fugitive Slave Law came in no small part from their perception that the "judge" was not bound by the accustomed rules of evidence or constrained by the ordinary safeguards of criminal or civil procedure. He was, by design, a kind of chartered tyrant. Thus Ellis' emphasis on the presumption, not indeed of innocence but of freedom, was meant to impress arbitrary authority with its pertinence as a guide to conduct. So anomalous were fugitive slave cases from a legal standpoint that defense lawyers could not—or claimed they could not—confidently rely on "the plain principles of justice and law." "In these cases," Ellis said, "no one knows what ground he stands upon." And so he now explicitly appealed, by way of supplement, to "the instinctive feeling of common fairness and humanity," addressing the court in its presumptive capacity as a human being. This was not advertised as higher law doctrine.

> Sir, you sit here, judge and jury, betwixt that man and slavery. Without a commission, without any accountability, without any right of challenge, you sit to render a judgment which if against him no tri-

bunal can review and no court reverse. He may be dragged before you without any warrant; you must proceed without any delay; without any charge, on proofs defined only as such as may satisfy your mind, you may adjudge, and your judgment to surrender will be final forever. Therefore [the presumption of freedom] will commend itself to your Honor's reason and justice. The mind that is to decide a matter involving questions of law and fact will not fail to weigh all these questions with the greater care the greater the chances of error and the dangers of its result, and, in this case, require the claimant to prove his case beyond a possible doubt.[2]

Ellis seemed to be speaking in a way to occupy time, as though hoping to get to the end of the day without committing himself too much. Delay and obstruction had always been the policy of the Vigilance Committee, but now it looked very much as though he was unprepared, as claimant's counsel had suggested all along, to offer an affirmative defense. In fact his opening statement, in which the whole of the defense case was eventually laid out, filled the remainder of the Monday session and spilled over into Tuesday. He attacked the insufficiency of the record of the Virginia court, pointing out its lack of specificity; the fact that it was a transcript from the record, not a copy; that it could not be held to be a judicial record at all; that it did not "certify the proof," as required in the act of 1850. The complaint and warrant as issued by Loring were illegal on similar grounds. The claimant's evidence in general tended to show only that the prisoner "rendered no acts of service to the claimant" and that he was "by hearsay said to have been born of a mother, also not shown to have rendered any service to Suttle." Suttle's unadorned claim of ownership—as to mother or to child—made no prima facie case.

On the matter of Burns's alleged admissions while in custody, Ellis cited a Southern legal opinion that had been designed to effect a wholesale exclusion of slave testimony. In the language of the Southern court:

The master has an almost unlimited control over the body and mind of his slave. The master's will is the slave's will. All his acts, all his sayings are made with a view to propitiate his master. His confessions are made, not from a love of truth, not from a sense of duty, not to speak a falsehood but to please his master, and it is in vain that his master tells him to speak the truth and conceals from him how he wishes the question answered. The slave will ascertain, or which is the same thing, think that he has ascertained, the wishes of his master and moulds his answer accordingly. We therefore more often get the wishes of the master, or the slave's belief of his wishes, than the truth. And this is so often the case that the public justice of the country requires that they should be altogether excluded.

This was the perhaps the most philosophically interesting as well as the most tactically important of the defense arguments. The routine intimidation of man by man under the regime of slavery was plainly incompatible with a legal system predicated on legible motives and free and responsible actions. The preservation of law therefore required that the logical consequence of that regime be bracketed and excluded. Few jurists were willing to inquire very deeply why property in slaves should give rise to such systematic legal anomalies— why it was always making for "special cases"—for fear that they should have to conclude that slavery itself was radically unmanageable under the law, that the institution was for some reason inconsistent with it, and that anything that lay organically outside the law had to be regarded, quite simply, as illegal. The strained pretense that it was not lay at the bottom of all the political anxieties of the 1850s. The defense of slavery had increasingly to proceed by panic and patchwork, and by offering laws, like the Fugitive Slave Bill, that defied general principles of legality. This the abolitionist lawyers understood; the effect was to throw them back on a major effort to clarify essential traditions in the law, which they identified with a central enshrinement of democratic principles of freedom and civil liberties. This was the great ironic service that slavery rendered to America in the 1850s.

The major threat to freedom and civil liberties was the special empowerment of individuals beyond the point where their capacity to harm others was restrained by law. This had always been the situation of the slaveholder; it was now also the situation of Edward G. Loring, as Ellis politely and obliquely said:

Whatever rules you may choose to adopt in this case, whether in relation to your own powers, the construction of the statute, the admission or the weight of evidence, they ought to be such that it would not be possible for a man actually free, one of our own citizens, to be hustled off, sacrificed under the fall of the presumptions under which the laws place him for protection.

The extreme vagueness of the rules governing the conduct of a fugitive slave commissioner not only put him on his own resources, but made him the prime example of everything generally objected to in the arbitrary power concentered in "aristocratic" judges as compared with the diffusion of power in democratic juries. The freedom of Anthony Burns, Ellis seemed to recognize, lay at the mercy of the commissioner's personal whim, so long as there was nothing like real law—or nothing but slave law—to shape the outcome.

Ellis then offered the suggestion that what Suttle and Brent had shown relative to Anthony Burns might, with no better standard of proof than they proposed, be as convincingly shown in regard to any free black resident of the Commonwealth of Massachusetts, presuming the corrupt will to do it. In other words, such claiming, even if it were countenanced by the law, could not be legally distinguished from kidnapping. And where there was no distinguishing, there was no difference—a conclusion already acknowledged in the lingua franca of the abolitionists.

Ellis hammered away at the anomalous nature of the law. Everyone thought of the Fugitive Slave Law as a provision for interstate extradition, but it set standards within states as well: suppose that Suttle laid claim to a free resident of Richmond. Loring's ruling should be one that confirmed the need for careful, objective proofs; else that free man in Richmond would be at the mercy of the unencumbered dictation of a slaveholding commissioner. The standard of proof that Ellis urged was calibrated to his sense of the gravity of the issue: any hypothesis but that which the claimant sought to establish had to be perfectly excluded, and every fact certified "beyond any reasonable doubt whatever." The legal presumption of freedom had to be granted to all residents of Virginia born after 1785, rebuttable only by a showing of continuous ownership thereafter. The law was dangerously lax in other respects as well: it was a defect, for example, that it required only one witness—in this case Brent. Ellis quoted Deuteronomy 19:15 in favor of two or three witnesses as the assurance of safety, which number, he pointed out, juries rightly and instinctively preferred.

Turning to the facts of the case, Ellis pointed out that on claimant's showing Burns was mortgaged; only the mortgagee had legal title; only John M. Tolson had a right to recover. It was established in law that "a mortgagor, even if beneficially interested, could neither maintain trover for the goods mortgaged, nor assumpsit for their proceeds." Not only was Burns mortgaged, but he was leased, "and if the right of reclamation depends on the present right of possession, the lessee alone can have that. The Bill of 1850 only authorizes the person holding, the person to whom the service is due, to reclaim; therefore the lessee [Millspaugh] is the one to recover."

It was also a settled point of "the general law of nations," according to Ellis, and a specific implication of the 1850 law, that the claimant could not recover if there had been no escape. "Now they choose to show that the prisoner fell asleep on board a vessel in the bay in a slave state, and a breeze came to waft him away out on to the high seas and into the safe port of a free state. It was a boon to him. It made him free. He finds himself here without escaping . . . He has gained something, but not illegally. The master has lost, but that is his fault, in not being a better keeper."

Early in his address Ellis had repudiated opposing counsel's suggestion that the defense had no argument save against the law itself. He had then said that though he personally hated this law, he had never overtly opposed it, but had rather "done something to stay resistance to it," referring thus elliptically to his having blocked Higginson in the Vigilance Committee meetings in 1851. "I stand here for the prisoner," he proclaimed, "under and not against the law." And yet now, toward the end of his opening argument, he carefully laid out some dozen reasons why the Fugitive Slave Law could and should be held unconstitutional. He indicated that the option of such a ruling was still available to Loring despite the claimant's position that the matter had already been adjudicated. The law was only four years old, Ellis pointed out, "hardly yet trusted alone out of doors." There were indeed opinions affirming its constitutionality, but many fewer than were commonly supposed, and of these, a large portion were technical and not truly on point. Those that were ought to be understood as having been determined by political motives and not by sound legal reasoning.

In the course of "unsettling" the law in this way, of getting Loring to regard the question as an open one, Ellis expanded on the implications of how the law was situated politically. It was generally understood in 1850, he asserted, that the measure was not principally offered on the grounds of its intrinsic legal merits, but "as part of a system of grants and concessions, the best to be attained, to be acted on with a view to the political relations not of the parties but of the country." Without directly mentioning the Nebraska Bill, Ellis alluded to the way "all is changed now." He knew, of course, that resentment over the Nebraska Bill had for many found expression in the view that the repeal of the Missouri Compromise effectively released the North from *all* compromise and hence from all particular compromise measures. But this was not to be Ellis' position. The jolting change in the political climate effected by the Nebraska Bill simply made it clear how poisonous were all laws that consulted artificial, short-term political advantage at the expense of sound legal principles. He was not inviting nullification as a sort of counterreformation policy (as some radicalized Whigs were), but urging careful scrutiny of the laws to discriminate between the transient and the permanent in legislation. Operating from a Transcendental construction of the law as a thing ideally insulated from politics, a thing that functioned, when it functioned best, only by such internally consistent logic as was forever true, just, and fit to be obeyed, Ellis now urged on Loring the duty to reject the extrinsic political contamination and restore to the law the kind of purity and rational symmetry that would not have to be enforced at the point of a government bayonet.

Ellis listed his reasons for supposing the Fugitive Slave Law to be unconstitutional, though he had first to get round the argument of Webster and the opinion of Shaw that the 1850 law had to be constitutional because the very similar law of 1793 most assuredly was. He therefore confined his reasons to features unique to the more recent measure, citing, for example, its explicit rejection of trial by jury; its suspension of the writs of habeas corpus and *de homine replegiando* ("Coke would think all this required a new Petition of Rights"); its extralegal creation of a new class of judges ("This position has never been answered; the knot is only cut"); its violation of the Fourth Amendment protection against unreasonable searches and seizures; and its violation of the Fifth Amendment guarantee that no one shall be deprived of liberty without due process.

Much of what Ellis said was standard theory with the abolitionists, so that not even those who agreed with it were borne away by its force—but everyone, friend or enemy of the defense as they might be, was thrown into excitement by Ellis' concluding announcement of their affirmative defense. He would prove that the prisoner had been in Massachusetts from March 1, directly contradicting the testimony of Brent, who claimed to have seen Suttle's Tony in Richmond on March 20.

There would be an alibi.

On March 1—a Wednesday—the clerical petition against the Nebraska Bill was drawn up and Theodore Parker signed it. Emerson was home in Concord composing his address "The Fugitive Slave Law," expressing for "students and scholars" his wish that "they know their own flag, and not stand for the kingdom of darkness." On that day in Cambridge, in his mansion on Tory Row, Longfellow read Sumner's latest speech, and judged that while "it may not keep slavery out of Nebraska, it will keep it out of many hearts forever." From the Senate Chamber in Washington, Sumner wrote to Dana bemoaning "the discord among Anti-Slavery brothers" at home and predicting that "we shall soon close up in close ranks again."[3]

On that day Anthony Burns, barely recovered from the chill, cramp, and starvation of his long, dark ocean transport, went out into the streets of Boston in search of work. Coming down Washington Street near the Commonwealth Building, scanning for black faces among the sparse crowds of bundled-up pedestrians, he spotted a man, no better dressed than himself, who seemed approachable. He struck up a conversation and learned that the man's name was William Jones and that he was a day laborer sometimes at City Hall and at other times at the Mattapan Iron Works near his home in South Boston. But today, as on many days, he did not work at all. Burns asked if he knew of anyone who might be looking for help in a store. Unaccustomed to New England winter weather, Burns wanted indoor work, but he wasn't particular. When Jones asked him what he could do, he answered, as he had answered so many times on the hiring grounds, that he could do most anything.[4]

Jones, a mildly eccentric fellow, full of crotchets and peculiarities, perhaps slightly insane, but certainly very friendly and accommodating on this occasion, took Burns to Mr. Russell's bootblack shop nearby, not so much to find work, it seems, as to get Russell to write an entry in the private memorandum book that the illiterate Jones always kept on his person. Russell obligingly made a notation to the effect that when Jones began washing windows at the Mattapan Works—as he was to do a few days hence—he would take his new friend on as an assistant at eight cents a window.

Jones and Burns then went to John Favor's carpenter shop at 49 Lincoln Street and spent the better part of an hour in conversation, though there was no work to be had. Fresh out of leads and having nothing better to do, Jones went off "to fool," as he called it, at an apothecary shop in the United States Hotel at the corner of Lincoln and Beach. Burns tagged along. After a brief period of loitering, they went to a clothing store in Essex Street operated by Stephen Maddox, a black man, who also handled seasonal contracts for various kinds of outdoor work—window washing, carpet shaking, and so forth. But Maddox said that he didn't expect to have any jobs before the first of May. The two men walked aimlessly about the city for several hours more and ended up at Jones's home at nightfall. Neither one had eaten; Jones at least was unconcerned, for he never ate more than one meal a day.

The next morning he took Burns with him to City Hall, where he spoke to Cyrus Gould, the custodian, about work for himself. On Friday, March 3, Jones and Burns went to the Mattapan Works and discussed the window-cleaning job with the boss, Mr. Sanger; they also spoke to George H. Drew, bookkeeper and paymaster, who asked Jones if the man with him was his brother. "All men are my brothers," Jones replied.

They began work the next day. The job took the better part of a week. At the end of the first day, Burns was not sure that the $1.50 he got from Jones was quite as much as was due him, and he spoke to Drew about it. (In fact the sum was all, to the last penny, that Jones had been given that day.)

After the work in South Boston was done Burns assisted Jones on odd jobs at City Hall. These stints, however, came to an end on March 18, at which time the two men parted company.

More than two months later, on May 25, Jones heard about the arrest of a fugitive slave named Anthony Burns. Someone had read to him from a newspaper account. He thought the prisoner might be the man he had befriended, but he couldn't be sure because he had called that man "John and Jack, or any short name that came handy." However, he went that day to the Police Court and to the Municipal Court to see what he could find out; there he spoke to some policemen who told him what little they knew of the matter. On Friday, rather mysteriously, Jones, who had once lived in Virginia, went to see Suttle at the Revere House and seems to have got an interview. In the evening he attended the Faneuil Hall meeting and went with the crowd to the Court House. There he fell in with a policeman whom he knew (he seems to have known several policemen rather well) and after the riot hung around the square to "protect city property."

On Saturday he tried to get into court to confirm his suspicion that Anthony Burns and the man he knew were one and the same. But the military, who were keeping abolitionists out, were not letting ragged black men in. At some point, perhaps on Saturday, Jones applied to Watson Freeman for a permit to see Burns in his cell. The marshal refused, saying that no one, not even his master, was allowed access.

At noon on Sunday Jones was in the crowd in Court Square and got a good look at Burns, who had his head out the window, acknowledging his supporters below. Jones again went to the Revere House to confer with Suttle, though for what purpose no one now can say. He later indicated that he might have seen Suttle in Virginia, but he did not know the man, nor had he spoken to him before this week.

Either on Sunday evening or on Monday morning, Jones presented himself at Ellis' office and gave the defense its best chance of prevailing.

🔥 RICHARD HILDRETH

[I]t is but now that Democracy and Despotism face to face, like Gabriel and the Arch-enemy, make ready for a desperate and dreadful struggle.

RICHARD HILDRETH

If the practical effect of antislavery as a reform movement had to depend solely on the disinterested moral righteousness and sympathetic feeling of the white population, things might have worked out rather differently than they did. The moral argument, especially as Garrison shaped it, had made considerable headway with the general, nonactivist Northern public since 1831, but it operated more immediately on private feeling than on public policy, emphasizing as it did the personal coming out from the corruption of church and state. Numerous consciences were thus set at rest by the conviction that slavery was wrong—yet it remained, blessedly, a distant wrong, like Russian serfdom. The moral argument was further shut up in the private realm by the decision to cordon off antislavery from politics (no voting, no Union with slaveholders), somewhat as Roger Williams had sought to conceal religion from politics as a thing too valuable, too essentially private, to be entrusted to the conflicting motives of worldly men. Like the "higher law" itself, Garrison's uncompromising moral stance had to operate, if it was to operate at all, from outside or above the sphere of contention. His consciously secessionist position made converts by drawing them out of the possibility of real contact with what they opposed and into a segregated compound of ideological purity. Indeed, one impetus to action on the part of the radicals of 1854 was the sense not that Garrison had failed, but that he had succeeded: that the moral argument and the theoretical convictions it sustained had as much popular force in New England as they were ever likely to attain.

A certain gratifying and cost-free style of emotional response was also in place, particularly after 1852 and the success of *Uncle Tom's Cabin,* that taught the people how to *feel*—if ever the occasion for feeling should arise. What had yet to be induced was a conviction of the substantial presence of slavery. Either the moral reach of the people had to be extended outward or the sin had to be imported into the private sphere and exemplified. "I have lived all my life without suffering any known inconvenience from American slavery," said Emerson in March of 1854, but immediately added that for him the immunity had ended when Webster foisted the Fugitive Slave Law on the country. The Fugitive Slave Law was one form of presence because it required, at least hypothetically, the active participation of Northern citizens in maintaining the Southern institution. The fugitive cases were another, more concrete form of presence, yet prior ones, at least in Boston, had not been generally shared in, but had been entrusted to those supposed most immediately concerned—to the abolitionists in the Crafts and Sims cases, to the blacks in the Shadrach affair. In each event the public had found a way to affiliate with the wrong side even while expressing its disapproval of slavery and its resentment at the intrusion. Hundreds of private citizens had spontaneously volunteered to escort Sims to the ship that would carry him back to Georgia; they were glad for a chance to support Webster and the Union, but were indifferent or even professedly hostile to slavery itself—as Webster was. The people had been more relieved by the temporary nature of the disruption than galvanized by contact with it. The most advanced of the antislavery workers kept alive on a steady diet of slave rescues, but the mass of the people were conscious of no continuous emergency.[1]

The privacy of the moral argument had latent within it a limitation on the production of activists and reformers. Like the more familiar and conventional religious instruction that it mimicked, the moral argument against slavery tended to assume that every man's duty was to seek first his own salvation rather than his brother's. Safety was the watchword. Even Mrs. Stowe's answer to the question "What must I do?" was an evangel of inwardness: you must see to it that your feelings are right. There is a daring, culturally unfeminine presumption in the publicity or outer-directedness of reform concerning which a high degree of suspicion would always exist. Even so good and angry a reformer as Charles Dickens was alert to its potential for conflict with the private sphere: "I do not go with Mrs. Jellyby in all things," said Mrs. Pardiggle in *Bleak House,* Dickens's best-seller of 1854. This suspicion is even more emphatically marked in Hawthorne's *Blithedale Romance* of 1852. And once it appeared with memorable conciseness when a young lady asked Emerson if it were not true, as she had heard, that reform is always in bad taste.[2]

This reticence, these misgivings, had to do with an informing private construction of the moral world, abetted by the typically constricted extent of most New Englanders' contact with the world at large. (The socially limiting effect of "woman's sphere"—not a national or regional convention—was held to enhance morality at the expense of public influence; women became reformers only by violating conventional gender roles and emerging into a larger world.) Those moral duties most vividly present to the New England imagination touched on members of one's family and on those with whom one dealt in social and business relationships; as Emerson ironically suggested in "Self-Reliance," the point regularly looked to was "whether you have satisfied your relations to father, mother, cousin, neighbor, town, cat and dog—whether any of these can upbraid you." In some respects, the difference between the reformers—the "young men with knives in their brains," as Emerson called them—and the others was less a matter of absolute moral conviction than of the effective size of the world they acknowledged.[3]

In discussing his transition at this time from proslavery Virginia Methodist to antislavery reformer, Moncure Conway spoke of being emancipated from an extremely narrow vision of moral relevance:

In Methodism my burden had been metaphysical,—a bundle of dog-mas. The world at large was not then mine; for its woes and wrongs I was not at all responsible; they were far from me, and no one ever taught me that the earth was to be healed except at the millennium. The only evils were particular ones: A. was a drunkard, B. a thief, C. a murderer, D. had a cancer, and so on.

Conway's superseded moral style was by no means the special product of his Southern background or a function of his youth. If there could be said to be anything like a broadly typical American approach to ques-tions of morality, it lay in this monitory Protestant attachment to in-timidating examples, a system not of crusading engagements, but of the warnings, proscriptions, disciplines, and avoidances that kept one, by design, on the straight and narrow path—if not, indeed, indoors al-together. The attack on slavery might then depend on that quality Thoreau called "extra-vagance," a revolution in the moral imagination coordinate with taking possession of a larger world than one seemed to have a natural claim to. Frederick L. H. Willis, a distant relative of Hamilton Willis and a frequent houseguest of the Alcotts, credited his youthful conversion to abolitionism with introducing him "to a much broader sphere of life than I could have otherwise attained." This sense of a liminal glory was widely shared by the abolitionists, both by those who were glad to find themselves thus suddenly powerful and by those who more disinterestedly sought to empower others. The key signature in all this was a desire for a larger sphere of action—what might be called emancipation in general. Conway and many of his contempo-raries were convinced that Emerson's writings had effected that revolu-tion for them, had delivered that larger world.[4]

If it was in this sense the job of antislavery workers to raise the Northern public out of its curious absorbing localism and set it to gaz-ing past the circle of the near horizon, they soon found the manufacture of larger worlds a congenial occupation, sometimes a Transcendental one, sometimes not. The invention of a world, as in the model invention of 1776, was simply a matter of creating or refashioning affiliations, and there are as many ways of going about that job as there are worlds that result. To whom, they asked themselves, can one feel connected and responsible? In how many different ways can allegiances be ex-pandingly redefined so as to include the cause of the slave?

One answer was to see the slave as a fellow laborer in the common world of work. The development of this world is related to the nascent labor movement. The argument over who had it worse, the plantation slave or the "free" Northern mill hand, had the unintended effect, on the one hand, of dramatically transcending racial categories and, on the other, of making antislavery a model for labor reform.

Another answer was to see the slave as the characteristic victim of a foreign power hostile to oneself—in effect as the enemy of one's enemy. The development of this world is related to the tragically co-alescing impulses toward sectionalism and nationalism.

The motivational advantage of these new worlds from an antislav-ery standpoint lay in the commonalities of interest between white North and black South that for the first time distinctly and convinc-ingly emerged, and in the fact that the complications of racial preju-dice—that tendency to define "black" as "other," which had all along bedeviled the moral argument—were largely evaded.

At the time of the Burns trial, the book most prominently advertised in the pages of the *Liberator* was a worldmaker of the sort just de-scribed: *Despotism in America,* by Richard Hildreth, a member of the Boston Vigilance Committee. First published in 1840, this revised and much-expanded edition was issued by John P. Jewett, another Committeeman and the publisher also of *Uncle Tom's Cabin.* The book is a pioneering formulation of what Eric Foner has called the "Republican Critique of the South." Neither particularly distin-guished nor altogether original, *Despotism in America* nevertheless pre-sents a powerful and ideologically coherent mythology of regional dif-ferences that, as Foner's generic term implies, proved immensely influential with Republicans, who began to organize themselves into a political party in the summer of 1854. Though Hildreth's concep-tion of the significance of the regions performed the bulk of its cul-tural work in the hands of these Republicans and remained in circu-lation long enough to help in a general way to shape postwar policies of reconstruction, it was first offered as a contribution to antislavery theory.[5]

Hildreth's appeal to his readers is predicated on a rather simple re-gional chauvinism, but he leaves it more complexly theorized than he finds it. Slavery and the Slave Power are not just foreign and distant in relation to New England, but constitute a threatening and desper-ate linked companion, in whose hands a large portion of the future of

New England lies. The binary or contrasting nature of the argument effectively ties the poor crippled South to the modern energetic North in an unstable Union of mutually defining oppositions, a contest, in fact, for control over the meaning of America. The conjunction is conceptually important because while Hildreth's polarizing argument could easily underwrite a disunionist project, its overt purpose is to forestall sectional antagonism through the abolition of slavery, returning the Union to health under a restored (reread or reinterpreted) Constitution. That Constitution, as Hildreth reveals it, is a pro-freedom, not a pro-slavery, document, and the values it contends for are vastly more important than the Union itself: "Perish the Union; let it ten times perish, from the moment it becomes inconsistent with humanity and with freedom!" The real struggle, however—and one that is manifestly destined to succeed—is to make that progressive constitutionalism triumphant through all the states.[6]

In taking this tack, Hildreth legitimizes a prevailing impressionistic Northern view of Southern cultural backwardness, first by locating its cause in the disastrous effects of slavery and then by giving this theory of causation a special (free labor) ideological supplement that appeals more to Northern self-interest than to any suppositional or abstract righteousness.

Hildreth makes it clear throughout the exposition that he regards slavery as a profound moral wrong, and yet the critique is predominantly economic, showing that the slaveholding system is practically incompatible with progress and the production of wealth—the future that New England sees for itself. The portrait he paints of the South is that already well established by travelers unsympathetic to slavery, including, currently, Frederick Law Olmsted. The general air of dilapidation and poverty (the poor condition of fences is often and particularly alluded to), the concentration of wealth in a very small class of plantation owners, the dependence on agriculture to the exclusion of manufacturing, the culture of the shiftless poor whites, the lack of schools, the suppression of free speech, the romantic militarism of the planters, the feeble showing of the region in science and letters, even the rapidly declining fertility of the soil—all the manifold elements of what amounts to a cultural catastrophe—Hildreth traces to the singular relation of master and slave, which he defines, not metaphorically but actually, as an eternally protracted state of war. The Southern landscape and the Southern psyche are alike war-ravaged.

"For the sake of brutalizing others, they have sought to barbarize themselves."[7]

Hildreth notes that slavery arose as "a substitute for homicide" at that historical moment when it was discovered that a defeated enemy might be more useful alive than dead. But a captive enemy never ceases to be an enemy, watches for an opportunity to escape, is kept in place only by the captor's constant recourse to intimidation and force, and presents a standing threat to the security of the enthralling power. Tethering an enemy to one's own home assures that war and not peace will be the all-suffusing theme of existence. Thus the Southern anxieties about slave revolts: "all their lives, the sword has been pointed at [the slaves'] hearts, and if they in any way succeed in grasping it by the hilt,—what wonder if they use it?" In conventional political theory such a state of permanent war is precisely the condition that society came into existence to preclude. Social governance by force majeure is therefore to be seen as a barbarous, prehistoric mode of proceeding, the precise opposite of the progressive regime of Northern republican freedom. Thus when Ellis is threatened by a bayonet-wielding soldier on the Court House steps, what he sees is not just a momentarily bothersome incongruity but a more than symbolic representation of the system of slaveholding; appropriately, he complains of the invasion of a foreign barbarism into that "temple" held sacred to reason and justice.[8]

As a victim of kidnapping, as a man unlawfully detained, the slave makes, of course, a reluctant and unprofitable servant from an economic point of view, especially as compared with the free Northern worker, whose labor is speeded by incentives. Obviously this comparison shifts the argument from race to class. The systematic exploitation of the working class is inconsistent with the survival of republican values. Slavery is justified by its apologists on racial grounds with the argument that the Negro is too depraved, by nature, to be suffered to go free; Hildreth's attack on slavery is justified on class grounds with the argument that their "depravity" is an immediate effect of their exploitation: "To expect, as between masters and slaves the virtues of truth, probity and benevolence, is ridiculous. Slavery removes the very foundation of those virtues"—for both classes. The "great social experiment" going on in the North is to see what happens when labor is educated and encouraged to become skillful; according to Hildreth the concurrent Southern experiment is to see what happens when the laboring class is mentally and emotionally devastated by unceasing coercion. "It is a common remark at the South, that the more intelligent a slave is, the more unquiet, dangerous, and troublesome he is. The remark is just." Hildreth calls the deliberate withholding of literacy and education "slavery's second growth," or "the murder of the soul." It is the spiritual echo of what is done to the bodies of the slaves, dictated by the logic of class warfare and required by the ongoing theft of the slave's labor. Clearly this is outrageous to Hildreth on purely moral grounds, but he is also concerned to show its perverseness as a means of securing a productive labor force.[9]

The object of this inhumanity in the Southern system is of course to keep the slave at tasks that he has no private motive to perform: eventually, Hildreth observes, no one *but* the slave is working. "Wherever slavery exists, labor comes to share the degradation and contempt of servitude, while idleness is regarded as the peculiar badge of freedom." This is the very heart and essence of the Freesoil message, as well as of the emergent "Republican critique of the South." Labor is the real currency of the middle class; where that currency is devalued, that class cannot exist or will never arise. Where labor is shameful, civilization has no future. The struggle to exclude slavery from the territories becomes for many a movement to preserve tolerable conditions for Northern workers; if it happens also to put a lid on sin, so much the better. Here, then, is where slavery involves the interests of the white population of both regions, quite apart from their moral views. In Hildreth's analysis slavery simply cannot coexist with free labor, but drives it out; whatever gumption might originally have existed among nonslaveholding Virginians, he suggests, has long since fled over the Blue Ridge:

> The poor whites of the old slave states have hitherto found a resource in emigration. All of them who had any spirit of enterprise and industry have quitted a home where labor was disgraceful, and in the wide regions beyond the mountains have attained a comfortable livelihood, and have amassed wealth by means which however innocent or laudable, they could not employ in the places where they were born, without a certain degree of self-abasement.

Precisely this motive for emigration had operated in the case of the father of William Herndon, Lincoln's law partner in Illinois, as

Herndon himself confided to his hero, Theodore Parker, in 1856.[10]

This helps to explain why many white Northerners who could muster no particular empathy for slaves or sympathy with abolitionists could become exercised about the extension of slavery into the territories; or why Abbott Lawrence could claim with some rational expectation of being believed that the groups of New England emigrants being sent out to settle Kansas in 1854 contained no abolitionists. What was at stake in the "Nebraska fraud" was the preservation of a system of free labor on which rested the future prosperity of the nation, all prospects for upward social mobility, and the progressive culture of a middle-class democracy—to say nothing of the availability of Western land to Northern adventurers.

One rather lurid incident that illustrates the mixture of antislavery motives under the weight of this concern involves the death of "Buffalo Bill" Cody's father, who, about the time that Anthony Burns was arrested, laid claim to a homestead near Fort Leavenworth. One day soon afterward he was compelled to address a crowd of pro-slavery Missourians on the only subject then being talked about. He proceeded to declare his Freesoil views, saying that he had been one of the pioneers of the recently organized state of Iowa, and that he had then "voted that it should be a *white* state—that negroes, whether free or slave, should never be allowed to locate within its limits." He believed in letting slavery remain "as it now exists," but he would work to see his dream for Iowa realized in Kansas. The speech was not well received. Isaac Cody died from the stab wounds he suffered on that platform.[11]

One of Hildreth's reasons for revising and reissuing his *Despotism in America* in 1854 involved the work he had done the previous year on his *Theory of Politics,* based on the socialist thought of Robert Owen. Hildreth had come to see in a new light the important social benefits that accrued when the conditions of labor were personally advantageous to the laborer. He thought he saw in the culture of New England—in its educational opportunities, its artisanal democracy strongly flourishing in its villages, and its diversified and decentralized economy—a general ideological commitment to advancing the position of the worker. To Hildreth the Northern part of the Union looked a great deal more like Owen's New Harmony experiment than either looked like the South, despite what proslavery apologists were saying about New England wage slavery, and, for that matter, despite what Melville was saying in "The Tartarus of Maids," this spring of 1854, about the exploitation of female labor in the mills. Northern society had gone far toward achieving many of the more valuable results aimed at in such deliberate utopian experiments as Brook Farm and Alcott's Fruitlands. "If in the Northern States of the American Union there exists a degree of political equality of which the world offers no other example on so large a scale, the equal distribution of property throughout those states, is not less striking and remarkable." Indeed Hildreth saw America as engaged in a great unresolved social experiment pressing toward "the equal distribution among all the members of the community, of freedom, property, knowledge, social advantages, and those other good things which make up the mass of human happiness." This was not only what the Constitution, properly understood, had committed the country to; it lay, in Hildreth's view, at the root of all governmental legitimacy everywhere. The South had opted out of this experiment, setting legitimacy and legality equally aside, in electing to conduct its own experiment with aristocracy and "Despotism." Its system promoted none of the three objects aimed at by legitimate governments: security of persons and property; civil and political freedom; and social, political, and economic equality. The promise of America and the prestige of nationalism, Hildreth implied, rested with the triumph of principles now exclusively gathered, in a somewhat defensive posture, in the North. The South, so long as it held to slavery, was a dangerous renegade, insufficiently disengaged from the Old World and profoundly untrue to the renovating example of the American Revolution (that overarching signifier at the Burns trial); yet the South was to be commiserated with and encouraged back into the American fold, its tragic apostasy having gone so far toward accomplishing its own pitiful destruction.[12]

Indeed, the South had constructively seceded from "America" already—which is to say, from that new world that Hildreth saw as coming into being in fulfillment of the idea of democracy. Like Emerson, Thoreau was generally in accord with this view, understanding progress to consist in the movement "from an absolute to a limited monarchy, from a limited monarchy to a democracy." In the "progress toward a true respect for the individual" betokened by that still-unfolding historical process, the antidemocratic Southern states (in Hildreth's view "aristocracies of the sternest and most odious kind") were purely anomalous. Hildreth's modest proposal was that the South should cease to make war against its laboring class, should join and not oppose the clear design of history, and should emulate the empowering conditions of labor that were ever more clearly emerging in the free air of the North.[13]

It is of course impossible to develop a "critique of the South"— Freesoil, Republican, or otherwise—without at the same time reinventing the North along equally ideological, not to say mythological lines. One logical and clearly foreseen consequence of Hildreth's argument was the encouragement given to Northern labor agitation by its linkage in theory with antislavery work. One of the reasons why Worcester was so forward in the Burns matter and in antislavery in general was the presence there of a vital culture of artisans, mill workers, and shopkeepers. From the moment of Burns's arrest it was understood that help was to be looked for not from fashionable Boston, where capital and corporations held sway, but from "the country," particularly from Worcester, the "heart of the Commonwealth."

Among the crowd of rioters at the Court House on Friday night was a twenty-three-year-old friend of Martin Stowell named Ira Steward. A machinist by trade, Steward had earlier been fired from the Draper Works in Providence, Rhode Island, for agitating against its standard twelve-hour work day. The exploitation of the industrial working class lay open to most of the arguments advanced against slavery, and Steward, more than anyone else of his generation, became effectively obsessed with the analogy. Within a decade he became the leader of the movement for an eight-hour day and, drawing on his antislavery experience, worked out a systematic economic theory in its defense. His theory differed from the arguments of other labor reformers in resting the case squarely on the beneficial effect of lowering the rate at which surplus value was extracted from the labor force. While others argued that happy workers would compensate for shorter hours with higher rates of productivity, Steward used the work-day issue as a means to enlarge labor's ownership stake in the work it did. It was an antislavery model of labor reform, complete with a full recognition of the disparate interests of labor and capital.[14]

Steward's concern to raise the standard of living among workers was consistent with Hildreth's definition of the middle class as the site of a natural democratic equality:

It is an observation as curious as it is important, [Hildreth wrote] that in countries in which industry is respectable, and where the fruits of labor are secure, property always tends toward an equal distribution . . . It appears then that in civilized communities, the natural tendency of things is toward equality. Inequality can only be maintained by artificial means; by laws which give to some individuals exclusive advantages not possessed by others, such as laws of primogeniture, of entail, laws conferring hereditary rights and privileges; laws creating monopolies of any and every kind.

Steward wished to redress the balance of power between labor and capital, so unequal under the twelve-hour system as to resemble slavery. Giving workers leisure time and higher effective wages would make them consumers, which would bring on more production and employ other workers; in order to maintain profits while keeping prices down, capital would introduce newer and more efficient production methods. In the resulting general progress, the social and financial inequalities between capitalists and laborers would diminish, and eventually the working class would take over the means of production. Steward was the only one of the Court House rioters whose works are known to have been read by Karl Marx.[15]

It is not clear that Hildreth's *Despotism in America* is necessarily or intrinsically a roadmap to revolution. To some extent it can sustain a conservative or a radical reading, depending on the political emphases one brings to it. And yet as the product of a culture of romantic reform, the book is concerned to discriminate sharply between the natural and the artificial in society, and in so doing becomes profoundly subversive of certain pillars of the status quo. The questioning of categories in Hildreth's book seems most consequential on the general subject of contract. Was it a contract that the North entered into in ratifying the Constitution, and, if so, is it a binding term of the contract that the parties should honor slavery in perpetuity? In an artificial system of legality contract becomes the only moral obligation: "and this contract, we are told, must be preserved inviolate, or government is at an end, and chaos comes again." The main argument of Webster and the Union-saving element had all along been predicated on the sacred nature of contracts. Yet to Hildreth,

These opinions respecting law and government involve, indeed, the inconsistency and absurdity of supposing that men have power, by arrangement and convention, to make that artificially right which naturally is wrong—an inconsistency and absurdity which there have not been wanting able writers to expose . . . They have shown clearly enough, that law, so far as it has any binding moral force, is and must be conformable to natural principles of right; indeed, that in this conformity alone its moral binding force consists; and that so far as this conformity is wanting, what is called law is mere violence and tyranny, to which a man may submit for the sake of peace, but which he has a moral right to resist passively at all times, and forcibly when he has any fair prospect of success. Such, indeed, was the principle upon which the American Revolution was justified.[16]

Revolution is understood as the reassertion of a natural order in which the prolonged stresses resulting from forced and artificial inequalities are resolved. Hildreth specifically calls attention to unnatural contracts—and their veneration as contracts—as the main prop of social injustice. The Constitution (whether read as underwriting democracy or despotism) is the American ur-Contract and will therefore be at the center of any second revolution, but its central place in American life also makes it inevitable that all obligations and arrangements will be seen as versions of contracts, legitimate or illegitimate, as between slave and master, labor and capital, husband and wife. Hildreth speaks in effect for the whole movement of romantic reform in America in destabilizing or unsettling the very notion of contract and its sacred inviolability. "It has been triumphantly shown, that the very essence and substratum of contract is, mutual benefit. Contracts, whether in law or morals, have no binding force without a consideration. Men cannot bargain away either their own rights or the rights of others. All such pretended contracts are void from the beginning." Contracts have to square with eternal notions of equity; even contracts that start out just and satisfactory may become void in time as conditions change and the equations of "mutual benefit" disappear. It is an application of the rule against perpetuities to contract law, such as Jefferson may have had in mind when he suggested that government be reinvented every generation. If one wished to exert a revolutionary pressure against an ossified system, one could do worse than, by attacking the essential notion of contracts, to bring all the parties to all agreements back to the negotiating table.[17]

THE
BOSTON SLAVE RIOT,
AND
TRIAL
OF
Anthony Burns,

CONTAINING THE
REPORT OF THE FANEUIL HALL MEETING; THE MURDER OF
BACHELDER; THEODORE PARKER'S LESSON FOR THE DAY;
SPEECHES OF COUNSEL ON BOTH SIDES, CORRECTED
BY THEMSELVES; VERBATIM REPORT OF JUDGE
LORING'S DECISION; AND, A DETAILED AC-
COUNT OF THE EMBARKATION.

BOSTON:
FETRIDGE AND COMPANY.
1854.

Press of J. S. Potter & Co., 2 Spring Lane and 130 Washington Street.

Cover, *The Boston Slave Riot and Trial of Anthony Burns,* 1854

Clockwise from top left: Ralph Waldo Emerson, 1854; Walt Whitman, July 1854; Henry David Thoreau, 1854; Henry Wadsworth Longfellow, June 1854

Clockwise from top left: Theodore Parker, 1853; John Greenleaf Whittier, ca. 1855; Lewis Hayden; Thomas Wentworth Higginson, 1857

Clockwise from top left: Jerome Van Crowninshield Smith, 1854; Richard Henry Dana Jr., ca. 1849; Leonard Grimes; Edward Greely Loring

Map of downtown Boston, ca. 1854

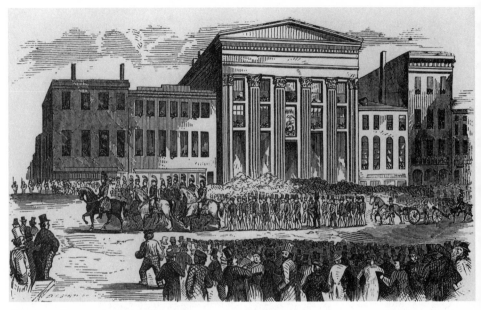

Marshal's posse with Burns

AMERICANS TO THE RESCUE!

IRISHMEN UNDER ARMS!

AMERICANS! SONS OF THE REVOLUTION!! A body of
SEVENTY-FIVE IRISHMEN, known as the

"COLUMBIAN ARTILLERY!"

have VOLUNTEERED THEIR SERVICES TO SHOOT DOWN THE CITIZENS
OF BOSTON, aided by a company of UNITED STATES MARINES, nearly
all of whom are IRISHMEN!! and are now under arms to defend Virginia
in KIDNAPPING A CITIZEN OF MASSACHUSETTS!!!

AMERICANS! These Irishmen have called us

"COWARDS! AND SONS OF COWARDS!!"

Shall we submit to have our citizens shot down by

A SET OF

VAGABOND IRISHMEN!

Broadside, ca. May 28, 1854

Twelfth Baptist Church, Southac Street

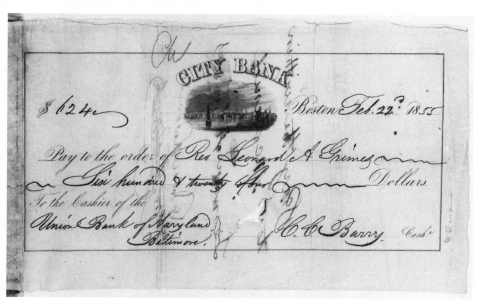

One of two checks used to purchase Anthony Burns

Anthony Burns (upper right) with Oberlin's "Preparatory Class," 1855

The Fugitive Slave Not Rescued.—To drive away the mob is a hard thing, but to drive away all tan, pimples, and freckles from the skin, use the Balm of Thousand Flowers; that is warranted to do it or no pay taken. For sale by Fetridge & Co., the proprietors, and all respectable druggists.

ADVERTISEMENT IN THE *COMMONWEALTH*, May 30, 1854

From breakfast to bedtime, the hours of this bustling Anniversary Week were filled with councils and conventions large and small. The mornings were specially devoted to business meetings, so that at 8:30 on this Tuesday morning, when Hamilton Willis made his way to the marshal's office at the Court House to negotiate with a slaveholder, his route not improbably took him past the Freeman Place Chapel, where at that hour were assembled the financial officers of the Society for the Relief of Aged and Destitute Clergymen.

After the brusque dismissal of yesterday's note, Willis was gratified, if slightly surprised, to find the Virginian politely receptive to new overtures. Suttle indicated that although he "wished to take the boy back," he was prepared to sell him afterward, adding that he wanted to see the result of the trial. Willis had already decided that Suttle would not be stampeded by hints that he might lose his property before he could sell it. His ownership might be undermined by Loring's decision or by a rescue, and his own life was palpably in danger so long as the trial lasted. Yet however much such fears might weigh with Suttle, Willis made no reference to sinister possibilities. Instead he granted that Suttle's title to Burns was "clear enough," and proposed to acknowledge the fact by buying the man regardless of the outcome of the hearing. Willis knew full well that there was nothing in the law to prevent Suttle, following an adverse ruling from Loring, to have Burns rearrested on the spot and brought before another commissioner. It was not a criminal trial, so no concept of jeopardy, much less double jeopardy, applied; indeed, the process could be repeated indefinitely, or so long as Suttle's cash and brazen courage held out. Credible rumor had it that George T. Curtis stood ready to hold court in case of need.

Willis presented his offer as coming not from abolitionists, but instead from "some of our most respectable citizens," men who had no interest in obstructing the law, but who simply wanted to put a stop to an "unpleasant case." He told Suttle this was how most people regarded the matter, and read him a letter from George Baty Blake, who was offering unlimited funds on these ostensibly apolitical grounds. Suttle agreed, but with certain stipulations not entirely satisfactory to Willis; Suttle explained why he could not accept without conditions, and Willis agreed. It was nearly a contract, then, when Hallett arrived at the marshal's office and called Suttle aside. They spoke for a few minutes in earnest low tones. At length Suttle returned to Willis and said, "I must withdraw what I have done with you." Willis turned in exasperation to the interfering Hallett, who merely pointed to the discoloration on the floor where Batchelder died, and said, "That blood must be avenged."

The newspapers thereafter called Hallett "the avenger of blood."[1]

When Willis stepped out of the office and out of the building, past armed guards at the famous door, the crowd in Court Square seemed swarming in the brilliant morning light. Obstruction and the massing of bodies were the themes of Anniversary Week.

From behind an office window across the square at 39 Court Street, lawyer Tracy Cheever surveyed the identical colorful scene and afterward wrote in his diary: "For several days a crowd of people, including negroes, negro wenches and red-hot abolitionists, has been gathered around the Court House, and has blocked up our entryway, sidewalk &c so as to prevent all business." The routine circulation of clients through the Court Street law offices had been choked off, but the state judiciary had shut down, too, judges and court officers unwilling to be jostled or to present credentials to surly lieutenants. Still, many people, including even Lemuel Shaw, placed the blame for the suspension of "business" on the federal government and its military, not on the citizens of Massachusetts, who had arguably as much right to the entryway and sidewalks as the lawyers did. Looking at the crowd through his window (the frame, as it were, of his profession), Cheever saw, exclusively, groups of ineligible petitioners, people who for different related reasons fell outside the law, who didn't recognize its force, and who weren't sustained by it. He saw them at all only because they didn't belong at the Court House, and he took it as the sign of a very bad law that it had brought them here, gathered noisily under his window this workday morning.[2]

Melville's "Bartleby," written less than a year earlier, provides a tempting context for Cheever's lawyerly way of seeing and reckoning.

His diary entry continues: "The expense of sending back this poor negro into slavery who probably is not worth a dollar a day, as a laborer, to any body, will be some $15 or $20,000, and possibly more." It was of course an inevitable way of sizing up a suit at law—whether the cost of litigation bore a reasonable relation to the assets in question—and Cheever was coming to the conclusion that the Vigilance Committee was bending all its efforts to promote: cheapen a man by reducing him to the value of his labor, and the consequence is . . . he becomes too expensive to keep. It was the ironically compensatory upside of the commodification Melville deplored, another antislavery argument conveniently independent of anybody's sympathy or goodwill and effective with the many strangers to moral reasoning.

After thus reckoning the cost, Cheever examined the subjective aspect of the case:

> The general feeling of Boston citizens is a strong desire that he may escape from his Master & the Officers, and reach Canada—while a year ago and before the passage of the Nebraska Bill men would have executed the Fugitive Slave Act with alacrity, if not willingness—Now no man will raise a finger to help the claimant but large numbers of U.S. troops are requisite to prevent his victim from being torn from the custody of the law and hurried off to some place of safety.

And how has this change come about? Have the good people of Boston learned treason from Mr. Garrison? Or sympathy from Mrs. Stowe? Have they learned from Frederick Douglass a new way to reckon the value of a black man? Who, in Dana's phrase, taught them to call Anthony Burns the *person* at the bar?

> This comes of the recent gross breach of faith on the part of the South, with the treacherous aid of a few Northerners, (who, indeed are never wanting to the mean service of slave extension) recently perpetrated by the passage of the Nebraska-Kansas Bill—I trust that by some hook or crook, every fugitive slave may be able to give the South the slip, until the doleful experience shall cause them to lay aside forever that gross public immorality, which impairs the good faith of fair contracts.

So, after all, here is a sort of friend of the slave, who turns out to have more in common with the "negroes, negro wenches and red-hot abolitionists" than his window-gazing self imagines. The repudiation of the Missouri Compromise, a long-standing agreement between the sections, had got him thinking about "fair contracts" in a way that excluded support for the Fugitive Slave Law. If he no longer saw that support as a contractual obligation under the Compromise of 1850, the blame lay not in him but in the poison of Southern faithlessness.

He had done nothing to invite this conclusion, while much in his temperament resisted it. On Friday night, for example, he had felt no impulse to go to Faneuil Hall, much less to the Court House. He had gone instead to the Howard Athenaeum to see the celebrated Mrs. Mowatt, his favorite actress, in *Armand*. There would not, he knew, be many more chances to enjoy the romantic, vaguely titillating work of this still-young widow, for she was leaving the stage at the end of her Boston engagement to marry William Foushee Ritchie, the influential editor of the Richmond, Virginia, *Enquirer*, who was even now declaring his opinion that the Athens of America had become "a den of wild beasts."[3]

 TUESDAY, MAY 30

[A]ll the assurance of the claimant and his friends gave place to unfeigned anxiety and alarm, while wonder and hope played over the countenances of those who sympathized with the prisoner.

CHARLES EMERY STEVENS

Tuesday was a very good day for the defense. The immediately evident fact that the promised alibi witness was a very dark, not overly prosperous black man merely confirmed suspicions on the claimant's side that some fraudulent testimony was about to be given. As William Jones approached the stand, Hallett whispered loudly, "Here comes a witness that [Theodore] Parker has got to perjure himself." Suspicion fell on Parker not just because he was Boston's most outspoken opponent of the Fugitive Slave Law, but also because he was on good terms with the entire black community, including many who were members of his own church.[1]

Jones testified at length about his encounter with Burns on March 1. He rehearsed in detail their movements on that day and gave the names of the various people they met. He described the stint of window-washing at the Mattapan Iron Works beginning on the fourth and produced his "memorandum book," which was offered, but not admitted, into evidence. All during the testimony Wendell Phillips' stomach was in a knot: he was sure that some of the man's "little imperfections and peculiarities" would emerge and overthrow his credibility. But Jones proved a stunningly effective witness and equal to Seth Thomas' extensive cross-examination. Trial-watcher Hannah E. Stevenson, a friend of the family of Theodore Parker and a boarder at their home, jubilantly concluded that Mr. Jones was "in his own person 'the great cloud of witnesses' spoken of."[2]

Second to testify for the defense was George H. Drew, bookkeeper at the Iron Works. He remembered Burns as having been with Jones on March 4, fixing the date by reference to his account book. He had given Jones $1.50 that day, the first of several payments that continued at intervals until March 18, some time after the last windows were washed. He particularly remembered Burns because the man had questioned him at the time about the correctness of the payment. When Drew first entered the courtroom he had recognized Burns and believed that Burns recognized him as well, since the prisoner's eyes had appeared to follow him fixedly as he moved to his seat. On cross-examination he couldn't say that he recalled seeing the scar on Burns's cheek that day at the Iron Works and supposed that Burns must have approached him with his head turned aside; still, he had no doubt that the man who had accompanied Jones was the prisoner at the bar.[3]

The third witness, James F. Whittemore, was one of the directors of the Mattapan Iron Works and a member of Boston's Common Council. He recalled seeing Burns at work on March 8 or 9, the day or the day after he returned from a month-long trip to the West. He was perfectly certain of the identity because he had noticed at the time both the scarred cheek and the mangled hand. A few days since, he was told by Rufus Putnam, a machinist at the Iron Works, that the fugitive slave in custody was the man who had been working with Jones. When he and Putnam came to court on Monday to confirm the identification, Whittemore was satisfied. He had gone with Putnam to Ellis' office this very morning and was then and there served with a notice to appear.

Dana, on redirect, established that Whittemore was a lieutenant in the Pulaski Guards (Company C, 5th Regiment of Light Infantry, Massachusetts Volunteer Militia, then on duty), and that he was not an abolitionist or a Freesoiler, but a Hunker Whig.

Stephen Maddox, the black owner of the clothing store visited by Jones and Burns on March 1, then testified, fully corroborating Jones's account of the visit. Edward Parker's cross-examination revealed that Jones had recruited him as a witness, that he and Jones had had some conversation about the event, and that he had spoken of it this morning in Ellis' office. Parker also elicited the information that Maddox had attended the Faneuil Hall meeting on Friday and that he had afterward joined the crowd at the Court House for about twenty minutes.

Other witnesses corroborated Jones's story. William C. Culver, a blacksmith, had seen Burns at the Iron Works. John Favor, the black master carpenter, very distinctly remembered the visit of Burns and Jones, fixing the date to the best of his recollection as between March 1 and 5. Rufus Putnam, the machinist, testified that Burns had been at the Iron Works when he began his own work there during the first week in March. He had been asked by Drew, the bookkeeper, to present himself at Ellis' office. H. N. Gilman, a teamster, remembered Burns by the scar on his face; he had seen him just after payday, which was March 1. Horace W. Brown, currently a Boston policeman, had been employed as a carpenter at the Iron Works before quitting on March 20; he recognized the prisoner as the man who had assisted Jones. "I remember the scar on his face."[4]

For the first time in the case the outlook for Burns seemed hopeful. Suttle had clearly and specifically stipulated that he was looking for a slave who had escaped from Virginia on or about March 24, and who had last been seen in Richmond—by Brent—on March 19. Could a commissioner turn over a man who had so clearly been in Boston three weeks earlier? Not if he was looking for a reasonable pretext to liberate him. Not if he was feeling the immense pressure of public opinion. Not if he had been persuaded by defense arguments that the claimant's case had to be held to the most rigorous standards of proof in the identification.

Samuel May was ecstatic. Though he had been barred from the courtroom, he had been able to follow the proceedings from his position in the crowd outside, and when court was adjourned at 6:00 he dashed off a note to Higginson in Worcester:

Several men, black & white,—the latter men of *repute*—have positively sworn to seeing & employing Byrnes here from the 1st to the 8th of March—and the complaint says he escaped the *24th March*. On this point, R. H. Dana Jr. feels (I understand) a good deal of hope, and others, cool & intelligent, think so too.[5]

Hallett's suspicion of perjury was universally shared on the claimant's side. Seth Thomas contrived to understand that while the black witnesses were lying, the white witnesses were simply mistaken. One of Suttle's volunteer bodyguards, Charles C. Jones, a Georgian studying law at Harvard, wrote home to his parents at the end of this crucial day:

> It is yet quite doubtful whether the Negro will be sent back or not. The commissioner, Judge Loring, one of our professors, wants firmness. The case is as clear as the noontide sun. Six witnesses have been introduced today in the defense, who testify that they saw Burns in Boston *more than three weeks* before ever he left Virginia, while he was yet in the employ of Mr. Brent, who hired him from Colonel Suttle, and who is now with the latter in Boston. *Flat perjury.* My blood boiled at this Negro testimony, at the vile epithets heaped upon Colonel Suttle and his friend hourly in the courthouse by counsel . . . Secret meetings are held by abolitionists with the avowed purpose of finding persons who will appear as witnesses and swear to anything which they are instructed to do. Do not be surprised if when I return home you find me a *confirmed disunionist.*[6]

Even Burns's supporters seem to have been more comfortable with black testimony when it was backed by white corroboration. When Phillips recalled this turn in the case less than a year later—in testimony before a committee of the state legislature—the crucial part played by the black witnesses seemed to slip from his memory.

Southern and Southern-sympathizing observers of the trial were sure that people capable of mounting a murderous assault on federal officers would not stick at the mere suborning of perjury; neither did they doubt that a poor black roustabout could be induced to say whatever circumstances demanded. While there is finally no reason to doubt the genuineness of the alibi testimony, Phillips and the defense team understood the grounds for skepticism and relied rather more on the prestige of James Whittemore than on the detailed recollections of William Jones. The presumption was general that it was difficult to get a white man, with a reputation to protect, to lie for a fugitive slave.[7]

And yet not impossible, as Mrs. Mowatt's fiancé pointed out in the

Richmond *Enquirer,* the South's leading newspaper:

> The latest accounts of the legal proceedings consist chiefly of perjured
> statements of a large number of suborned witnesses in support of Mr
> Weller's favorite plea of "halibi."—This last phase of the case is pecu-
> liarly Bostonian. They have little regard for the Gospels there, and
> seem to have a charter as illimitable as the winds to swear to what they
> please; provided it be in behalf of runaway negroes, and in overthrow
> of the laws and Constitution of the Union.
>
> The advices we publish show with what high hand the Boston peo-
> ple are playing the game of treason.

And yet the only plausible explanation is that Brent lied to Suttle
about seeing Burns in Richmond on March 19, a lie to cover his incompetent supervision and, no doubt, Millspaugh's own long delay in
notifying Brent. He had not foreseen the difficulties that this story
would eventually present, but now he stuck to it, as he had to.[8]

TREASON

[The Burns case] completely revolutionized public sentiment regarding the
evil of slavery and its far-reaching control over the North, attaining a point
beyond which it could not go.

BENJAMIN P. SHILLABER

The Boston *Post* was the semiofficial organ of the state Democratic
machine and, along with the Boston *Journal,* among the most extreme
of the city's anti-abolition papers. It routinely supported President
Pierce's administration and measures, of course, but B. F. Hallett's
control of its editorial content gave its coverage of the Burns affair a
personal animus. On Tuesday, May 30, it commented on the "almost
unparalleled excitement" in the city the day before:

> The abolitionists and their confederates did all they could, to subserve
> the cause of mob law! Their treasonable meeting at Faneuil Hall was
> not enough. It was not enough that Parker, and Phillips, and their as-
> sociates excited the passions of their deluded dupes up to the pitch of
> destruction and murder, nor that seditious hand bills stared the passers
> by at the corners of the streets. Bodies of men from distant towns came
> in to the city to aid their detestible [*sic*] work, and the consequence was
> that all day our city was the scene of great confusion.

What these bold, bad men are doing, is nothing more nor less than committing treason.

One had to take charges of treason seriously when they emanated from the district attorney's paper, which now quoted Daniel Webster's definition of that crime as he derived it from the Shadrach case: "I say if they resolve to resist the law, whoever may be attempted to be made the subject of it, and carry that purpose into effect, by resisting the application of the law in any one case, either by force of arms or force of numbers, that, sir, is treason."

It was clear that Hallett had set his sights on Theodore Parker, though he was willing to take down any number of others along the way. The *Post* article quoted the opinion of the Boston *Journal* that "There was not a man on the rostrum at Faneuil Hall on Friday evening, whose hands are not dyed in the blood of James Batchelder, but if any one is more guilty than another, it is the Rev. Theodore Parker, for it was he who put the motion to adjourn to Court Square."

Other prosecutions were contemplated as well. Stephen Higginson arrived in Boston on Tuesday to investigate rumors that a warrant had been issued for his brother's arrest. He checked in at the Brattle House and managed quickly to confirm the truth of the reports that had been conveyed to Worcester the day before by William F. Channing. Channing now wrote that the evidence against Higginson "was in the hands of the police court," adding that certain unnamed officials had decided to give Higginson advance warning. Samuel May understood from this that Higginson was being invited to flee the country, and he began to make preparations to that end on his friend's behalf. Dana supposed that there was more than enough evidence to convict Higginson and told him that "if you seek safety you had better go." John Andrew's advice was to "get out of the way for the present, [and] *not* give yourself up." Higginson, still unsure whether the pending indictment would be for riot, murder, or treason, settled himself with the thought that, in the present excitement, no arresting officer could venture safely to Worcester. Channing and others desired "that there may be no resistance to legal process." Higginson's mother expressed the same hope.[1]

Those already under arrest—the Court House rioters—appeared before Judge Abel Cushing of the Police Court at 11:00 on Tuesday, but the arraignment was put off until Friday because the results of the coroner's inquest were not yet available. In his letter to Higginson, Channing noted that "further arrests" would probably result from the inquest, and asked his cousin to "Tell this to our colored friend [apparently Lewis Hayden] who went up to W[orcester], I believe, within two or three days."

When in the course of time Higginson actually was indicted for "High Treason," he boasted to Maria Weston Chapman that such had "always been considered the crime of a gentleman."[2]

Charlotte Forten, young, black, and female, could not aspire to treason, high or low, but from her home in Salem looked forward instead to attending the Antislavery convention the next day in Boston, biding her time meanwhile by anxiously brooding on the Burns case and finding vent for her feelings in Elizabeth Barrett Browning's poem "The Runaway Slave at Pilgrim's Point." "How powerfully it is written! . . . It seems as if no one could read this poem without having his sympathies roused to the utmost in behalf of the oppressed."[3]

The poem is a dramatic monologue in which the female speaker, evidently on her way to Canada, has improbably paused at Plymouth Rock to commune with the "pilgrim-souls" and to pour out to them the violent melodrama of her own history. As in Whittier's currently popular "Sabbath Scene," Browning's strategy is to divide the villainy of slavery from the suffering it causes, representing the one as national and masculine, the other as personal and feminine. The "pilgrim-souls," an important but ambiguous point of mythic reference, are appealed to because of their foundational experience as fugitives from tyranny; they, too, were displaced persons to whom freedom was life itself. Such experience and personal testimony, however, are supposed to be no longer current in the white world, and are represented as an empty mark on a wild and desolate seaside landscape. If the love of freedom survives into the mid-nineteenth century as an emotional fact, it is to be read exclusively in the maddened feelings of the hunted slave.

Admired as prototypical fugitives, the Pilgrim patriarchs are also hated as white progenitors. In a kind of reverse fall, the sins of "their hunter sons" are visited on the national fathers, the Massachusetts fathers. Generation, in this poem, whether forbidden to blacks or indulged by whites, is reduced to a function of tyranny: the fugitive's own lurid story is that her Southern white master killed her slave lover, then raped her; she gave birth to the rapist's son, but then murdered the child when she observed with horror "the *master's* look" in its pale infant face.

The poem is not in all respects a very good one, but its melodramatic themes clearly resonated for Forten, situated as she was, politically and emotionally, before the engrossing spectacle of the Burns case. If it is treason to have the blood of Batchelder on one's hands, as she might have read that morning in the *Post*, why does the blood of slaves make no traitors? Indeed, why does it seem more apt to make patriots? The theme of the physical wounding of the slave is prominent in Barrett Browning's poem, as it is in much of the more visceral antislavery literature. At one point the slave protagonist speaks to her pursuers:

> I am not mad; I am black.
>   I see you staring in my face—
> I know you staring, shrinking back,
>   Ye are born of the Washington-race,
> And this land is the free America,
> And this mark on my wrist—(I prove what I say)
>   Ropes tied me up here to the flogging-place.

The moral authority of suffering is that it can always "prove what it says," an elementary task to which the white male inhabitants of "free America" (sons of an always truthful slaveholding father in this overdetermined poem) are clearly not equal. The response of Barrett Browning's heroine to her floggers is diametrically opposed to that offered by Stowe's Tom to Legree: she does not cry out under torture, but "cursed them all around / As softly as I might have done / My very own child." That child, of course, she tenderly wished dead, so it is not a tremendous leap in the next few lines to her call for a general uprising of the slaves, to "end what I begun!"

The wounding and the sexual predation seem designed to reinforce the fiction that the slave, as the invention of the slaveholder, is and must be a purely physical and instinctual being. Tom's "victory" over Legree consciously explodes that fiction precisely by taking seriously the primacy of the spiritual. He refuses to be defined by an earthly master as a mere animal to be scourged. But that is not the tactic taken in the poem. The Christian doctrine of returning love for hate is, to be sure, the inevitable point of reference, but the protagonist specifically declines it:

Whips, curses; these must answer those!
    For in this Union you have set
Two kinds of men in adverse rows,
    Each loathing each; and all forget
The seven wounds in Christ's body fair,
While He sees gaping everywhere
    Our countless wounds that pay no debt.

The speaker seems, perhaps in the incoherence of her grief, to have forgotten her immediately preceding call for a slave rebellion ("lift up
your hands, / O slaves, and end what I begun!"). "Curses" seem an emotional compromise between a problematical physical rebuke and that
unlikely Christian-Stoic forbearance that Stowe advanced or that
Whittier was even then pressing on "our colored friends." Between the
resort to violence and turning the other cheek, between the physical
and the spiritual, lay the parody of both: the hard words, the melodramatic words, that bore witness to the wounding. That's, to be sure,
what the entire poem is—a curse and condemnation, a wail in words (as
its author thought) "too ferocious, perhaps, for the Americans to publish." Thus while the poem *seems* to enter the debate over violent versus
Christian means in the antislavery struggle, its mark of gender is that it
comes out squarely for cursing, for saying what one feels.[4]

The humanity of the poem (not any religious appeal or superhu-
manity) is its conscious claim to attention, and that humanity in turn
is predicated on a literal reading of the exhausted, misused slave body.
The wounds are the more horrific for their banality. They are not the
wounds of Christ, and have no redemptive powers. They are just
slashed skin and quick pain: marks read very much in the spirit in
which they were inscribed.

Our wounds are different. Your white men
    Are, after all, not gods indeed,
Nor able to make Christs again
    Do good with bleeding. *We* who bleed
(Stand off!) we help not in our loss!
We are too heavy for our cross,
    And fall and crush you and your seed.

If the oppressed slave becomes the rooted-for physical anti-Christ,
who falls rather than ascends, who crushes rather than redeems, she is
only such a Christ as infernal slavery makes. Yet the poem, in its
strongest moments, allies feeling with the reality and triumph of the

physical, with, again, retributive justice, and by implication with a rejection of the higher reaches of Christian response, as though sympathy, in the immense difficulty of its awakening, requires that the slave be seen as a wounded and woundable animal. It is as though the poet had asked herself what the strongest, most vivid basis for sympathy might be, given that the maximum of aroused sympathy was the goal (as Forten sensed), and concluded that nothing could be presented as having greater emotional reality than the effects of physical cruelty. Stowe, in *Uncle Tom's Cabin,* demonstrated that this was not an inevitable choice. The maximum pressure brought to bear on Tom consisted in the attempt to dislodge him from truth and character, compared to which the physical abuse was as nothing; the effectiveness of those scenes at Legree's plantation depends on the reader's capacity to grant ontological reality to such religious "abstractions" and, simultaneously, to dispense with the racist notion that blacks are consigned by racial fate to a physical, instinctual realm where, by definition, they must be unmotivated by ideals. Tom's wounds *were* redemptive, as Stowe was careful to point out and as American women by and large chose (or perhaps needed) to believe. One secret of the popularity of *Uncle Tom's Cabin* was that it saved Christianity just when antislavery threatened to empty the churches.

Burns was quite routinely seen as a Christ figure, whose suffering and betrayal, whose very wounds, were a precondition to his supporters' intensest sympathy. The highest pitch of abolitionism was accounted religious in its transformative effect on its acolytes and volunteers, and so the slave's passion and his looming crucifixion were vicariously entered into in this reviving spring of 1854. His enemies were the Judas Iscariot and Pontius Pilate of State Street. Roman legions guarded him. *Ecce homo,* as Phillips virtually said.

❧ POLITICS AND FORCE

What is the difference between Colonel Suttle and Russian Salve?

The slave owner inflicts *Flesh Wounds,* and the other cures them and is good for *Burns.*

ADVERTISEMENT IN THE *COMMONWEALTH,* May 31, 1854

On Wednesday, the last day of May, the weather turned cold as the wind blew in from the ocean. Mayor Smith, as if in response to the general cooling, instructed Benjamin F. Edmands, commander of the militia, to demobilize half his force: "one military company will be amply sufficient, from this day, till further orders, to maintain order and suppress any riotous proceedings—acting in concert with the police." In fact Smith had been for some time deeply concerned about who would pay for all these men under arms. He had repeatedly pressed the matter with Hallett and Freeman, but their assurances of federal reimbursement came back hedged and equivocal. This morning, at last, the district attorney telegraphed to Washington to find out definitely if what he'd been telling the mayor was true or not; the president had replied: "Incur any expense deemed necessary by the Marshal and yourself for city military, or otherwise, to ensure the execution of the law." With this statement in hand, Hallett and Freeman began, in effect, to issue orders to the mayor:

> We deem it necessary, that when the decision of the Commissioner is to be given, which will probably be tomorrow morning, the avenues and streets around the Court House should be cleared of the crowd, and an ample military force be on guard to preserve the peace of the city, and prevent riot or personal outrages, which are then to be anticipated, whatever may be the decision.
>
> And we further deem it necessary, that, if the Marshal with his posse is required to pass through the streets of the city, they should not be crowded upon, molested, or placed in a position of defence which may render it necessary to protect themselves by a resort to arms. And this requires the whole military and police force of the city to preserve the peace of the city, and prevent riot and assaults upon the officers of the law, in the discharge of their duty.
>
> We repeat what we have before said, that the United States officers do not desire you to execute the process under the fugitive law of the United States, which devolves on them alone in the discharge of their duties, but they call upon you, as the conservator of the peace of the city, to prevent the necessity of conflict between the posse of the Marshal, and those who may attempt to resist them by force while in the lawful discharge of the duties required of them.

A few hours later, when Hallett and Freeman became aware of Smith's earlier and independent order to Edmands to have half his troops stand down, they requested that "two companies of Light Infantry to be on guard for the night, and until further orders." It was done.[1]

If Mayor Smith thought this show of force excessive, President Franklin Pierce clearly did not. Determined that the situation should be kept under control, the president this morning, through Jefferson Davis, his secretary of war, ordered the Army's adjutant-general, Colonel Samuel Cooper, to go to Boston, empowered to attach to the marshal's posse as much military force as he thought necessary, including two companies of U.S. troops stationed in New York that had been on alert for the last forty-eight hours. Colonel Cooper was well suited to this task: he was favorably known to the secretary as the brother-in-law of one of Davis' closest friends in Washington, Virginia Senator James Murray Mason, author of the Fugitive Slave Law. Mason, a power in national Democratic politics since 1847, had enormous personal influence at the White House so long as Pierce was in it. While it seems impossible to determine just how active he may have been behind the scenes in the Burns case, it is virtually certain that he was acquainted with Colonel Suttle, since both their families had long histories of residence in Stafford County, and Mason is known to have kept a close watch on Stafford politics.[2]

Charlotte Forten, accompanied by Sarah Remond, came in from Salem to attend the convention of the New England Anti-Slavery Society at the Melodeon. They were disappointed to find as they approached the great hall fewer indications of public ferment than they expected, but still they sensed that "much real indignation and excitement" lay beneath the surface. In fact business had been largely suspended in the heart of the city, and hundreds of men and women were holding a constant sad vigil in Court Square. The papers continued to put out frequent special editions, keeping the newsboys on the streets in a constant uproar.

Momentarily joining the crowd at the Court House, Forten paused to consider that it was "now lawlessly converted into a prison, and filled with soldiers, some of whom were looking from the windows, with an air of insolent authority which made my blood boil." She and her older companion passed on to the meeting, only to find that "the best speakers were absent, engaged in the most arduous and untiring efforts in behalf of the poor fugitive." Missing Phillips, Garrison, and Parker, she nevertheless heard speeches by Sarah's brother, Charles Lenox Remond, and by Stephen S. Foster and his wife, Abby Kelley. The latter, at the morning session, urged the women to support their husbands and brothers in "our just and holy cause."[3]

Ann Warren Weston was one of many Garrisonians whose patience and principles were being sorely tested by the Burns case. She boycotted the meeting, feeling that "they had better adjourn it, first in order to be at Court Square and second because it is a pity to have unadvised absurd talk. For the Abolitionists to be discussing non-resistance and kindred topics at such a time was not profitable." Yet not all the talk was about passive resistance. A Mr. Prince of Essex was advocating a plan for establishing secret societies throughout the Commonwealth for the express purpose of harassing and opposing the slavehunters. Edmund Quincy offered the opinion that such meetings as the present, in their compulsive enshrinement of eloquent speaking, were nevertheless "the laboratories where revolutions are commenced." He pointed out that the revolution that claimed the head of Charles I had begun not in 1642, but much earlier, among the Puritan ministers who educated a people to their rights; and that the American Revolution had begun not in 1775, but much earlier, when in homes and churches discussion of colonial grievances trained up a generation to act for liberty. And "now," he said, "we are preparing the way for a new and greater revolution."[4]

Throughout the day, fragmentary bulletins arrived from the Court House, and by these means Dana's long summation for the defense peppered the meeting with bursts of encouragement.

Charlotte Forten dined this day at the Garrison home, where indeed she would always be a welcome guest. She was not only the young friend and housemate of Garrison's closest black ally, Charles Remond of Salem, but the niece of Robert Purvis, a wealthy black abolitionist, and the granddaughter of James Forten, the pioneering reformer who had taught Garrison early and convincingly about the evils of colonization. At this midday meal, Charlotte thought Garrison "spoke beautifully in support of the non-resistant principles to which he has kept firm," and conceded that he was "indeed the very highest Christian spirit." And yet it was an ideal almost entirely beyond her reach, "for I believe in 'resistance to tyrants'" (as she wrote that day in her journal) "and would fight for liberty until death."

As she returned to Salem at the end of the day, she was "sick at heart" at the sight of soldiers patrolling the Boston streets on horseback, "ready at any time to prove themselves the minions of the south." For the sake of getting home at a reasonable hour, she missed the evening session of the antislavery meeting, at which Abby Kelley Foster put her famously undomestic side on display. She delivered a stinging rebuke to the Freesoil party, suggesting that its past sins of coalition made it forevermore an unreliable vehicle in the crusade. Addressing Henry

Wilson, who had come over from the Freesoil Convention at the Music Hall to curry favor with the Garrisonians, she demanded to know "what security has anyone in giving his vote to the Free Soil party, that we shall not be helping the worst pro-slavery men into office?"

> Heretofore we have seen the Free Soil party coalescing with the Democratic party, electing George S. Boutwell, a timid doughface, to the Governor's chair, and helping to place *Caleb Cushing* (!), the vilest pro-slavery man anywhere to be found, on the Supreme Judicial Bench of the State. Who can assure us that we shall not, by and by, see them putting that wretched tool of slavery, Benjamin F. Hallett, into office?

"I ask these questions in good faith," she said, "and not from any wish to cavil." But she had put her finger on the very thing that had crippled and now killed the party; and to make the moment yet more dramatic, she had asked her questions of the very man who in 1851 had designed and put in motion the fatal strategy of exchanging for the election of Charles Sumner the entire moral stock of the Freesoil movement. The boost it had given to Salem's Caleb Cushing, a Hunker Democrat, had come back to haunt the radicals, for Cushing was now Pierce's attorney general and, as many supposed, was calling the shots in the Burns case. The internal party divisions caused by the coalition had never healed. The Freesoil party had not grown, even under the provocation of the Nebraska Bill, but for the past three years had led, like the Whig party, a sort of posthumous existence, coming only now—this week in fact—to a consciousness of its own demise. The theme of its convention this year was the need for a whole new start, for "the formation of one great Northern party for freedom."[5]

❦ DANA'S ARGUMENT

The same faculty of seeing and describing which caused him to make his mark in "Two Years before the Mast" at the age of twenty-two, enabled him to produce the effects on bench and jury which he indisputably did produce at forty. It was not his grasp of legal principles, though in this regard he was not wanting; it was not his command of authorities, for that he did not have; it was his combined courage and tenacity, and his faculty of seeing things clearly himself, and then making others see them as he saw them.

CHARLES FRANCIS ADAMS

The Wednesday court session opened at 9:00, and a few last rebuttal witnesses were brought forward. One man, William R.

Batchelder—a relative, perhaps, of the dead guard—was called for the purpose of reporting a private conversation he had had with Jones, but the defense's objection to it was sustained, and neither Batchelder nor Jones was ever recalled. Benjamin True, one of the marshal's guard who had been with Burns in the jury room since the arrest a week ago, was then called to testify about certain conversations with the prisoner. This testimony was also objected to, but Loring allowed it. In the end, True alleged only that Burns had told him that he "had been here about two months, perhaps a little short of that," before which time he had been in Richmond, Virginia. He damaged the claimant's case rather more than he helped it, however, by admitting that Burns had seemed "intimidated" the night of his arrest, before and after speaking with Suttle. In an attempt to undo that damage, True testified that he "never threatened him or held out any promises to him; [he and the guards] endeavored to treat him well; gave him newspapers, oranges, oyster stews and candy when he wished them." Asked what use the newspapers might have been to the prisoner, True replied that "he can read and write."[1]

Counsel for the claimant rested their case.

Dana rose from his seat and began what would be a four-and-a-half-hour summation for the defense. He had only a brief outline for a guide, scribbled on one side of a half-sheet of notepaper, yet he rarely looked at it, and his whole performance gave the impression of brilliant improvisation.[2]

Addressing the commissioner, he said:

> I congratulate you, Sir, that your labors, so anxious and painful, are drawing to a close. I congratulate the commonwealth of Massachusetts, that at length . . . by leave of the Marshal of the United States and the District Attorney of the United States . . . her courts may be reopened, and her Judges, suitors and witnesses may pass and repass without being obliged to satisfy hirelings of the United States Marshal and bayoneted foreigners, clothed in the uniform of our army and navy, that they have a right to be there. I congratulate the city of Boston, that her peace here is no longer to be in danger. Yet I cannot but admit that while her peace here is in some danger, the peace of all other parts of the city has never been so safe as while the Marshal has had his posse of specials in this Court House. Why, Sir, people have not felt it nec-

essary to lock their doors at night, the brothels are tenanted only by women; fighting dogs and racing horses have been unemployed, and Ann street and its alleys and cellars show signs of a coming millennium.

He then offered congratulations to the U.S. government, whose representative, Hallett, could return to more appropriate duties, his presence at court no longer needed for purposes of intimidation. Dana alluded to Hallett's outburst on Monday morning, saying that while the commissioner was of course unmoved by it, still it was a matter of regret that he had not silenced the district attorney at once. Dana also congratulated the officers of the Army and Navy, "that they can be relieved from this service, which as gentlemen and soldiers surely they despise, and can draw off their non-commissioned officers and privates, both drunk and sober, from this fortified slave-pen, to the custody of the forts and fleets of our country, which have been left in peril, that this great Republic might add to its glories the trophy of one more captured slave."

These congratulations, he said, were given in expectation of a favorable end to the trial, seeing that the prisoner, who was manifestly free a week ago, continued free by presumption until overwhelming evidence showed otherwise. Yet if the decision was to be for slavery, better that the trial should continue for the remainder of the prisoner's life.

The maxim that it is preferable for nine guilty men to go free than for one innocent man to suffer unjustly is generally held to by jurists in cases of murder, where a single life is balanced against the interest of an entire community.

> How much more should it be applied to a case like this, where on the one side is something dearer than life, and on the other no public interest whatever, but only the value of a few hundred pieces of silver, which the claimant himself, when offered to him, refused to receive . . . We have a right, then, to expect from your Honor a strict adherence to the rule that this man is free until he is proved a slave beyond every reasonable doubt, every intelligent abiding misgiving, proved by evidence of the strictest character, after a rigid compliance with every form of law which statute, usage, precedent has thrown about the accused as a protection.

Cases at law are decided by varying standards of proof. A "preponderance of the evidence" will determine the outcome in petty cases, but higher standards apply as the seriousness of the matter escalates. Charges of murder must be sustained "beyond a reasonable doubt." To justify any standard of proof more stringent than this, it needed to be shown that the remanding of a man to slavery was an action yet more terrific than a conviction for murder. Thus Dana spent some time showing that "It is not by rhetoric, but in human nature, by the judgment of mankind, that liberty is dearer than life." Men willingly place their lives at risk for many reasons; often they make choice of death in preference to "poverty, disgrace, or despair," but who in all the world ever sought for slavery or captivity?

Dana's statement to the contrary notwithstanding, his argument, in both the strength and weakness of its appeal to nature, was profoundly rhetorical throughout. Given that the Burns "trial" was not a suit at law, but a mere administrative hearing for which no standard of proof had ever been set, Dana's analogy to a murder trial might seem like an attempt to reconcile the proceedings with established judicial practice. Actually, as the recourse to analogy in itself implies, it was a flagrant excursion out of positive law into natural law, a dangerously unmapped realm of ethics and psychology where precedent and legal convention would have less force than a rhetorical address to the conscience. Because the de facto standard of proof in the case was whatever satisfied the mind of Edward G. Loring, this rhetorical maneuver of Dana's was both forceful and appropriate. The guiding assumption on the defense side had been that no judge who was not a monster would remand Burns if he had an alternative and felt free to pursue it. Dana clearly saw that if he were to secure Burns's liberty, he would, in the first instance, have to free Judge Loring, who might yet claim to be a sort of slave to the law, with no will of his own. Thus Dana put it to him that at the very heart of America's most oppressive law was an ambiguity (respecting proof) wholly favorable to freedom. Whatever discretion the commissioner had was directly tied to that ambiguity, and in conscience and the law of nature was the freedom now to select a threshold of proof that would allow the promptings of a healthy conscience to be realized and the freedom of Anthony Burns to be affirmed.

Dana then laid out the elements of the case that the claimant had to make out. "Col. Suttle says there was a man in Virginia named Anthony Burns; that that man is a slave by the law of Virginia, that he is *his* slave, owing service and labor to *him;* that he escaped from Virginia into this State, and that the prisoner at the bar is that Anthony Burns. He says all this. Let him prove it *all!* Let him fail in one point, let him fall short the width of a spider's thread, in the proof of all his horrid category, and the man goes free."

As Dana moved through these separate points, he advanced from the possibility of mistake to the likelihood of mistake, culminating in the legal and logical certainty of mistake, at last subsuming under this umbrella of error the whole of the claimant's case. As to the central issue of identity, how common, said Dana, how well known, were instances of mistaken identity. "One of the earliest and most pathetic narratives of Holy Writ is that of the patriarch, cautious, anxious, crying again and again, 'Art thou my very son Esau?' and by a fatal error, reversing a birth-right, with consequences to be felt to the end of time." Mothers of sailor sons gone on long voyages have taken in strangers, confusing them for kin. The commissioner himself has found it difficult to identify Harvard classmates at reunions. "We have the Comedy of Errors. Let us have no Tragedy of Errors, here!" Dana went on to point out that in the first case brought under the Fugitive Slave Law, a man had been arrested in Philadelphia, adjudged a slave, and sent under guard to his master in Maryland—only to have the master refuse delivery of a man he had never seen before. Other such mistakes had occurred.

Dana asserted that evidence on the point of identity came wholly from Brent, who had not often seen the slave since 1847, when he last hired him and when Burns was sixteen or seventeen years old. "The record they bring here describes only a dark complexioned man. The prisoner at the bar is a full blooded negro. Dark complexions are not uncommon here, and are more common in Virginia. The record does not show to which of the great primal divisions of the human race the fugitive belongs. It might as well have omitted the sex of the fugitive." Had the record meant to identify the prisoner, it would not have contented itself with an understated reference to "a scar on his right hand." "A scar!" said Dana contemptuously. "The prisoner's right hand is broken, and a bone stands out from the back of it, a hump an inch high, and it hangs almost useless from the wrist, with a huge scar or gash covering half its surface." Seeing that his right hand is the chief property his master has in him, such a calamity would be well remembered by him. If we suppose that the record fully describes the man sought, or that Brent's testimony does, which refers only to "a cut," then the prisoner is not the more subtly disfigured slave who escaped.

Dana then went into the grounds for supposing that Brent and Suttle picked out the prisoner in default of the real fugitive because they could not return to Virginia empty-handed: "Remember the state of feeling between North and South; the contest between the slave power and the free power. Remember that this case is made a State issue by Virginia, a national question by the Executive. Reflect that every reading man in Virginia, with all the pride of the Old Dominion aroused in him, is turning his eyes to the result of this issue. No man could be more liable to bias than a Virginian, testifying in Massachusetts, at this moment, on such an issue, with every powerful and controlling motive on earth enlisted for success."

Brent's feeble testimony and the catchall Virginia record ("which is probably still only Mr. Brent on paper") are impeachable on the supposition that Brent may not have recalled Anthony Burns particularly well, which indeed would account for the surprising vagueness of the descriptions. The one point on which Mr. Brent is clear and certain is that he saw the man in Richmond on March 20. "He persists in his positive testimony, and I have no doubt he is right and honest in doing so." Yet the prisoner could not be the man Brent saw, since he was in Boston from the first day of March, as shown by the unshaken testimony of William Jones. "Of this your Honor cannot, on the proofs, entertain a reasonable doubt."

Dana reviewed the testimony of the alibi witnesses, pausing to emphasize Whittemore's Hunker Whig politics and his connection to the Pulaski Guards, both to show his utter lack of radical bias and, not incidentally, to provide the Hunker Whig on the judicial bench with a model of nobly disinterested behavior. The force of the alibi witnesses lay precisely in their numerical advantage over the solitary Brent. One man may be mistaken, said Dana, but six or eight independent identifications coinciding on the other side cannot be. "If we had the burden of proof, should we not have met it? How much more then are we entitled to prevail, where we have only to shake the claimant's case by showing that it is left in reasonable doubt?"

Yet, though it was clear enough to his own judgment that the two sides could not have been identifying the same individual, Dana owed it to his client not to rely on this showing alone. Suppose, then, that all the defense testimony has been thrown out. Has the claimant made his case? Has it been shown that the prisoner owes service and labor to Colonel Suttle? The claimant, perhaps, will say that he does not need to, that the record of the Virginia court is by law decisive on the points of slavery and escape; and yet, Dana pointed out, it is so only if the claimant avails himself of section 10 of the Fugitive Slave Law, which provides for the *ex parte* determination of the points of slavery and escape in the state from which the slave escapes. But in the present case, the claimant, by introducing Brent's testimony, elected to go forward under section 6, which provides that testimony on all three points (slavery, escape, and identity) be received in the state in which the fugitive is found. Claimant cannot now switch tactics and receive the benefit of section 10. "We say that the two proceedings cannot be combined. The jurisdiction and duties of the magistrate are different in the two cases. The rights of parties are different."

It seems that Thomas and Parker had made a hopeless legal muddle out of Suttle's initially straightforward case by mixing kinds of proof. Dana explained:

Even if the record can be combined with parol proof, it can hardly be contended that it is conclusive against proof the claimant himself puts with it. When the statute says it is conclusive, it means that the defendant is not admitted to contradict it by proof. But if the claimant introduces proof which overthrows [the allegations of the record], can he contend that it is conclusive? If he proves that the right to the certificate is in Millspaugh, and not in Col. Suttle, can he fall back on his record and claim a certificate for Col. Suttle? If he proves that the man did not escape, can he fall back on his record, and claim a certificate for an escaped fugitive?

For these reasons and for others Dana asked the commissioner to "confine this record . . . in the straitest limits. It deserves a blow at the hand of every man who meets it." And yet if the commissioner admits it, "we have objections to offer . . . from the nature of its contents and form." Among its many deficiencies, the record does not allege that the slave "escaped into another State. Unless he has escaped *into another State,* the *casus foederis* does not arise. And how is your

Honor to know that he did escape into another State? The only evidence you can legally receive [if the record is admitted] is on the point of identity. If you proceed strictly by the record, you are without evidence of one great fact necessary to call into action the constitutional powers."

To illustrate the illegality of granting a certificate to the claimant in this case, Dana imagined the conversation that would ensue between Suttle and Millspaugh when Burns was brought back to Richmond:

Millspaugh: Why are you carrying my man about the country? I have not asked or desired you to do any such thing.

Suttle: But I have a certificate from a Commissioner in Boston certifying that he is now owing me service and labor, and authorizing me to take and carry him off.

Millspaugh: Then the Commissioner did not know that I had a lease of him.

Suttle: Yes he did. Mr. Brent let that out. It came very near upsetting our case. But we got our certificate, somehow or other, notwithstanding.

Dana then imagined Millspaugh's reaction on hearing from Suttle, in the alternative, that he had been refused the certificate: "To be sure you were. Did you not know law enough to know, you and Brent together, that you had no right to the possession and control of the man I have hired on a lease? Did you suppose the Boston commissioners would have so little regard for this species of property in Virginia as to give it away to the first comer?"

Then, too, Brent, "in his simplicity, thinking he was all the time proving prodigious acts of ownership," has let it out that Burns was mortgaged to one Tolson—which also, as a settled point of law, eliminates Suttle's standing in any action to recover. He has no right to say to Burns that he may or may not come or go. He has, compared to the lessee, or mortgagee,

nothing to say about it . . . If the man is not returned to him at the end of his lease, let him look to his bond. Let him not come here, to Massachusetts, disturb the peace of the nation, exasperate the feelings of our people to the point of insurrection by this revolting spectacle, summon in the army and navy to keep down by bayonets the great instincts of a great people, haul to prison our young men of education and character, and . . . cause the blood of a man to be shed. Let him look to his bond! If he must peril life, disturb peace, outrage feelings and exasperate temper from one end of the Union to the other, let him do it for something that belongs to him, not for a mortgaged reversion in a man. Let him look to his bond!

The only evidence on the point of escape—evidence introduced by the claimant—shows that no escape occurred. Unrebutted testimony indicates that the leaving was involuntary, indeed unconscious. Nor is there any evidence that the leaving was contrary to the wishes of Millspaugh. The story of Burns's falling asleep on board the ship at Richmond had come from Burns himself at second hand through Brent. While a favorable legal construction could be put on that story, it was linked in the same narrative with more damning admissions, and just as Dana had objected to the introduction of the testimony at first, so now he urged Loring to give the statements as little evidentiary weight as might be. What the prisoner had said was demonstrably tainted by fear and intimidation. Dana reminded the judge that he had seen the prisoner the next morning and had concluded then that he was not, even then, in a fit condition to be tried. How much more liable would he have been the evening before, when just arrested, to be terrified and coerced by a man who meant to enslave him for life and who offered to make him "no compromises"?

Dana had been speaking for a little less than four hours when he turned at last to the constitutional argument, which had figured so largely in Ellis' opening remarks. Though he believed that the Fugitive Slave Law was indeed unconstitutional, he had little expectation that Loring would have the courage or independence to agree. The matter had apparently been settled in 1851 when Lemuel Shaw rejected the argument of Robert Rantoul in the Sims case. Shaw's opinion had been the first and was, ever since, the controlling sustention of the law's constitutionality. Dana, who had assisted Rantoul in the design of that argument, proposed now to restate its terms "only as a continued protest." Rantoul's argument rested on five points: (1) that the commissioner is made a judge in a manner inconsistent with constitutional provisions, (2) that the Constitution provides for trial by jury in cases where property rights and rights of personal liberty clash, (3) that Congress has no power to confer authority on state courts to manufacture evidence that shall be binding on courts in other states, (4) that such evidence is incompetent because the fugitive is unrepresented at the taking thereof and is subsequently barred from challenging it, and (5) that the law as a whole is an unconstitutional extension of the powers of Congress.

That said, Dana concluded:

> You recognized, Sir, in the beginning, the presumption of freedom. Hold to it now, Sir, as to the sheet-anchor of your peace of mind as well as of his safety. If you commit a mistake in favor of the man, a pecuniary value, not great, is put at hazard. If against him, a free man is made a slave forever. If you have, on the evidence, or on the law, the doubt of a reasoning and reasonable mind, an intelligent misgiving, then, Sir, I implore you, in view of the cruel character of this law, in view of the dreadful consequences of a mistake, send him not away, with that tormenting doubt on your mind. It may turn to a torturing certainty. The eyes of many millions are upon you, Sir. You are to do an act which will hold its place in the history of America, in the history of the progress of the human race. May your judgment be for liberty and not for slavery, for happiness and not for wretchedness; for hope and not for despair; and may be the blessing of Him that is ready to perish may come upon you.

 ## Thomas' Argument

The black man will have his day, and I want him to have it peaceably, else he will be obliged to use force . . . And if that necessity is resorted to, although I should regret it, yet in the great cause of human rights I should rush into the battle as gladly as I would to a bridal-feast.

SETH J. THOMAS, 1842

Lead attorney Seth J. Thomas summed up for the claimant's side. His principal and strongest argument was that under the Fugitive Slave Law the Virginia record was simply determinative on the points of slavery (that is, Suttle's ownership of Burns) and escape. Absolutely nothing that was said on these matters, nothing that *might* be said, whether in reference to Millspaugh's lease, Tolson's mortgage, or Burns's falling asleep on shipboard, had the least relevance or legal weight, for the record by law precluded any searching into these subjects. They were settled matters, and the court had only to satisfy itself on the point of identity. Was the prisoner at the bar the man named in the certificate?

We have put in, said Thomas, the testimony of Brent, who has known Burns from childhood, who "had him in his own employ, and had leased him to others, for several years, during all which time Col. Suttle claimed to own him, and treated him in all respects as his slave. We put in also Burns' admissions that Col. Suttle was his master." There was further, on the point of identity, the description in the record, which, though the defense calls it imprecise, is enough in all likelihood to distinguish this man from, say, every other black man in Boston. "There can be no doubt that he is of *dark* complexion—the suggestion is that he is very dark. It is certainly no misdescription, and is sufficiently exact." He has a scar on his cheek and another on his hand. If it is suggested that he also has a fracture of one of the bones in his hand, it is still also a scar. Moreover, the age and the height of the prisoner answer to the description in the record.[1]

Thomas then spent a considerable time reviewing the alibi testimony, acknowledging that it was, "of course, clear that this man could not have been both here and in Virginia from the first to the nineteenth of March." The eccentric illiterate, William Jones, became in Thomas' portrayal a clever, resourceful conspirator and perjurer. Since Burns had escaped on or about March 24, his encounter with Jones on Washington Street must have occurred rather later than the date sworn to. Thomas supposed that the encounter had actually happened, presumably in April, and that Burns's asking a stranger on the street for work and his going home with that stranger to board were eminently consistent with a recent escape from slavery in Virginia. Jones had learned directly from Suttle that his man had escaped on the twenty-fourth, so Jones went about convincing as many people as he could that the colored man with whom he had in fact cleaned windows at the Mattapan Works in early March was his later friend, this very same Anthony Burns. In this plan, according to Thomas, Jones was innocently abetted by a number of softhearted misremembering white men and culpably abetted by at least one conscious black liar, Stephen Maddox.

Thomas then pounced on the empty spaces in the defense case: if the prisoner was not Suttle's Tony, escaped from Virginia to Boston, whence came he here? "Where was he in February or January, or last year? Where was he born? Where has he been living?" The defense, believing their job was to shake the case of the claimant, who bore the whole burden of proof, had downplayed this question, asserting that "he may have come from New York or Cincinnati or Canada." It was not their business, they supposed, to build a biography. But Thomas now asked why, if he was in fact from any of these places, they chose to name three and not stick to one. The defense had suggested that the prisoner might have relatives in the place he came from, relatives who were, perhaps, fugitives who would be at risk if their location were known. But Thomas was not buying any of this. His counter-suggestion was that the defense was grossly negligent if it failed, for any such scruples, to produce the prisoner's Northern relatives. More likely, he said, "the sisters are all in Virginia."

"But say these witnesses show that Brent is wrong in testifying that he saw Burns in Virginia on the 19th. Suppose this to be so; what then? The date is immaterial." The supposition that Brent was mistaken in the date still left all three elements of the case in place and satisfactorily proved. It still left intact Brent's testimony in regard to the prisoner's identity—the testimony of one who had known him a great deal better and a great deal longer than all the alibi witnesses together. Brent might be mistaken, and so might the defense witnesses; but one man knew the prisoner's identity with absolute certainty—the prisoner himself—and his admissions have made it clear that he somehow knew Brent in the past. "How?" asked Thomas rhetorically.

Satisfied that he had proved the claimant's case "in three ways—by the record, by the testimony of Brent, and by the admissions of the defendant," Thomas passed on to a brief defense of the constitutionality of the Fugitive Slave Law, rehearsing the well-known argument that the act of 1793 had been consistently upheld, and that the 1850 law, differing little from that, had itself been upheld by the Supreme Judicial Court of Massachusetts, as well as "by every judge before whom a case under it has arisen."

"There I leave it. And if constitutional, and the claimant has a valid claim, why shouldn't he have the benefit of it? What sort of a law is that which professes to protect one in his right of property, but which, when practically applied to a state of facts contemplated by it, from being objectionable to a class of persons, fails to secure such right?"

Having, he said, some further points he wished to argue, Thomas asked, in view of the lateness of the hour, to be allowed to finish his remarks tomorrow. But Loring wanted the arguments concluded this very day, since the circuit court was to occupy the room on Thursday. Thomas therefore simply recapitulated points already made, ending by saying that the record "is conclusive of two facts, that the person owed service and escaped. That record, with the testimony of Brent and the admissions, prove the identity. I take leave of the case, confident in the proofs presented, confident in the majesty of the law, and confident that the determination here will be just."

As Dana listened to Thomas' argument, his contempt for his opponent steadily mounted. The "argument was poor," he would write that evening in his journal. "Indeed, he is a small pattern of a man in every way, moral and intellectual." For long moments at a time, as Thomas spoke, Dana watched the commissioner's face for signs, but the uncertain glimmers of approval or repugnance were too faint for interpretation. He thought he learned more from observing, as he had done during his own argument, just when the commissioner was taking notes and when he was not. For his own part, Dana took only one note during Thomas' closing: at the bottom of the scrap of paper on which he had blocked out the topics for his own far longer summation, he had scribbled: "If not [a] slave why not show it?"[2]

Court adjourned at 4:00 until Friday at 9:00, when Loring would give his decision.

 ## CONSPIRACY

I certainly should be perfectly willing to go to Prison in such a cause—as I should be willing to have you go.

<small>LOUISA HIGGINSON TO HER SON, THOMAS WENTWORTH HIGGINSON, MAY 31, 1854</small>

In all probability our Brother Burns will be liberated and the Government be satisfied with having spent $50,000 to preserve the Laws.

<small>LOUISA HIGGINSON TO T. W. HIGGINSON, JUNE 1, 1854</small>

The Vigilance Committee kept in more or less continuous session at Tremont Temple throughout the week, and on Thursday Moncure Conway again joined the group. The feeling at the meeting was that Dana and the alibi witnesses had done their work well, and although it was clear that Loring now had all the basis he might need to refuse the certificate, his will to do so remained very much in doubt. Many supposed that he would prefer to avoid the popular odium sure to follow on a bad decision, but others were convinced that if he had any such sensitivities, he would have resigned his place long since. It seemed that the decision would now rest less on any compulsory logic in the law than on the personal character of the judge. Loring had a reputation for humanity, derived from his solicitude toward widows and orphans in the Probate Court. He was generally thought an affable man, fond of dinner parties and entertainments, and had many old friends among the Whigs, including not a few, such as Palfrey and Sumner, who had in recent years embraced the Freesoil movement. Horace Mann, another "Conscience Whig," had been among Loring's very closest friends since their days together at the Litchfield Law School. And yet, in 1850, when the Fugitive Slave Law was being debated, Loring had praised the measure in a series of articles in the *Daily Advertiser,* while his friend Mann, successor to the congressional seat of John Quincy Adams, had denounced the law and Webster too. They rarely communicated thereafter. Mann had gone off to Ohio to be the first president of Antioch College, and Loring had fallen (to what extent remained as yet unclear) under the spell of his Curtis kin, the still hard core of the remaining Webster loyalists.[1]

The Vigilance Committee had to plan for an adverse ruling. Rescue schemes were discussed, but no one knew whether, if Burns were remanded, he would go by land or sea. Nor did they know whether he would be guarded in transit by federal officers or held in the unassisted custody of Suttle and Brent. A group headed by Austin Bearse considered boarding the transport ship—if there was to be one—on the open sea, but this image of antique piracy and flashing cutlasses was a little more than most of the reformers could take. "All sorts of plans are discussed," said William F. Channing in this day's dispatch to Higginson. "Some may be attempted. Most of our friends are tired out, but today's rest will refresh them."[2]

When Conway left the meeting to return to Cambridge, he was accosted in the street by three or four men whom he didn't recognize. "I am told that you are acquainted with the two slaveholders," said one. Conway admitted that he was. "Can you not call on them and find out the number of their room in the Revere House?" Flushing at the thought of what they intended, Conway issued a brief "No" and walked off. He later supposed that had Brent known of his conduct in this incident, "that it had lain in my hands to endanger him and Suttle," he—Conway—would have been less severely ostracized than he actually was when he returned to Virginia shortly thereafter.³

There were enough reasons, however, for the Virginians to hold a grudge against the young man. He was still confided in by his Southern comrades at Harvard, including some who were now close in Suttle's confidence. From these Conway had heard that Suttle meant, if Loring should rule against him, to have Burns seized, with or without a new warrant, and brought by force back to Virginia, trusting there to be able to make out a legal justification. This course of action, Conway had been told, had been urged on Suttle by B. F. Hallett. Presumably Hallett was not responsible for another detail of the plan: that Suttle would pack the courtroom on Friday with Virginians, one or more of whom was to have the task of shooting Theodore Parker during the scuffle. Early on Thursday morning Conway and a professor of his from the Divinity School, the Reverend Dr. George E. Ellis of Charlestown, came to the law office of Ellis' younger brother, Charles, to inform him of these rumors, which Conway felt he had on good authority. Lawyer Ellis took the reports seriously—all the more because he had implicit faith in the defense's case and expected—as did a great many others—that the prisoner would be set free on Friday morning.⁴

Near versions of the story about Suttle's plans had been afloat since Wednesday. Even in Worcester, Higginson had heard the tale. "It is rumored (& well endorsed)," he wrote to his mother, "that the U.S. government has telegraphed from Washington to *take the man, legally or otherwise.* This leaked out and was posted in handbills all over the city." The handbills read:

> NEW DANGER!
> It is now rumored that the Slave-holder intends to carry off Burns by the aid of hired ruffians after the Commissioner shall have set him at liberty.
> CITIZENS, STAND GUARD!⁵

At the heavily attended Freesoil meeting on Wednesday at the Music Hall, a note outlining Suttle's supposed intentions was handed up to New Hampshire Senator John P. Hale at the rostrum. He read it to the assembly, but then quieted the sensation by claiming not to believe it. He wanted their attention fixed on the prospect that the law would be carried out—executed, one way or the other, "in violation of the dearest rights for which men had sacrificed their lives. It was as though the blood of martyrs had not been shed, and the constitutional principles given to man never had graced the statute-books of any nation."[6]

The rumor that Suttle would not abide an unfavorable decision well suited the temper of the time and place, reinforcing the impression that federal law had a tendency to become of no effect when it stood in the way of Southern purposes, while remaining inflexible in the face of Northern grievances. It seemed entirely plausible that Suttle would ignore a ruling that set Burns free, because the South had shown just such revisionary force mere days before in the repeal of the Missouri Compromise. Hale might not have believed the news about Suttle, but he read it anyway, painting the slaveholder as a low conspirator against law, fair play, and conscience. In fact the Fugitive Slave Law did not proscribe anything now charged in rumor against Suttle, who could have put Burns through this legal mill an indefinite number of times; indeed, he could have carried him off under his own private power. All the elaborate machinery of the hearing was provided as a mere assistance to the slaveholder in the recovery of his errant property; it was up to the slaveholder to decide whether he needed this assistance or not. As a veteran antislavery lawyer, Hale knew this. His expression of disbelief was a calculated effort to have any favorable ruling received by the public as a weighty and enforceable judicial determination that Burns was a free man and a legally protected citizen of Massachusetts. Whether it would be that in fact depended entirely on how the people responded.

The public mood, especially prone just now to fears of alien conspiracies, had a marked shaping effect on the Freesoil convention and made it something of a turning point in the political history of Massachusetts and the North. Its angry and determined tone was wholly owing to the Burns affair, and although party organizer Frank Bird stated that its purpose was not "to operate especially upon the fugitive case now before Commissioner Loring," that case dominated the discussion and by comparison threw Kansas into the shade. Bird understood the need to energize the Freesoil party by purifying its ideology, or, if its history of compromise now made that impossible, then to organize a new party "which shall be as true to Freedom as the South is to Slavery." In making that appeal, he did not refer to the Kansas-Nebraska Bill or the repeal of the Missouri Compromise; instinctively he found the "hot button" issue nearer at hand. "Why is it," he asked, "that to-day you cannot get an official, straight-forward opinion from any lawyer, Whig or Democrat, in this city, that the old writ of personal replevin is a legal process? From the Governor to the Attorney-General and City Solicitor and Mayor, not a man will stand up firmly for the enforcement of this old Massachusetts law." When the people needed convincing that freedom was in peril, Bird described a conspiracy of Southern tools in Northern places; it was Court Square and State Street, not the Indian frontier—Burns, not Kansas—that made the living, present case.

The keynote speaker at the Freesoil convention was Ohio's Joshua Giddings, the most feared and respected antislavery voice in Congress. He had come to the Music Hall straight from Judge Loring's courtroom to say that in his thirty-four years as a practicing attorney he had never seen such a spectacle and hoped never to see one again. He said they had no use for such proceedings on the Western Reserve and spoke of a recent episode in which a U.S. marshal, bent on kidnapping a black man from his home, had been sent packing. He sympathized with the prostrated citizens of Massachusetts. He could not, he said, do justice to his feelings on this subject—to see a people controlled by powder and ball here in the middle of the nineteenth century! Force might be expected in the despotic governments of the Old World, but not under the free government of America, where, it was said, the people made their own laws. The theme of his speech was that the key to the recovery of lost power, the remedy for the diminished political self-determination made manifest this week, was to unite under the banner of freedom. The Burns trial, he alleged, "was concocted at Washington," yet in the people's reaction to it he was "more impressed than ever before that there is but one feeling and one principle at the North, and that is in favor of liberty."

It was the Anthony Burns case as much as anything else that made it seem so, that made popular support for "freedom" appear an opportune rallying point for a Northern political organization, though, as it happened, that organization was not to be the exhausted Freesoil party, which, at the age of six, had already too much history.

People were beginning to wonder why Harriet Beecher Stowe was saying nothing. Anniversary Week in Boston had always been like a family reunion for the Beechers, and Harriet was in Boston again this year, in from her famous Stone Cottage at Andover with her husband, Calvin

Stowe. Her father, Lyman, and her brother Edward along with Professor Stowe were in attendance at Thursday's ministerial conference at Meionaon Hall, a meeting dominated as usual by the Congregationalists. As a religious group, the Congregationalists were perhaps the least vocal about slavery, or, rather, of the Protestant sects they harbored the greatest amount of proslavery opinion; yet today they had put aside their routine business in order "to consider the duty of the pulpit in the present crisis." Professor Stowe, a solid scholar but also, by most accounts, a rather strange man, addressed the assembly to say that "I pretend to no great things, but I here say that this beard don't leave this chin until the repeal of the fugitive slave law is secured." The boldness of this announcement was not lost on Hallett's *Post,* which remarked the next day that the public "will be sorry to hear of this determination, for it has long been thought that the professor's *beard,* and *pants,* too, could be more appropriately worn by another member of his family." Such comments imply that Harriet Beecher Stowe was being looked to for an opinion on the Burns case, but they also explain, perhaps, why she chose not to give one.[7]

Ann Warren Weston maintained that "It would have looked better if she had shewn her face to the people in Boston," but Mrs. Stowe and the Beechers were keeping a low profile and "have abode," as Weston suggested, "where Napthali did pretty much"—which is to say, on the remotest outskirts of the kingdom of Israel. In fact Mrs. Stowe's time was much taken up with applying the last touches to her next work, a quiet book of European travels titled *Sunny Memories of Foreign Lands.* Made rich by *Uncle Tom's Cabin* and richer still by last year's *Key to Uncle Tom's Cabin,* Mrs. Stowe was not now eager for controversy. She could only have felt chastised by the explosive anticlerical reaction to her Nebraska petition and so, as would appear, set herself on a course of disengagement from politics. The public waited for a new word, and yet, having taught the people how to see Anthony Burns, she had no more to say.[8]

There was certainly no shortage of talk. While Calvin Stowe addressed the ministers, Nathaniel H. Whiting held forth at the antislavery meeting on the Garrisonian theme of the corrosive effects of union with slaveholders. A self-taught, unpretentious shoemaker from South Marshfield, long active in reform, Whiting had come into Boston specifically to monitor the Burns trial. A dozen years earlier Emerson, having heard him speak against the traditional authority of the Bible at a reformer's convention in Chardon Street, had picked him out from obscurity and published him in the *Dial.* It may be that Whiting's head was turned on that occasion, finding himself put forth as Emerson's model of the popular democratic orator. "A plain, unlettered man," Emerson had written, "leaving for the day a mechanical employment to address his fellows, he possesses eminent gifts for success in an assembly so constituted."[9]

Another Emerson protégé addressed the antislavery meeting in its afternoon session. Caleb Stetson had known Emerson since their student days at Harvard and had been one of the most regular attenders at the Transcendental Club from 1836 to 1840. He and Emerson had worked together in 1845 to oppose the annexation of Texas, a measure against which, in the general rally of the Northern intelligentsia, he had pronounced in his own voice an "everlasting No." More conservative in his religious views than many of the Transcendentalist ministers, Stetson was nevertheless classed by Emerson among "the sons of hope." This day, before the antislavery meeting, Stetson spoke against halfway measures. He said that between things that are radically opposite to each other, such as slavery and freedom, right and wrong, there can be no compromise. In all such attempts the right perishes and the wrong remains; freedom will disappear and slavery and oppression will be guaranteed a victory. He thought the time had come to adopt "a system of entire *excommunication,* and refuse all intercourse with the slave-holder and kidnapper, with the violators of oaths and the breakers of promises." He meant a social and political excommunication, a breaking off of the collusive support tendered by the Northern cotton interest and assorted doughfaces. "As for excommunication from the church, I fear it is useless to speak of that. I fear that all honest men will soon turn round and excommunicate the church."[10]

While this was going on, while the assembled leaders of the Congregational Church flung tepid curses at the government, while the Universalist Reform Society discussed disunion and the Massachusetts Home Missionary Society proposed sending Freesoilers to Kansas, while the Hutchinson family was singing "Let the bondman go free" at the antislavery meeting, while Richard Henry Dana spent the day writing out his closing argument for the newspapers, and while Anthony Burns and Martin Stowell sat in jail cells at the top and bottom, respectively, of the Court House, Watson Freeman made his way this Thursday afternoon to Edward G. Loring's office, intent on finding out how the decision would go. He explained to the judge how vastly different the security measures would be in either event, and that he needed timely information if he were to prevent a calamitous outrage against law and order. The threat to the physical safety of his men—and to that of the citizens of Boston—placed him under a great responsibility, et cetera.[11]

According to a later statement by Dana, who was not present, Loring "positively refused, and said that no man should know [the decision] until it was pronounced." But Wendell Phillips and Theodore Parker always maintained that the decision had been privately divulged to the claimant's side at 4:00 that afternoon. Around 9:15 that evening, a man named John M. Way came to Charles Ellis' house to say that Watson Freeman had just told him that Burns was to be sent back. Not surprisingly, Freeman's own story, after the fact, was that he had been kept in the dark with everyone else and forced to make his preparations in the alternative.[12]

Thursday afternoon at 4:00, Joseph K. Hayes, police captain in charge of Station No. 5 but temporarily assigned to City Hall, had seen a document outlining the "order of movement, &c., if Burns is carried away." Very few people seem to have known or suspected that Hayes was actually a spy, a member of the Boston Vigilance Committee who had infiltrated the police department and was reporting back to the radicals. Although he held a responsible and visible place in the ranks of the force, he had been employed by the city for only one week. Some of the abortive rescue plans had proposed to make a more aggressive use of his inside position.[13]

Thursday evening there was a meeting at the office of Mayor J. V. C. Smith, attended by General B. F. Edmands, commander of the state militia, Major Dulany, commander of the Marine contingent from Charlestown, Marshal Freeman, District Attorney Hallett, and Peter Dunbar, the Customs House boss who had recruited the marshal's guard. Edmands was clearly nervous about his position in this unpopular affair. Speaking later of this meeting, he said, "I distinctly declined to place my troops in any way as a part of the escort which should convey Burns from the Court-house to the wharf, and I further stated that I considered myself as only acting under the precept of the Mayor, for the purpose of aiding the civil authorities in keeping the peace of the city." Indeed, all of those present knew that it was illegal—a violation of the "Latimer Law"—to use state or city personnel to assist in slave cases. But then it had been to the same degree illegal to use state buildings to jail fugitive slaves. The pretense was here firmed up that tomorrow's "keeping the peace of the city"—the task assigned to the police and the state militia—was a thing wholly unrelated to helping get Burns out of town or preventing a rescue. And Edmands wanted to be officially on record as understanding that.

Marshal Freeman had conferred privately with the mayor several times during the day, the last time at 11:00 P.M. His movements had been observed by Hayes.[14]

In Salem the Unitarian minister Octavius B. Frothingham, an admirer of Emerson and later the first historian of the American Transcendental movement, was in a state of anguish over the Burns case. He already knew the topic of the coming Sunday's sermon, knew that it would fall on the polite ears of his wealthy congregation like the blast of a cannon, but tomorrow's news would determine just how uncomfortable he should have to make them. His congregation included a small number of Salem's relatively large black population, all of whom were awaiting the outcome of the trial with keenest interest. These were people Frothingham knew and liked. This evening he officiated at the marriage of one of these black parishioners, Helen S. Putnam (niece of Garrison's protégé Charles L. Remond), to Jacob D. Gilliard of Baltimore. In his prayer he alluded to the trial, acknowledging what could not be ignored, and, as Charlotte Forten, one of the guests, recalled, "spoke in a most feeling manner about the case" in conversation with the groom. Still, "the wedding was a pleasant one," Forten wrote that evening in her diary; "the bride looked very lovely; and we enjoyed ourselves as much as it is possible in these exciting times. It is impossible to be happy now."[15]

"BAD FRIDAY": JUNE 2

The liberty of America was never in greater peril than now . . . Which shall conquer, slavery or freedom? That is the question. The two cannot long exist side by side.

THEODORE PARKER

Suttle and Brent checked out of the Revere House early in the morning and, before the downtown streets began to fill with people, made their way to the Charlestown Navy Yard. There a government barge took them out to the U.S. Revenue Cutter *Morris* anchored in Boston Bay. They would remain all day aboard the ship.[1]

By 6:00 A.M., crowds had started to gather at the Court House.[2]

Shortly afterward, Major General B. F. Edmands, having finished his breakfast, arrived at his headquarters at the Albion Hotel. His militia troops had reported by his order to their respective armories and were now beginning to march through town to mass at the Parade Ground on Boston Common. Converging there from points throughout the city, the columns of troops made their presence known by martial music of fifes and drums. At about 7:30 Edmands began reviewing his troops: Companies A and B of the 1st Battalion Light Dragoons, 153 rank and file under Major T. J. Pierce; eight companies of the 5th Regiment of Artillery, 339 men and guns under Colonel Robert Cowdin; eight companies of the Fifth Regiment Light Infantry, 280 men and guns under Colonel Charles L. Holbrook; three companies from the 3d Battalion Light Infantry, 112 men and guns under Major Robert I. Burbank; and the 80-man Divisionary Corps of Independent Cadets, commanded by Lt. Colonel Thomas C. Amory.[3]

At 7:30 a heavy brass cannon, drawn by a pair of horses, was brought into Court Square by a detachment of the 4th Regiment U.S. Artillery and turned over to a squad of U.S. Marines. This "formidable piece of ordnance," loaded with six pounds of grapeshot, was set up at the southeast corner of the Court House and trained on the crowd gathering in Court Street. ("Last Friday," said Parker, "you saw the cannon! One day you will see it again grown into many cannons.")[4]

At 8:00 a notice posted at the Court House was attracting a crowd of its own. A "man in a white hat" read it out to the milling throng, who responded with a chorus of hissing and groaning:

TO THE CITIZENS OF BOSTON.

To secure order throughout the city, this day, Major General Edmands, and the Chief of Police, will make such disposition of the respective forces under their commands, as will best promote that important object; and they are clothed with full discretionary powers to sustain the laws of the land. All well-disposed citizens, and other persons, are urgently requested to leave those streets which it may be found necessary to clear temporarily, and, under no circumstance, to obstruct or molest any officer, civil or military, in the lawful discharge of his duty.

J. V. C. Smith, Mayor.
Boston, June 2d, 1854.

The city was now under martial law and would remain so until late in the afternoon.[5]

At 8:45 Dana entered the Court House and directly approached the marshal. In answer to Dana's questions, Freeman said that he had no idea what the decision would be, but that he had made arrangements to meet any eventuality. He declined to say what his plans were if Burns should be remanded to Suttle, but indicated that he had no second warrant and no intention of arresting the man if Loring were to set him free. In that event, Dana said, he would himself escort Burns out of the building.[6]

Dana took his place in the courtroom, glancing at the prisoner, who was already in his seat. The lawyer was startled to see his client decked out in a rather fine new suit of clothes. For a week Burns had appeared in the same coarse outfit he had worn the night of his arrest. Now he was resplendent in a "new hat of the latest fashion, new cut coat, vest, pants and gaiter boots." Dana didn't know what to make of it. He couldn't see the telltale marks and scars at all, but only the unaccustomed clothes and how they set off the man's tall and muscular form. He had to admit that Burns was an impressive-looking fellow.[7]

Loring came in at precisely 9:00. Everyone in the crowded room rose, searching the Judge's features for clues to the decision. The reporter for the *Liberator* thought he looked "haggard and care-worn, and evidently pressed down by a deep sense of the heavy responsibility weighing upon him."[8]

At that moment Edmands' troops, led by their officers on horseback, began moving off the Parade Ground to take up assigned positions along State Street between Court Square and the docks. They were to keep State Street clear and to block all the intersecting avenues. From this moment on there were to be no more fifes and drums, no more regimental banners in the van; it was to be muskets and fixed bayonets and crowd control.

Loring strode to his desk with a sheaf of papers in his hand and took his seat. The packed room settled in with much nervous throat-clearing and scraping of wooden chairs on the bare wooden floor.

Outside, a company of 1st Regiment of Light Infantry, Massachusetts Volunteer Militia, was clearing the square. Among the people now being pushed back was the Reverend Thomas Whittemore, editor of the *Trumpet and Universalist Magazine,* who supposed that all this military activity surely meant that Burns was doomed. Having heard that the officer in charge was named Samuel Adams, Whittemore approached him to ask if he was a descendant of the Revolutionary hero. The officer, whose name is listed as Samuel G. Adams, replied impatiently that he didn't know—and turned back to his business, completing the sweep of the square by 9:30.[9]

Loring had begun to speak, addressing first the constitutional objection. "Whenever this objection is made it becomes necessary to recur to the purpose of the statute." He said that the Fugitive Slave Law "purports to carry into execution the provision of the Constitution which provides for the extradition of persons held to service or labor in one State escaping to another." Like the Fugitive Slave Law of 1793, the law of 1850 did nothing more or less than implement a constitutional requirement.

> If extradition is the only purpose of the statute and the determination of the identity is the only purpose of these proceedings under it, it seems to me that the objection of unconstitutionality to the statute, because it does not furnish a jury trial to the fugitive, is answered; there is no provision in the Constitution requiring the identity of the person to be arrested should be determined by a jury. It has never been claimed for apprentices nor fugitives from justice, and if it does not belong to them it does not belong to the respondent.[10]

In addressing the question of whether slave law commissioners were an unconstitutionally created class of judges, Loring decided that the whole of their duty was ministerial rather than judicial, that they differed from those appointed to act under the 1793 law only in being fewer and better qualified.

As to the argument that the record of the Virginia court was given unconstitutional authority over proceedings in Massachusetts, Loring held that Article IV of the Constitution grants Congress the right to prescribe what "effect" the records and judicial proceedings of a state court shall have beyond its jurisdiction. "This express power," said Loring, "would seem to be precisely the power that Congress has used in the Statute of 1850."

The remaining litany of constitutional objections Loring disposed of by summary allusion to Shaw's decision in *Sims*. These points "are settled," Shaw had said, and Loring now repeated, "by a course of legal decisions which we are bound to respect, and which we regard as binding and conclusive on the Court."

Loring then made clear what weight he was prepared to give to "the wise words of our revered Chief Justice" in that case. The paragraph he quoted from Lemuel Shaw (7 Cushing, 318) perfectly summarizes the historical mythology of Webster in his last phase, and of the Hunkers, his cohorts—a mythology that looks upon the enslavement of blacks as an indispensable precondition for American nationality:

> Slavery was not created, established, or perpetuated by the Constitution; it existed before; it would have existed if the Constitution had not been made. The framers of the Constitution could not abrogate Slavery, or the rights claimed under it. They took it as they found it, and regulated it to a limited extent. The Constitution, therefore, is not responsible for the origin or continuance of Slavery— the provision it contains was the best adjustment which could be made of conflicting rights and claims, and was absolutely necessary to effect what may now be considered as the general pacification, by which harmony and peace should take the place of violence and war. These were the circumstances, and this the spirit in which the Constitution was made—the regulation of slavery so far as to prohibit States by law from harboring fugitive slaves was an essential element in its formation, and the Union intended to be established by it was essentially necessary to the peace, happiness, and highest prosperity of all the States. In this spirit and with these views steadily in prospect, it seems to be the duty of all judges and magistrates to expound and apply these provisions in the Constitution and laws of the United States; and in this spirit it behooves all persons, bound to obey the laws of the United States, to consider and regard them.

Anthony Burns sat stock still, never taking his eyes off Loring. Outside, the Marines ostentatiously went though the motions of loading and firing their cannon—without discharging it—meaning to impress the crowd with their speed and dexterity. The police were beginning to make arrests.

Loring was not insensitive to the fact that the question before him had its moral side, whatever the law of the matter might be. "It is said that the statute, if constitutional, is wicked and cruel." In reply, Loring quoted Shaw again, who was himself quoting his predecessor as chief justice, Isaac Parker: "Whether the statute is a harsh one or not, it is not for us to determine." He took cognizance of the argument (which had been raised more out of court than in) that the law was so wicked and cruel that no good man would involve himself in its administration. "Then into what hands," he wondered aloud, "shall its administration fall? . . . Will those who call the statute merciless commit it to a merciless judge?"

Here was hope.

"If the statute involves that right, which for us makes life sweet, and the want of which makes life a misfortune, shall its administration be confined to those who are reckless of that right in others, or ignorant or careless of the means given for its legal defence, or dishonest in its use? If any men wish this, they are more cruel and wicked than the statute, for they would strip from the fugitive the best security and every alleviation the statute leaves him."

Having clarified his own position and determined that the statute was constitutional, Loring now turned to the facts of the case. That Burns owed the claimant service in Virginia and that Burns escaped from that service were conclusively established by the record of the Virginia court under section 10 of the Fugitive Slave Law. "Thus these two facts are removed entirely and absolutely from my jurisdiction," leaving the prisoner's identity as "the only question I have a right to consider."

He weighed Brent's testimony against that of the alibi witnesses, allowing that the former came from a single source "standing in circumstances which would necessarily bias the fairest mind" (echoing Dana's characterization), and allowing also that the coinciding testimony of the several defense witnesses was manifestly free of bias. Testimony on both sides was from individuals "whose means of knowledge are personal and direct," but in Loring's opinion that of the defense witnesses was "less full and complete than that of Mr. Brent." He was prepared in effect to call this swearing match a draw and to look elsewhere for decisive evidence.

"In every case of disputed identity there is one person always whose knowledge is perfect and positive, and whose evidence is not within the reach of error, and that is the person whose identity is questioned, and such evidence this case affords. The evidence is of the conversation which took place between Burns and the claimant on the night of the arrest."

Loring went over Brent's version of this conversation in detail, beginning with Burns's greetings, "How do you do, Master Charles" and "How do you do, Master William." He repeated Suttle's questions and gave Burns's answers in turn. "Something was said about going back. He was asked if he was willing to go back, and he said—Yes, he was."

Burns heard himself thus speaking falsely and shook his head vigorously, desperately, in denial, knowing it was not his place to speak even now. What he had said was not what the judge said. His voiceless "No" was seen throughout the courtroom, and it provoked sympathy. But Loring pushed on and said that this evidence supported Brent against the alibi witnesses and so tipped the balance in favor of the claimant's side that "my mind is satisfied beyond a reasonable doubt of the identity of the respondent with the Anthony Burns named in the record."

"On the law and facts of the case, I consider the claimant entitled to the certificate from me which he claims."

🌿 THE CORTÈGE

A tyrannical statute and a weak judge!
   The decision was a grievous disappointment to us all, and chiefly to the poor prisoner. He looked the image of despair.

R. H. DANA, JOURNAL, JUNE 2, 1854

Loring ordered the courtroom cleared, though Burns, standing, remained behind in a cluster of the marshal's guard. He looked different now; something incredible had been settled about him. A number of Vigilance Committee members stopped briefly to commiserate. Most of these Burns had not met before, like Dr. Henry Bowditch or John L. Swift, the young man whose booming voice had summoned the crowd to the assault on the Court House. Swift recalled the scene:

> It happened to me to be present when the case was closed. I heard with my own ears that decision fall from the lips of Judge Loring. I looked upon Anthony Burns during that procedure—I saw him, as word after word came out from the mouth of that Judge which forged the fetters for his limbs. He listened with all the eagerness of a man who knew his unhappy condition . . . As I looked upon him, I thought of the few months he had known liberty—the struggles he had undergone to attain it—and then how soon he was to return to the house of bondage. Then, sir, my blood boiled within me. There stood a man, accused of

no crime, charged with no misdemeanor—I hope that the attorneys who plead against him, and the Court who decided adverse to him, may appear before Heaven as pure and unstained as that man!—and all he asked of Massachusetts, a State boasting of its sovereignty—rich beyond rivalry—prosperous even to excess—powerful and mighty—all he asked of the State was, that in that trial, where all that was valuable to him in life was at stake, he might have the same privileges which would be granted to parties in a suit involving twenty dollars.

While the commissioner was signing the certificate, Swift joined the small group of shamefaced handshakers moving mournfully past the prisoner. Futility needed at last to express itself, which, after the long ceremony of the law, seemed human enough: "I took him by the hand," Swift remembered:

> It was a strong and manly hand. I looked into his face. He was struggling to keep back the emotions of his heart. I held the hand and gazed into the face of a man who was a slave on my native soil. It was too much for me—to my inmost soul I felt the deep degradation of that moment. Not only had Anthony Burns been deprived of his rights, *I* had lost something—had lost the proud privilege of saying that I had life and being in a free commonwealth; and from that hour, I pledged the efforts of one life to prohibit slavery in the State of Massachusetts, and wipe out the deep disgrace and dishonour of that transaction.[1]

Dana and Grimes, together with Alexander Thayer, a reporter for Horace Greeley's *Tribune,* stayed behind with Burns while the others left. For a whole hour Grimes kept up a constant flow of earnest, consolatory talk with his parishioner. To the newly adjudicated slave he explained that it was all a mere point of honor with the government to have him returned and that Suttle was willing to sell him just as soon as he got him home. Burns said he was afraid that once removed he would be forgotten by his Northern friends and that if he were sold—as indeed he expected to be—he would be sold not to friends, but "down the river" on account of his weak hand. He had run away in the first place, he said, to avoid just that. Indeed, Suttle *had* tried to sell him, and would have done it, but there had been no takers. He understood that Master Charles looked on him as damaged goods and wouldn't be at all particular about what kind of situation he put him in. That was the worst of it: being put to a job he didn't know well. For years he'd been encouraged to say on the hiring grounds that he could do almost anything, but he had always known it wasn't so. Getting into unaccustomed work had maimed his hand—had well nigh killed him. In imagination he could see it happening all over again.[2]

Grimes tried the best he could by talking and by praying to keep the man's sunk courage up.

The bells of Boston's churches tolled. And as news of the decision spread by telegraph, bells tolled in towns throughout the Commonwealth.

At 11:00 Burns was returned to his cell. Dana and Grimes went with him and stayed a few minutes, assuring him that they would come back and be with him when he was taken down to the cutter. On his way out, Dana stopped to inform Watson Freeman of this purpose and was dumbfounded when the marshal objected. Dana insisted that criminals going to execution were always permitted to have their clergymen and counsel with them. Freeman went off to confer on this point—"with the officers in command of the troops," as Dana remembered it—and came back with a flat refusal. In that case, said the disgusted lawyer, he and Grimes would go and take their leave of the prisoner now. And yet, when they tried to speak with Burns apart, at the window end of the jury room, the guards did not, for once, retire back toward the door, but hovered round and listened. Frederick D. Byrnes, a "broken down man, of an impeached reputation," known to everyone as "Auger-hole" Byrnes, was the most forward of this officious crew—perhaps because he was deaf. Benjamin True, the deputy in charge, said that their orders had been changed, that conversations now had to be monitored. Rejecting those conditions, Dana explained in a few words to his client why he had to leave so abruptly. Grimes followed suit, first pressing on Burns his own address and that of Deacon Pitts, in the event that he might be allowed to write from Virginia.[3]

About this time Wendell Phillips arrived to say farewell. When they met it was Burns who spoke first: "Mr. Phillips, has everything been done for me that *can* be done? *Must I go back?*" Phillips' reaction to the question was a complex, indirect survey of the ironies: "I went over in my own mind the history of Massachusetts. I thought of her schools, her colleges of learning, her churches, her courts, her benevolent and philanthropic institutions, her great names, her Puritans, her Pilgrims, and I was obliged to say, 'Burns, there isn't humanity, there isn't Christianity, there isn't justice enough here to save you;

you must go back.' Then I vowed anew before the ever-living God I would consecrate all the powers He had given me to hasten the time when an innocent man should be safe on the sacred soil of the Puritans." Perhaps it really had been about the Puritans all along, about the sacred, mythological soil of sovereign Massachusetts. Even Elizabeth Barrett Browning, in her Florentine villa, had guessed as much.[4]

Hallett wired the president's private secretary, Sidney Webster: "The Commissioner has granted the certificate. Fugitive will be removed to-day. Ample military and police force to effect it peacefully. All quiet. Law reigns. Col. Cooper's arrival opportune." Outside, beyond the cleared square where Grimes and Dana now paced, the crowds in the streets doubled and redoubled. As many as 50,000 people waited restively for a glimpse of the slave in irons.[5]

When Loring's decision came down, the mayor told his assembled police captains that they and their men were to proceed to their assigned positions along State street, close any businesses that remained open, and move the crowds back along the intersecting avenues; if they met with any difficulty, they were to "take care of their own lives, for the military company in State street had orders to fire on the people without notice."[6]

At 11:00, as Burns climbed the stairs for a last hour in the lockup, Captain Joseph K. Hayes tendered his resignation from the police force in a letter handed personally to the mayor. He believed that Smith, who had seemed at first to support the protesters, was now taking orders from Hallett and Freeman. On the strength of that belief, he had spent much of the morning at City Hall monitoring Freeman's movements in and out of the mayor's office. Now, as he said in his letter, he had "received an order which, if performed, would implicate me in the execution of that infamous 'Fugitive Slave Law.'" It was, in other words, an illegal order.[7]

The newspapers were bringing out special editions by the hour, so the resignation became known immediately, and Hayes was a hero before Burns was ever moved. No hint would leak out that his dramatic gesture was linked in any way with the Vigilance Committee or that Hayes was a member. Four days later, Harriet Beecher Stowe would present the ex-captain of police with an inscribed copy of *Uncle Tom's Cabin* in honor of his "noble example . . . of preferring worldly loss rather than a loss of manhood and honor." By then he was back at his old job as chief of security for Tremont Temple, so it is doubtful that he suffered much loss of any kind. Still, the tokens and testimonials poured in. One of the more substantial gifts of money was raised by Ednah Dow Cheney, friend of Bronson Alcott and Moncure Conway and one of the organizers (together with Lucy Stone) of this day's disrupted meeting of the New England Women's Rights convention. Speeches in Hayes's honor were given by Theodore Parker and William Lloyd Garrison. Charles Sumner assured him in a letter that he had done right: "To help enslave a fellow man in Boston cannot be less heinous, in the sight of God, than to do it on the coast of Congo." C. M. Ellis said of Hayes, "In this act of yours, New England spoke"—raising as a rhetorical question the issue of who spoke in the counteract.[8]

The mayor had been distinctly unhappy about the resignation because it threatened a serious derangement in Chief Taylor's plans for crowd control. Smith tried to dissuade Hayes from ruining his career (as he supposed), but his hands were too full just then to spend much time in pleading. He had instead to dash off a note to General Edmands at his post on the Common: "The U.S. Marshal informs me, officially, that he shall be ready to move the escort at precisely half-past 12 o'clock, and you will therefore govern yourself accordingly. Please inform him when all is in readiness."[9]

Smith's note also carried a cryptic postscript—"The boat is at T Wharf"—which alluded to another antislavery defection, as much talked about in the aftermath as the Hayes resignation. Earlier arrangements had the Cutter *Morris* docking at Long Wharf, but the government was at the last minute denied landing rights by Boston shipping magnate John H. Pearson, a man notorious for his prominent role in the capture and return of Sims in 1851. The government was put to some inconvenience by this gesture and had to scramble to come up with an alternative; yet far worse and more hurtful, from their point of view, was Pearson's change of heart. His going over to the abolitionists a repentant sinner made a sharp and forceful political statement. It was the most visible break in the ranks of the wealthy Boston Hunkers and a sign of more to come. "We went to bed one night old fashioned, conservative, Compromise Union Whigs," said Amos A. Lawrence, "and waked up stark mad Abolitionists." A petition for the repeal of the Fugitive Slave Law had been posted at the Exchange and was quickly filled with the names of Boston's commercial elite.[10]

Up and down Court Street and State Street black bunting appeared at the windows, first, it was said, at the Court Square office of John C. Park, a distinguished attorney and commander of the Ancient and Honorable Artillery. Soon the brick facades of buildings all the way down to Commercial Street were dressed in mourning. Rather than endure the danger and commotion on the sidewalks, women gathered in disproportionate numbers at second- and third-story windows in shops and offices along State Street; from these windows they hung out their shawls and mantles as the gloomy flags of their disposition, of hopeless black stuff woven. In addition to the milling thousands on the sidewalks, hundreds more stood on the rooftops gazing down. Work ceased at the Custom House, and merchants and speculators emerged from the Exchange to join the mass. The Woman's Rights Convention adjourned, and ladies in bloomers streamed out of Tremont Temple. Though many of the onlookers were from out of town, radicals and conservatives alike were stunned by the public display and by the altered sentiment of Boston it implied. Henry Bowditch called it a miracle, pointing out that "'Hunker Whigs' and Democrats vied with each other in cursing the whole affair. During the whole day," he said, "I met with but two persons who upheld the proceeding. We formed a ring around these and hissed and hooted them."[11]

Proslavery sentiment was undoubtedly less rare than that. Wendell Phillips and Theodore Parker, who had been together much of the week, left the Court House together. From out of the crowd an excited voice emerged, connected to a leveled arm and pointing finger: "There!" came the cry, "there go the murderers of Batchelder!" Overcome with shame and disgust at Loring's decision and preoccupied with sympathy for Burns, Parker had no thought, kind or cruel, for the dead proslavery Irishman or his ghost. This rude reminder of what the diehard opposition thought—at such a moment—was just about more than the feisty minister could take. A fight nearly broke out.[12]

If, from the scene of this disturbance, one turned to the east and glanced down the line of march toward the harbor a third of a mile away, one could see, near at hand, above the heads of the colorful pinned-back crowd, the landmark Commonwealth Building with its strange tentlike penthouse. This building, one of the tallest secular structures in Boston, housed the offices and printing plant of the city's Freesoil newspaper and was this day the vantage point favored by the radicals for viewing the coming cortège. It seemed to be entirely covered in black cambric. From the upper story six American flags, themselves draped in black, were hung flat against the building's several sides, making one vast national monument of grief and mourning.[13]

Hundreds were gathered at the windows of this building, waiting for the slave to pass, in the meantime watching the infantry (or the visually more interesting plumed cavalry) as they worked to define the street and worked to define the crowd. One of these watchers was Martha Russell, of North Brainford, Connecticut, a writer of New England local-color stories for the Washington-based antislavery journal, the *National Era*. She had been visiting at the home of her kinsman, John Denison Baldwin, editor and business manager of the *Commonwealth*, who a week previously had signed the petition for the use of Faneuil Hall. Baldwin's quiet but central place in the culture of Boston Freesoilism would soon prove useful to Miss Russell, who found herself, just then, confronting a distinctly stratified or politicized literary marketplace. It was Vigilance Committeeman John P. Jewett who in 1856 published her *Stories of New England Life*, after it was turned down, despite Whittier's recommendation, by James T. Fields, of the prestigious house of Ticknor and Fields. Whittier had thought her work more intense and more thoughtful than that of the popular Ticknor author Fanny Forester—whose death in Hamilton, New York, at the age of thirty-seven, would be announced in tomorrow's papers. Today it was Martha Russell's job to deck the national flag in mourning and to hang it out the window.[14]

Below, she could see an outsized coffin, painted black, with the word "Liberty" emblazoned on it. Raised up on ropes above the street, making an ironic triumphal arch for the new Roman legion, this funereal item was the day's most conspicuous piece of protest symbolism. It had been procured by Dr. Thomas P. Knox, who made a precarious living offering medical assistance to the poorest of Boston's black population. More than a year previously, following the death of his infant son, he had come to Boston from Hyannis to take up this mission. He and his wife, having read *Uncle Tom's Cabin*, had connected their own grief (as they were meant to) with the grief of the broken families of slaves. His wife, Angelina J. Knox, now wrote a poem to her husband:

> I love thee well—thy wife and child
>   Are dear to thee as life;
> But, go! for God's sake rescue Burns—
>   Forget thou hast a wife![15]

Diagonally across the street from the Commonwealth Building was the law office of John Albion Andrew, member of the Vigilance Committee, future wartime governor of Massachusetts, and, today, lead counsel for the Court House rioters. This office was another favored gathering place for the friends of the slave, and it too was festooned in black. Ann Warren Weston described the scene in a letter the following week: "I went last Friday morning to Mr. Andrew's office with the most entire hope that Burns would be released. How could I think that Edward Loring could be so terrible a fool, when no decent man *who respected evidence,* could have done otherwise than set him at liberty. This was the popular expectation." News of the stunning decision was brought in by Samuel Johnson, Unitarian minister at Dorchester, who happened also to be a close friend of Higginson's since their days together at the Harvard Divinity School. Andrew's office quickly filled up. Higginson's father-in-law, Dr. Walter Channing, was there along with his nephew, William F. Channing, Edmund Quincy, and a score of others. Off in a corner, Boston Alderman Abel Dunham was "breathing out threatenings and slaughter against the Mayor who had called out this great military force without any consultation."

> At 10 o'clock from above the C[ourt] H[ouse] as far as one could see and down as far as one could see on State St. was one dense and tossing crowd. The windows of every office and place of business were full, the shops shut. The cavalry companies, *Mass[achusetts] companies,* ordered out by the poor little witless small pox Smith, made their appearance. They were received with the loudest groans and hisses, shouts of "Kidnapper! Slave Catcher! Shame! Shame!" . . . For my part, I was sitting in a little side room with Edmund [Quincy] beside me and whenever any cadets or Col. [Thomas C.] Amory [commander of the Corps of Cadets], or any [of] those wicked gentlemen appeared, we called out, Shame and Shame at them in our most expressive and scornful voices. Edmund varied it by the words "Nigger catcher" when he wished to make himself especially odious.[16]

Quincy knew that his nephew Sam was one of the cadets. In a letter a day or two later, he advised him to "drop the name" that he had "disgraced." Many of the soldiers and officers were deeply mortified to be recognized, called out, and cursed by name.[17]

Ann Weston seems not to have known (or from her vantage point not to have noticed) the Reverend James Freeman Clarke, who arrived at Andrew's office from that morning's Unitarian meeting—or two other men: Harvard Divinity student Moncure Conway and Albert G. Browne Sr., the father of a son in jail, Andrew's client, charged with riot for having covered Higginson's retreat from the Court House door with a thrown rock. Andrew himself was in the office for a while around noon, determinedly working at his desk and refusing to acknowledge by any lament or protest what was already an accomplished fact. He had to appear for the rioters before Judge Cushing at the Police Court in a couple of hours, a session originally scheduled for 9:00 A.M. but put off by the excitement.[18]

Lower down the line of intended march, Samuel May, born during the first year of the American Revolution, now seventy-eight years old, a picturesque old man with long white hair, joined his sons in running a rope from the roof of his hardware store at the corner of State and Broad streets to the building opposite, from which he hung two large American flags, union down. A man in the crowd protested the shopkeeper's dishonorable treatment of his country's flag and threatened to tear them both down, but May stayed firm in the ensuing discussion of what patriotism required this day.[19]

The Vigilance Committee had hoped that there would be an interval following Loring's decision when Burns would be in Suttle's private custody, at which time they hoped to get a writ of replevin and serve it—with emphasis. But as it happened, Suttle had exercised his rights under the Fugitive Slave Law, and Burns would have a federal escort all the way to Virginia. Five deputy U.S. marshals were detailed for this purpose, including the notorious Asa Butman. Wendell Phillips mistakenly supposed that this arrangement involved some chicanery or collusion on Loring's part, while Dana mistakenly believed that an opportune interval had in fact occurred, but that no one had been willing to serve the writ. In any event, the last chance for a legal remedy had now passed.[20]

Hamilton Willis made a final attempt to secure Burns's freedom by purchase. With Suttle incommunicado on the *Morris,* Willis approached Thomas and Parker at the Court House, offering again to pay whatever might be asked and to receive Burns either there in State Street or on board the cutter, at the owner's option. Parker was willing to go to Suttle and make the arrangements, but he expected trouble from the marshal in getting permission to board the ship, which (thanks to Pearson) was still riding in the bay. Willis consulted with

Freeman and found that the marshal had no objection to the plan, but Parker, conferring simultaneously with Hallett, was informed that Suttle had made an unambiguous commitment not to sell until after his arrival in Virginia. No doubt he had, though such was also the position that Hallett had been promoting, on orders from Washington, all along. So it seemed that the last chance to keep Burns in Massachusetts by peaceable means had also passed. Willis shortly afterward made an offer to a member of the Vigilance Committee to provide a boat for a rescue. But it was too late for that as well.[21]

Watson Freeman sat nervously in his office and waited for two hours to get word from Edmands that the military situation was under control. At length, hearing nothing, he ordered Edmands to report to him in person. The general, a State Street druggist in civilian life and secretary of the Boston Academy of Music, dashed on horseback from the Common to the Court House and presented himself, explaining that his troops were ready but that the police were disorganized, having left important locations wholly unguarded. His own men had been given orders to reinforce only those positions previously taken up and cleared by the police. Freeman told the general to work it out with the mayor—and quickly.[22]

By 2:00 the militia units had plugged the gaps, and Edmands sent word to Freeman that all was in readiness.

Burns was brought downstairs and out into the bright sunlight through the east door of the Court House, where his shiny new boots made their first acquaintance with the sacred soil of Massachusetts. The new clothes looked fine, a forty-dollar parting gift, as it turned out, from his jailers, who probably knew that slaves got such outfits only when they were being dressed up as merchandise. Burns, who had lodged a strenuous and successful protest against being handcuffed, took his place with Freeman at the center of a hollow square composed of the marshal's guard. Each man of this guard wore a pistol by his left hand and in his right held a government-issue cutlass in a vertical position before him. Thus Burns was described as "hemmed in by a thick-set hedge of gleaming blades." The guard was described as "exceedingly apprehensive."[23]

Ahead of this group was a company of U.S. Marines; ahead of that a company of U.S. Infantry, in for the occasion from Newport, Rhode Island; ahead of that, in the very front, was a company of men on horseback, Boston's "National Lancers." Behind the marshal's guard was a company of Marines, followed by the horse-drawn field piece, manned by six members of the 4th Artillery Regiment. This detachment was escorted and guarded by an additional platoon of Marines. The procession started off at a quick-step at 2:30. Immediately the crowd tried to force its way into the column between the Marines and the rear-facing cannon, but it was forced back by mounted Lancers and other militia units.[24]

Dana could not move in the crowd without attracting attention and what seemed to him the excessively hearty cheers of the people, yet, bumped and jostled, he managed to follow his client at a distance. He was still far to the rear when the procession reached the wharf; what happened there he never saw, but turned off and headed back to his office, where he spent the afternoon in preparing a copy of his closing argument for publication in Saturday's paper.[25]

The procession was a solitary black man walking down the middle of the busiest street in Boston on a Friday afternoon encased in a moving white army. It passed first by the Old State House, near where Crispus Attucks fell at the time of the Boston Massacre—when, as some remembered, State Street was still called King Street. Here a company of cavalry, as ordered, fell into the rear of the column, keeping the inrushing crowd off the cannon and its guard. High up in the nearby Commonwealth Building, Martha Russell sat by the window and watched:

> Did you ever feel every drop of blood in you boiling and seething, throbbing and burning, until it seemed you should suffocate? Did you ever set your teeth hard together to keep down the spirit that was urging you to do something to cool your indignation that good and wise people would call violence—treason[?]
>
> I have felt all this today. I have seen that poor slave, Anthony Burns, carried back into slavery!

She had a good view along Court Square to the west, which appeared to be "one sea of swaying, moving heads"; to the east she could see all the way down State Street to Commercial Street and the Custom House at the head of Long Wharf. She took note of Sam May's two flags and the "black drapery" sprouting everywhere. She watched as the great black coffin was carried in and observed the struggle of the police to confiscate it—"but the men who brought it, aided by the crowd, were too much for them."[26]

In her lengthy report to her cousin, written that day, Martha Russell took the clergy to task, and the nominal Christians they led, for all the pious temporizing in the religious meetings of Anniversary Week:

Mind, I do not censure the clergy entirely for all this; they are but the mouth-pieces of the parishes generally; but I do censure the rich and respectable Christian people here. They did not want the man to go back; they would even have bought him (I am glad they couldn't) a dozen times over, but it was law, and he must go back. If they had but used their private influence with the mayor, with the commissioner, the slave man need not have gone back. Why, General [Henry] Wilson told me yesterday that he and Dr. [Samuel Gridley] Howe went to _____ and begged him to use private influence in favor of the slave, and they were met with excuses, deprecations of the law; but it was law he obeyed. If Henry Wilson had been governor of Massachusetts that slave would never have been sent back . . . I believe such men as Garrison and Theodore Parker are better Christians than men like them. When Garrison got up the other night in the anti-slavery convention he foretold exactly the infamous decision that would be given by the commission[er], and exclaimed in his deep, earnest tones: "Why art thou cast down, O my soul; why art thou disquieted within me; hope thou in God." And added: "In Him do I trust." I felt, let men call him what they will, that man is a Christian.

She went on to describe the procession as it passed before her astonished eyes, giving vent to her anger and amazement at the use of "the city troops with loaded muskets and fixed bayonets" and her disdain for the "ruffians and rowdies" who comprised the marshal's guard.

In the midst of these walked the poor slave, and do you know, cousin, I could have shot that marshal with a right good will, and never been at all troubled at the memory of the deed. I felt such a hardness within me when I thought of him . . . When they had passed, then I wanted to cry, half in joy, half in sorrow and shame; joy to think so many hundred troops were necessary to take one poor black man from Boston; shame that he needs must go. I had only to look around me from the spot where I stood to read the most eloquent history of Massachusetts. On the east rose the majestic spire of Bunker Hill Monument; to the north the great dome of the State House; on the west the spire of Old South Church, and scarcely at the distance of an arrow's flight the cupola of Faneuil Hall. Beyond stretched the beautiful bay of Massachusetts, dotted with white sail and dimpled over with green islands, and over all arched the blue, loving sky of June. In face of all this the deed was done.

Not done without incident, however. From the Commonwealth Building someone produced a shower of cayenne pepper over the troops, and someone else tossed a bottle of sulfuric acid, which, just missing the ducking head of lawyer Joseph W. Coburn, shattered harmlessly on the pavement. Elsewhere on the line of march a cavalryman's horse was bayonetted and had to be destroyed. Another horse was likewise killed when a truckman tried to drive his freight wagon through the police lines. A black man carrying two pistols in his belt was arrested and taken to the Center Watch House.[27]

Sitting at the counter of his father's hardware store, Samuel May Jr. was answering a letter he had just received from Higginson:

> Dear Mr Higginson,
>
> I am now here awaiting the sad procession expected soon to move down Court Street, State St, and Long Wharf, to the U.S. Revenue Cutter "Morris," wherein our poor, outraged brother Anthony Byrnes is to be borne back to Virginia soil, and to be cast into the slave-pens which are the principal characteristics of that old Mother of States. As you will have heard, Commissioner Loring has remanded Byrnes into the hand of his claimant. The Mayor early this morning issued a proclamation

At that moment the soldiers came, interrupting his writing, and then, as a friend described it, "old Sam and his three sons ran out with the most violent hisses and outcries so that the military doubled up their fists at them."[28]

> —here I was called off, and I have seen the cortege—first came a body of troop, with drawn swords; then a large force of police and marines with drawn swords; surrounding a hollow square of the same, in the midst of which walked Byrnes with a face calm and manly, tho' very serious. Next came a large brass field-piece with artillery men, loaded to the muzzle and ready to be discharged, if needed. Then came a force of infantry. And, ever and anon, as the people rushed in behind, and on all sides, with groans and hisses, and many with cheers, companies of mounted horsemen would rush down the streets, dividing and scattering them for a time. *He has gone!* and Boston and Massachusetts lie, bound hand and foot, willing slaves, at the foot of the Slave Power, the most cruel and accursed despotism this poor world has ever been oppressed by. He has gone to the tender mercies of the Slavetraders.

Dr. Henry Bowditch was there in Sam May's store, together with his teenage son, Nat, and his brother, the lawyer William Ingersoll Bowditch. Twice they had seen the troops make feints at the unruly crowd with leveled bayonets, and once they had seen the cavalry charge—"Parisian style"—with drawn swords. It seemed clear to them as they watched that the state militia alone preserved Burns from rescue. "The small corps of villains"—meaning the marshal's guard—"would have been overwhelmed." The same conclusion appeared the next day in virtually all the papers: in the *Commonwealth* it was evidence of the illegal and immoral deployment of the state's military power, a sign of guilt and perfidious weakness in Mayor Smith and Governor Washburn—while in the *Post* it was a satisfying demonstration that a strong militia is the safeguard of the laws. Dr. Bowditch concluded: "The people now are more ripe than ever for revolution." Already, as he stood watching the cortège, he was laying plans for his secret "Anti-Man-Hunting League," the purpose of which would be to kidnap the kidnappers.[29]

Across the street a single black man kept desperate pace with the advancing center of the procession, pushing through the crowd to keep up, distracted, frantically hurling insults at the troops, cursing and gesticulating wildly. What he was doing was more than enough to get him shot under General Edmands' orders, but the police got to him first, wrestled him to the ground, and took him into custody. It was William Jones, the alibi witness. As he was led off, the crowd cheered.[30]

Samuel Gridley Howe was on the sidewalk, perhaps out of sight of this incident. "The most interesting thing I saw in the crowd," he wrote soon after to Horace Mann, "was a comely coloured girl of eighteen, who stood with clenched teeth and fists, and with tears streaming down her cheeks,—the very picture of indignant despair. I could not help saying, 'do not cry, poor girl—he won't be hurt.' 'Hurt!' said she, 'I cry for shame that he will not kill himself!—oh! why is he not man enough to kill himself!'" Howe was deeply shocked by the fierceness of this notion, coming as it did from such a pleasing, picturesque, sentimental slip of inoffensive negritude, but the more he thought about it the more he liked it. Yes, emphatically, this was a good idea. "There was the intuition, the blind intuition of genius!" wrote Howe: "had he, then and there, struck a knife into his own heart, he would have killed outright the fugitive slave law in New England and the

North." He must have thought the girl was offering a solution to *his* problem. In fact, he hadn't a clue to what she meant.[31]

One wonders if it might not have been Charlotte Forten whom he had run into that day, who was sixteen then and regarded as "a handsome girl, delicate, slender, and with a finely chiseled countenance which revealed in the lightness of the skin a trace of white blood among her ancestors." She would write that evening in her journal:

> Our worst fears are realized; the decision was against poor Burns, and he has been sent back to a bondage worse, a thousand times worse than death. Even an attempt at rescue was utterly impossible; the prisoner was completely surrounded by soldiers with bayonets fixed, a cannon loaded, ready to be fired at the slightest sign. To-day Massachusetts has again been disgraced; again she has shewed her submission to the Slave Power; and Oh! with what deep sorrow do we think of what will doubtless be the fate of that poor man, when he is again consigned to the horrors of Slavery. With what scorn must that government be regarded, which cowardly assembles thousands of soldiers to satisfy the demands of slaveholders; to deprive of his freedom a man, created in God's own image, whose sole offense is the color of his skin! And if resistance is offered to this outrage, these soldiers are to shoot down American citizens without mercy; and this by the express orders of a government which proudly boasts of being the freest in the world; this on the very soil where the Revolution of 1776 began; in sight of the battle-field, w[h]ere thousands of brave men fought and died in opposing British tyranny, which was nothing compared with the American oppression of to-day . . . I can write no more. A cloud seems hanging over me, over all our persecuted race, which nothing can dispel.[32]

Bronson Alcott watched the procession "sadly." He confided to his journal that he was "ashamed of the Union, of New England, of Boston, almost of myself, too." That day's spectacle had made a difference in his life: he vowed, in what amounted to a break with Garrison, to vote—to vote for the first time in his life. "I must see to it that my part is done hereafter to give us a Boston, a mayor, a Governor, and a President, if, indeed, a single suffrage or many can mend matters materially." Perhaps the country could be saved from slavery if better men were in office—"yet something besides voting must do it effectually."[33]

The procession was nearing the end of its march. When it arrived at the Merchants' Exchange, the very heart of commercial Boston, the militiamen posted there indulged their cruel wit with a chorus of "Carry Me Back to Old Virginny," a popular minstrel song. It was later credibly reported that these soldiers—along with a good many others—were drunk. It is not surprising that much attention was paid to the inebriated condition of the men under arms, since the temperance movement, especially strong following the adoption of the Maine Law, enjoyed wide support in antislavery circles. One officer, Colonel Isaac H. Wright, leader of the Massachusetts troops during the Mexican War and now commander of a company of Light Dragoons, was held up to special ridicule for falling off his horse while trying to run down a citizen. He compounded his infamy shortly afterward by protesting the passage of a state law that offered to interrupt the traditional whiskey rations for the troops. But reform held on this point, and guns and liquor were officially separated in government policy: Jefferson Davis, as secretary of war, would abolish liquor rations for the regular army in November of this year.[34]

The procession at last reached Commercial Street near the docks, and had to make a sharp turn to the left just where the crowd was thickest and most boisterous. This was predominantly a rough shirt-sleeve crowd of sailors and dock workers, supplemented at the last moment by a rush of onlookers from the Custom House. This crucial section of the route—indeed the whole of Commercial Street from Market to State—was guarded by militia Company A, Fifth Regiment of Artillery, under Captain Thomas C. Evans, a man who by this time had lost all patience with the public. Evans assaulted a heckler named Haskell, cutting him on the hand with his sword. When Haskell demanded to know what Evans' business was, the captain cried, "to kill just such damned rascals as you are!" The situation was markedly worse than anywhere else along the line. Too many people were being forced into too small an area; teamsters trying to get their wagons across the street were daring the soldiers to fire. At one point, Evans ordered his men to face about and present arms, and seemed to have every intention of giving the order to shoot, when a superior officer, Major John C. Boyd, interfered, seeing that the mob was about to yield. Nevertheless, various people were badly beaten, including William Ela, a druggist's stockboy in from Roxbury on an errand. The bottle of ink he had been told by his employer to purchase was mistaken by the soldiers for vitriol and stricken from his hand; the boy was so severely butted about the head by the musket-wielding troops that the crowd had to intervene to save his life. The Reverend Whittemore witnessed the assault: after interrogating Captain Adams, he had followed the procession all the way down from the Court House, and some weeks later testified when Ela sued the city for leaving him brain-damaged, as Dr. Bowditch himself testified he was.[35]

The procession reached T Wharf at last, and Burns was put aboard a steamer, the *John Taylor,* for transport out to the *Morris* at Minot's Light. Considerable delay occurred as the soldiers labored to mount the cannon on the aft deck of the boat under a continuous volley of curses from sailors all around. At 3:20 the steamer left the wharf, threading its way among the many small craft that had massed in the harbor to bear witness.[36]

 ## GOING HOME

'Tis over now—the darkest day—
Return we in the twilight's gloom;
We've seen th'oppressor bear away
The victim to his doom.

GEORGE W. PUTNAM, "TO COMMISSIONER LORING"

I think no great public calamity, not the death of Webster, not the death of Sumner, not the loss of great battles during the War, brought such a sense of gloom over the whole State as the surrender of Anthony Burns.

GEORGE FRISBIE HOAR

It was time to go home. The Reverend George Osgood of Standish, Maine, one of thousands of New England pilgrims in for the conferences of Anniversary Week, had been distracted and overwhelmed by the slave case. Now he would take back to his people a message different from any he had thought to come for. Heading out the harbor, heading north, the country preacher gazed—almost, but not quite, from Burns's perspective—at the spectacular receding city: "How glad I was to look back from the Portland Steamer on that Friday evening and watch the sun as it went down over the smoke and dust of the City and then set round and red behind Bunker Hill Monument, which seemed to stand like a bar in its centre." He was glad because, having seen firsthand all the moral drama of the day, he concluded that the people, "beneath their love of order and peace, had a still deeper love for freedom and a deeper hatred of slavery than they had known before."

His own antislavery sentiments had been sorely tried that morning by the sectarian evasions of the Unitarian conference, "where quite a number of speakers spoke of faith and love and told a great many excellent truths which were very beautiful," but which—though indeed he remembered James Freeman Clarke's prayer for the slave—gave him an opportunity to play the part of the Lone Concerned: "I had the rudeness to rise and break the calm and beautiful current of their feelings by telling them, that I believed in man! in the man created in the Image of God, the man into whose bosom cometh the true light, that lighteth every man that cometh into the world, the man for whose sake Christ lived, toiled, suffered and died. The man who for no crime but the natural depravity (of which sin God was the Author) of having a skin darker than our own, was imprisoned in Boston!"[1]

Out-scattering from Boston that evening were a multitude of such private purposes—angled, cracked agendas, trivial ones and important ones—to which had been subordinated in settled righteousness a renovated solidarity with the slave. If Osgood thought, with many besides slaveholders, that black skin was God's lasting blight and curse on one of Noah's sons, then antislavery was a holy generosity, a testimony at once to Christ's redemptive power and to our own magnanimous way of overlooking the divine discreditation. Feeling an interest in the imperiled slave was good in itself, but better yet, it seemed, for ends still more remote. To look at the slave was always in some way to overlook him. Such polite racism as Osgood's made it inevitable that he should care more for the religious abstraction (the key to his own professional identity) than for any particular "Image of God," however threatened.

It takes some getting used to—this notion that an approach so self-centered, so "interested," so evidently wide of the mark, can be a legitimate style of caring. It seems to erase the object of solicitude or to sink it in other matters. Yet this style is pretty much what the masculine culture of New England had to work with in 1854, and indeed the male leaders of opinion worked with it, on the whole, rather effectually. To do this style justice, it might be understood as a way of balancing self and other: if it looks at times as though the pitiful object of attention is being made use of to advance the personal goals of a relatively privileged insider, it may also be seen as a means by which selfishness mitigates its lack of contact with an outside—how, in other words, it develops *toward* an authentic generosity. It is not, after all, the perfection of indifference.

The coastal steamers out of Boston were full that evening, and so were the inland trains: full of men and women, full themselves of stories to tell at home in Providence, New Bedford, Worcester, Essex County, and the North Shore. Anthony Burns would serve for a time as a bond of neighborhood. The poet Whittier, unable for the past week to wander far from his sickbed, found himself greeting the outbound cars at Amesbury:

> I heard the train's shrill whistle call,
>   I saw an earnest look beseech,
>   And rather by that look than speech
> My neighbor told me all.

Having been misunderstood and misread when he tried in prose to explain to Dr. Bowditch his desire to have a moral and physical presence in Boston, he would now make a poem that no one could misconstrue, a statement owing much of its force to the fact of his not having been there. Absence had meant not seeing, and yet the spectacle, even in the aftermath, promoted looking over speaking, merged meaning with feeling and put both beyond the reach of words.

> And, as I thought of Liberty
>   Marched hand-cuffed down that sworded street,
>   The solid earth beneath my feet
> Reeled fluid as the sea.

In his absence, Whittier stands for all those who would receive the news as an appeal to the imagination, where, if anywhere, the passing shadow and act could have a lasting life. The permanent or persistent event would be a shaped and molded thing—a work of art, in other words, constructed by a presence merely imaginative, or by a process more akin to bringing the thing into one's home than of leaving one's home for its sake, as Martin Stowell had tragically done (Stowell, who thought he had killed a man, and would never go home again).

Burns was not handcuffed, as Whittier might have known had he been there, but the inaccuracy betokens a connection between imaginative freedom and humane compassion that could only have been damaged by exposure to the actual event. In imagination, the particular victim subsides (or expands) into a representation of Liberty—not the slave's liberty, but Liberty in general—shackled and held in by what can never be generalized or lifted clear of the detail, the handcuffs. The very incongruity of the emblem is disconcerting, even dizzying, putting all solid certainty into a state of fluid chance.

> I felt a sense of bitter loss—
>> Shame, tearless grief, and stifling wrath,
>> And loathing fear, as if my path
> A serpent stretched across.

Describing the feeling of a chance encounter with a snake, Emily Dickinson chose the memorably evocative phrase "zero at the bone." But this poet on this occasion wants to suggest the limits of language, not its power to express feeling, pursuing the theme he started in the first stanza. An important part of the "loss" he has suffered (and is now suffering) is that of the poet's privilege both to have feelings and to name them. The evil is felt, not seen, and the response—"tearless grief" and "stifling wrath"—suggests the compounding of strong emotions by the impossibility of expressing them adequately. Indeed, the emotional constriction is very much like Liberty in handcuffs. In the exasperated inarticulateness of the lines, language is represented as exceeded, and the party of the word, in the figure of the poet excluded from the scene of action, is at a genuine crisis.

> All love of home, all pride of place,
>> All generous confidence and trust,
>> Sank smothering in that deep disgust
> And anguish of disgrace.

Many of the reactions to the Burns case remind us how common it was to suppose that all of politics—perhaps all of law and government—is in the end to be viewed as a defense of the home. The American Revolution was, in the public's estimation, fought from and over a few million private homes. All that ever changed in the controversies of politics were the ideas about what secures the home or what threatens its value. What mainly persists is the strength and sensitivity of this home-loving, home-protecting motive, by which a particular legal travesty in Boston can seem to undermine the granite foundations of houses throughout the Commonwealth. The commitment of the state to a policy of injustice, or its refusal to defend its established liberties, casts a pall over its whole territory, directly touching the basis on which homes are held sacred.

> Down on my native hills of June,
>   And home's green quiet, hiding all,
>   Fell sudden darkness like the fall
> Of midnight upon noon!

Recollections of the previous week's eclipse suffuse the poem. Home is natural and normative; a sudden unseeing is what descends out of nowhere upon it.

> And Law, an unloosed maniac, strong,
>   Blood-drunken, through the blackness trod,
>   Hoarse-shouting in the ear of God
> The blasphemy of wrong.

An apocalyptic image: is Law the bringer of darkness or is it merely shielded by this blindness of unnatural night? And shielded from whom? What champion will vindicate the ways of God against the laws of man?

> "O, Mother, from thy memories proud,
>   Thy old renown, dear Commonwealth,
>   Lend this dead air a breeze of health,
> And smite with stars this cloud.

> "Mother of Freedom, wise and brave,
>   Rise awful in thy strength," I said;
>   Ah, me! I spake but to the dead;
> I stood upon her grave!

Whittier's poem, titled "The Rendition," shapes the event as threat but at the same time conveys the powerlessness of language to oppose it.[2] The bardic invocation of New England's traditionary "Gray Champion" to rise up and defend the cause of liberty fails. The "loss" is not just of the quiet, secessionist enjoyment of home. It is not an individual loss at all but turns out to be that entailed by a broad encompassing principle of death, general throughout the land, which utterly changes the ground we stand on. The speaker's hope and trust had been vested in the continuity of old, historic virtues, but these are now honored in their names only. The marrow of divinity has not survived the worship service. In the end, the poet can imagine a better result than reality provides and can even state that result in language, but the poem is manifestly incomplete, a hollow form of words to be filled, completed, and made effectual, if at all, by the realized will of the people, who may yet rise up and again defend their homes. The party of the word dead-ends into the party of deeds at the point of revolution.

Dana finished the foreshortened, authorized version of his closing argument and sent it off to the Boston *Traveller* by 8:30 that evening, then went to the Parker House for tea with court reporter Horace Gray. There they happened to meet Vigilance Committeeman Anson Burlingame, who, seeing that the nine o'clock omnibus had already left, offered to walk Dana out to his home in suburban Cambridge. As they strolled up Court Street toward Bowdoin Square, Dana thought he caught a glimpse of some commotion out of the corner of his eye, but it was not warning enough to prepare him for the crushing blow that followed, delivered across his right eye from behind as he turned. The force of it shattered his glasses and sent him staggering into the street. He was never sure afterward whether he had actually fallen to the ground or lost consciousness; his recollection was of the passersby who tended to his bleeding wound and explained to him what had happened. Meanwhile Burlingame took off after the pair of attackers. These he pursued through Allen's saloon to the alley in back, then into a gambling den on Stoddard Street, where he was finally turned back by a group of rowdies who meant to protect their own.[3]

The assailants, with certain of their friends—all of whom were discharged and paid-off members of the marshal's guard—had been celebrating the reenslavement of Burns in Allen's saloon when they spotted Dana coming up the street. Two of them, Luigi Varelli and Henry Huxford, fell in behind the lawyer and his friend, and at the moment of the attack, Varelli grabbed Dana's walking stick and pushed Burlingame aside while Huxford delivered the blow, perhaps with his fist, probably with a billy club.

Varelli, known around town as Louis Varell, Louis Bieral, Louis Clark, or "Spanish Lew," was the leader of a Boston crime syndicate involved in gambling, prostitution, illegal liquor sales, "horse-racing, dog-fighting, prize-fighting, and other equally reputable employments." Born of Portuguese parents in Valparaiso, Chile, and banished from San Francisco by that city's Vigilance Committee, he had come to Boston in 1852. Shortly thereafter he was tried and acquitted for the murder of his paramour, whom he was alleged to have thrown off the Charlestown bridge. When Watson Freeman found himself in need of a large number of intimidating men to serve in his personal guard, he turned naturally to Peter Dunbar of the Custom House and to Luigi Varelli of Stoddard Street.

Henry Huxford, an Irishman who also used the name Bill Sullivan, was a sometime prize-fighter and all-around thug; he was employed by Varelli as an enforcer, or, in the language of that day, a "shoulder-hitter." Despite Dana's publicly expressed view of the marshal's guard, Huxford held no grudge against him, but consented to the attack merely to ingratiate himself with his boss. Huxford was soon arrested by a tough little bounty-hunter named "Cocky" Heath who was in it entirely for the reward that the city was offering. Shortly after his arraignment, however, Huxford fled to New Orleans, skipping bail posted by Varelli, whose involvement in the assault was not yet suspected. Varelli's standing in the criminal world depended on not being successfully crossed by underlings, so he boldly joined forces with Heath to procure Huxford's extradition back to Boston and, further, arranged the perjured testimony that sent Huxford to prison for two years. It had to be perjured testimony, since the real witnesses whom Varelli could easily have produced might have implicated him in the attack.[4]

This cowardly assault by lower-class immigrants was easily discriminated in the public mind from the heroic assault on the Court House, mounted by sons of Puritans. Sympathy flowed in upon the battered lawyer, the proslavery style was clarified, and with nothing worse than a black eye and a few chipped teeth, Dana joined the roster of antislavery martyrs. Yet his brother-in-law wrote to say that "a lawyer, sworn to support the Constitution of the United States as the Supreme Law of the land, who indulges in such seditious sneers at that Law as I was sorry to see in your exordium—sooner or later and in one way or another, upon general principles of retributive Justice, will receive a thwack for it somewhere. I am happy that your thwack is no worse." Dana saved this letter.[5]

Another drama was taking place during the evening of that dramatic day. Even as Dana was being mugged in Court Street, the curtain was up at the Howard Athenaeum for the final appearance of Mrs. Anna

Cora Mowatt, thirty-five-year-old darling of Boston playgoers and by any measure the preeminent actress in America. As was customary in the theater, the last performance of the run was a benefit for the lead actor; but this was to be not only her farewell to Boston, where her career had begun a dozen years before, but also a farewell to the acting profession itself, for the still sprightly and alluring widow was four days hence to marry William Foushee Ritchie, editor of the Richmond *Enquirer,* the abolitionist-denouncing "Democratic Bible" of the South.

Anticipating the close of her career, she had two months before published her memoirs with Ticknor and Fields. By now the *Autobiography of an Actress* had sold 20,000 copies, augmenting her already substantial celebrity and contributing to the importance of today's performance. Tracy Cheever, the lawyer who had watched the crowds in Court Square through his office window, was determined to attend, "resolved from my interest in her romantic and almost heroic life, and the virtues of her character, to be present and hear the last words pronounced by her from the stage." Indeed "the virtues of her character" were the core of her appeal; entering the world of acting as a respectable and educated young middle-class lady, she had been personally responsible for breaking down much of the old moralistic prejudice against the theater, and in particular made women comfortable about attending. Her audiences were still predominantly masculine, however: a great many men, like Cheever—or Ritchie—found her comparatively refined and delicately emotive manner deeply charming. Cheever succeeded this day in getting his ticket, though the fierce demand and swarming crowds had driven the scalpers' price for box seats up to an unheard-of twenty dollars. It is not recorded what the going price was for tickets to the black gallery in this segregated theater. Charlotte Forten's friend Caroline Putnam, whose daughter was married the day before in Salem, had once been roughed up by the manager of the Howard Athenaeum when she had refused to sit where she was told. And he had a policeman's help in doing it.[6]

This evening Mrs. Mowatt would play Parthenia in *Ingomar,* as she had done many times before. She was always emotional on benefit nights, however, and she had more reasons than usual to be anxious now. Ending a long and wearying tour, she was headed to a new life and a new home where she would have slaves to command. She would, tomorrow, leave Boston for Virginia, if by a different route than Burns was taking, still, like him, to join the household of a slaveowner. Mrs. Mowatt was no abolitionist, but she was, for all her moderate and accepting views, a Northerner, a child of New York. Apparently willing to give slavery a try—even to embrace it as a part of new duties—she nevertheless felt the institution was unsound, unfortunate from a moral standpoint, and destined in the fullness of time to disappear.

No one can say what was on her mind that night, but it is certain that the performance was a rocky one. Parthenia took an undignified tumble in the second act, so severely injuring her arm as to lead her to think it was broken. She troupered through the final act with her arm in a sling. When the performance was over the applause was loud and long drawn out. Mrs. Mowatt stepped up to the footlights and, after quieting the audience, made a speech of farewell, in the course of which she pointed to the remarkable progress Boston had made in improving the moral climate of public dramatic performances, one reform, at least, that she had consistently encouraged. She was probably referring most of all to the action of Josiah Quincy, who as mayor eight years earlier had outlawed the third or prostitutes' row in the legitimate theaters. No aspect of public life, it seemed, was immune from the standard of private morality.[7]

Mrs. Mowatt proceeded immediately to New York and to her wedding, which was attended by Democratic Senator Stephen A. Douglas, author of the Kansas-Nebraska Act. Mrs. Ritchie and her new husband honeymooned at Fauquier Springs, Virginia, within a few miles of the church to which Anthony Burns still belonged but was not at the moment attending. Her new and rather splendid home in Richmond was before long an unhappy one, and it would seem that Mr. Ritchie's special fondness for the slave girls had much to do with the difficulty. Before the Civil War broke out, the couple were living apart: in fact Mrs. Ritchie fled the marital home and took up residence in Europe. Yet in Virginia, before this breach developed, she had found the great mission of her later life: working with an invalid Southern matron, Ann Pamela Cunningham, and with the nation's greatest orator, Edward Everett, she became strongly identified with the movement to purchase and restore the Mount Vernon estate of George Washington, America's ur-home.[8]

🌿 REPUBLICANS

[A] *politician* in the service of a *party* cannot be trusted.

CHARLES SUMNER TO HORACE MANN, AUGUST 5, 1850

On Saturday Whittier wrote to William Lloyd Garrison, with whom, in 1833, he had cooperated to form the American Antislavery Society. It was Garrison who at that time had diverted Whittier from a farmer's life and given him the mission that first made and still sustained his reputation as America's foremost antislavery poet. Despite the profound disagreement that had grown up between them over the usefulness of political action in abolition work, Whittier wrote to him and renewed his subscription to the *Liberator*.

He said that he agreed with Garrison's published remarks at the previous week's antislavery convention in regard to the present duty of the friends of freedom.

> We must do what has never been done, convert the North. We must use this sad and painful occasion for this purpose. We must forget all past differences, and unite our strength . . . Get the people of the State right, and there will be no more of those hateful Commissioner trials; but around every inhabitant will be thrown the protection of just laws.

To Whittier and to thousands of others who meant to look on the Burns case as a catalyst for new or renewed effort, it seemed clear how dangerous, how destructive of all liberty, the attachment to Webster's Union had become. The emancipation of the slave would never be realized if the idea of liberty—which flourished in New England if it flourished anywhere—were to find itself in retreat or wholly offered up for tranquillity's sake. "If I had any love for the union remaining," he wrote to Garrison, "the events of the last few weeks have 'crushed it out.'" Still he could not bring himself to Garrison's position of immediate and absolute disunion:

> I do not forget that the same power which is needed to break from the Union may make the Union the means of abolishing slavery. At any rate, what we want now is an *abolitionized North*. To this end Unionists and Disunionists can both contribute. At least, let us have *union among ourselves*. In our hatred of slavery, our sympathy for our afflicted colored brethren, and in our indignation against the oppressor, we are already united,—and let us now unite, as far as may be, in action.[1]

Action. Had Higginson somehow redefined the term for Whittier? Was Higginson not, in the desperate heroism of a grand failure, a forerunning hint of that champion whom the poet was invoking? Surely he was something like that figure of militant liberty, who (if not dead, if not part of the unreturning past) might yet be expected to rise awful in his strength and "smite with stars this cloud." Higginson, it seems, was thinking along the same lines, and wondering if his Quaker friend altogether meant what he was saying. The poem was not yet published, but he had seen Whittier's retraction in the *Times* of his ambiguous letter to Dr. Bowditch, and wondered whether its proscription against violence didn't amount to a disavowal of himself. He wrote to Whittier, and on Sunday Whittier replied: "Reproach thee, dear friend!—God forbid. If I cannot counsel other than passive resistance to that accursed law,—I love and honor not the less those who act from their deep impulses of humanity. Believe me (whatever may be thy feeling towards myself) thou art dearer to me than ever."[2]

Whittier's pacifism was profound and genuine, but that it was also under siege made him distinctly uncomfortable. How odd, he may have thought, that poetry and the artistic imagination should accommodate with such ease things that continued unresolved in the conscience. Poetry seemed in its very nature to value heroic confrontation and was better adapted to issuing calls to arms than to airing real scruples over how the evil was to be beaten back. As Emerson was writing now in the privacy of his journal, "Liberty is aggressive. Liberty is the crusade of all brave and honest men. It is the epic poetry, the new religion, the chivalry of all gentlemen. This is the oppressed Lady whom all true Knights on their oath and honor must rescue and save." The Burns case and Higginson's act were imperious new variables reforming the sense of what heroism and courage were; they gave standards to every man's unavoidable rephrasing of the question, what was to be done? The greatly increased plausibility that a revolutionary physical intervention would prove necessary became something that one's fears had to be adjusted to. Some of this thinking—all of it experimental, to be sure—can be glimpsed in another of Emerson's journal entries of 1854: "I am here to represent humanity: it is by no means necessary that I should live, but it is by all means necessary that I should act rightly. If there is danger, I must face it. I tremble. What of that? So did he who said, 'It is my body that trembles, out of knowing into what dangers my spirit will carry it.'" Everyone's sense of what "doing something" could mean had received an unsettling shock, allowing for an inrush of that idealism of which poetry approved.[3]

A few days after sending off his letter to Higginson, Whittier published a brief article in the *Commonwealth* titled "A Convention of the People." In it he called for the formation of a new political party out of the ruins of the old—which, it would seem, is what he had meant in inviting Garrison to unite with him in action. In the article he wrote that "the eyes of the people of the North—of Massachusetts at least—must now be fully opened to the true character and designs of the slave power. They have seen and felt what slavery is. The iron has been driven deep into their souls. A darker, sadder spectacle than that exhibited in Boston last week, the sun of the nineteenth century has never looked upon." In proposing a fusion of Freesoilers, anti-Nebraska Whigs, and Democrats, Whittier observed that "Massachusetts is called upon to take the first step in this great movement." Here was the beginning of the Republican party in Massachusetts.[4]

It belonged to the apocalyptic temper of that time that disaster was welcome and the upheavals preluding revolution were actively encouraged. No painful, disorganizing event but held out to the radicals the promise of the last collapse of an unacceptable old order. A new appreciation for the usefulness of death and defeat took general hold and quite eliminated the sense of discouragement. Dana, for example, wrote to Edmund Quincy on June 5: "The issue has been unfortunate for the poor fugitive, but I firmly believe that the entire transaction, from its beginning to its ending, has been over-ruled for the best purposes of impression on the feelings and understandings of men." Dana's father, who had attended all the sessions of the trial, wrote on the same day: "There must be a Northern Power, saying nothing about Whig or Demo. or Free-Soiler; but Richard thinks the time is not yet come to organize regularly, that the leaven must work more first." Ellis, too, was encouraged; he thought that "it matters little what the cause is that starts the slide; once in motion, it must go on."[5]

Others thought the time *had* come for regular organizing, and the first and unlikeliest among these was Ralph Waldo Emerson.

Like Thoreau, Emerson had stayed at home in Concord during the excitement. He had been working with the exceptionally resistant materials for his next book, *English Traits,* and was frustrated with his lack of progress. Deep in his work, he wrote no letters at this time and discouraged all visitors but family. His eldest daughter, Ellen, aged fifteen, was at home on vacation from her boarding school in the Berkshires, and Emerson would give to the narrow circle of family and Concord neighbors what time he could spare from his writing. His private journals express his anger and disgust over the slave case, and no doubt his wife, Lidian, with her long-settled antislavery views, was no less upset. Of her reaction we know only that on June 18 Emerson described her as "my poor broken-to-pieces wife," and that on the Fourth of July following, she got her husband's permission to drape the gateposts at their home in black. Ellen's vacation must have been seriously darkened by the emotional tenor at home by the time she had to return to school on June 5, when her father escorted her to the railroad depot at Boston. It was the first time in more than a month that Emerson had been in town. He met Alcott that day, who must have spoken to him of what he had seen and done the momentous week before.[6]

On June 9 Emerson wrote his first letter ever to Charles Sumner, a letter of commendation and encouragement for the senator's noble but unavailing speeches against the Nebraska Bill. On the sixteenth, Emerson was back in Boston, on his way to Cambridge for a rare dinner with Longfellow. While in the city, Emerson encountered the changed opinion that Dana and others had remarked on and "was edified, as never before, by the conversation of lawyers and merchants. They were stung by being cheated,—cheated and insulted by the riffraff of the streets . . . I came home," he said in this second letter to Sumner, "with more confidence in the future of Massachusetts than I have felt for many a day." He concluded this letter, sent on June 17, with a paragraph commending their mutual friend Higginson, saying, "It is only they who save others, that can themselves be saved."[7]

By this time Emerson was caught up in a plan, apparently hatched between himself and his neighbor Samuel Hoar, to convene a mass protest meeting at Concord Town Hall on June 22, a meeting to organize antislavery feeling in the state and at the same time protest the Kansas-Nebraska Act. Emerson spent this entire week "collect[ing] the materials," getting posters printed, and writing letters of invitation as head of the Committee of Correspondence. He was also on the committee that drew up the resolutions, which were subsequently printed over his name in the *Liberator:*

> *Resolved,* That the citizens of Concord, whose fathers were among the first to resist the tyranny of 1775, will not be the last to resist that of 1854.
> *Resolved,* That the passage of the Nebraska and Kansas bills by the

present Congress, is an unprovoked and wanton outrage upon the principles and feelings of the freemen of the North and West, and destroys all confidence in the integrity, good faith and honor of the national government.

Resolved, That the Compromise of 1820 was in the nature of a compact between the slaveholding and non-slaveholding States, and inasmuch as that compact has been repudiated by one party, the other party is thereby absolved from all the obligations supposed to be imposed by it. Therefore,

Resolved, That the free States are at full liberty to resist the admission of any slave State into the Union hereafter, and that it is their solemn duty so to do.

Resolved, That the whole system of compromise measures has received a fatal stab in the house of its friends, and the Fugitive Slave Law of 1850 was a part of that system, and cannot stand without that support. Therefore,

Resolved, That the Fugitive Slave Law of 1850 must be repealed.

The Concord meeting urged a united opposition to further encroachments of the slave power and finished by calling for a general convention of all who could support these resolutions, to be held at the Hanover House in Boston on July 7.[8]

That meeting and the one in Concord were the first in Massachusetts specifically designed to bring into existence a new antislavery party, but the Whigs who might have joined still hoped that in this newly altered climate their own party could be made a vehicle for antislavery; the result was that those attending both of Emerson's conventions were mainly Freesoilers. The Boston meeting, which Emerson attended with Samuel Hoar and his son George on the seventh and eighth, ended feebly when it was learned that a yet larger and more promising convention was to be gathered later in the month at Worcester, organized by Seth Webb Jr., the lawyer who had been so active about the edges of the Burns case and who had, at last, put the battering ram to the Court House door. On July 20 the new party was born and baptized at Worcester—indeed, in the same building where, six years earlier, the Freesoil party had sprung to life. The Worcester Republicans called for a nominating convention in September, which in due course put Henry Wilson forward as its candidate for governor.[9]

This infant party, as George F. Hoar later said, was but a continuation of the old Freesoil party under a change of name. If the attempt at a genuine political fusion was widely conceded to be a failure, it was not, as the fall elections would show, a sign that the people were unprepared for wholesale change. The initial weakness of the state Republican party was that, in its challenge to established party allegiances, it was not quite radical, not quite novel, not quite angry enough. A more powerful solvent was required than a group of Freesoilers under any name could supply in undoing the structure of government—even if it did have all the best and most polished speakers. Henry Wilson was far from alone in recognizing at this time that "the demolition of the Whig and Democratic parties by the American [or Know-Nothing] party might produce a political chaos out of which a new and better creation might soon spring." The radicals, standing consciously at the point of crisis and praying for chaos, saw that the most advantageous next development was the utter destruction of what has come to be known as the "Second Party system" in American politics.[10]

CARRIED BACK

"Master Charles, what are you going to do with me?"
"What do you think I *ought* to do, Tony?"
"I expect you will sell me."
Col. Suttle replied that Anthony had caused him great expense, that his lawyers' fees alone had been four hundred dollars; but he left unanswered the slave's anxious inquiry.

CHARLES E. STEVENS

We rejoice at the recapture of Burns, but a few more such victories and the South is undone.

RICHMOND *ENQUIRER,* June 2, 1854

The *Morris* met with a patch of heavy seas between Cape Cod and Long Island, and because the traveling was uncomfortable, Suttle and Brent transferred to a passing steamer inbound for New York, to continue the trip by land. Burns and the five deputies continued on, arriving at Norfolk on June 10. The most famous slave in America was met at dockside by the mayor, who had him immediately escorted to the city jail; the deputies, meanwhile, were treated to a fancy public dinner. Burns was "quite communicative," according to the Norfolk *Herald,* about his disappointment with life in Boston. He was reported to have said that there were many unemployed Negroes there. The sailors on the ship that took him north had told him he was headed for a land of milk and honey and would want for nothing in the city, yet it took him a month to find any work at all, and in the meantime he was "half starved and ragged as a buzzard."

> None of his abolition friends cared for him until they found out that he was a "runaway nigger," and then they were ready enough to help him. A common nigger there (he said) was of no account with them—he might starve and rot; but if he was only a "runaway," they were almost ready to fall down and worship him. "Look at these clothes," said he, pointing to the elegant dress suit he had on—"do you think they would have given them to any common nigger? Shugh!"

Anthony Burns was home. He had not forgotten how to talk to white men in the South.[1]

On June 12 he was transported by the steamer *Jamestown* to Richmond and spent the next ten days in jail, while the deputies, following a second dinner in their honor, headed back North. On June 22 Brent at last arrived on the scene and ordered Burns incarcerated in the notorious slave-pen operated by Robert Lumpkin. This was a massive three-story brick building just outside the city, situated on an acre of ground and enclosed by a high barricade topped with iron spikes. Burns was handcuffed and chained at the ankles, thrown into a hot, unventilated room six feet by eight feet immediately below the roof, and left there for four months. His daily fare was a single portion of cornbread and putrid bacon; water was supplied once a week in a bucket. Because his chains and manacles never came off, neither did his clothes. There were no toilet facilities.[2]

Alexandria Va
27th June 1854
Hamilton Willis Esqr—

Sir

I have had much difficulty in my own mind, as to the course I ought to pursue about the sale of my man Anthony Burns to the North. Such a sale is objected to strongly by my friends and by the people of Virginia generally, upon the ground of its pernicious character, inviting our negroes to attempt their escape, under the assurance, that if arrested and remanded, still, the money would be raised to purchase their freedom. As a Southern man and a slave owner I feel the force of this objection and clearly see the mischief that may result from disregarding it.

Still I feel no little attachment to Anthony, which his late elopement, [with] the vexation and expense to which I have been put, has not removed, and I confess to some disposition to see the experiment tried of bettering his condition.

I understand the application now made to purchase his freedom, does not come from the abolitionists and incendiaries who put the laws of the Union at defiance, and dyed their hands in the blood of Batchelder, but from those who struggled to maintain law and order.

Now that the laws have been fully vindicated (although at the point of a bayonet) and Anthony returned to the city of Richmond, from which he escaped; and believing that it would materially strengthen the Federal Officers and facilitate the execution of the laws in any future case which might arise, and influenced by other considerations to which I have referred, I have concluded to sell him his freedom for the sum of fifteen hundred dollars.

When in Boston, acting under the extraordinary counsel of Mr. Parker, one of my lawyers, I agreed to take twelve hundred dollars if paid at a fixed period. The money was not forthcoming at the time agreed upon, and I then, being better advised, determined the law should take its course.

By the course pursued of violent, corrupt, and perjured opposition to my rights, the case was protracted for days after my offer to take twelve hundred dollars; consequently my expenses were generally increased, I presume materially so as to my attorneys, to whom I paid from my private purse four hundred dollars.

Now as I am not a man of wealth and am bound to have a moderate regard for my private interest, it will readily be seen that twelve hundred dollars at the time I agreed to take it, would have been better for me than fifteen hundred now.

In reply to your question about [Burns's] character, I have to say, that I regard him as strictly honest, sober and truthful. Let me hear from you without delay. If you accede to my terms, I will on receipt of the money deliver him in the city of Washington with his free papers, or I will send him by one of the steamers from Richmond to New York.

Very Respectfully,
Charles F. Suttle[3]

Leonard Grimes tried to reassemble the pledges he had gathered before, but he came up short. Those who "had struggled to maintain law and order" had apparently made as much of a point as they meant to. Buying slaves was not looked upon as a viable tactic by the abolitionists, who likewise had points to make. Grimes went to Hallett again and told him that since he had been responsible for the failure of the purchase at the lower price, his offer of a hundred dollars should be raised to four hundred, to make up the difference. This Hallett declined to do, but he did stand by his earlier pledge. Parker and Thomas supposed that Suttle was honor bound to take $1,200. That, whether he had the money or not, is what Grimes offered in his letter to the slaveowner.

No word ever came back from Alexandria.[4]

KNOW-NOTHINGS

Under ordinary circumstances, a clandestine political party would have lacked mass appeal, but 1854 was not an ordinary year.

GEORGE H. MAYER

An antislavery hardliner yet a tactical pragmatist, Henry Wilson understood that the fledgling Republican party was by no means powerful enough to make him governor, so he tried that summer to secure as well the nomination of the American party, more popularly known as the Know-Nothings, or "the Order." Wilson had joined this group back in March, while it was still a secret society of handshakes and passwords, spiced with a dollop of pseudo-Masonic mumbo jumbo—long before it emerged as an independent political party. Membership in the lodges had increased gradually until the end of May, when, with the passage of the Kansas-Nebraska Act (and the coinciding Burns trial), the movement took off in a manner that would have been spectacular had it not been an astonishingly well-kept secret. From his inside position Wilson was able to foresee that by November its electoral power would be formidable indeed.[1]

The Know-Nothings, however, gave the gubernatorial nomination to Henry J. Gardner of Boston, an old Hunker who had recently bolted from the Whigs, among whom he had long been known as "that Jackass." Indeed he had been pried loose from his party, as had many others, by Nebraska, thence to be drawn toward Know-Nothingism by the magnetic appeal of anti-Catholic nativism. When

Gardner told party operatives that he could be offered to the convention as one who conscientiously supported their antislavery and temperance planks, a good many were suspicious. "Hum!" said one: "How was it when he ran as a pro-slavery, Fugitive Slave Law, Webster Whig, against me for the Common Council and beat me?" "Hum!" said another, "how was it that not very long ago I was compelled to throw the brandy bottle out the window to keep him from drinking any more?"[2]

In exchange for Wilson's support (and for Wilson's last-minute withdrawal as the Republican nominee), Gardner agreed to support him as the Know-Nothing candidate in the senatorial race. So in 1854, as in 1851, the more weakly positioned of the two deal-makers—and the more radical—got to be a United States senator, demonstrating again how taken for granted it was that state politics mattered most. North or South, it was a states' rights environment, and loyalties were first of all local. This was one reason why in Massachusetts the Burns case resonated so profoundly, and why for many it had been more shattering than Kansas-Nebraska.[3]

Such was the feeling even outside the Know-Nothing party. At the Whig convention in August, eighty-three-year-old Josiah Quincy labored under a loaded conscience to insist to his party that Nebraska was not the point, that it was merely another development in a Southern strategy whose purpose had been clear for years. "It is not that burthen which most presses upon my mind," he told the Whigs. "There is another, nearer home, more immediate, more important, and more insupportable." After describing the deployment of state and federal troops in the Burns rendition in a way to make it sound like a military occupation, Quincy added: "This scene (thus awful, thus detestable) every inhabitant . . . of this Commonwealth may be compelled again to witness, at any and every day of the year. . . ."

> There is not a Negro in the South that can be compelled, even by his master, to cut the throat or blow out the brains of his brother Negro. Yet, so long as the fugitive-slave obligation remains in the Constitution, there is not a militia-man in Massachusetts who may not be compelled to-morrow to cut the throat or blow out the brains of a fellow-citizen, at the will of the basest Southern slaveholder.

Quincy was asking the Whigs to undo the mischief that Webster had caused and to assert that Massachusetts, in its sovereignty, would be henceforth absolved from being "the field-drivers and pound-keepers for the black cattle of the slave-holding States." The party was to take a stand and repudiate the Fugitive Slave Law: "Are you the sons of the men of 1776?" he asked. But the Conscience Whigs had already left the party.[4]

The election that fall left all observers stunned and reeling; it turned out to be a rout of unparalleled magnitude for the Order, made all the more remarkable by the party's previous invisibility. Its strength, veiled behind the walls of a thousand secret lodges, emerged in a single day and quite overthrew the government. George F. Hoar conceded that Gardner had "organized with great skill and success the knave-power and the donkey-power of the Commonwealth," which accounted for his taking 63 percent of the vote in a four-way election. In addition to the governor's mansion, the Know-Nothings had captured the State House, carrying every seat in the upper house and all but three out of more than 400 seats in the lower. The eleven-man congressional delegation elected that fall contained no Whigs, no Democrats, and no Freesoilers. And by the beginning of the next year, Henry Wilson, elected by the new state legislature, was headed to Washington to take his place by Sumner's side.[5]

No state election had ever seemed more like a popular coup d'état. "Nothing like it can be found in the political history of the country," marveled the *Liberator*. "Even now, with the figures staring us in the face, it seems almost incredible." "There can be no doubt," Henry Wilson later wrote, "that the rendition of Anthony Burns, with all the attendant circumstances, the superserviceable zeal of the Boston officials, and the unseemly alacrity of the President in ordering a national vessel to bear a single friendless man, of a proscribed race, back to that servitude from which he had so bravely but vainly striven to escape, largely contributed, in New England at least, to the overthrow of the politicians and parties that upheld the Slave Power."[6]

The Democrats had been particularly blamed for Stephen Douglas' Kansas-Nebraska Act and for the dough-face policies of Pierce and his attorney general, Caleb Cushing: this party was soundly rebuked. The Whigs, now little more than a residue of organized Websterism, had been especially blamed for the Fugitive Slave Law, its legal defense, and its continued enforcement: this party was at last destroyed. A thoroughly aroused electorate had risen up and with the only instrumentality available—the American party—had swept the slate clean of politics as usual, breaking the decades-old domination of arrogant Boston Whiggery and of the controlling money power that lay behind it.

Governor Gardner was quick to deliver on his nativist agenda; among his first actions was the dissolution of the Irish militia companies. Thinking to take advantage of this newly sympathetic climate, a number of black men in Boston, Robert Morris prominent among them, combined to form their own militia company, the Massasoit Guards. They failed to win official recognition, but managed to maintain themselves nevertheless. Unwilling to be regarded as a "*caste* company," they chose to "invite to their ranks any citizens of good moral character who may wish to enrol their names."[7]

The men elected to the state legislature that fall were a colorful group of the rankest political amateurs. Abolitionists and anti-Nebraska men took their seats in the State House beside ranting anti-Catholic bigots, self-righteous prohibitionists, America-firsters, and astonished philanthropists. Farmers, tradesmen, ministers, and lawyers, they were all alike freshmen, alike ignorant of parliamentary procedure and strangers to organization and the wielding of power. Outgoing Whig Governor Emory Washburn, who had been pilloried for his inaction in the Burns case, presided at their swearing-in, at the end of which he took his leave, saying, "Now, gentlemen, so far as the oath of office is concerned, you are qualified to enter upon your duties." The Reverend Daniel C. Eddy, author of *Angel Whispers; or, The Echo of Spirit Voices,* a currently popular book of consolation for the bereaved, was, "in the confusion," elected Speaker of the House. Eddy was a Boston Baptist minister who was sure that the aggressive designs of the Slave Power and the Catholic conspiracy against New England's free schools were cut from the same cloth. "Roman Catholics," he said, "should be taught that our only object is to guard our own liberties and do them good."[8]

The Massachusetts legislature of 1855 was for years known as "the Hiss legislature," after Representative Joseph Hiss, who, while out conducting surprise inspections of convents to ferret out suspected kidnapping and sex crimes, saw fit to charge the state for the hotel and liquor bill his own mistress had run up. And yet, for all that was undeniably raw, gross, and comical about this assembly of dilettantes, it probably was, as Henry Wilson said, "the most radical antislavery State legislature ever chosen in America." The ex-Freesoilers among them clearly saw their chance and acted on it. "Never did we have such an opportunity as this," wrote Dr. James W. Stone to Charles Sumner as the session opened. An early Freesoiler and member of the Boston Vigilance Committee, Stone was now a Know-Nothing leader in the State House.[9]

The newly empowered Know-Nothings proved to be at once a vehicle for reactionary anti-Catholic, anti-immigrant sentiment and an engine of exceptionally progressive reform policies. The party passed a series of remarkable bills in 1855, among which was by far the most extravagant Personal Liberty Law ever devised. This enactment provided for the writ of habeas corpus in all cases in which a person was restrained of his liberty; ensured that in the resulting trial by jury verdicts would be unreviewable; defined more strictly the nature and quality of the evidence that a claimant would have to supply in discharging his burden of proof in the case; declared *ex parte* depositions inadmissible; stipulated that "no confessions, admissions or declarations of the alleged fugitive against himself shall be given in evidence"; made it illegal for anyone to act as counsel for the claimant; made it illegal for any state official to act as a federal slave law commissioner; appointed state commissioners to defend people claimed as fugitives; and established heavy fines and terms of imprisonment for kidnapping, to be imposed whenever a claimant turned out to have detained anyone falsely. When Governor Gardner was presented with this bill he had it reviewed by Chief Justice Lemuel Shaw and state attorney general John Clifford, neither of whom hesitated to pronounce it obviously unconstitutional. On these grounds Gardner vetoed it, but the legislature overrode. According to the historian of the personal liberty laws, "No cases arose under the Massachusetts law of 1855, and it is not difficult to understand why."[10]

The same legislature received petitions from more than 12,000 people from every part of the state, a high percentage of whom were women, demanding the removal of Edward G. Loring as judge of probate. Fewer than 1,500 names (all men and mostly from Boston) were gathered in protest of the movement. The matter was referred to the Joint Committee on Federal Relations (chaired by Sumner's friend Dr. James W. Stone), at whose hearings in February and March Phillips, Parker, Hildreth, and Swift testified with considerable gusto. Little effort was made to disguise the fact that this was a political witch hunt, designed to put Loring "on trial at the bar of the People" without so much as alleging an impeachable offense, and indeed for conduct unrelated to his performance as a state official.[11]

Dana was alarmed by what Loring's removal would mean for the independence of the judiciary, a cause that appealed irresistibly to his underlying conservatism, and so, to the general surprise of the public, he testified on Loring's behalf, all the while conceding (what he had already publicly stated) that the judge was weak, open to influence, and wrong on the law. It was suggested to Dana in rebuttal that Loring's removal for his political offenses would not threaten the independence of the judiciary, for the simple reason that he was not being removed for any act belonging to the repertoire of state judges. The message that Loring's removal would send to state judges was narrow and unproblematical: they should not contravene the will of the Commonwealth by making slaves out of free men.[12]

By a divided vote, the committee recommended Loring's removal, and the House and Senate concurred. Yet again Gardner demurred, and since the procedure of removal by address was merely advisory to the governor in his appointive power, the matter was dropped. It would be renewed, however, in subsequent years, and Loring was finally ousted in 1858 when a similar legislative appeal was made to Governor N. P. Banks.

A far more radical measure adopted by the Know-Nothing legislature was an act empowering juries in criminal cases to decide both the law and the facts. It was an appeal from the head to the heart, a democratic affirmation of the private judgment of the people against the overweening power of judges, who were now looked upon—as they had often been looked upon before and during the Revolution—as the tools of arbitrary power. It was also, of course, an advertisement for jury nullification, since juries gave no reasons for their decisions, and acquittals were inevitably sustained by the principle of double jeopardy. The new law was, further, an attack on the professional character of the legal system, something that became clear in subsequent complaints about the measure. It was contended that such juries as this law promoted would usurp the place of legislators and make law ad hoc. Such juries—mere citizens—were not learned in the law; they would displace men "whose labor and whose duty it is to study and determine these questions." Which, to be sure, was precisely the point.[13]

The much-derided Hiss legislature abolished imprisonment for debt, passed progressive child labor legislation and a married women's property act. It came close to abolishing the death penalty and even closer to mandating a ten-hour work day. Furthermore, on April 28, 1855, the legislature put an end, officially, to the system of separate colored schools in Boston. This act, vindicating the arguments of Robert Morris and Charles Sumner before the unsympathetic Whig Lemuel Shaw, was greeted with much rejoicing in the Sixth Ward. Later in the year, at his church on Southac Street, Leonard Grimes hosted a public testimonial for William Cooper Nell, the black leader who had worked most unremittingly for the measure.[14]

CATHOLICS AND ANTI-CATHOLICS

Among the many exciting events that marked the progress of the year 1854 in Boston, was the advent of Gabriel and his horn.

EDWARD H. SAVAGE

God save the Commonwealth of Massachusetts.

PATRICK DONOHOE, BOSTON *PILOT*, November 25, 1854

In the short course in American history, the Know-Nothing party has come to stand quite simply for anti-Catholic bigotry and nativist intolerance: in sum, for the kind of irrational hostility toward minorities that no modern society can well afford. It is more than a little surprising, therefore, to find the Know-Nothings of Massachusetts not only militantly committed to protecting African-American citizens but also, for the moment, the single most powerful and effective means of promoting their interests. Ethnic exclusionists are not usually associated with progressive ideas, yet this Know-Nothing legislature, to cite one more instance of its openness to radicalism, came within a hair's breadth of selecting Theodore Parker as its chaplain.[1]

Certainly there were in the Know-Nothing movement a great many who cordially despised Catholics and Irishmen in the trite and vulgar ways of stereotypical ethnic prejudice, and who needed no more reason to vent their hostility than the mere fact of cultural difference or some cloudy sense of economic challenge. Steps were in fact taken by the new state government to deport Irish paupers (a goodly percentage of the total immigrant stream) and to institute a twenty-one-year residency requirement for foreign-born voters. And yet, in regard to the workplace, recent historical studies have shown that the

Know-Nothings were not a labor party—not, as one might have supposed, a party of young and resentful Yankee mill hands displaced by a more exploitable foreign work force. Nor were they a party of the ignorant (its name notwithstanding) or of the poor. As their electoral mandate implies, they received support from voters of all classes, occupations, and levels of education and income. Their spokesmen raised no labor issues in complaint against the Irish, nor did the party emerge at a time of economic distress.[2]

Although Irish immigration peaked during the years 1850–1854, New England anti-Catholicism was no recent development, nor even a nineteenth-century one; its roots ran long and deep in the region's Puritan past. Indeed, the persistence of anti-Catholicism over time implies an underlying reference to ideological content and suggests that its emergent ethnic dimension was in an important sense accidental. That Massachusetts could trace its colonial origins to the revolutionary impetus of the Protestant Reformation was still, in 1854, acutely felt, especially among the more liberal clerical leaders of public opinion. Radicals in Massachusetts in the summer of 1854 still, after a fashion, maintained what the generation of William Bradford and John Winthrop had affirmed more than two centuries before: that the most glorious of all social experiments had been entrusted to the English Protestants of the New World, that of moving mankind forward against the conservative drag of the Catholic Church. The manifest difficulties of making the Boston Irish allies in that fight did not prevent the abolitionists from trying: one finds Garrison and Phillips, for example, holding out to them the example of Daniel O'Connell, the antislavery Irish nationalist, trying thereby to form a revolutionary solidarity between oppressed white colonial and black colonial populations. This strategy did not work, and Catholics in Massachusetts, though they supported revolution in Ireland, remained avowedly and programmatically conservative in their new home. They successfully opposed the 1853 constitutional revision, denounced Emersonian Transcendentalism and Garrisonian abolitionism (along with romantic reform in general, which smacked of Erastianism), and at the same time conspicuously supported the civil authority and the law of the land, including slavery. A desperately poor and persecuted minority, the foreign-born Catholics of Massachusetts were committed to being unprovocative "good citizens," and they would have nothing to do with reform or with social experimentation. Because Irish adopted citizens looked to the U.S. Constitution as their shield and shelter in a hostile land, they were prone to set down those who called it "an agreement with hell" as fanatics and "nigger-worshippers."[3]

In his Fourth of July sermon (which referred frequently to the Burns trial), Theodore Parker said what was then very often said on the Fourth of July: "We are now making the greatest political experiment which the sun ever looked down upon." That experiment was, first and foremost, the establishment of a democratic society, a "government of all, by all, for all" (as Lincoln read in Parker's works), which would give practical effect to the free and independent private judgment of educated men. America was to be a nation that honored work because it honored individual character and accomplishment rather than inherited privilege, concretions of power, or the tyrannical exploitation, as in slavery, of the labor of others. It was to be a state founded on "industry, and not war," a "great, noble-hearted commonwealth, a nation possessing the continent, full of riches, full of justice, full of wisdom, full of piety, and full of peace." Parker's vision was of a continental America unfolded on the modern, progressive, New England model—yet it was also an elaboration of recognizably Puritan values. One of his main points in the sermon was that the Catholic Church opposed every aspect of this quintessentially Protestant design.[4]

There is no evidence that Parker, who disliked political parties in general, significantly cooperated with the Know-Nothings (indeed, he warned of the danger they represented), but his anti-Catholicism, in its broader ideological aims, was hardly distinguishable from that of the Know-Nothing leaders. Parker, Wilson, and Burlingame, for example, were convinced that the immigrant Catholics represented a potentially dangerous and very alien ideology, yet they agreed in disavowing an intent to exclude or degrade anyone politically on the basis of religious belief. "I am glad the Catholics come here," said Parker. "Let America be an asylum for the poor and the downtrodden of all lands." Religionists of every sect should find in America "free opportunity to be faithful each to his own conscience"—implying that such freedom was a Protestant, not a Catholic, value. He was glad that Catholics came to America because the presence of the Roman Church in New England was valuable in maintaining, through its opposition, a necessary alertness and zeal in the Protestants' ideal social vision. It was easier, that is, to sustain the Reformation if there were a reasonable number of Catholics in the vicinity. Parker, who had been virtually expelled from the Unitarian conference more than a decade earlier for his Emersonian radicalism, knew what it was like to be silenced by the official culture, and he knew as well that debate and open exchange were not just nobler, but in the end more effective, weapons in the fight against untruth than censorship and oppression. "If, with truth and justice on our side, the few Catholics can overcome the many Protestants," he said, "we deserve defeat."[5]

Protestantism still found it necessary to define itself in a struggle with the Catholic principle, which, for its part, persisted in denying to Protestantism the status of a religion at all. Orestes Brownson, who converted to Catholicism in 1844, had earlier been a Unitarian minister, a member of the Transcendental Club, and a friend and colleague of Emerson and Parker. By the 1850s, as the editor of and principal writer for *Brownson's Quarterly Review*, he had become the most prolific and respected Catholic spokesman in Boston—perhaps in all of America—and Parker's most indefatigable critic. In Parker Brownson claimed to see the characteristic acting out of Protestant irreligion. He had taken the basic Reformation idea—the attack on extrinsic authority—to its last, self-erasing extreme. He denied the plenary inspiration of the scriptures. He denied the supernatural authority of Jesus and disbelieved in miracles. He called original sin a superstition and found mankind to be good by nature. Free will was what he believed in and the right of the individual to satisfy his own conscience in points of religion as in all other matters. It was Brownson's view that Protestants, in their pride and rebelliousness, had abandoned everything that made religion religious, and that in this process of abandonment no one had gone further than Parker, that exemplary radical.[6]

This Catholic critique served as well to subvert the "higher law" doctrine advanced by Parker and other antislavery men. Brownson affirmed that indeed a higher and more universal law than the American Constitution had been established by God and that in its presence no conflicting human statute could command the least assent. But who was to say what this higher law was? Sunk in the rejection of external authority and sustained only by a respect for one's own opinion, the Protestant could rely on nothing but a private and personal assessment of the question—and yet no one's opinion was better or more authorized than another's. The Catholic, as Brownson eagerly pointed out, was spared all the trouble arising from the mislocation of authority in the individual: his inerrant Church simply told him what God's law was. "For us Catholics, the fugitive-slave law presents no sort of difficulty," Brownson declared. Citizens are "bound to obey the civil law till they can bring a higher authority than the state, and a higher than their own private judgment, to set it aside as repugnant to the law of God. This higher authority they [Protestants] have not, and therefore for them there is no higher law."[7]

But Parker's notion of democracy invited and embraced what Brownson feared; in the absence of a central instructional authority, there would indeed be contention. (Was he not glad to have the Catholics come?) Contending opinions were an environmental necessity of freedom; they were, Parker thought, a guarantor of progress rather than a sign of anarchy. Bereft of most traditional supernaturalism, Parker was yet enough of a Transcendentalist to believe that justice, for example, had an ultimate sort of power and an authority not less directive for being uncontained by institutional structures. Its power to draw to it the consciences of men was in itself a divine government, sufficient to assure that the right could not be kept down forever. As Emerson believed, so Parker believed, that nature (as well as nature's analogue in the soul, the private, unperverted moral sense) were organized in such a way as to favor, reward, empower, and establish good on the one hand, and to repel and defeat evil on the other. This Emersonian belief—that good was general and powerful and prevailed unceasingly, while evil was local and temporary—lay at the core of the New England Protestant concept of progress, just as it was also embodied in Sumner's Freesoil slogan, "Freedom Is National; Slavery Is Sectional." For Parker, in his private judgment, it was enough to know that the Catholic Church had no quarrel with slavery to conclude that it had a less reliable access to the higher law than he did himself. What had a man a conscience for, Parker might have asked, if not to use it?

Brownson's case against Parker amounted in the end to a cry of alarm against the chaos sure to follow when every man judges the law. Free society was now and always would be, in Brownson's Catholic view, an ungovernable Pandemonium of men self-erected into uncompromising godhood—a flat and ludicrous failure. As it happened, that was the same conclusion reached by slavery apologist George

Fitzhugh in the book he was writing that summer in Richmond when Anthony Burns was driven past his window on the way to prison. Free society, Fitzhugh said, was a failure; its undirected laissez-faire capitalism made any humane concern for the uncompetitive worker incongruous and impossible. Indeed he may have been thinking of the Burns riot when he quoted Thomas Carlyle's snide one-liner on America's liberal democratic institutions—that they amounted to "anarchy plus a street constable."[8]

Both sides in the Catholic-Protestant controversy at this time (as argued in the press rather than in the streets) agreed that the main line of division ran through this question of the right of private judgment. One side was democratic and the other antidemocratic. One was open and dialogic, the other closed and monologic. One side opposed slavery, the other supported it. Parker claimed in his sermon to have been told that "there is not in all America a single Catholic newspaper hostile to slavery." Dana's friend Anson Burlingame, who was to be elected to Congress that fall as a Know-Nothing, asserted that not one priest had signed Mrs. Stowe's clerical petition against the Nebraska Bill. Support for slavery was appalling in itself, but the spectacle of such unanimity convinced many that it was orchestrated by a regime not just antidemocratic, but totalitarian and coercive with respect to its inmates and secretive and subversive with respect to its enemies—reviving with new force the old antisacerdotalism of Puritan New England.[9]

The quality of attention bestowed on Catholics in Massachusetts at this time was surely owing in part to the feeling that groups hostile to the Protestant values of New England had powerful hidden agendas and were playing the political game, with remarkable success, in unaccustomed ways. Political power in America, as the Freesoilers had been saying for years, reposed in the hands of a tiny minority of distant slaveholders whose names no one knew, who were full of secret designs against Mexico, Texas, Nebraska, Cuba, Haiti, and, indeed, New England itself. Antislavery thought of itself as communicating openly in public forums like Faneuil Hall; as resisting censorship, speaking out bravely before hostile mobs and opposing political gag rules; as arguing for free speech and the right of petition for redress of grievances—while the government in Washington seemed to conspire with treacherous effectiveness against the life of the Missouri Compromise or, at will, to control Boston by secret telegraphic communiqués to B. F. Hallett. The Irish Catholics—who, if not in active league with the Slave Power, at least put no obstacles in its way—had their own hidden agendas, forwarded—or so it seemed to the Yankees—by a veritable culture of secrecy, running from the Jesuits (established in Boston in 1829) and the ever-fascinating convents (the Ursuline convent in Charlestown had been burned by a nativist mob in 1834, partly incited by Lyman Beecher's anti-Catholic sermons) through the whole question of the foreign control of their political power down to the nature of their alleged campaign against the free schools. The correspondingly secret nature of the Know-Nothing organization may have been a kind of paranoid acknowledgment of the perceived tactics of its opponents and is further evidence of how the culture, under revolutionary pressures, came to feel the futility of open covenants openly arrived at.[10]

The bottom layer of the Know-Nothing appeal was a parody or crude restatement of the neo-Puritan ideology at the top, and it amounted to a thinly varnished invitation to cultural war. In several distinct ways the Burns trial amplified this invitation. Class and ethnic tensions were given free rein in the vilification of the marshal's guard. In the constantly reiterated emphasis on an Irish affinity for liquor, violence, vice, and slavery, a low ethnic prejudice, masquerading as a racial prejudice, was deployed in an idealistic crusade against human bondage. Then too there had been intense and general unhappiness over the fact that the predominantly foreign-born U.S. troops (military service was a mode of naturalization), together with the Irish companies of the state militia, had been the ready instruments of oppression and had conducted themselves throughout as arrogant, insulting forcers of conscience. They had been armed by the government, it was said, to shoot down Protestant defenders of liberty. A great deal of facile stereotyping, even among the most highly educated, followed from the commonly held view that the Celtic population could be and were to be distinguished from the Anglo-Saxons at the level of race. Thus, as Emerson said in the book he was writing at this time, "Race avails much, if that be true which is alleged, that all Celts are Catholics and all Saxons are Protestants; that Celts love unity of power, and Saxons the representative principle."[11]

When Anthony Burns was arrested in Boston, a ragged, distracted Scottish-American eccentric named John Orr had just been released from jail in Worcester, where he had been held for incitement to riot. His life's work was to travel about the northeastern states on foot distributing anti-Catholic and Know-Nothing handbills, passing the hat, and lecturing on street corners about the perils of Irish immigration. He had arrived in Worcester fresh from vandalizing the church in Chelsea that Brownson attended. Wherever he went he announced his arrival by tooting on a little brass horn he carried, from which practice he was known simply as Gabriel. Wherever he went, riots broke out. His arrest in Worcester had been a sore point with the men of the local Know-Nothing lodge, many of whom, including its president, were shortly afterward among the rioters at the Boston Court House. In fact Gabriel himself had gone to Boston and was indirectly responsible for a fracas in Endicott Street on May 28 in which two of his Know-Nothing supporters were severely beaten by a band of exasperated Irishmen. A few weeks later, on June 23, Gabriel was in the Catholic mill town of Lowell, where, with a protective bodyguard, he held forth before a large crowd on the South Common near St. Peter's Church. The sisters at nearby St. Patrick's girls' school had sent their charges home and were themselves barricaded in the cellar, fearful of another such invasion as the Know-Nothings had recently made at the convent school in Roxbury. Violence followed in the wake of Gabriel's departure—violence serious enough for Lowell's mayor to read the riot act and to ban public assemblies. Regarded in the main as a mere nuisance by the police and dismissed as a simple lunatic by sober Protestants, Gabriel was in fact a cause of grave alarm to the entire Irish community. On July 3 the Catholic church in Milton was blown up.[12]

Pressured from below by the popular demagoguery of Gabriel with its vision of the evil to be avoided, and from above by Parker's advanced neo-Puritan reform theology with its vision of the good to be embraced, the Protestant clergy of Massachusetts felt called upon to formulate their middling positions. One who did so in a thoroughly typical and illustrative way was the Reverend Eden B. Foster, pastor of the John Street Congregational Church in Lowell, whose sermons delivered the Sunday following the Gabriel riots linked Catholicism to the depredations of the Slave Power in Nebraska and the Burns case.

His morning sermon on June 25 was a jeremiad titled "The Rights of the Pulpit."

There are times when the law of God is broken by a nation and its rulers, with such gratuitous and wanton disregard of truthfulness and justice, that God is likely to speak, it may be in mercy, leading men to repentance; it may be in severity, pouring upon them his condign and terrible judgments. At such a time the word of God needs to be unfolded in its political aspects.

In response to Mrs. Stowe's anti-Nebraska petition, Stephen Douglas had taken the floor of the Senate to pour contempt on the "political preachers" of New England, dismissing them as ignorant meddlers and advising them to remember what topics rightly belonged to the sacred desk and indeed to their capacities for research. The ministers were, almost to a man, infuriated by this implied muzzling of conscience. Foster quoted Douglas in the sermon as saying, "If we recognize three thousand clergymen as having a higher right to interpret the will of God than we have, we destroy the right of self-action, of self-government, of self-thought, and we are merely to refer each of our political questions to this body of clergymen. Here is a great principle subversive of our free institutions." Right, said Foster: to believe otherwise "is simply and purely the Papal usurpation," but to affirm freedom of conscience in general is to extend it to ministers, who should therefore be in, not out of, the political arena. Their influence would not be a priestly authority (as it demonstrably had been in the past), but they would be listened to wholly for the value of whatever truth they spoke.[13]

Foster continued: "Our country has, within a few weeks past, been the witness of scenes more amazing and alarming than any other events which have happened since the foundation of the Republic." He went on to arraign the government treachery that sold Nebraska. That idyllic region (which had previously escaped everyone's attention), soon to be blasted and blighted by slavery, had been free by nature and had held out the promise of being "a pleasant home" for the settler. Foster covetously described it as a place

> where the breezes of Heaven have freely played, and the light of Heaven has freely shone, and the accumulations of Heaven have freely gathered for long centuries . . . a place sacredly dedicated to freedom; where men who toil for their living, and rejoice in the dignity and fruits of their labor may find an asylum and a blessed home, and where with wife and children around them, with churches and schools on every side, with books and presses, and refined society at hand, with

the protection of just laws, and the enjoyment of varied comforts, and the solace of religious hopes they may happily live and joyfully die, and leave at last to their children the same rich inheritance which God had given to them.

Under the defining pressure of real events at home, Kansas and Nebraska had become an ideal "world elsewhere," a frontier of the social imagination to be filled up as the Canaan-become-Israel of a free and independent class of American workers.[14]

But here and now was the Burns case, an urban nightmare and dark antithesis of Foster's dream of progress. It is necessary to quote Foster's sermon at some length to convey the flavor of the ministerial response, the breathless piled-up detail, suggestive of a personal presence that week in Boston, the inevitable contextualizing references to the Revolution, the sentimental forecast and prophecy with regard to Burns, the sense of unprecedented civic challenge and its religious resonance:

On Friday, the 2nd day of June, at three o'clock in the afternoon, a poor, unbefriended, unhappy negro, after having been seized in the city of Boston, upon false pretenses, and tried without judge or jury, and sentenced, against conclusive evidence of an alibi, to be remanded as a fugitive slave to his Southern claimant, was taken into a hollow square of armed men, with drawn cutlasses, and loaded muskets, and gleaming bayonets on every side, and trailing artillery following behind; and from the Court House, by the marshal and his posse of one hundred and twenty-five men; by the chief of police and his whole constabulary force; by twenty-two companies, making a military power of more than thirteen hundred armed men, was this wretched victim of a colored skin transported to the revenue cutter, Morris, and thence, still under the authority of the United States government, carried to the South, there to die prematurely by torture, or by excessive toil, or of a broken heart. Never before, since British hirelings stood in the streets of Boston and shot down unarmed and unoffending citizens, has that city been under martial law and military siege. Never before, since the blood of the Revolution was shed, have the streets of Boston been blockaded, and the business of Boston suspended, and the free expression of opinion coerced by cannon and sword, by the menace and the terror, and the death-dealing power of the military arm. These things bring reflecting citizens to a pause; they bring Christians to their knees; they bring all who love their country and who value freedom to inquire, under what rule are we living? What is before us? What holy truths have been neglected, and what false principles inculcated to bring about these terrific realities? And what duties in such a crisis as this devolve upon us?[15]

First, the duty to repeal the Fugitive Slave Law; for otherwise "Freedom in this country has received a mortal blow." The Fugitive Slave Law "is not designed simply or mainly to hold the black race in subjection," Foster argued, "but to place in bondage the white race of the North. It is a restriction on our Saxon blood, and Saxon will, and Saxon liberties. It is to restrain the education, conscience, and independence of our children. It is to limit our free speech, free thought, free worship, and free action." Nothing, according to Foster, now mattered more than the repeal of the Fugitive Slave Law.[16]

In his afternoon sermon, titled "Perils of Freedom," he addressed himself mainly to the wicked Kansas-Nebraska Act—wicked because, among other things, it "renders aid to the plottings of the Romish hierarchy."

> Everything indicates that there is a struggle coming on in this country between the principles of Protestant liberty and Romish power . . . But what I wish especially to remark in this connection is, the alliance between Slavery and the Roman Catholic religion in this strife. Their spirit is one, the spirit of bigotry and intolerance in Church and State, the spirit of dictation over the conscience and our politics. Their principles are in perfect harmony, principles which establish an aristocracy, which introduce special privileges, which perpetuate the power of caste. Their aims are identical, the purpose to set up their own ascendancy and to subject all opinions and interests to their rule . . . Slavery and Romanism have joined hands in firmest league . . . This is shown by the whole Catholic vote at the last election [when the Freesoil-designed revision of the state constitution was defeated], by the course of Bishop Hughes [New York Archbishop John Hughes, author of *The Decline of Protestantism and Its Cause* (1850)], by the astounding proclamations of Brownson; by the position of the entire Romish priesthood, not a man of whom signed the protest against the Nebraska Bill, not a man of whom gives his voice or his vote against the extension and perpetuity of Slavery; and by the uniform tenor of the Catholic journals which are constant and insidious in their assaults upon republican liberty, and in their defense of Slavery's demands . . . The Nebraska Law gives to both these forces an immense advantage, wrenching away from the hands of Freedom one of her most potent weapons of defence, and placing in the hands of Slavery and of Romanism a two-edged dagger with which to stab liberty to the heart.[17]

How difficult to say at what point in the downward trending from idealism to demagoguery the value of a crusade has at last leached out. In the wake of the Burns case every convert to antislavery found by the specific gravity of his character his own peculiar level, with just the mix of motives and just the suitable style to arm and invigorate him as he looked about for something—anything—to *do*.

🌿 WALT WHITMAN

Our white brethren everywhere are reaching out their hands to grasp more freedom. In the place of absolute monarchies they have limited monarchies, and in the place of limited monarchies they have republics: so tenacious are they of their own liberties.

J. W. C. PENNINGTON

On May 31, the day of final arguments in the Burns case, Walt Whitman turned thirty-five, and he supposed, as all poets since Dante have done, that half his life was gone. Yet there must have been some doubt that day whether he was really a poet at all, since over the first half of his life he had written in rhyme so scantily and, as he glanced back, so little to his satisfaction. He had felt that dissatisfaction as long ago as 1847, when he had begun in a few detached fragments to experiment with free verse, deliberately rejecting the conventional meters that so easily made a pretty ringing song of conventional hobbled thought. Those first fragments of free verse had been about the unbeautiful topic of slavery. "I am the poet of slaves, and of the masters of slaves," he had said then, declaring his identity with the subject. And yet of late he had not been writing poetry at all.[1]

If not a poet, then, was he a journalist? Over the years he had committed to print a certain amount of ephemeral nonpartisan fluff and a larger quantity of partisan bluster in the Democratic papers he had edited, but he and the Democrats had come at last to a parting of the ways—over slavery. He had supposed that the Wilmot Proviso, which would make the territories got from Mexico forever free, was intrinsically a Democratic measure. He supposed it was a logical sequel to the prohibition of slavery contained in the Northwest Ordinance, framed in 1787 by his lifelong hero, Thomas Jefferson. But the party disagreed, nominated an anti-Wilmot man (Lewis Cass) for president in 1848, and had Whitman removed from the editorship of the *Brooklyn Daily Eagle,* which paper then reverted to Hunkerdom. That year, along with other radical New York Democrats, called Barnburners, Whitman became a Freesoiler, hoping to elect favorite son Martin Van Buren. For a while he edited a paper for the new party, but he was permanently out of that line of work by 1850, the year of the great disgust over the Compromise, the last year in which Whitman had put a poem into circulation—a poem about politicians who compromised on slavery.[2]

He had spent the last four years unexpressively, out of politics, alternately loafing and reading and doing stints as a carpenter building houses. But it was impossible to be entirely out of politics. Even the loafing and the building were irresistibly convertible into antislavery gestures, were indeed for Whitman the necessary acting out of his free labor ideology. All working, all not-working, and all the conditions of both had meaning foisted on them by the everything-opposing point of reference that slavery made, so that in all sorts of unexpected ways white American life came to be construed as not-black-slave life. (Thoreau supposed that his freedom depended on his ability "to live deliberately," but when Emerson wanted to commend that state, he would say: "Hurry is for slaves.") Whitman's loafing and building belonged to the antislave persona of the sovereign citizen-laborer, to that insouciant, undominated, working-class vision of himself that, when he got it down just right, would make *Leaves of Grass* a document to dazzle and convert backsliding Democrats. To Whitman, as to most Northern white males, being antislavery meant taking a class position and upholding a certain notion of free life; it did not seem to require a moral or racial position, except perhaps secondarily, as an implication that presented itself. Being antislavery seemed to mean deepening one's commitment to the dignity of independent labor, and thus also, for Whitman, it meant speaking (as he had done many times) for the interests of the millions of mechanics, farmers, and operatives who made up "the grand body of white workingmen" in America.[3]

Whitman's thirty-fifth birthday found him living in Skillman Street in Brooklyn in a house he had just built but didn't own, in which he would spend hours poring over the just-published, just-purchased nine-volume edition of *The Writings of Thomas Jefferson.*[4]

He was also following the Burns trial, day by day, in Greeley's

Tribune (which also reported, later that summer, that the ubiquitous Gabriel was tooting his horn in Brooklyn).[5]

Whitman might have reacted to another fugitive slave case occurring at the same time in Manhattan, in which the brother and nephews of the Reverend Dr. J. W. C. Pennington, the most highly respected black leader in New York, had been arrested in the predawn hours of May 25, arraigned, and rushed back to slavery before the same day ended. But it was the slow-developing, public-facing Burns case, drenched in the symbolism of its Boston venue, that proved evocative, that stirred Whitman's blood and made him a poet again. Throughout this thirty-sixth year, beginning thus with a return to slavery, the loafing and the reading and the housebuilding all receded behind a revolutionary commitment to free verse, and when it was over, Walt Whitman published his first book of poems, *Leaves of Grass,* on Independence Day, 1855.[6]

Among the twelve distinct poems in that volume was Whitman's untitled response to the Burns rendition, a poem he would eventually call "A Boston Ballad." Like much of his earlier poetry, and unlike virtually all that came afterward, it is a topical marshaling of irony and satire. The naive eyewitness speaker who serves as the poem's narrator has been drawn to what he supposes is a patriotic, Fourth of July style military parade. "Here's a good place at the corner," he says. "I must stand and see the show." There is no reference in the poem to Burns, who is overwhelmed to the point of invisibility by his military escort. The actual reason for the "show" is thus wholly suppressed, with the result that Whitman's narrative persona at first simply gives himself up to feelings of jingoistic pride at seeing "the President's marshal," "the government cannon," and "the federal foot and dragoons." "I love to look on the stars and stripes," he says. "I hope the fifes will play Yankee Doodle."[7]

The speaker's attention is almost immediately troubled, however, by a duplicate parade of the evoked ghosts of Revolutionary War soldiers: "antiques of the same come limping."

> The old graveyards of the hills have hurried to see;
> Uncountable phantoms gather by flank and rear of it,
> Cocked hats of mothy mould and crutches made of mist,
> Arms in slings and old men leaning on young men's shoulders.

Unnoticed by the living crowds, these ghosts vent their wordless gestural rage on the parade of their unworthy descendants. They make motions of ineffectual protest, as though desperate to interfere on Burns's behalf. But, not having seen the cause and center of the parade, Whitman's spectator cannot comprehend or interpret their reaction. Why are they not impressed as he is? He interrogates them, speaking in effect directly to the eighteenth-century fathers, asking at last, "Is this hour with the living too dead for you?"

With that question a new regime of ironic understanding descends on the speaker and infuses the poem.

> Retreat then! Pell-mell! . . . Back to the hills, old limpers!
> I do not think you belong here anyhow.

He can, however, think of one thing that does belong here. He proposes that an official delegation be sent from Boston to London:

> They shall get a grant from the Parliament, and go with a cart to the royal vault,
> Dig out King George's coffin . . . unwrap him quick from the grave-clothes . . . box up his bones for a journey
> Find a swift Yankee clipper . . . here is freight for you blackbellied clipper,
> Up with your anchor! shake out your sails! . . . steer straight toward Boston bay.
> Now call the President's marshal again, and bring out the government cannon,
> And fetch home the roarers from Congress, and make another procession and guard it with foot and dragoons.

The symmetry of the matched processions suggests a certain equivalence in Whitman's view between exporting live men as slaves and importing dead men as monarchs. Both actions belong to an identical paradigm of tyranny (Hildreth's "Despotism"), based on a confusion, once gloriously clarified by the fathers but remystified since, about what is native and what is foreign, what genuinely belongs "here," and what does not.[8]

To the extent that the poem has a specific accusation to make, it is that the commitment to a Revolutionary ethos of egalitarian democracy and republican liberty had been lost sight of in an aristocracy-creating scramble for commercial gain. Although Boston had already been surpassed by New York as the commercial center of the country, it still prided itself on its traffic with England (in particular) and on the elegant tall clipper ships it built to maintain that commerce. The Whigs who for years had controlled the state and who controlled it still were known for defending its commercial interests—mainly its cotton manufacturing—by placating the South. This was the only reason once-Revolutionary Boston could now have for sending a man into bondage. To them the Fugitive Slave Law had been the lynchpin in a final adjustment of those sectional differences that threatened their industrial economy; they had rejoiced in its passage and had given all thanks for it to Webster. What they had bought for themselves in this exchange took four years to become evident: they are here represented as surrounding the rendition of a slave with a carnival atmosphere.

There is, in Whitman's indictment, more than a little of Jefferson's suspicion of the social and political effects of manufacturing as a way to wealth and perhaps as well some of Jefferson's sense of the damage done to action, activity, and enterprise when the responsibility for the production of value is sloughed off onto the shoulders of the slave. Certainly there is a good deal of Jefferson's dislike of England's aristocratic society—to the point of Whitman's overlooking the fact that England, not America, was now the slave's free haven. At the end of the poem, when King George's skeleton has been reassembled, his ribs glued back in place, and the crown restored to his empty skull, the newly vassalized Yankee, the eponymous Jonathan, is told: "here is one of your bargains."

What is finally more interesting than Whitman's Jeffersonian critique of the Burns case, however, is the curious absence from it of Burns himself. Whether by deliberate intent or otherwise, the poem becomes a spectator's lesson about not seeing. As in Herman Melville's great story about slavery, "Benito Cereno" (completed by April 1855), the slave protagonist is the one of all the characters whose perspective is pointedly ungiven, though he is in both cases the proximate cause of all that happens.

An argument could be made that the omission of the black center in these two slices of white life is a conscious rhetorical strategy designed to appeal to readers on familiar ground without confronting them with the racial divide. Antislavery, in this argument, does not require knowledge of the victim but, consigning victimization to the realm of God's or nature's mysteries, can go forward among whites on the accidents of self-interest.

Certainly it was the intention of antislavery writers to multiply reasons for opposing slavery, but there is cause to suppose that the invisibility of the black man in certain antislavery works is structural, intrinsic to the discourse, and not the calculated trick of a calculating writer. Like Hildreth's *Despotism in America,* Whitman's poem is an example of the political construction of the antislavery argument, and the power of such discourse to compel assent—or to confront a subject at all—is inevitably related to its partialities and limitations and to the existence of territory outside its purview. The crisis of 1854 comes down to the fact that American politics was operating *on* the black population as a force utterly alien to them: the procession down State Street, a piece of consciously designed government-issue symbolism, loudly proclaimed this fact. So long as "politics" remained the exclusive province of white male voters, the discourse appropriate to it (and engendered by it) would remain structurally incapable of entering into the world of the object and registering the plight of the slave. If Mrs. Stowe had stunned the world by seeming to make such an entrance, she accomplished the feat by attacking and renouncing, not by taking up, the discourse of politics. As it was, the only way to represent slavery *as* a political issue was to show its secondary effects on the white world of acknowledged political constituencies.

In this manner, slavery threatened to become a thing that happens to white people. The Worcester *Spy,* perhaps the most progressive paper in Massachusetts, ran an article on June 13 titled "Who Is To Blame?" concluding that "We are the slaves and vassals of the South, and we have been made so by the servile, money-getting, cotton-spinning, compromise-making citizens of our own State." The New York *Post* seemed to agree, saying that if Boston had once been the "Athens of America," it was now "the City of the Seizers."[9]

[H]ow many Christian ministers to-day will mention him, or those who suffer with him? How many will speak from the pulpit against the cruel outrage on humanity which has just been committed; or against the many, even worse ones, which are committed in this country every day? Too well do we know that there are but very few, and these few alone deserve to be called the ministers of Christ, whose doctrine was "Break every yoke, and let the oppressed go free."

CHARLOTTE FORTEN, JOURNAL, JUNE 4, 1854

To-day, ministers are preaching as never before.

THEODORE PARKER, JUNE 4, 1854

On the day of Pentecost, fiery tongues rest on their heads, courage and conviction enter their hearts—they are heard by every man speaking to him in his own tongue, united, strong, brave, hopeful, loving—they go forth, to conquer the world.

JAMES FREEMAN CLARKE, JUNE 4, 1854

Two days after the rendition, on June 4—Whitsunday—the pulpits of New England resounded with discourses on the Burns case, on Kansas-Nebraska, or on both together. Only a small portion of these sermons was ever published, but among those that were the ones most eagerly received and most widely read were composed by men intellectually in Emerson's debt. New England Transcendentalism was working out its antislavery vocabulary. There was *Massachusetts in Mourning* by Higginson, preached at Worcester; *The New Crime Against Humanity,* delivered by Parker at the Music Hall; *The Rendition of Anthony Burns,* given by James Freeman Clarke at the Church of the Disciples; *The New Commandment,* by Octavius Brooks Frothingham at Salem; *Legal Anarchy,* by John Weiss of Watertown; and, a week later, Samuel Johnson's *The Crisis of Freedom,* preached at Lynn.

Higginson appeared that morning as a hero before the excited congregation of the Free Church at Brinsley Hall, home of the Worcester Freedom Club and momentarily the center of antislavery in Massachusetts. The tone of the address hovered between a sadness over slavery's triumph and a righteous anger that urged toward revolution. He spoke defiantly from a text in Jeremiah ("Shall the iron break the Northern iron and the steel?") but confessed that "to-day is, or should be . . . a day of funeral service—we are all mourners—and what is there for me to say?" He wondered whether there was "any disinterested love of Freedom left in Massachusetts," but thought it a matter of congratulation that at least freedom "did not die without a struggle, and that it took thousands of armed men to lay her in her grave at last."[1]

That the issue had got past the talking stage was a thing to be thankful for: "Words are nothing," Higginson said, "we have been surfeited with words for twenty years." Concerned to vindicate his own course of action, he said that men must consecrate to the Right not the higher faculties only, but "our proper manly life on earth" as well. "Our souls and bodies are both God's, and resistance to tyrants is obedience to Him." He supposed that had the attack on the Court House been better supported it might have succeeded by force, yet without bloodshed or "the death of that one man." Aware that many in the audience had doubts about the morality of physically coercive means, he wished it understood that "calm, irresistible force, in a good cause, becomes sublime." The sublimity was shown in the capacity of heroic action to be represented symbolically: "The strokes on the door of that Court House that night . . . went echoing from town to town, from Boston to far New Orleans, like the first drum beat of the Revolution—and each reverberating throb was a blow upon the door of every Slave-prison of this guilty Republic." If the self-importance of this declaration sounds slightly hysterical, no doubt Higginson *was* excited, yet he knew his own act as a public performance, knew that it was, in one way or another, on all men's minds just then. Some in his congregation had literally heard those symbolic strokes; all well knew that their minister had. Physical experience was coming back to be the source and signifier of the moral symbolic; rhetoric was being regrounded in action. Such was the effect looked for.[2]

Mere words without a proper backing were a poor support for any people. In light of the Burns case, asked Higginson, would words forestall a military despotism?

> What is your safeguard? Nothing but a parchment Constitution, which has been riddled through and through whenever it pleased the Slave Power; which has not been able to preserve to you the oldest privileges of Freedom—Habeas Corpus and Trial by Jury!

The power of ideas was emigrating from language toward a new embodiment in realities more palpable: "We talk of the Anti-Slavery sentiment as being stronger; but in spite of your Free Soil votes, your Uncle Tom's Cabin, and your New York Tribune, here is the simple fact: *the South beats us more and more easily every time.*" Freedom may have a reliance on words, but it takes all "the best eloquence and literature of the time, to balance the demoralization of a single term of Presidential patronage."[3]

The remedy was revolution:

> At any rate my word of counsel to you is to learn this lesson thoroughly—*a revolution is begun!* not a Reform, but a Revolution. If you take part in politics henceforward, let it be only to bring nearer the crisis which will either save or sunder this nation—or perhaps save in sundering . . . For myself, existence looks worthless under [the ascendancy of the slave power]; and I can only make life worth living for, by becoming a revolutionist . . . I see, now, that while Slavery is national, law and order must constantly be on the wrong side. I see that the case stands for me precisely as it stands for Kossuth and Mazzini, and I must take the consequences.

Higginson's particular recommendation as to the position the people should take was to "fall back on first principles" and then make those principles felt by asserting them. Thus, first, they should make Worcester free: "No longer conceal Fugitives and help them on, but show them and defend them. Let the Underground Railroad stop here! Say to the South that Worcester, though part of a Republic, shall be as free as if ruled by a Queen! *Hear, O Richmond! and give ear, O Carolina! henceforth Worcester is Canada to the Slave!*"

In this jeremiad Higginson was giving the Free Church a near version of what Emerson had always maintained: that power lies not in numbers but in the dedication of the forlorn hope that men make who plant themselves indomitably on the truth, defying custom, circumstance, and the whole world besides. Transcendentalism, deployed as antislavery, becomes revolution.[4]

As Higginson spoke that day to Worcester, so Theodore Parker spoke to the world. The Boston minister knew he had a national and an international readership, and used his sermon deliberately to fashion the historical record. An unusually long sermon as delivered, "The New Crime Against Humanity" was further added to for publication; it gives a full account of the affair as its author saw it, with historical reference to the position of Massachusetts on slavery and with much recurring emphasis on the personal culpability of Edward Loring.

Parker's attention to personalities lay at the heart of his popularity as a piquant and controversial minister, and at the heart also of his unpopularity among those who felt it the duty of clergymen to speak softly and carry no sticks. In the world as Parker's theology constructed it—an unpredestinated world without miracles, where faith meant active striving for an ideal, not passive obedience to external instructions—human character counted for much. Just as Parker would say in his concluding paragraph that "There is power in human nature to end this wickedness," so he believed there was fault in furthering it. At bottom he wished to understand and make clear to others how such an event as the rendition of Anthony Burns could have happened. He did not blame the people generally ("I believe . . . in the nobleness of man") and pointed out that "Not a single pro-slavery measure has ever been popular with the mass of men in New England or Massachusetts." That these measures consistently became controlling in Massachusetts he laid to the door of the leader class, to the immense prestige of Webster, to the cowardice (as he forthrightly called it) of Edward Everett, and more generally to a hard-hearted indifference to freedom and justice on the part of Boston's men of wealth and fashion. More specifically, in the Burns case, did he blame the weak pliancy of Governor Washburn and Mayor Smith and the servile party spirit of Hallett and Freeman. But above all he blamed the moral blindness of Edward Greely Loring, "the prime mover." "He was not obliged to be a commissioner," said Parker in this day's sermon. "He was not forced into that bad eminence . . . If Mr. Loring did not like kidnapping, he need not have kept his office. But he liked it. He wrote three articles, cold and cruel, in the *Daily Advertiser,* defending the Fugitive Slave Bill." Even had he kept his position, he could have declined the particular case, as other commissioners had done—as Hallett himself had done in the Craft case. Everything in Loring's behavior identified him as a responsible and voluntary agent, unlike, say, the marshal's guard, whose perfidious conduct was less a cause for despair simply because they "were tools, not agents."[5]

Positioned as he was, Loring ought to have been an exemplar of the freedom he enjoyed. Receiving its benefits in full measure, he ought to have been its advocate and defender. Yet there was something in Loring's culture that, while freeing his action, had corrupted his character. Something, in Parker's view, had loosened the man's hold on the higher law of God and made him, in effect, morally insane. The madness had shown itself in numerous instances of prejudicial conduct during the trial: in the favorable view of the claimant's case implied in Loring's pretrial statement about the likely outcome; in his ruling certain evidence and admissions in or out; in construing as he did the probative value of certain evidence; in permitting the claimant to switch in midtrial from the sixth to the tenth section of the law; in giving credence to the testimony of a biased witness over unbiased ones, and so forth. None of these actions had been forced on him; each testified to Loring's willful pursuit of an outcome favorable to slavery and damning to freedom. Why would a man do such a thing?

The sermon suggests that Loring's behavior was both tragic (destructive of "confidence in humanity") and at the same time deeply mysterious. Parker frankly wondered at it, holding it up as an instance of undoubted voluntarism and therefore of culpability, but only hinting at the reasons behind it. Most slave commissioners, in Parker's view, had man-stealing in their bones and operated from "an osteological necessity." But in the case of Loring, a carefully turned-out product of Massachusetts institutions, appearances had seemed to promise a different result. "His breeding and his culture, his social position, his membership in a Christian church"—all were factors tending to preclude moral insanity—unless, that is, each of these had become pathological in themselves. The isolating privilege of Boston's favored genealogies, the practical atheism of Boston's commercial culture, the proslavery views of Boston's churches had long been among Parker's targets, and they now seemed to have found their representative man, their apotheosis, in Edward Loring, the scapegrace judge of probate.[6]

Parker's skewering of the commissioner's moral character comes to focus on the kinds of mistakes that result from installing the "lower law" in place of the higher. What is at issue is Loring's faith in that which he has not merely sworn to uphold but which he has gone on to make a thorough fetish of.

> Imagine the scene after man's mythological way. "Edward, where is thy brother Anthony?" "I know not; am I my brother's keeper, Lord?" "Edward, where is thy brother Anthony? "Oh, Lord, he was friendless, and so I smote him; he was poor, and I starved him of more than life. He owned nothing but his African body. I took that away from him, and gave it to another man!"
> Then listen to the voice of the Crucified—"Did I not tell thee, when on earth, 'Thou shalt love the Lord thy God with all thy understand-

ing and thy heart?'" "But I thought thy kingdom was not of this world."

"Did I not tell thee that thou shouldst love thy neighbor as thyself? Where is Anthony, thy brother? I was a stranger, and you sought my life; naked, and you rent away my skin; in prison, and you delivered me to the tormentors—fate far worse than death. Inasmuch as you did it to Anthony, you did it unto me."

The shock comes from Parker's way of finding "Anthony" in the Bible, where other Christians simply do not and cannot. That Parker could locate him there shows how the movement of liberal Christianity (the campaign of the Transcendental ministers, with its roots in Emerson) had, for some, delivered the "Sacred Scriptures" from the status of an inviolable fetish, a relic "not of this world." The Bible—a form of Constitution—seemed to gain power by losing it; to Parker and other Transcendental ministers, it was something that could be "gone into" to the degree that authority for its meanings was transferred to the reader. Loring's problem was that he had, after all, been segregated from the higher law culturally: on the one hand by his reification of the lower law and, on the other (presumably), by a conventional superstitious regard for scripture as a thing fixed, closed, dogmatic, and delivered, the Bible as taught in the proslavery churches. The connection between these two susceptibilities was a point of character, a feeling of personal incompetence and a desire for help from the outside. The cure for this moral insanity was self-reliance, not unlike that which Andrew Jackson had shown in saying that he supported the Constitution—"as I understand it."[7]

Parker's radicalism, from one point of view, amounted simply to a certain orientation toward texts, a decision not to grant them inordinate or tyrannical powers, but instead to meet them with an Emersonian demand for simultaneous quotation and originality. This strategy of self-reliance is evident at another passage in the sermon, in which Parker examined exactly the most derivative and precedent-respecting portion of Loring's decision: his citation of Lemuel Shaw's opinion on the constitutionality of the Fugitive Slave Law. Parker imagines what Shaw might have said in defense of the old Roman practice of martyring Christians:

The torture, persecution, and murder of Christians was not created, established, or perpetuated by the constitution; it existed before; it would have existed if the constitution had not been made. The framers of the constitution could not abrogate the custom of persecuting, torturing, and murdering Christians, or the rights claimed under it. They took it as they found it, and regulated it to a limited extent . . . the provision [for persecuting, torturing, and murdering Christians] was the best adjustment which could be made of conflicting rights and claims to persecute, torture, and murder, and was absolutely necessary to effect what may now be considered as the general pacification by which harmony and peace should take the place of violence and war, [etc.].

When law is not submitted to conscience but is accepted on the recommendation of men in high places or regarded as in itself an ultimate authority, then the right of private judgment (on the basis of which the Protestant religion was loudly distinguishing itself from the Catholic) is trampled upon, tyranny is erected, and freedom fails. Then bad laws enjoy an equality with good laws.[8]

The absurdity of the position that law exacts obedience (a function of slavery) rather than judgment (a function of freedom and personal character) is made clear in yet another of Parker's free quotations, this time of the entire trial, with the creative introduction of yet another aggressively independent variable:

Suppose Colonel Suttle had claimed the mayor and aldermen of Boston as his slaves; had brought a "record" from Alexandria reciting their names, and setting forth the fact of their owing service, and their escape from it; had them kidnapped and brought before Mr. Loring. According to his own ruling, the only question he has to determine is this: "the identity of the persons."

Innocent free persons are in danger of being enslaved whenever a weak judge consents, as a matter of general policy, to be overruled by whatever is law at the moment. The point is not that such a thing *could* happen, but that it already *has* happened.[9]

"Every time a good speech on the great issue was made," said William Herndon, "I sent for it. Hence you could find on my table the latest utterances of Giddings, Phillips, Sumner, Seward, and one whom I considered grander than all of the others—Theodore Parker." Herndon and his law partner, Abraham Lincoln, were in fact engaged at this time in a lengthy study of the slavery question, trying to see their way through the collapse of old parties and the rise of new ones. Long a reader of Parker's works, Herndon had opened a personal correspondence with the Boston minister less than a month before, admitting that "you are my ideal—strong, direct, energetic, charitable." On June 11 he wrote again to say that he was spreading the gospel of Parker's works and of Emerson's works to everyone he met. "I hope you will write out your New York speech and your late Boston sermon. The country needs moving with an eloquent and enthusiastic power. If you write out and publish please send me a copy."[10]

🔥 If We Feel Not

The transcendentalists were quite universally abolitionists, for their philosophy pointed directly towards the exaltation of every natural power.

O. B. Frothingham

If Transcendentalists were busier than others in shaping opinion in the spring and summer of 1854, it has to be acknowledged that their activity also had its recoil in a reshaping effect on them. Arguably none of them survived the effort. At least they were not afterward what they had been before, which is perhaps no more than one expects in a revolution. Emerson and Thoreau, for example, who were now more willing to speak out on public issues, were prepared by the events of this year to endorse the militant measures applied by John Brown and others in Kansas and at Harper's Ferry.

The Transcendental movement, centering always on Emerson, had long been a prolific source of ideas—perhaps the most prolific in America—but its appeal, like that of Puritanism, was at bottom emotional rather than intellectual: it fed a starved appetite for authenticity and offered a feeling of relatedness to what was permanent in the nature of the universe. In a busy, bustling, trivial nineteenth century, it alleged an affinity between the simple separate person and the realization of principles. It opposed all that obscured this connection and embraced everything that announced it. It was exhilarating and new-making precisely to the extent that Americans had resigned themselves, as Thoreau would have it, to lives of quiet desperation.

After 1850 it was antislavery that focused this message most clearly, showed the relation between discouragement and slavery on the one hand and hope and freedom on the other. Emerson's central contribution had been to extend a general permission to the people to doubt the efficacy of their mossbacked institutions as vehicles of hope and to trust their own instincts as independent social critics. It was, explicitly, a call to leave derivative or secondhand experience behind and enter into authentic agency or freedom. The reward for doing this was to find oneself in a new world.

"The antislavery agitation," said the Transcendentalist minister O. B. Frothingham,

> was felt to be something more than an attempt to apply the Beatitudes and the Parables to a flagrant case of inhumanity—it was regarded as a new interpreter of religion, a fresh declaration of the meaning of the Gospel, a living sign of the purely human character of a divine faith, an education in brotherly love and sacrifice; it was a common saying that now, for the first time in many generations, the essence of belief was made visible and palpable to all men; that Providence was teaching us in a most convincing way, and none but deaf ears could fail to understand the message . . . Then, if ever, we ascended the Mount of Vision.[1]

Any philosophy predicated on openness is always at risk of being overwhelmed by what it is open to. The old churches had been a schooling in a faith once (long ago) delivered to the saints, who had, perhaps, "beheld God and nature face to face"; but that primary relation had lapsed, and now, as Emerson said, we see only second hand, "through their eyes." Transcendentalists like Parker, Higginson, and Clarke had "come out" from that church to found experimental churches of their own or, like Emerson and George Ripley, to pursue experiments even less recognizably Christian. Now, if the empty and rejected husk of orthodox religion had failed to free the slave and showed no sign of ever doing so, perhaps it was up to the slave to save the churches, pouring lost life back in. As Frothingham later recalled, the antislavery men "made real the precepts of the New Testament."

> Their clients were the poor, the lowly, the disfranchised, the unprivileged, against whom the grandeurs of the world lifted a heavy hand. They were champions of those who sorrowed and prayed, and this was enough to win sympathy and disarm criticism. It was a great experience; not only was religion brought face to face with ethics, but it was identified with ethics. It became a religion of the heart: pity, sympathy, humanity, and brotherhood were its essential principles. At the

antislavery fairs all sorts and conditions of men met together, without distinction of color or race or sex. There was really an education in the broadest faith, in which dogma, creed, form, and rite were secondary to love; and love was not only universal, but was warm.

Whatever delusions there may be in all this, it is clear that without the general encouragement of Transcendentalism, without its assault on institutions or its invitation to subjectivity and authentic action, antislavery might never have been seen as an occasion for religious renewal or become popular on that basis. As it was, erstwhile Unitarians, wandering among the black folk at the antislavery fair, could feel (as they had wanted to feel since Puritan times) like first-century Christians. Emerson's prescription for the churches had been "first, soul, and second, soul, and evermore, soul. A whole popedom of forms one pulsation of virtue can uplift and vivify." Parker believed the same.[2]

Frothingham's sermon on the Burns case was in many ways the most remarkable of them all. The text was not from Jeremiah (the nationalistic choice of Higginson and Clarke) but from the gospel of John: Christ's announcement of the "new commandment" to "love one another." This injunction had been given to Christ's followers that they might be known as veritable disciples to "all men"—known not by their subscription to any doctrine or by the performance of any rite, but simply by the love and charity they bore to others.

Before Frothingham had finished his sermon, however, he was in deep trouble with his congregation. They had found offensive the proposition that the churches had failed of this sign of discipleship; they did not like to hear the word *Christian* put in quotation marks. "It is the simple truth," said Frothingham, "that christians of all sects have, and still do, substantially reverse the principles of Jesus." These nominal Christians "care more for dogmas than they do for charity." "The Christian Church universal of this country,—I state but a commonplace truth,—is blind and indifferent to the most hideous institution now existing under the sun." There is "too much truth in the saying, that the church has been the great obstacle" in the way of abolition, though "the churches . . . deem themselves no less christian on this account."[3]

Last week in Boston, he went on to say, while ministers of all the denominations gathered to dispute about Trinity and Unity and to find out the best mode of instructing children in the doctrines of the gospel, *"Christ himself,* in the person of one of the least of his disciples, was arraigned before Pontius Pilate."

> There sat the procurator on his tribunal; there were the mercenary sol-diery, filling the avenues . . . there stood the prisoner bound and guarded; and what was his crime? Why, he had declared himself a *king:* the king of his own person . . . "Art thou such a king?" he is asked. "I am a king." Then come the false witnesses with their testimony . . . A message arrives from the Southern headquarters, saying, "if thou let this man go, thou art not Caesar's friend" . . . All this goes forward in broad day, for successive days, in a city crowded with people who had come up to the great passover festival. The prisoner is condemned; and ere that mighty concourse of christians has dispersed, his insulted form, manacled and guarded by nearly two thousand armed men, is led along our modern *via dolorosa,* toward the place of infamy and pain be-yond the city. What a commentary this upon the christianity of chris-tendom; the christianity of the puritan city, the "paradise of divines"!

Frothingham's congregation was getting distinctly uncomfortable. Some had walked out by this time.[4]

He addressed the question of what one might have done—ought to have done—last week in Boston. What could Jesus himself have done? The answer is a wild blend of Emerson and Harriet Beecher Stowe, a sort of sentimental Transcendentalism:

> I cannot tell . . . Questions of conduct are always perplexing, even in trifling matters. No one can judge for another . . . One thing we all can do: we can feel as Christians should; if we feel not, we can do nothing; and it is because we feel not, that we do nothing. And after all, feeling is doing. Feeling will express itself in characteristic ways. What is in us *must* come out of us. If nothing comes out of us, there is nothing in us. If the effect we produce be evil, it is vain to pretend that the cause that produces it is good; that pity expresses itself in indifference, mercy in callousness, and humanity in inhuman allegiance to inhuman statutes. Judge the tree by its fruits.

Had the nominal Christians been authentic Christians, none of the evil work of that week could have gone forward. A wolf, it is seen, may enter the very fold of Christ and without causing protest or re-sistance steal one of the sheep, yet there is a great deal of bleating if the form of the service is so much as questioned.[5]

So Frothingham had said at the time, and so he subsequently discovered—for he was so distraught over the Burns case that he refused to offer communion to his lukewarm (or openly hostile) congregation. They rejected his sermon ("It is not what Christ taught that saves the world," explained one of the parish, "but what he was and did"). Their resentment over the sermon was amplified by the omission of communion into a conflict that could not be resolved short of the minister's departure, so he divided the rest of his pastoral career between Jersey City, New Jersey, and New York City. Eventually he wrote a biography of Theodore Parker and the first book-length study of New England Transcendentalism.[6]

As Parker's and Frothingham's sermons suggest, there were not a few ministers in Boston inclined to take a different view of slavery. Those who were cavalierly said to be "proslavery" in fact with few exceptions professed dislike of the institution, but were willing to let Southerners do as they pleased and were certainly unwilling to jeopardize the Union over some scruple affecting none but blacks. Parker seems to have been right in suggesting that these men presided disproportionately over the fashionable churches. One whom Parker particularly liked to talk about in this connection was Ezra Stiles Gannett, successor to the great William Ellery Channing at the Federal Street Church. Among the most prominent of Gannett's congregation was the slave commissioner George Ticknor Curtis, who was alleged to have helped Loring in the framing of his decision.

Gannett was by all accounts a kindly and generous if unspeculative man who had been present at the organization of the Unitarian denomination in 1825 and who continued ever afterward to feel a proprietary interest in its welfare and that of its clergymen. He was uncomfortable with controversy and avoided political topics in the pulpit. By temperament and conviction he was a man of peace. At the time of the passage of the Fugitive Slave Bill he claimed to be convinced that the measure preserved the country from fratricidal war and, in the threatened extinction of the American Union, from the collapse of the last best hope for human progress. His fear of war, it may be, spoke more loudly to him than his regard for justice, for he knew even then that slavery was a "sin." Further, he found himself defending the conduct of his slave-catching parishioner against statements by fellow ministers that the law "could not be administered with a pure heart or unsullied ermine." Mr. Gannett was sure that Mr.

Curtis' motives were of the highest, his ermine immaculate. To Parker it seemed the situation could stand to be expressed otherwise: "A parishioner of my brother Gannett came to kidnap a member of my church; Mr. Gannett preaches a sermon to justify the Fugitive Slave Law, demanding that it should be obeyed; yes, calling on his church members to kidnap mine, and sell them into bondage forever. Yet all this while Mr. Gannett calls himself a 'Christian,' and me an 'infidel.'"[7]

During Anniversary Week of 1854, while the Burns trial was going on, Gannett never suspected that one of his houseguests, the Reverend John Parkman, was a member of the Boston Vigilance Committee, and so he dealt freely in judgments on the fanaticism of the abolitionists. "What is one man against the preservation of the Union?" he asked; "what good is going to come of all this excitement?"—so that Parkman was forced at last to require that there be no more talk on the subject. On Friday, when Parkman returned to the house from watching the procession, Gannett asked him if it was true that Burns had been sent back. Told that it was, Gannett collapsed in tears.[8]

In the immediate aftermath, Gannett said that the decision to send the slave back was "right," but he was annoyed and upset that a group of schoolgirls in his charge had contrived to witness the rendition. Perhaps, he was tempted to think, it was better after all to defy the law. "No, obey now!" he decided: "but the revolution must come, and such a general revolution is not disobedience." His daughter asked him what he would do if a fugitive should come to his door. "I have thought of that," he said. "I should shelter him and aid him to go further on to Canada, and then I should go and give myself up to prison, and insist on being made a prisoner, [and] accept of no release. For I have decided what to do as an individual against the government, and therefore I should abide the result."[9]

Having decided what to do as an individual, Gannett brooded for a week over what to say as a minister. On June 11 he delivered his *Relation of the North to Slavery,* a statement in which one can see all the psychic violence by which a bold new conviction is wrenched from a history of compromise:

It is the relation which we shall in future hold to Slavery, that was brought before us by the occurrences which so painfully agitated this community for many days, and at last drew tears from the eyes of men, and harsh words from woman's lips; it is the relation in which we shall allow ourselves hereafter to stand towards Slavery, that demands serious and Christian thought. For this is not purely a political question; it has its moral side, and religion and Christianity are entitled to examine it as entering within their domain.

He hoped there would be no imputing of "moral cowardice" to any whose conduct had evinced loyalty to principle, even mistaken principle. He touched on some of the standard proslavery arguments: there are, he said, "thousands of masters at the South who believe Slavery to be a logical deduction from sure premises, and a fair inference from Christian truths." Likewise it is "equally wrong to charge upon all masters harsh usage or cold neglect of their slaves. In many families they are treated with uniform kindness." Neither should we judge the matter from extreme examples on either side, as *Uncle Tom's Cabin* would have us do. It is not from portraits of incredible piety or inhuman cruelty that we should construct our views on this important topic. That slavery is "ineradicably wrong and bad" cannot be a function of the particular style given it by particular masters, but is wholly owing to the irresponsible ownership of one human being by another: such alleged property right needs to be denied categorically.[10]

In this crisis, some part of Gannett wanted to leapfrog over the Freesoilers and demand the abolition of slavery in the South itself: "an immediate adoption of measures for the final liberation of every man, woman, and child, now regarded as transferrable property, is what a correct view of duty would obtain from the Southern master." And yet this duty could not be enforced by the national government or be required of one state by another, for states' rights had to be respected under the Constitution, and no policy should be interfered with so long as it is "kept within the boundaries of the State in which it originates, and does not invade the constitutional rights of any citizen of another State." Until revolution comes, resolving society back into its original elements, we are limited to "passive resistance" to such laws as would "violate our consciences to obey." It would "be fatal to integrity and purity of character," Gannett said, to allow obedience to human law to supplant "our respect for what we believe to be the requisition of God." Therefore, given that it is both immoral and impolitic to fight for justice, we may yet elaborately suffer for it. "Painful as may be the struggle, we must not disturb the public peace for the sake of redressing a private wrong."[11]

How Gannett got the idea that slavery was after all a "private wrong" is difficult to say: perhaps it simply *felt* so to him. In fact the sermon's painfully contorted arguments and embarrassed scruples show more than anything else the extreme pressure that events had put on pacifist principles and how those principles, if adhered to, were bound to make a hash of any response to the urgent conflict between conscience and the law. The quality of Gannett's argument, the surfaced motives, and the distressed, helpless feel of it all assist us in seeing why the appeal of nonresistance was diminishing, and how John Brown and civil war could be waiting in the wings.

Gannett concluded with a number of suggestions as to what was to be done: first, make no further compromises with the South; second, use the political process to repeal whatever in the law is repugnant to the conscience; third, oppose the westward extension of slavery; and fourth (and most significantly), "rescue our own soil from being trampled by those whose attempts to reclaim their fugitive servants are conducted in a manner to wound our sensibilities and provoke our passions." This last point was the one that most drew the attention of Slave Commissioner Curtis as he sat glowering and sour-faced that Sunday morning in his pew. What Gannett meant was that the men of Massachusetts, in order not to have their sensibilities wounded, in order to avoid having their passions provoked and displayed, ought to pass a rigorous Personal Liberty Law, the effect of which would be to compel the South to regard the law of 1850 as they had once regarded the law of 1793—that is, as a thing of no practical utility. If the South proved unwilling to do that and kept up its outrageous slave-catching forays, then the North would have to decide if the Union was worth preserving under such conditions. Gannett did not think the South would be so rash, but if it meant to press the point, he was prepared, then, for disunion.[12]

Curtis felt that he had been publicly betrayed and humiliated by a friend. In his anger and disgust he wrote a three-part article in rebuttal and had it published in the *Courier,* a Hunker Whig sheet, and then again as a separate pamphlet. His fundamental charge was that of disloyalty: in effect, of rebellion if not treason. "The evidence exists all around us," he wrote, "that there is now a strong disposition here in Massachusetts, to treat the government of the United States, at least in regard to one of its functions, as if it were a foreign power, whose authority over us we may and ought to bring to the test of actual resistance." Curtis was particularly troubled that the American Revolution should be rhetorically co-opted by those who, he believed, sought the dismantling of the federal Union. The frequent assertion that there was a similarity between conditions now and those that had sparked the Revolution of 1775 implied, of course, that the federal government was a tyranny that had to be cast off. "We shall probably find," he wrote, "that the sooner we get rid of the notion that there is any resemblance between our relations to the government of the United States, in this matter, and our former relations with our mother country, the more freely and truly will our moral perceptions be able to operate." He pointed out that we had no representation in the government that imposed the Stamp Act and the Boston Port Bill, nor had we acknowledged in the first place the right of Parliament to legislate for the colonies. The government we defy now, however, is ours—as truly ours "as the government of our separate state is."[13]

Curtis analyzed with great skepticism the feasibility of such disunion as Gannett proposed. No state—and Massachusetts least of all—would be suffered to leave the Union peaceably. If "the North" were to secede, the constituent states would first have to agree, and if the question were nakedly put—will you surrender fugitive slaves or dissolve the Union, break up the government, and take the consequences?—Curtis supposed the answers were unlikely to be unanimous for disunion. But nullifiers could not go even that far "without coming into collision with the forces of the United States, [or] without passing over the dead bodies of their own kindred, and friends, and neighbors."[14]

In his second installment, Curtis began by quoting Article IV, section 2, paragraph 3 of the Constitution in order to demonstrate that what Gannett was proposing was that the South should voluntarily forgo a specifically defined right in the security of its property. The moral question that Gannett posed had to extend to the nature of our behavior in the face of a solemn promise made. That our Northern fathers made an agreement in accommodation of their Southern colleagues might not preempt the moral argument, but the continuing duties imposed by that agreement had to be considered.[15]

The principal duty that the law imposes on the private citizen,

Curtis said, is light enough: it is no more than to avoid interfering with the federal officers who do the work. "We have no responsibility, not even of a moral kind, in the act that is done."[16]

Curtis was annoyed that people could not seem to mind their own business, and he was fed up, too, with the childish rhetoric of the opposition. "Dr. Gannett seems to feel that there is some kind of desecration of our soil, in permitting a fugitive slave to be arrested upon, and removed from it."

> Undoubtedly, our soil is consecrated to Freedom. But is it consecrated to Freedom for *all men?* What consecrates it to Freedom at all? Is it not so consecrated by *the Law?* And is it not so consecrated just so far as the Law has impressed that character upon it, and no farther? We presume that this will be admitted by all. The soil of Massachusetts is not consecrated to Freedom by the general sentiments or feelings of its inhabitants;—it is consecrated to Freedom by *the Laws* which they have ordained for its government, and just so far as those Laws determine the condition of those who are on it . . . It is impossible for the state to make a law which shall consecrate its soil to the Freedom of men, who are made by the Constitution of the United States incapable of acquiring freedom by coming within our jurisdiction. The proposition is not true, therefore, that our soil is consecrated to the freedom of all men. There are certain men who are excepted from this advantage by the operation of the fundamental and paramount law of the country, which determines the character of our soil *as to them;* and while this remains so, there can be no desecration of our soil by removing those persons from it.

Returning to the morality of the question, Curtis pointed out that all states had a natural and unquestionable right to exclude undesirable persons. "Without this right, no state or nation could protect itself, or its people, from foreign vice, or the infections of disease, or from foreign pauperism." The terms of the argument seem to be shifting here a little, but this observation still belongs to the general point that Massachusetts soil is not free to all.[17]

Like Dr. Gannett, and like "most of us," Curtis refuses to make "an absolute judgment" that slavery is everywhere and always a sin or that the slaveholder is everywhere and always a sinner. We cannot certainly know that God is an abolitionist. And just as this uncertainty prevents us from fitting out ships for rescuing slaves from Virginia, so we should not presumptuously use state law for the same purpose.[18]

The final installment of Curtis' argument is given over mainly to issues of legal history, imputing to Gannett a sorry ignorance of the reasons why the Fugitive Slave Law of 1850 was made stronger than the law of 1793, and why the South would not stand idly by and watch it be gutted. Around this argument is woven another, amounting almost to an *ad hominem* attack, which implies that Gannett and the many others who now speak as he does are simply being hysterical, that their refusal to stay the course is not a matter of logic and principle at all, but of unmanly squeamishness. Gannett's solicitude about "sensibilities" and "passions," he suggests, is morally misplaced. If during the week of the Burns trial sensibilities and passions were dangerously excited, the fault lay not with Suttle for coming after his property, but with the Massachusetts men who in the madness of their fanaticism murdered a federal officer.[19]

🔥 FOURTH OF JULY

What, to the American slave, is your 4th of July? I answer; a day that reveals to him, more than all other days in the year, the gross injustice and cruelty to which he is the constant victim.

FREDERICK DOUGLASS

At home in Concord during the Burns trial, Thoreau was busy loafing at his ease, quite literally "observing a spear of summer grass," as his journals tell us. He was also observing the riot of the cankerworms in the black cherry trees and in a general sort of way supervising the "revolution of the seasons." He could not spare the time to come to Boston, preferring instead "to be present at the birth of shadow" in the first expansion of young leaves. He very much blamed "such a time as this" for dragging his attention away to the poisonous vulgarity of the newspapers, but he read them and took the measure of the Burns case from Boston's proslavery sheets as well as from the *Liberator* and the *Commonwealth*. On the day of the rendition, he took his mother and sister on a boat ride along the Assabet to Annursnack.[1]

On the next day arrived two Worcester friends, H. G. O. Blake and Theo Brown, who had undoubtedly come from Boston. That weekend, indoors and out, they talked about justice and heroism, themes that kept them coming back to the name of their mutual friend Higginson. For Thoreau, it was an occasion to find fault with fame:

> In some cases fame is perpetually false and unjust. Or rather I should say that she *never* recognizes the simple heroism of an action, but only as connected with its apparent consequence. It praises the interested energy of the Boston Tea Party, but will be comparatively silent about the more bloody and disinterestedly heroic attack on the Boston Court-House, simply because the latter was unsuccessful. Fame is not just. It never finely or discriminately praises, but coarsely hurrahs. The truest acts of heroism never reach her ear, are never published by her trumpet.

In fact until June 10, when he was arrested, Higginson was the reverse of famous, his secret close-guarded by friends and kept from the ears of the police. Thereafter it was evident that he, unlike his more obscure co-defendants, would be the focus of useful publicity in a political trial. At this point Lucy Stone suggested that, for fame's sake and for the sake of the cause, it would be best altogether if the minister were convicted and hanged.[2]

Thoreau had his own reasons for thinking about fame at this time. Since March he had been reading and revising galley proofs for *Walden,* expecting publication in June, recalling all the while the failure of his first book just five years before. No, fame was never just, never discriminating: people were "so occupied with the factitious cares and superfluously coarse labors of life that its finer fruits cannot be plucked by them." Concerned about the reception of *Walden,* he had nevertheless learned to curb his longing for general approval and to expect little or nothing in the way of commendation. Besides, there was nothing heroic—comparatively speaking—about publishing a book. He would put that work aside, delaying its appearance until August, and speak out on the Burns matter.

Thoreau's speaking fell somewhat accidentally into a struggle over ideological ownership of the Fourth of July. On June 4, when Thoreau in his journal compared Higginson's heroism to that of the mock-Indians of the Revolution, Higginson, in his *Massachusetts in Mourning,* was calling for the cancellation of Fourth of July ceremonies in Worcester. It would be a mockery, he felt, to rejoice much at this time in the nation's freedom. Four days later, the Boston Vigilance Committee called on all the towns of the Commonwealth to imitate "the worthy example of the City of Providence" and omit the usual celebrations. Then,

> As if to glory in their shame, and wantonly to outrage heaven and earth, the City Authorities of Boston,—*fresh from the kidnapping of Anthony Burns,*—have made the most extensive preparations to celebrate the Fourth of July with all the pomp and circumstance of a hollow, man-stealing patriotism, ending with a costly display of fireworks in the evening, in which such bitter mockeries as *"America is free,"* and *"statutes of Liberty and Justice,"* (!!) are to be emblazoned in fiery forms, for the admiration of a people in vassalage to Southern slave-hunters and slave-drivers!

In response—or simultaneously—the Massachusetts Anti-Slavery Society called for a counterdemonstration, "A Grand Mass Meeting of the Friends of Freedom," to assemble at a picnic ground in Framingham to hear such speakers as Garrison, Phillips, Charles Remond, Stephen S. Foster, and Lucy Stone. While certain newspapers condemned the abolitionists for trenching on the national jubilee and for "getting up funeral processions and parading about the coffins and chains," others were determined to

> Raise no starry banner—tears of shame its brightness dims!
> On its silken folds, blood-written, see the names of BURNS and SIMMS!
> Did it wave above the "Acorn" as the guardian of the sea?
> When it floated o'er the "Morris," did it set the captive free?

Or yet to

> Tear down the flaunting lie!
>   Half-mast the starry flag!
> Insult no sunny sky
>   With this polluted rag!
> Destroy it, ye who can!
>   Deep sink it in the waves!
> It bears a fellow-man
>   To groan with fellow-slaves.[3]

Such forthright clamor over symbols, with its suggestion of a displacement of antagonism, reminds us that the clamor over Burns had truly and all along been a fight of the same sort: all of it seems to confess in its rhetoric that there is something at the center that cannot be directly got at or contended with and so is practically absent. From this comes the impression that all the respondents individually, all whose attention had been drawn by Anthony Burns and his difficulty, had more or less "missed the point" and got angry, by default, with something nearby. We can make out, in a rough way, what it is that prevents a particular individual from responding pertinently and so becoming, as we may say, heroic and famous. In looking at the event retrospectively, which is to say with some illusory sense of having seen the whole of it, what we in fact see most are the limitations of the actor's approach—how that is fatally delimited by a culture that makes this person a Democrat or a Freesoiler and that one religious or careful of his reputation, makes this one concerned about labor and that one about law, and how their approach makes their action small and partial. Granting that history is the sum of these contingent disappointments and granting that history is eminently worthwhile on that confession, still no narrative can be assembled that fails altogether to suggest the standard by which we know and judge these actions (as we surely do) as partial. Irresistibly we look for the one who least "misses the point," the hero for whom the center is not empty or who succeeds, somehow, in plausibly filling it.

At Framingham, Thoreau came closer than anyone else to naming that center, closer than anyone to defining the quality of displacement and deference in the rhetoric of all the others.

When Independence Day arrived, however, time was short, and there were many who wished to address the meeting. Besides the featured speakers, the crowd heard from a number of others who, like Thoreau, had come forward too late for publicity. Sojourner Truth and Abby Kelley Foster spoke that day, as did John C. Cluer, a Court House rioter, and Moncure Conway, giving his first antislavery speech. None but the main speakers, however, got much attention in the press afterward, and of these Garrison may be said to have stolen the show by recourse to spectacle. He first read the Declaration of Independence, then discussed the contrasting principles embodied in the Fugitive Slave Law, Edward G. Loring's decision, and Benjamin R. Curtis' charge to the grand jury defining the treason of Parker and Phillips. Finally, to give the source of all this latter-day corruption, he read the proslavery clauses in the Constitution. He thereupon burned all these documents (except the Delcaration) one after the other, saying after the last, "So perish all compromises with tyranny.

'And let all the people say *Amen!*'" Which, of course, with only a smattering of protest, they did.[4]

Phillips, who would shortly be arrested, said to the crowd at Framingham:

> When [the work of this summer] is done, I will be proud of the old Bay State. I used to be proud of her. Time was when I took on my lips the name of the old Commonwealth with a glow of conscious pride that gave depth to the tones of my voice, and an added pulse to the heart. I was proud of her; but my pride all vanished when I saw that old Indian on her banner [the flag of Massachusetts] go floating down State Street with the Slave Brigade, with Ben Hallett and the U.S. Marshal and a chained slave beneath him. I have lost all pride in Massachusetts till she redeems herself from that second day of June. Let us roll up a petition, a hundred thousand strong, for the removal of Judge Loring.[5]

Recalling that day of pastoral exhortation, Austin Bearse, captain of the *Moby-Dick* and doorman for the BVC, said, "They kindled Liberty's altar flames till the bush glowed with her divine presence." Moncure Conway recalled: "That day I distinctly recognized that the antislavery cause was a religion." It was altogether a very satisfactory affair.[6]

That Thoreau's speech went so largely unnoticed may be owing to the fact that he gave a much shorter version than was afterward published. However that may be, Garrison noticed it, asked for the manuscript, and printed the complete text in the *Liberator* on July 21. Horace Greeley noticed it there and copied it into the New York *Tribune* on August 2 with an admiring headnote that acknowledged its peculiar authenticity:

> The lower-law journals so often make ado about the speeches in Congress of those whom they designate champions of the Higher Law, that we shall enlighten and edify them, undoubtedly, by the report we publish this morning of a genuine Higher Law speech—that of Henry D. Thoreau at the late celebration of our National Anniversary in Framingham, Mass., where Wm. Lloyd Garrison burned a copy of the Federal Constitution. No one can read this speech without realizing that the claims of Messrs. Sumner, Seward and Chase to be recognized as Higher-Law champions are of very questionable validity. Mr. Thoreau is the Simon-Pure article.

There are many points of similarity between "Slavery in Massachusetts" and other contemporary statements. As many another outraged onlooker had done, Thoreau attacked the commissioner, the governor, the mayor, the military, and the newspapers; but although he did all this very wittily and memorably, the distinctive significance of the address (and what entitles it to Greeley's encomium) is the self-consistent point of view from which the judgments come. At the most basic level, there is in it none of the struggle and perplexity apparent, for example, in Gannett's sermon of conversion, for the simple reason that there is no conversion: the address draws as much on journal material from the Sims rendition of 1851 as from entries inspired by Burns. Nor for that matter is it anywhere at odds with "Resistance to Civil Government." Unlike many—perhaps most—of the commentators on the Burns case, Thoreau is not arguing with himself, though it may be, as some have suggested, that he now understands his position a little better than he had.[7]

Such fundamental consistency is important because Thoreau's main topic and allegation is that the point of view adopted by others is quite ordinarily compromised, sometimes comically, more often tragically. And every compromise he identifies is caused by the individual's ceding some of his autonomy and liberty to the state or to the institutions of the public culture. Men suppose, for example, that voting helps: "The fate of the country," he said, as though in response to Phillips, "does not depend on how you vote at the polls—the worst man is as strong as the best at that game; it does not depend on what kind of paper you drop into the ballot-box once a year, but on what kind of man you drop from your chamber into the street every morning." Men suppose that they can untangle the present dilemma by tracing the history of the Constitution: "The question is not whether you or your grandfather, seventy years ago, did not enter into an agreement to serve the devil, and that service is not accordingly now due; but whether you will not now, for once and at last, serve God,—in spite of your own past recreancy, or that of your ancestor,—by obeying that eternal and only just CONSTITUTION, which He, and not any Jefferson or Adams, has written in your being."[8]

In general, Thoreau believes that the besetting mistake, even among ardent reformers, is that the higher law is taken for a sort of court of appeals—a part of the public sphere to bring sin to—rather than occupied as a home and dwelling place.

Since 1850, when Seward introduced the term into the senatorial debate over the Compromise measures, abolitionists had appropriated "the higher law" in an increasingly routine way to endorse the righteousness of opposing slavery. In this they were abetted by a class of men who supposed that the currency of "higher law" doctrine would (even more than "natural law" doctrine) help to promote their theological or evangelical goals. The tendency in both cases was to arrive at an instrumental application of the concept. Nominally it was an ultimate form of constitution; practically it was a means to a particular end, as can readily be seen from the restricted contexts in which the term comes up. But the notion (without the name) had been a central defining element in Emerson's aggressively noninstrumental thought—and in Thoreau's—for decades before Seward spoke. In the thought of the Transcendentalists, as in that of philosophical idealists generally, the concept of a law higher than any that space and time could show had been extensively explored, not as a tool for blocking the Compromise of 1850, but in the broadest possible sense of freeing slaves or (what is the same thing) producing a free point of view.

There is an implication in this that no point of view can be truly free that is also predominantly instrumental—that if freedom is wanted for a particular person, group, or purpose, the point of view that wants it is mortgaged to the prospect as well as to the means of bringing it about. Garrison is perhaps an instance of this ironic sort of slavery, a point that was not lost on his detractors then or now, or on those, like Hawthorne, who satirized reformers for seeming, in their monomania, too much like the blind leading the blind. Sumner is perhaps in his own way another instance. Yet no one criticized this sort of self-immolating commitment to a purpose more than Emerson, who valued "sphericity" over excessive development in one direction, who supposed that one was freer (not more enthralled) the higher the law one obeyed, and who supposed that we were the rightful inheritors of the *whole* universe, culpable only when we retreated, voluntarily, into a corner.

Yet Higginson attacking the Court House was a hero to Thoreau, as in a year or so the militant John Brown would also become. The point about these men, from Thoreau's perspective, is that they did not wait to gather majorities, but responded as free men answerable to a conscience that could not abide the presence of evil. Had they consulted the practicalities a bit more, they might not have acted at all. In both cases failure—as Thoreau shrewdly noted—was precisely the indicator of the hero's contempt for instrumentality and of the peremptory quality of the call of the higher law. Failure is *often* more heroic than success and more useful to the human race for putting it in mind of the value of having the higher law for a motive and for demeaning the cheap and partial efficacy of a reliance on tactics, policies, and confederates.

"They who have been bred in the school of politics," Thoreau announced, "fail now and always to face the facts." Instrumentalists, Freesoilers, tacticians, anti-Nebraska men, lovers of policy, those who would reform the outsides of things, men whose revolution was not permanent but occasional, "put off the day of settlement indefinitely, and meanwhile the debt accumulates." The slave does not need the "half measures and make-shifts" of the politicians; what he needs is freedom and an end to scheming and deferring.[9]

In a very special way, Thoreau stood before the Framingham crowd to represent the very freedom that the slave was denied, the freedom that, in Thoreau's view, Massachusetts had not protected and defended because, when all was said and done, the state had not thought to value it. The state did not value freedom or personal liberty because, having so rarely seen these qualities exemplified, it did not understand them. (Thoreau had a book in press that would wake his neighbors up and acquaint them with a life of "extra-vagant" freedom.)

"Slavery in Massachusetts" was not to be the response, once more, of a slave to a slave case, but a report issued from free soil about conditions there. The judgments would not sound like the heading of a petition, but would have the quality of prophecy and doom. To be free is to be unimplicated, which in turn is the best and perhaps the only perspective from which one can see that in the present case servile behavior has been passing itself off as authority. Being free means, furthermore, speaking with olympian disdain of that masquerade. In the best-remembered passage from the speech, Thoreau said:

> Massachusetts sat waiting Mr. Loring's decision, as if it could in any way affect her own criminality. Her crime, the most conspicuous and fatal crime of all, was permitting him to be the umpire in such a case. It was really the trial of Massachusetts. Every moment that she hesitated to set this man free, every moment that she now hesitates to atone for her crime, she is convicted. The Commissioner on her case is God; not Edward G. God, but simple God.

The Transcendentalists' stock-in-trade was to startle their readers with an altered point of view. Their business was to see things differently and to persuade us that the difference was finally that between our slavery and their freedom, our customary allegiance to a lower law and theirs to a higher. Readers who liked their work found it instructive, liberating, revolutionary. Here Thoreau puts Edward G. Loring in his place, not by offering an opinion of his actions, but by seeing him as a pathetic substitute God, whose ridiculousness was supported by a population all too eager to vest him with powers not his own. The law becomes a system whereby people, having ceded questions of right and wrong to petty officials, are thrust into the position of merely hoping that right will prevail—a situation that does not, in Thoreau's view, accord with the original relation of free men to the moral world.[10]

Thoreau's idea is that slavery, or unfreedom, subverts and reverses everything (hence the prevailing tone of irony in all his published work). Just as Hildreth had found that slavery was "illegal" because it was philosophically inconsistent with basic legal principles and therefore unregulatable by anything resembling law, so in Thoreau's writings we recognize regimes of freedom by their ironic or antithetical relation to regimes of slavery. "The law will never make men free," he says; "it is men who have got to make the law free. They are the lovers of law and order, who observe the law when the government breaks it." This makes sense and is to be distinguished from anarchy only on the assumption that the higher law is inscribed in the conscience of those free men who independently regulate their conduct by it. Freedom then means the ability to sustain allegiance to the highest law and to resist the inverting forces of compromise.[11]

The address concludes with a call to action: "We have used up all our inherited freedom," he said, alluding to what makes the Fourth of July, for most Americans, a mainly commemorative ritual. "If we would save our lives, we must fight for them." He is very explicit about the life that has been lost: "I feel that my investment in life here is worth many per cent less since Massachusetts last deliberately sent back an innocent man, Anthony Burns, to slavery. I dwelt before, perhaps, in the illusion that my life passed somewhere *between* heaven and hell, but now I cannot persuade myself that I do not dwell *wholly within* hell."

I walk toward one of our ponds; but what signifies the beauty of nature when men are base? We walk to lakes to see our serenity reflected in them; when we are not serene, we go not to them. Who can be serene in a country where both the rulers and the ruled are without principle?

The remembrance of my country spoils my walk. My thoughts are murder to the State, and involuntarily go plotting against her.

He wants the serenity, the remembered country, and voluntary control over his thoughts restored. For all his self-reliant individualism, he cannot claim in the best of mortal times to have lived wholly within heaven on any strength of private rectitude. The moral condition of society matters, as this case tells him, for to the extent that unprincipled behavior announces itself in others, he finds himself drawn out, implicated, and unfree. The failure in one man to honor freedom, it turns out, is the whole source of slavery in another—and Thoreau will not make that mistake himself. He is here this Fourth of July to publish freedom and make it famous.[12]

He ends his address, as he was to end *Walden,* with a hopeful turn to the rebirth of nature in spring—what he had been devotedly studying in his eccentric freedom during the trial. He mentions a white water lily he had recently seen, an emblem of purity in which he found a reassuring pledge that the "integrity and genius" of nature were yet "unimpaired," and that "there is virtue even in man, too, who is fitted to perceive and love it." Thoreau presents himself not as one who, like so many of the others, can feel free only while contentiously demanding it, but as one for whom it is a permanent value, routine and domestic—as one who can speak from it as well as for it. The lily—or nature—is a standard that puts mean actions to shame and "suggests what kind of laws have prevailed longest and widest, and still prevail." To know such a standard is immediately to know "how inconsistent your deeds are with it." The larger, higher, and more independent that standard is which you use, the more free you are of inferior and compromising points of reference and the less likely, in the end, to crucify Anthony Burns.[13]

LETTERS FROM HELL

[I]t is a sad thing to reflect, that the gold of Massachusetts can do what its laws cannot,—give a man his freedom.

JOHN L. SWIFT

On Sunday, July 9, Concord organized its own Vigilance Committee in a meeting attended by Waldo and Lidian Emerson, Thoreau's parents, and by a number of others active in the antislavery movement.

Thoreau himself went that day to Fair Haven by way of "Hubbard's Bathing-Place." The committee decided to sponsor a weekly series of public meetings on slavery and, "to open them with eclat," Emerson was to invite Theodore Parker to give the inaugural lecture.[1]

On July 17, three days before the birth of the Massachusetts Republican party at the Worcester convention, the first group of Kansas emigrants left from Boston under the auspices of the Massachusetts Emigrant Aid Company. This scheme to colonize Kansas with antislavery men—and thus to control it for freedom under the principle of "squatter sovereignty"—was the project of Eli Thayer of Worcester, assisted by Samuel Gridley Howe and Worcester minister Edward Everett Hale, together with Amos A. Lawrence, the leader of Boston's Cotton Whigs, who supplied financial and managerial support.[2]

By this time Higginson and the other Court House rioters, including Martin Stowell, were out on bail, their trials postponed because prosecutions under the state liquor law (the so-called Maine Law) had been given precedence over all others by legislative decree, with the result that the courts were overwhelmed and the criminal justice system was nearly in chaos. On August 1 a number of these bailed rioters attended the celebration of West Indian Emancipation—a regular antislavery holiday—at Abington, Massachusetts. There Charlotte Forten heard Higginson for the first time, heard him say, rather as Thoreau had said, that he hated the Fugitive Slave Law "not because it is unconstitutional . . . but because it is *infernal*." Forten was impressed by him: "he is very fine looking," she wrote, "and has one of the deepest, richest voices I have ever heard." She was much pleased, too, with the "genial, warm-hearted" Johnny Cluer and his broad Scots accent.[3]

On this day, also, the pioneer party of the Emigrant Aid Society arrived at the present site of Lawrence, Kansas, and began to erect a settlement.[4]

Eight days later, *Walden* was published. "We account Henry the King of all American Lions," said Emerson. "He is walking up and down Concord, firm-looking, but in a tremble of great expectation." The letter by Emerson containing this announcement went on to note that "people believe that the recoil from the last outrage will work long . . . The reliance for ousting Washburn and Whiggery in Mass. is mainly on the 'Know Nothings.'"[5]

That summer, Richard Henry Dana won a famous victory over

Bridget Donahoe, a schoolgirl of Ellsworth, Maine, who had been expelled for insisting a bit too strenuously on her right to read the Douay Bible rather than the required King James Version. In his argument on behalf of the local school district, Dana said:

> It is the policy and the principle of our people to absorb and amalgamate into ourselves the strangers who come among us for a permanent home, and to give them equal rights. But if any portion of them insist on keeping up, to the utmost, national and religious distinctions, and in making extravagant and exclusive claims, and thus that two-fold hostility of race and religion is drawn into action, whatever form the contest may take, they must know that it must end, and that soon, in their entire defeat, and probably, as human nature goes, in a state of things worse for them and less creditable to us, than we now have.

The prophecy was thoroughly fulfilled after Dana returned to Boston. Bridget Donahoe's priest, the Reverend John Bapst, became the victim of a nativist mob, was tarred, feathered, and ridden out of town on a rail.[6]

A month later, Dana got what he never expected: a letter from Anthony Burns in prison.

> Richmond August 23th 1854
> My Dr Mr Danner I take the opportunity to rite you A few Lines and I hope that thay will fine you in Physician Good health Peace and hapness and Mr ellis and to all of My friends and Brothern one and all of them I am Glad to say that I am yet A Live through mercy of God and the Lord Jesus Christ that he hath kept me until Now through much Sufferings I am Glad to say that if what you all my friends did for Me could Not keep me from coming Back in to A Land of death it Did dow Sum Good for My suffering moot have Ben ten hundre times greter then it is But I am yet Bound In Jail and are waring my chings Night and day But is Waitinge for Som kinededliver to Come that I May Bee DeLivered & the Man or Men that Brought me here sad that thay was going to By Me But I dont heir No More a Boute it and I think that it is the Last that I shall heir thay tole My oner to Not Let you all have Me But I am for Sale And if you all my friends will please to healp your friend this Much i will Bee to you all A friend all My days And if you will get Sum of your friends to come to Alexandra and not to say that he come from Boston and inquier where Mr Suttle keep Store And Ask him if hath Sole his man and what he will take for him that he wood Like to By Me and you can get me Low he wood take $800 dollars for me Now & I pray in the name of the Lord that you

will Bee to healp me out suffereinge one time please Anthony Burns
dont rite to me until I tel you[7]

When Burns was thrown into his "cubby hole" he had a pen and some
stationery secreted on his person, but no ink. In the first weeks of his
confinement, he had managed with the aid of a spoon to cut through
the floorboards behind the trapdoor—the sole entrance to his cell—
so that when his jailer came in (as he rarely did), the excavation was
covered. This hole gave Burns access to other slaves in the room
below, and it was through their help that he eventually procured some
ink. He wrote with his hands manacled; then, when he saw a black
man pass in the street below, he threw the letter out the barred window, weighted with a piece of brick chipped from the wall. The letter had been addressed to "Lawyer danner Boston / Massachusetts" and
was at first misdelivered to James Dana, a very distant relative.[8]

For months afterward nothing more was heard. Burns's maltreat-
ment finally made him sick enough for the jailers and Suttle to relent.
He was given some medical attention, spruced up, and, sometime in
November, put on the auction block in Richmond. There, with Suttle
in attendance, the notorious fugitive stood for more than an hour
while the crowd angrily jeered and taunted him. Bids were very slow
in coming. Finally it occurred to the auctioneer to advertise Burns as
a minister of the gospel. That helped, since religious slaves were often
docile and obedient, but in the end the successful bid was only
$905—from David McDaniel, a cotton planter and dealer in horses
and slaves (or, alternatively, "a horse-racer and gambler by profession") from Rocky Mount, North Carolina. He cared not at all about
Burns's religion: it was a financial speculation.[9]

To avoid the mobs, McDaniel took away his purchase in the middle
of the night. He told Burns he was under no circumstances to go about
the plantation spreading the gospel to the slaves: "If you want to preach
to anybody," he said, "preach to me." Burns flatly refused to be limited
in this matter, but declared that he would in all other respects be a
faithful servant and not run away so long as he was treated well. Mc-
Daniel is said to have liked the forthrightness of this reply. On arriving
at the plantation, Burns was put in charge of the stables.[10]

Shortly before Christmas, Dana got another letter:

My Dear Mr Daner I take the opportunity to Now write you A few Lines
to inform you of my health I Am well at this time and hope that these few

Lines will fine you and all of my freands in physician health peace and hapiness have at tend you all the day Long I am Able to say that the god of your havenely father hath been with me even untell Now and he hath said that he wood ever bee A god for me & pray on that god May strinthen you all in that you try to dow he was A god in delivering of Many citys and he is the sam that he All ways was Mighty to dow this if we have the faith beleving in him that he will dow these things & dow Not hold your hand from trying for you know not when the Lord will deliver you all these mighty foars for Let us be hold egupt how that the Lord did bring them out and he is Still Able to deLiver More so pray on that your prayers May be heird through Much truble & I beleve that you all hath hird grate Many lies Abute what I did say but I trust that you will Not begin to think so you must expect to her all this Now

But god AlMighty wise he knows the truth pray for me that I might once More stept My foot on the Lands of that cuntry once more I cuold tell you all of many things & gave my Love to Mr Phillips and Mr Parker Mr elissye to all My friends and Brothern Brother Pitts and to Brother Cole the precher my best Love My Brother Grimes the preacher and tell them to write me one of theire texes each of them on[e] and all of you write to A Letter and all the News what is don and what is dowing in the city all write me soon As you can dow all you can for me

I hope to see you all agin please god pray for me untill I com agin to you all with the healpe of god I will Not write much more to you Now as the time is shorte & I am Living with A man who is A trader But he says that he will Not sell me I am tryinge to dow the best I can but if I can get the chance I will com Agin all ways Look for me and pray that the Lord will dow this But I say to you all my friends that theire is But one way to deliver me and many others you must do it with you soels god will helpe you to do it.

time is short the Letter will close you friend and Brother Anthony Burns write to me and call me James Black of Rocky Mount North Callina for if you call my name I will Not get it write Now to Me

pray for Me in all the chirches one and all Anthony Burns

call me James Black

North Callin I may get it

When I fine that I can get Letters from you then I Will write to you all the News and what I wount you to Dow for me & if you can cen A Letter to A friende of your in Richmond and get them to derect it Me in North Callina I can get it think for your self how to do it[11]

Burns's story became generally known in Rocky Mount, and one day a neighbor of McDaniel happened to write an account of the slave in a letter to her sister in Amherst, Massachusetts. This sister conveyed the information to a Baptist clergyman of that town, the Reverend G. S. Stockwell, who in turn wrote to McDaniel, asking if Burns might be purchased. When, early in February, an answer came back in the affirmative (the price was $1,300), Stockwell dashed off a letter to Leonard Grimes in Boston. McDaniel, he wrote, said that "Burns is still anxious for his freedom and he is willing to favor him if it can be done without any public excitement." A few days later Stockwell got another letter from McDaniel, threatening to sell Burns south if the deal wasn't settled quickly. Dismissing this as a bluff, Stockwell nevertheless wrote back agreeing to meet McDaniel in Baltimore on February 27 to make the exchange. He had evidently received word from Grimes by this time that the money for the purchase would shortly be in hand.[12]

On February 22 Charles C. Barry, cashier at Boston's City Bank and longtime secretary of the Pine Street Antislavery Society, drew two checks on the Union Bank of Maryland: one for $676, representing the amount that Grimes had raised by that time, and another for $624, which Barry, who was by no means wealthy, was advancing on his own. Most of this would be repaid to him as small contributions came in over the next two months.[13]

McDaniel had no easy time getting Burns to the meeting, for despite his efforts to keep his purpose secret, he twice had to face down a mob bent on thwarting the sale, once on the train to Norfolk, and once on board the steamer before it left for Baltimore. On the second occasion he was forced to stand in the companionway and hold off a crowd with his revolver. Nevertheless, they arrived at Barnum's Hotel in Baltimore in good time, Grimes having arrived two hours earlier, and the transaction was completed. The hotel owner, Isaac Barnum, had to be called in to vouch for Grimes in getting the checks cashed, and again to post a $1,000 bond, without which no railroad would agree to carry a Negro North, lest it be held liable for an escape. On his way to Baltimore, Burns knew only that Stockwell had been negotiating for his release; he was delighted but not surprised to find Grimes at the hotel: "I told you," he said to McDaniel, "I told you it must be Mr. Grimes." Stockwell arrived late, as the parties were leaving.[14]

The three men spent that night in Philadelphia, then went on to New York, where on March 2 Burns addressed a large audience at a black church, giving a full account of his experience. He prefaced his remarks by saying:

> My friends, I am very glad to have it to say, have it to *feel*, that I am once more in the land of liberty; that I am with those who are my friends. Until my tenth year I did not care what became of me; but soon after I began to learn that there is a Christ who came to make us free; I began to hear about a North, and to feel the necessity for freedom of soul and body. I heard of a North where men of my color could live without any man daring to say to them, "You are my property"; and I determined by the blessing of God, one day to find my way there.

He gave the same speech five days later in Boston's Tremont Temple, adding that his main reason for escaping was to be able to preach the gospel. Christ, he said, had long since freed his soul; it was up to him, now, to free his body and conform his life to his calling. When he was finished with the narrative of his capture, trial, and imprisonment, he said he hoped he might speak to them again on the subject of slavery.[15]

When Burns arrived in Boston, Dana was in the middle of his testimony at the State House before the Committee on Federal Relations, carrying on single-handedly the case against removing Judge Loring, and so he was too busy to see Burns. He was pleased with his testimony and with the courageous devotion to principle that his isolated performance suggested. "I feel, too," he wrote in his journal, "that I have been the means of bringing the Anti-Slavery sentiment of the state to a stand still." He had a glorious opinion of himself.[16]

Dana did not see his former client until the end of the month, after Burns had gone out to Amherst to join Stockwell, who had arranged to conduct him on a speaking tour. This project, however, was cut short when, on March 15, Burns fell dangerously ill in Brooklyn. Recovered, he returned to Boston, where, on the thirtieth, he at last got in to see Dana for several hours. Again he went through the details of his torture and imprisonment in Richmond and elaborated on McDaniel's relatively good treatment of him in Rocky Mount. Dana then pointed out to Burns the window of the cell where he had been kept, and took him back to the courtroom—from which, after the trial, the federal government had been permanently ejected by city officials.[17]

That evening, Dana marveled as he considered the magnitude of the issues and the insignificance of their pivot:

> What a change, and what a life for an obscure negro! One of several millions of obscure negroes, he escapes to Boston, and is as obscure there, when in a day, his name is telegraphed all over the Union, millions await the decision of his fate in anxious suspense, riots and bloodshed occur, the heart of a nation is aroused, over his body is the great struggle between the moral sense of a people and the written law backed by armed power— half a nation is humiliated and half a nation triumphant, as the scale is turned,—to him, freedom for life or servitude for life hangs in suspense, the die turns for slavery, bonds and imprisonment await him, but the eyes of a nation are on him, again humane hearts beat, and he is purchased to freedom, and now he visits the scene of his agony of trial, a hero, a martyr, with crowds of the learned and intelligent of a civilised community listening to his words! Who can tell what a day may bring forth! Who can tell what [are the] things and which are the men that are to move the world.[18]

🎗 TRIALS

And it becomes all to remember, that forcible and concerted resistance to any law is civil war, which can make no progress but through bloodshed, and can have no termination but the destruction of the government of our country, or the ruin of those engaged in such resistance.

BENJAMIN R. CURTIS

Despotism cannot happily advance unless I am silenced.

THEODORE PARKER

The legal repercussions for the protesters of the Fugitive Slave Law in the Burns case were complicated, because while a certain group faced charges of riot and murder under state law, a larger group, with much overlap, faced federal charges, arising in some instances from the same acts, of assaulting or interfering with a federal officer, a crime that could also be construed as treason. Although the state cases were postponed until April 1855, only then to be dropped at last, the federal government moved to seek indictments of its own. On June 7, shortly after the rendition, U.S. Supreme Court Justice Benjamin R. Curtis, presiding over the Circuit Court in Boston, instructed the federal grand jury on the law that made it a misdemeanor, punishable by a year in jail and a $300 fine, to obstruct federal officers in carrying out any legal writ, process, or warrant. Franklin Pierce and his attorney general, Caleb Cushing, wanted to make an example of the Faneuil Hall speakers, and so, to get at them, District Attorney Hallett expanded the case to include Parker and Phillips. Curtis, in his charge to the grand jury, carefully explained that guilt attached not only to those actively engaged in the obstruction but also to those who, at a distance, merely expressed a desire that the thing should be done.[1]

Theodore Parker later suggested that such a view of the law would criminalize everyone who had sympathized more with Burns than with Suttle, or more with freedom than with slavery—that it could criminalize and control those who dissented from other government policies. Placing speech in the category of proscribed action, Parker felt, was the desperate shift of a government reduced to having its unpopular way by force. He was prepared, if indicted, to "give them their bellyful."[2]

The grand jury, whose term had begun on May 15 and was now nearly expired, had been confronted by Hallett with a rushed and necessarily incomplete case: it chose not to find a true bill of indictment and was dismissed. The government presented the case again, however, in the October term, when Curtis' brother-in-law William W. Greenough just happened to turn up on the panel of jurors. (Parker had foretold this stratagem—for a stratagem it seemed to him—in his Fourth of July sermon.) This time indictments were returned against Higginson, Stowell, Phillips, Parker, Cluer, Morrison, Bishop, and Roberts. Parker and Phillips rejoiced in the opportunity to be heard. Higginson, glad that Parker and Phillips had been indicted, opted for an effective rather than a showy defense. Stowell, too obscure an individual to make political use of his trial, was simply scared, though his lawyer, John Andrew, assured him that the prosecution's case was impossibly weak. Their trials were scheduled for the following March, but to accommodate Justice Curtis, who would preside, they were later shifted to April. Assisting Hallett with the prosecution was Elias Merwin, B. R. Curtis' former law partner.[3]

In April, during pretrial motions, the defense team argued six separate flaws in the indictment, but Judge Curtis found another error, not noticed by the defense lawyers, and quashed the indictment against Stowell, which for procedural reasons had come up first. The flaw was a technical one: that Loring had not accurately and in form described his official status in the warrant under which the marshal had been authorized to seize Burns, and therefore it could not be maintained that he had been opposed in the course of enforcing a warrant "duly sworn out." The fact of the matter seems to be that the government simply could see no advantage in providing abolitionists with a forum for agitation or an occasion for martyrdom. Hallett entered a *nolle prosequi* in the other cases, all prosecution ceased, and the era of Daniel Webster's influence in the affairs of Massachusetts came formally to a close.[4]

One indicator of the importance of this failed prosecution—this conflict from which the government retreated—is that it directly inspired one of the most remarkable and flamboyant American books of the nineteenth century. As early as June, Parker had begun to sketch out a legal defense that, by the time it was clear he would have no occasion to argue it in court, had become a thorough treatise on the right of free speech, the wrong of slavery, and the nature of judicial tyranny. Disclaiming legal talent, Parker frankly said it was such a defense as a minister would make, "a Minister of the Christian Religion on trial for keeping the Golden Rule." The book as published in November 1855 was titled *The Trial of Theodore Parker for the "Misdemeanor" of a Speech in Faneuil Hall against Kidnapping.* The publisher, Little, Brown, was so alarmed at its irreverence that it withheld its imprint from the title page. Although the book's premise was that "Slavery is Plaintiff in this case; Freedom Defendant," the stance of the person charged was anything but defensive. He did not hesitate to affirm, for example, that the prosecutor and the judge, Hallett and Curtis, were in collusion, determined separately and together to serve the proslavery aims of a corrupt national government. These aims, according to Parker were, first, the "Extension of African Bondage," and, second, "the Destruction of American Freedom."[5]

The age-old design of promoting slavery and destroying freedom goes forward most efficiently—or perhaps only—when the judiciary is corrupt and despotic, as Parker illustrated at length through the example of English judges under the autocratic Stuart kings. One of Parker's many examples was the Puritan divine Alexander Leighton, who for the writing of *An Appeal to the Parliament, or a Plea Against Prelacy,* was in 1630 sentenced by the Court of High Commission, in the Star Chamber, to pay a fine of £10,000, then "to be set in the pillory, whipped, have one ear cut off, one side of his nose slit, one cheek branded with S.S., Sower of Sedition, and then at some convenient time be whipped again, branded, and mutilated on the other side, and confined in the Fleet during life!" Some of Leighton's horrified friends tried unsuccessfully to help him escape, but the only result was that "those who 'obstructed' the officer in the execution of that 'process' were fined £500 a piece."[6]

Through such examples, including some from colonial Massachusetts, Parker made out a case that the Puritan cause had been as much against the justices as against the bishops, that the cause of liberty of conscience and free speech belonged by historical descent to New England, and that whatever form political despotism might take, its first reliance would always be on prostituted judges, on such as Jeffreys and Scroggs, "infamous creatures, but admirable instruments to destroy generous men withal." Parker's argument (which would have been verbally addressed to Judge Curtis and would have been delivered while the hearings to remove Judge Loring were going on and while Richard Hildreth was assembling material for a book titled *Atrocious Judges*) points to the dependence of federal judges on the power of the proslavery national government and to those judges as instruments subversive of state and local jurisdictions. The federal bench is described in Parker's *Trial* as aggrandizing power at the expense of courts more responsive to the people, though Parker also had a bone to pick with state judges who behaved autocratically. The argument was populist and democratic—an appeal to juries against judges and to Massachusetts against the capital in Washington. Parker also subtly linked present-day federal judges—notably Benjamin Curtis—through their own culture of interlinked precedents, directly to the tyrannical Stuart judges, thereby tending to show that deferred appeals to authority, if traced back far enough, are often found to rest on a basis of illegality. Like Emerson and Thoreau, Parker was fond of showing that what seemed most solid and compulsory was smoke and mirrors after all.[7]

If the reliance of tyranny is on judges, then the reliance of freedom is on juries, and so Curtis was wrong and oppressive to rule, as he did in the trial of Robert Morris, that juries had to be strictly triers of fact. It was Parker's belief that "a fair and conscientious Jury will never do injustice, though a particular statute or custom demand it, and a wicked Judge insist upon the wrong; for they feel the moral instinct of human nature, and look not merely to the letter of a particular enactment, but also to the spirit and general purpose of law itself, which is justice between man and man." This position favoring jury nullification had recently been advocated by Lysander Spooner and by John P. Hale, but in fact, as Parker noted, constituencies of reform and revolution had a long history of protecting the right of trial by jury. It was a particularly useful tool in a colonial setting. Parker discussed, for example, the famous case of the New York journalist John Peter Zenger, whose newspaper was suppressed in 1734 for contending that the people's "liberties and properties are precarious, and that Slavery is likely to be entailed on them and their posterity, if some past things be not amended"—such as that "trials by juries are taken away when a Governor pleases." When Zenger was prosecuted for seditious libel, his attorney, Andrew Hamilton, argued that a jury would be rendered useless if it were confined to uncontested matters of fact (such as whether Zenger had published the words in question), while leaving it to the judge to determine whether those words were libelous. "That," said Parker, "would be to put the dove's neck in the mouth of the fox, and allow him to decide whether he would bite it off."[8]

Even as Parker wrote out this revolutionary argument for expanding the discretion of the jury (directly opposing the dicta of Justice Curtis), the Know-Nothing legislature was writing the same into Massachusetts law.

The Trial of Theodore Parker is a work of historical legal scholarship, full of brilliant, very pointed political and moral satire; it is also, in ways both strange and predictable, a very personal book. On the one hand, Parker was defending conduct that had his own name prominently on it; he felt as personally attacked in this prosecution as any man would who found his most central and sacred principles arraigned by authority as criminal. On the other hand, he had come to identify himself (as indeed others had) as perhaps the foremost spokesman for freedom in America. He was a public figure mounting a very public argument for the authority of the private conscience; although his personal delivery from official harm involved an important principle, the outcome of the trial mattered less in the end than his responsibilities to a large, widely dispersed audience. As early as February, William Herndon had written to urge Parker to write up his account of the trial, however it might end, "and send [it] out to the world."[9]

One fine thing about all the most interesting works of American literature at this time is that one can't quite say whether they are more egomaniacal or grandly disinterested. Making whatever allowances are necessary for rhetorical hyperbole, Parker's *Trial* may be said to deal as forthrightly and intelligently with important issues of freedom and the law as any work, perhaps, since the *Federalist Papers;* and yet because it is committed on philosophical grounds to the importance of the author's own moral perspective, or to the importance of the world as present to himself, it is elaborately tied to the topics, circumstances, and personalities of the Boston slave cases. The indictment, with its naming of himself as a responsible moral agent, no less than his own past conduct, has literally brought home to him the effect of abstract principles, and so he engages both cause and effect in an appropriately homely manner; the indictment, in other words, meeting with the behavior that is indicted, frees him to engage abstract principle with personal passion. So while it is true, as John Weiss said, that Parker's *Trial* "is *the* book which the future historian of these times will hunt for with eagerness and rejoice in when found," it is also energized by a very localizing animus toward the Curtis clan.[10]

Much of the last quarter of the book is given over to a history of the Curtises' involvement in all the major slave cases in Boston as far back as 1832, when Charles P. Curtis first appeared for a slavehunter. Four years later he and his cousin Benjamin R. Curtis argued for the slaveowner in *Commonwealth v. Aves,* a case in which they tried unsuccessfully to establish the principle that slaveowners sojourning in Massachusetts should, by legal comity, be secure in the possession of any slaves they happened to have with them: that is, that slavery should to such a degree be sanctioned and protected in Massachusetts.[11]

Parker discusses the clamorous public support given by Thomas B. Curtis, George Ticknor Curtis, Edward G. Loring, W. W. Greenough, and B. R. Curtis to the Fugitive Slave Law at the time of its passage, and details their involvement afterward in the cases of William and Ellen Craft, Shadrach, and Sims, examining even the libel suit brought by George T. Curtis against Vigilance Committee member Benjamin B. Mussey for having published an antislavery speech by Horace Mann that alluded unfavorably to the commissioner.

And then there was the Burns case, in which,

it is said, Mr. Loring, who has no Curtis blood in his veins, did not wish to steal a man; and proposed to throw up his commission rather than do such a deed; but he consulted his step-brother, Charles P. Curtis, who persuaded him it would be dishonorable to decline the office of kidnapping imposed upon him as a United States Commissioner by the fugitive slave bill. Benjamin R. Curtis, it is said, I know not how truly,—himself can answer—aided Mr. Loring in forming the "opinion" by which he attempted to justify the "extradition" of Mr. Burns; that is to say, the giving him up as a slave without any trial of his right to liberty, merely in a presumptive case established by his claimant.[12]

Parker concedes at one point certain estimable and respectable qualities in the family, particularly in its older members. "In the ordinary intercourse of society, where no great moral principle is concerned, they appear as decorous and worthy men."

But this family has had its hand in all the kidnapping which has recently brought such misery to the colored people and their friends; such ineffaceable disgrace upon Boston, and such peril to the natural Rights of man . . . Without their efforts we should have had no man-stealing here. They cunningly, but perhaps unconsciously, represented the low Selfishness of the Money Power at the North, and the Slave Power at the South, and persuaded the controlling men of Boston to steal Mr. Sims and Mr. Burns . . .

Gentlemen, they are not ashamed of this conduct . . . Three of the family are fugitive slave bill commissioners; one of them intellectually the ablest, perhaps morally the blindest . . . is the Honorable Judge who is to try me for a "Misdemeanor."[13]

Parker's flaying of the Curtis clan is attentive in a general way to the traditional role that kinship played in the management of state affairs, but there is also a Hawthornesque fascination with the mystery of the iniquity that runs in families. In the very unanimity of their conspiring the Curtis men make a good symbol of the oppression emanating from selfish privilege: the appropriate enemy of democracy—here as in Stuart England—would be a tight cabal of conscience-forcers united by hereditary distinction and useful to the party in power. Unlike the unsponsored Parker, these men had wealth and social position, rewards that latter-day Puritans no longer associated with the favor of God.[14]

But could Parker have known of the Curtis family secret? If he did, he held his tongue, and no one else spoke of it. In the memoir of Benjamin Robbins Curtis written in 1875 by his brother George, their father, Benjamin Curtis, is barely mentioned. He is the only ancestor, going back six generations in America, whose birth and death dates are not given in that work. Virtually all that is said about him is that he "was bred in the merchant marine," that he "made several voyages as supercargo, and afterwards as master," and that he married Lois Robbins in 1807. He was off on his voyages for so much of his brief married life that Mrs. Curtis continued to live in the home of her parents. He "died abroad" at so early a date that the younger son at least had no recollection of him.[15]

But in 1802—and for several years before that—he was at Rio Pongos on the coast of Africa, working to supply slaves to the South Carolina market. He was thus among the last Massachusetts men to sell Africans into slavery before the Atlantic traffic was closed in 1808. As a factor established at that location, he would receive cargoes of trade goods in exchange for slaves and other commodities. In one such transaction in July 1802, he found himself unable to supply slaves enough to cover his indebtedness and gave his note for the remainder, promising, "for value received," to supply "nine four foot slaves, thirty seven prime slaves," and other consideration to the value of $4,481.41.

Five years later the newly married Curtis was sued in Massachusetts by the holder of the note, a Charleston slavetrader named Greenwood, for its full amount. Curtis' attorney argued that the contract was unenforceable on the grounds that slavery was illegal in Massachusetts, branded by statute as "an unrighteous commerce." Chief Justice Isaac Parker held that the contract could be voided if "the commonwealth or its citizens may be injured" by its enforcement or if "the giving of legal effect to the contract would exhibit to the citizens . . . an example pernicious and detestable . . . founded on moral turpitude, in respect either of the consideration or the stipulation." Parker's decision was that because the contract met neither of these exceptions, the principle of comity, by which Massachusetts recognized the laws of other states, must govern. The contract was legal in South Carolina, presumably legal in Rio Pongos, and not, to the present court, immoral on its face. Curtis was therefore liable for $4,481.41 and costs. Less than two years after this, Curtis' youngest son, George, was born, and after that the father drops out of the record, leaving his wife (or widow) nearly destitute and leaving an eldest son to grow up to become the nation's leading expert on the principle of interstate comity with regard to slavery.[16]

In a schoolboy theme "On the Origin of Evil"—the earliest of his surviving compositions—Benjamin R. Curtis made his Unitarian upbringing manifest by rejecting the notion of innate depravity:

> Neither do I believe that the first man differed in any respect from others of his race, but that he had the same passions and inclinations, and was placed here in a state of probation for a better world, and that the sin of Adam, who was the father of all mankind, was any more the origin of evil than the sin of a father of the present day is the origin of the wickedness of his children.[17]

Benjamin Curtis, the obscure patriarch, is immortalized in court records but not in the memorials of his children. So far as can be inferred from the evidence, he had hoped to keep his accounts forever unbalanced in his favor by the trifling expedient of having his life declared repugnant to the people of Massachusetts. It was just this potential for elevating law over morality that the Puritans had anticipated in their marked prejudice against the legal profession. In the older theocratic Massachusetts every man had spoken in court for himself (as Parker proposed to do in 1855), avoiding the ventriloquism of the professional advocate and allowing the court a more direct view of the righteousness of the positions taken. Something like this was undoubtedly at the bottom of the neo-Puritan provision in the 1855 Personal Liberty Law prohibiting lawyers from appearing for slave claimants, a provision that was as much a rebuke to lawyers as an impediment to slaveowners.

A closely allied cause for Puritan concern was the temptation held out by a professionalized system of adjudication to find in a purely legal standard a self-sufficient resolution to questions of morality. In the course of his argument in *Commonwealth v. Aves* (the case of the slave Med), Benjamin R. Curtis had occasion to say that "whatever may be the law of England on this subject, by the law of this Commonwealth, slavery is not immoral." Indeed this had been the decision of Chief Justice Parker in 1802 (a case not offered as precedent in *Aves*), when the elder Curtis was forced to take pecuniary loss along with a moral endorsement of his actions. Morality, in other words, is not anterior to the law but a sort of manufactured consequence; indeed, unless this is admitted, as the younger Curtis went immediately on to show, the whole system falls:

> The court will hardly declare in this case that slavery is immoral, and that to allow the master to exercise the right claimed would exhibit to our citizens an example pernicious and detestable, when, before you rise from your seats, you may be called upon by the master of a fugitive slave to grant a certificate, under the Constitution, which will put the whole force of the Commonwealth at his disposal, to remove his slave from our territory.

Theodore Parker, who looked to the Puritans far more systematically than this opponent ever did, cited Curtis' argument for the morality of slavery, and expressed in his *Trial* a profound refusal to live in the world to which that argument belonged; in fact—as his arming of the Kansas emigrants and his support for John Brown showed—he was willing to bring on the revolution that would destroy that world. Shortly before his death in 1860, Parker wrote: "There is a glorious future for America, but the other side of the *Red Sea*."[18]

 ## ENDINGS

Ye are bought with a price; be not ye the servants of men.

I CORINTHIANS 7:23

ANTHONY BURNS

When Burns arrived back in Boston the second time, he had, in a not unimportant sense, left his slave past behind. His friends congratulated him, saying that he owned himself now and was as free as any man in the country. But for the time being "unowned" had to pass for "free," and such freedom as had a cash payment at the bottom of it would by tacit agreement be said to look like freedom based on natural right secured by laws. In other respects he would find that escaping from slavery was still a piece of unfinished business.

Some people's presumption was that he could still be bought as a slave—or at least as a man with a specific slave identity. Immediately upon Burns's release, P. T. Barnum wrote to Boston offering him $100 a week if he would simply regale the crowds at the New York museum with accounts of his experiences. Burns rejected this offer indignantly, saying, "He wants to show me like a monkey!"—but he fell in with the somewhat more decorous plans of Stockwell and others to have him exhibited in New England for the benefit of various antislavery societies. Later, Burns traveled with an abolitionist panorama, The Grand Moving Mirror of Slavery, a thing dreamed up by three businessmen from Lewiston, Maine. The line between show business and reform became less clear as movement figures became more popular and the issue of slavery ever more politicized.[1]

In a sense, because of his celebrity and usefulness, Anthony Burns had stopped being *a* slave only to become *the* slave. His identity, doubtful at the trial, was now fixed by his known history, while the public pretense that he might not have been a slave—that he might not *be* a slave—was summarily dropped. A Worcester businessman, Charles Emery Stevens, composed a book appropriately titled *Anthony Burns: A History* (1856), which added to an account of the events in Boston a brief biography of the subject based on personal interviews. The author's hope for the book, as indicated in its preface, was to help concentrate Northern antislavery feeling and to promote the chances of John C. Frémont, standard-bearer of the new Republican party, against Democrat James Buchanan in the November election. The book's subject, however, had other hopes: Burns personally sold hundreds of copies of this white-authored autobiography and used the income to support himself at Oberlin, where he enrolled on a donated scholarship in the summer of 1855. In various ways Northern sentiment sought to make what use it could of Burns's slave identity, an identity it had stoutly denied not a minute longer than the South maintained it.[2]

Southern apologists for slavery consistently spoke of the duty of educated whites to protect and direct the weak and vulnerable black population, who could no more make it on their own than children could. The same view was to a remarkable degree held by many "advanced" Northerners, who found ample justification in it to offer presumptuous and condescending direction of their own. For example, in the "Concluding Remarks" to *Uncle Tom's Cabin,* Mrs. Stowe elaborated on her plan to colonize Liberia with freed American slaves. It was a popular plan, one that Lincoln held onto until a very late hour. Stowe, however, considered that it would not do to send them off unprepared:

Let the church of the north receive these poor sufferers in the spirit of Christ; receive them to the educating advantages of Christian republican society and schools, until they have attained to somewhat of a moral and intellectual maturity, and then assist them in their passage to those shores, where they may put in practice the lessons they have learned in America.

The anonymous female donor of Burns's Oberlin scholarship, the faculty at Oberlin, or both, had just this idea in mind, for we find Burns, seven months into his studies, writing to Theodore Parker about the "heathen nations where I might, some day, do a great deal of good." Parker, however, like other radical abolitionists, rejected the whole idea of African colonization; he replied to Burns with the hazardous, if not foolhardy, suggestion that he might minister more profitably to blacks in the South. The impressible Burns replied: "I know that the field is large in the South, where many fear to go, but who knows but that the Lord is a-going to make of me a Moses, in leading His people out of bondage?"[3]

Despite the integrated classes and the ostensibly supportive and liberal atmosphere of Oberlin, Burns's time there must have been excruciatingly difficult. A sense of how he was welcomed may be gleaned from a brief article in the Oberlin *Evangelist* announcing his arrival: "He comes to Oberlin to prepare himself here, by study, for greater usefulness to his oppressed race. He has talents, and if through grace, he may be kept humble and can pass unpoisoned through so much notoriety, he may do great good. Few students need so much prayer in their behalf as those of color, upon whom many eyes are turned, and as to whom great expectations have been raised." In the spirit of experiment, then, a rather doubtful Oberlin would make him worthy of the freedom he already had.[4]

Although Burns was a confident and easy speaker, the written word was to him an enduring source of bafflement and shame. A white Oberlin classmate, J. A. Seitz, concluded that Burns was "the dumbest darkey" he had ever met. There is little reason to suppose that other classmates were much more generous. Meanwhile, Burns wrote to Wendell Phillips to say, "I am going on with Studys dowing the Best I can & I hope to take up Lattain in the fall." He hoped, too, that Phillips was praying for him, "that I may hold out faithful to the End."[5]

Burns understood that education was itself an escape from slavery, the royal road (if any there were) to a truly free identity; but all the while the old life kept insinuating itself in the most discouraging ways. Soon after his arrival at Oberlin, hoping to join the local Baptist congregation, he wrote to his former church in Virginia to ask for a letter of dismission. The response he got, several months later, took the form of a clipping from the Front Royal *Gazette,* setting forth the decision of the church at Union, Fauquier County, to excommunicate him for "disobeying the laws of God and men" in his escape. Surprised and wounded, Burns framed a careful reply in which he denied having broken anything that deserved the name of law and pointed out that Suttle had taken and held him by criminal force. He concluded:

> You have used your liberty of speech freely in exhorting and rebuking me. You are aware that I too am now where I may think for myself, and can use great freedom of speech, too, if I please. I shall therefore be only returning the favor of your exhortation if I exhort you to study carefully the golden rule, which reads, "All things whatsoever ye would that men should do to you, do ye even so to them; for this is the law and the prophets." Would you like to be *stolen,* and then *sold?* and then worked without wages? and forbidden to read the Bible? . . . Suppose you were to put your soul in my soul's stead; how would *you* read the law of love?[6]

Burns's enrollment at Oberlin was intermittent, partly, it would appear, because of money troubles, but also because he was concurrently studying at Fairmont Theological Seminary in Cincinnati. In 1859 he briefly served as pastor at a black church in Indianapolis, but left when it seemed that Indiana's Black Laws, prohibiting the settlement of free Negroes, would be invoked against him. Finally, late in 1860, he left for St. Catherines, Ontario, a town largely populated by fugitive slaves, where he became the regular minister of the colored Baptist Church. For a year and a half he worked to repair the dilapidated meetinghouse and to put the church's finances in order. He accomplished both before dying of tuberculosis on July 27, 1862. His last letter, written during his final illness and addressed to James Freeman Clarke in Boston, expressed regrets about the death, two years before, of Theodore Parker; it contained as well some brief incoherent comments on the conduct of the war and on the actions of General Grant. At the end, sliding toward death and impenetrable mysteries, he signed himself "Anthony Burns, Ex-Abolitionist: now thinks Lee a Better Man."[7]

There were testimonials at the time of his death that show he had been well thought of in his last, most northern home. "Since he left Oberlin and came over into Canada," according to the Reverend Hiram Wilson, "he has made good impressions where he lectured in various places." The Reverend R. A. Ball of the British Methodist Episcopal Church in St. Catherines said: "he was a fine speaker and was considered to be well educated. He was unmarried and very popular with the white people and the people of his own race." A tombstone, now gone, was inscribed:

In Memoriam
REV. ANTHONY BURNS
The fugitive slave of the Boston riots, 1854.
Pastor of Zion Baptist Church.
Born in Virginia, May 31, 1834.
Died in the Triumph of Faith in St. Catherines,
July 27th, A.D. 1862.[8]

ASA O. BUTMAN

The notoriety of deputy marshal Asa Butman, arresting officer in the Sims and Burns cases, got him into trouble in the fall of 1854, resulting, as Higginson said, in "the thorough frightening of one who had frightened so many."[9]

On Saturday, October 28, 1854, Butman arrived in Worcester, perhaps in pursuit of yet another fugitive, but more probably in search of evidence to be used against the Court House rioters, which case was then before the grand jury. He was recognized by the Worcester Vigilance Committee, who, supposing that he had kidnapping in mind, posted handbills to warn the black community. On Sunday night a crowd of sixty men led by Stephen S. Foster kept a rather noisy vigil outside his hotel, provoking Butman to emerge, at 3:00 A.M., pistol in hand, to demand they disperse. This stratagem did not have the desired effect; Butman was immediately arrested on a charge of carrying a concealed weapon and taken off to jail. The crowd at his Monday morning arraignment was even larger and more boisterous than at the hotel, and at one point, after posting bond, the defendant was momentarily engulfed by the mob, though soon enough rescued by the city marshal. Butman was especially vulnerable because Worcester's mayor, anticipating the provisions of the Personal Liberty Law, had issued orders to the police not to cooperate with (and hence not to protect) the federal officer.[10]

As the mob got larger and more angry, it fell to the leading abolitionists—Higginson, Stowell, Foster, George F. Hoar, Thomas Drew, and a few others—to save Butman, who by this time had made up his mind to forfeit his bond and "never come to Worcester again as long as he lived." Hoar spoke to the mob and pacified them to the point that he thought he could risk escorting the prisoner out of City Hall to the railroad depot half a mile away. The two men barely got out the back door and onto the sidewalk, however, before the crowd, now numbering between 1,000 and 2,000, surrounded them. Higginson grabbed Butman's other arm and was soon beating back attackers and fending off thrown objects. Drew took up a position in the rear, alternately pushing the crowd back, then turning to kick the deputy himself. Foster was yelling, "Boys, don't kill him—don't strike him—but abuse him as much as you can!" Foster was one of three white men arrested this day and charged with incitement to riot, but the only indictment finally returned—for simple assault—was against a black man arrested at the same time.[11]

Butman was taken to the depot, where he arrived "almost lifeless with terror," and was locked in the station privy to await the train. When it was estimated that this makeshift cell could not be defended as long as it would take for the next train to arrive, Butman was again led out through the pummeling of the mob and driven in a hack the forty miles to Boston, where, still in fear for his life, he reportedly went into hiding for several days.

No slavehunters came to Worcester after that, and the city was now satisfied that it had become what Higginson had sworn to make it: "Canada to the slave."

MARTIN STOWELL

Stowell never told Higginson—perhaps his closest friend—that he believed he had shot and killed a man. There weren't many people he could tell: he thought obsessively about the slug he was sure was in the coffin of James Batchelder, and he feared an exhumation. Thomas Drew, who had given Stowell the gun, and Simon Hanscom, who had helped to retrieve it, knew the secret, but they kept solemnly quiet about the matter for many years after Stowell's death.[12]

It would seem that for Stowell life after the Burns and Butman riots was intolerably quiet and domestic. He continued to work with Higginson and others in closing the tippling shops, but there was some strange intoxication of his own he could not overcome. It was not just the ardor of idealistic reform that stirred his blood: he had developed a fatal fascination with dangerous right-doing that no safe haven for slaves could ever satisfy. When the war in Kansas heated up, he left his wife and children to lead to the scene of action a party of thirty-one men, armed with state-of-the-art breech-loading Sharp's rifles supplied by Theodore Parker and William F. Channing. Leaving Worcester on June 30, 1856, they took the Northern route through Iowa and Nebraska, crossing into Kansas at Pony Creek on August 7 as part of Jim Lane's "Army of the North." Though he certainly meant to defend himself if it came to that and to do in any event what duty required, Stowell was not exactly spoiling for a fight: for the time being he was satisfied to be the owner of 640 fertile acres of prairie near the present-day town of Fairview. Like others in the emigrant party, Stowell hoped to better his condition through land acquisition, but this was by no means a typical pioneer expedition. One of Stowell's Worcester comrades, Richard J. Hinton, recorded his reaction to finding himself that August in Kansas:

> My heart is too full to find words to express my thoughts, and it seems hard to realize that we are on the prairie destined by the slave oligarchy to be blackened by the hell of men in bondage. But the good God who provides for all, in His infinite providence, will not let this evil "fall upon us and overcome us like a summer cloud." The fair prospects of humanity must not be blotted, nor the hope of the world blasted.[13]

In Kansas Stowell got to meet John Brown before Higginson did. As the leader of his group, Stowell had duties to report back to Massachusetts about financial matters and was on one occasion hard pressed to know what to do when he discovered that Osawatomie Brown had bounced a check for $100. In the end Stowell chose to regard it as a contribution. He admired the man but was glad just the same to be spared the trouble of collecting the debt. It was hard enough to keep the books balanced: their first settlement, which they had hopefully called Plymouth, had just been sacked by the Border Ruffians, and Stowell, serving as judge and military commander, was rebuilding the town, rechristened, in Revolutionary style, Lexington.[14]

Stowell did not prosper as a farmer. His homestead dwindled steadily to 180 acres before he abandoned it, and certainly his family never joined him there. He had become, it seems, permanently dislodged, a wanderer. For a while in 1860, he lived in New Jersey, but soon after migrated back west to Iowa, as may be inferred from the fact that he entered the Civil War among that state's troops. He was a sergeant major in the Fifth Iowa Cavalry when he died, at the age of thirty-eight, from wounds received in an obscure skirmish at Paris, Kentucky, March 11, 1862.[15]

THOMAS WENTWORTH HIGGINSON

After the collapse of the government prosecutions, Higginson went with his family for a recuperative vacation to the Azores, taking with him the printed sheets of Parker's *Trial* and, as he later recalled, a bound copy of Whitman's just-published *Leaves of Grass*. He seems to have preferred the former. When he returned to Worcester early in June 1856, he found that the scene of the revolution he desired had shifted to Kansas; preparing to get involved there, he wrote to assure Moncure Conway that "this was a great historic period" they lived in, and that "the future will leave no true man unhonored." Along with his friend Seth Rogers, head of the Worcester Hydropathic Institute, Higginson immediately organized the Massachusetts Kansas Aid Committee, a more militant version of Eli Thayer's company, and equipped the party headed by Stowell. Another group of emigrants from Worcester under Dr. Calvin Cutter had left shortly before Stowell's but was disarmed and turned back when they inexplicably defied orders and tried to enter Kansas through Missouri. It was this débacle that prompted Higginson to go out on two separate tours of inspection, on the second of which he saw Stowell for the last time, in his rude cabin at Plymouth. James Lane wanted to give Higginson a field commission as brigadier general in the fight against the Border Ruffians, but the Worcester minister felt he had responsibilities at home, to family, church, and revolution. Still, he was enormously encouraged by what he saw out West. "Ever since the rendition of Anthony Burns," he said, "I have been looking for men. I have found them in Kansas." Of these he particularly liked John Brown, "who swallows a Missourian whole, and says grace after the meat."[16]

The election of James Buchanan shortly after this Kansas trip simply confirmed Higginson in his commitment to revolutionary action.

He organized and led a major disunion convention in Worcester the following January. There his thoughts returned again to Anthony Burns: "Give us," he said, "another chance to come face to face with the United States Government . . . and see if we have not learned something by the failure . . . No sir! disunion is not a desire, merely; it is a destiny!" Antislavery opinion got no more militantly radical than in this effort to unite the violent and nonviolent abolitionists, and yet even Emerson, whose coolness Higginson had always enviously admired, had said the previous summer that if the election did not go for Frémont, then "nothing seems left, but to form at once a Northern Union, and break the old."[17]

The story of Higginson's membership in the "Secret Six" who backed John Brown in the last phase of his career is well known and in any event too complex to set forth here. Suffice it to say that of these six—Higginson, Theodore Parker, Frank Sanborn, George Luther Stearns, Samuel Gridley Howe, and Gerrit Smith—only the last two were not notable friends and admirers of Emerson. In December 1859, when Brown was executed, Emerson and Thoreau were among his most ardent apologists. While Higginson, together with Lysander Spooner and others, laid plans to rescue Brown, Emerson made an effort to intercede on Brown's behalf with Virginia Governor Henry Wise. Shortly after the execution, Brown's daughters enrolled in Frank Sanborn's school in Concord and boarded with the Emersons.[18]

When the Civil War broke out the disunionists became unionists, and Higginson, after weighing his duties to his invalid wife, raised a company of Worcester volunteers. While he was training these men, a letter came from Brigadier General Rufus Saxton, headquartered in occupied Beaufort, South Carolina, offering Higginson the colonelcy of the first regularly constituted regiment of freed slaves. Saxton had been persuaded to make the offer by his chaplain, the Reverend James H. Fowler, who, as a student at Harvard Divinity School, had been arrested during the Burns trial for his protesting. In due course, Fowler became chaplain of Higginson's black regiment.[19]

Higginson's attitude toward black people was a complex compound of ignorance, conscientious sympathy, and escalating fascination. Few white abolitionists—if any—developed a more searching interest than Higginson in the culture of black Africa or in African-American history. Beginning shortly after the Burns case, he published a number of articles on these topics, beginning with "African

Proverbial Philosophy" in *Scribner's* and including a series on American slave revolts in the *Atlantic Monthly.* His military memoirs, *Army Life in a Black Regiment* (1870), were as much a sociological study as a record of wartime exploits. None of these documents is free from condescension, but the effort in all of them is to enhance and complicate white estimates of the capacities—realized and potential—residing in the race. The insurrection articles, in particular, are to be understood in relation to John Brown's activities, and testify to Higginson's growing conviction that black courage and determination ought not only to be acknowledged but actually relied on in bringing slavery to an end. Such faith was scarce indeed in white America.

It is hard to know how important it was to Higginson's evolving racial views that at Beaufort he got to know Charlotte Forten well. She had come down at Whittier's suggestion to teach the freedmen and their children as part of the celebrated Port Royal experiment. When Higginson arrived (much to Forten's surprise and delight), she had been settled in for a month. They had become acquainted the year before in Worcester when she had taken the water cure under the direction of Dr. Seth Rogers, who was now, as it happened, Higginson's regimental physician. As Forten's journal shows, the three of them spent much time together, taking romantic moonlight rides among the magnolias when they weren't instructing freed Gullah slaves how to read and how to fight. Higginson and Forten shared a number of interests and were even reading the same books: the newest fiction, *Les Miserables,* and the poetry of Robert Browning, but also *The Life of Toussaint L'Ouverture,* and *The Colored Patriots of the American Revolution,* by Forten's Boston friend William Cooper Nell.[20]

After the War Higginson was a different man, in ways that might have been predicted. His radicalism had been, of course, completely sincere, but it had always been meant for the consumption of his own particular tribal culture of Anglo-Saxon New Englanders, which was now precipitating out of a sort of Jacobin freedom into the increasingly decorous discussions of the *Atlantic Monthly,* and so when the great occasions of the 1850s passed, he had little left but the audience he had tried to move. Emily Dickinson, a stranger to him, caught him by surprise at this turning point, asking, just as he was going off to war, if he would be her "preceptor." She had just read his *Atlantic* article, "Letter to a Young Contributor," and thought she saw affinities of principle and temperament between herself and this crusading public man who was strangely undisturbed by the idea of talent in women. Letters passed between the pair for years afterward, but Emily Dickinson could have got little more from the exercise than a sense of how a cosmopolitan, her elected emissary from a wider world, might react to her poetry of privacy. Higginson got from it a haunting.

In some ways the revolution of 1854 might be supposed to have culminated along with Higginson's radical activism when the Amherst poet's newest friend entered Jacksonville, Florida, at the head of his black regiment and before leaving saw it burned to the ground. The Jacksonville campaign, undertaken in large part to announce freedom to the slaves of east Florida, was for Higginson a kind of second chance, another storming of the Court House, writ large this time, and successful. He and his black assistants had got in at last, breaching more by surprise than by force the defended barricades of the slave power. It was an act of purest liberation. But once inside, the colonel found the place at heart a desert, 90 percent of the population gone, almost no slaves to free, and his victory hollow.[21]

Some power seems to have gone out of him then, so that all his long life after the war seems like a polite retirement dominated by autobiography. One sees the progressively diminished power in the correspondence with Dickinson, in which, though he is accorded a superior position by his sequestered petitioner, he is purely reactive. She requests instruction; he responds in a teacherly fashion with talk about the rules she breaks, all the while prizing what is "naive" or primitive in her stance. He was paternal toward this genius who could not appear in public, as he preeminently could. He was fascinated by her strangeness and by the unfathomable sources of the liveliness and energy of her elliptical speech; he thought her dazzling expression needed more correctness, more control and discipline.

It was the blacks all over again.

MONCURE DANIEL CONWAY

When Conway for the first time spoke from the abolition platform and listened to Garrison and Phillips and Thoreau, he knew that antislavery was a religion and that he was himself at last converted. Slavery, he knew, was just as rapidly becoming a religion in the South, and he sensed a holy war in the offing.

Conway graduated from Harvard Divinity School that month and proceeded in the fall to Washington, D.C., where he would preach as a candidate at the Unitarian Church. When he arrived, he was surprised to find a letter from his father in Stafford County warning him that it was too dangerous just then to come home. Months later, after it became evident that Conway's moderately applied antislavery views were causing no scandal, his father relented, and the son came for a visit. Approaching the house after dark, Conway was accosted twice by local slaves (probably belonging to his own family), who had not only heard about his involvement with the abolitionists during the Burns affair, but who now supposed that he meant to provide them with a means of escape. Conway was only mildly surprised that the slaves were so well informed about the Burns case; he was stunned, however, by their eagerness to flee to the North. Convinced that slavery was an immoral policy, he had nevertheless supposed that the slaves, in their ignorance, did not value freedom highly and were content with their lot so long as they were treated humanely. For Conway, as for many others, the basic appeal of abolition was that it gave to a certain group what it abstractly deserved, not what it expressly wanted or could efficiently use.[22]

The trouble that Conway's father at first expected and then assumed had passed off came in fact the next day, when Conway was confronted in town by a gathering of young men, including some former schoolmates. Their leader spoke: "Charles Frank Suttle says that when he was in Boston you did everything you could against him to prevent his getting back his servant Tony Burns, and that you are an abolitionist. There is danger to have that kind of man among our servants, and you must leave. We don't want to have any row." On his way out of town he got a similar lecture from his uncle, Dr. Valentine Conway, to whom he tried to explain that antislavery agitation was part of a worldwide movement for freedom, against the force of which the institutions of the South stood not the slightest chance of prevailing. Dismayed at this truculent opposition from friends and family, Conway retreated, convinced that he would never see Falmouth again.[23]

Not yet twenty-three years old, Conway devoted himself to his ministry in the capital, where his occasional antislavery sermons were listened to with professed respect by Associate Justice B. R. Curtis, among others. Feeling his way, the minister pressed the antislavery message more and more boldly until, following the assault of Preston

Brooks on Charles Sumner in the Senate chamber and the nomination of Frémont by the Republicans, Conway at last overtaxed the patience of his congregation and was dismissed from what he had come to call his "Church of Freedom."[24]

He went then to Cincinnati and a new church. Although there is no record of it, he might well have encountered Anthony Burns, who was studying and starving at the Fairmont Theological Seminary. He certainly continued to promote Emerson and antislavery, bringing his hero out to lecture and launching a magazine called, in a commemorative gesture, *The Dial.* But the outbreak of civil war put an end to all thoughts of literary journalism.

For more than a year Lincoln conducted the war as a Union-saving measure in response to Southern secession. During this time Conway was among the most vocal advocates for the position that the war was and would continue to be unconscionable so long as it was not in the immediate service of emancipation. In 1861 he published *The Rejected Stone; Or, Insurrection v. Resurrection in America,* the sense of which was that the Founders had rejected the stone of "Justice" in choosing to write the Constitution as a compromise document, that the North now practically advocated a revolution that would perfect the Constitution by eliminating slavery, and that the South was, as it had been for eighty years, in a position of mere rebellion, not of revolution, the only force still supporting the old antebellum concept of the Union. If Lincoln were to free the slaves (as he had power to do), he would create millions of black allies behind the rebel lines, and the Southern armies would reorganize themselves as a defensive home guard. Conway's book was very well received. The fact that it was written by a Virginian gave it special weight. Copies of its three editions were distributed to Union soldiers, and, at Sumner's suggestion, even Lincoln read it.[25]

The president might have been more receptive to Conway's argument had he been less concerned about the effect of such policy among the still teetering border states—and had he not countermanded a nearly identical policy when implemented by John C. Frémont on his own authority as military commander in Missouri. Conway continued to put the case for a revolutionized union as the outcome of the current crisis and chided Lincoln for his apparent willingness to restore a Union with slavery in it; he further pointed out to Lincoln the meaning of his having been elected as a Republican. The continuation of Conway's argument was delivered as a lecture at the Smithsonian Institution in January 1862, attended by Frémont, who was for the moment a far greater hero to the abolitionists than Lincoln. This lecture was repeated a few days later at the Philadelphia home of William H. Furness, where Lucretia Mott and others heard it and said that if its principles were widely publicized, it would "revolutionize the war." By the end of the month, Conway had traveled to Boston, spent a day in discussion with Emerson, and convinced him of the soundness of the plan for emancipation, which Emerson would publicly endorse a few days later in his own lecture in Washington in the same Smithsonian series.[26]

Conway's lecture was elaborated into a book, *The Golden Hour,* published in 1862 by Ticknor and Fields. However, it proved less popular and effective than *The Rejected Stone,* perhaps because the argument was repetitious, perhaps, as Conway felt, because it seemed too visionary to expect to find in freedom a remedy for war.

That December, death overwhelmed Conway's Stafford County home. The countryside that Anthony Burns had known so well was utterly devastated. The stately brick mansion of the Conways in Falmouth hard by the Rappahannock was converted by federal troops into a field hospital, and the amputated arms and legs of Union and Confederate soldiers were heaped in a great pile beneath the shattered and leafless limbs of the front-yard tree. Walt Whitman was there tending to the wounded and the dying and saw it all.[27]

WILLIAM J. AND FRANCES E. WATKINS

In the spring of 1853, when Watkins failed to convince the Massachusetts legislature that black men in Boston had a right to form a militia company, he removed to Rochester, New York, transferring his allegiance from Garrison to Frederick Douglass. Many black activists had a difficult time negotiating the ideological split between these two leaders, but Watkins' defection is especially significant, since his family had been allied with Garrison for more than twenty years. When he argued before the legislature that the right to bear arms extended to blacks, he was obliged to acknowledge the respectability and even the citizenship conferred by connection with the military, yet at the same time he felt compelled to apologize for the inconsistency of this position with his Garrisonian nonresistance and his peace principles in general. Unlike his more militant friends, Robert Morris and Lewis Hayden, Watkins had no interest in marching or handling guns. If he was militant about anything at this time, it was about integration and the duty of blacks to come up to white standards. That his measured and careful statement before the legislature should have been met with nothing but curt dismissiveness certainly helped to set him on the road to Rochester.[28]

When, with the death of Batchelder a few months later, blood was actually spilled, Watkins was far less careful to assert his pacifist principles and in fact joined Douglass in approving the resort to lethal violence. In an article in *Frederick Douglass's Paper* titled "Who Are the Murderers?" he asked (with a certain anatomical inaccuracy): "Is that man a murderer who sent the well-directed bullet through [Batchelder's] stony heart?" Had the kidnapper's victim been a white man, he recognized, such measures of defense would have been lauded universally. "We should certainly kill the man," he went on to say, "who would dare lay his hand on us, or on our brother, or sister, to enslave us. We cannot censure others for doing what we would be likely to do, under the same circumstances, ourselves."[29]

In the same issue, Douglass wrote an editorial titled "Is It Right and Wise to Kill a Kidnapper?" which opened with a broadly philosophical discussion of whether the right to life did not rest on the same ground as the right to liberty, and whether similar grounds of forfeiture did not exist in each case. "We hold," he said, "that when James Batchelder, the truckman of Boston, abandoned his useful employment as a common laborer, and took upon himself the revolting business of a kidnapper, and undertook to play the bloodhound on the track of his crimeless brother Burns, he labelled himself the common enemy of mankind, and his slaughter was as innocent, in the sight of God, as would be the slaughter of a ravenous wolf in the act of throttling an infant." Douglass conceded that submission and nonviolence might in some cases have a moral force in shaming aggression, but he was concerned that the failure of slaves to resist capture was beginning to be cited as evidence of racial inferiority. "Every slavehunter who meets a bloody death in his infernal business, is an argument in favor of the manhood of our race."[30]

Taken together the two articles suggest how the increasingly desperate situation of fugitives after 1850 was driving moderate black activists toward revolutionary violence, from which position they were more likely to identify with Douglass than with Garrison. Watkins' faith in moral suasion was in sharp decline as he became convinced of the need for action: in Rochester he worked much on the Underground Railroad, made speaking tours, conspired with John Brown, supported women's rights, and organized for the Freesoil and Republican parties.[31]

But if Garrison was losing such restless young men as William J. Watkins, he was not lacking for fresh recruits. In the summer of 1854, Frances Ellen Watkins came to Boston and placed herself under Garrison's protection, very much as her cousin William had done five years before. Although precise information is lacking about her early career, it would seem that just as William had come to involve himself as a Garrisonian voice in the school desegregation battle, Frances had determined in the wake of the Burns case to become active and vocal in the antislavery struggle. She gave her first speeches in August 1854, launching her notable career as an antislavery lecturer with appearances before friendly audiences in New Bedford and Providence. That fall, under the sponsorship of the Maine Antislavery Society, she traveled throughout New England with a white female companion and addressed gatherings in cities and towns almost every day. Before the year was out, Garrison's publisher, J. B. Yerrinton & Son, issued Watkins' first book, *Poems on Miscellaneous Subjects,* with a preface by Garrison.[32]

It was by no means easy at this time for women to make public careers for themselves. It was vastly more difficult for an unmarried black woman, who, to speak to power, had to cross racial and gender lines—and, not incidentally, to risk the disapproval of other blacks in doing so. Yet soon Frances Watkins was in considerable demand on the lecture circuit, her poems had gone through several editions, and her opinion was sought in the meetings of the Colored Conventions. Next to Sojourner Truth, Frances Watkins was the most effective and indefatigable of the black female antislavery speakers. Her career, launched in the shadow of the Burns case, survived the Civil War, flourished in reform work, secured her reputation as a writer, and culminated after forty years with the publication of the novel for which she is best known today, *Iola Leroy, or Shadows Uplifted* (1892).

It is clear that Frances Watkins' entrance into the public arena was strongly conditioned by what the men of her acquaintance were doing. It has been pointed out that her foundational statement of Christian social justice owed much to her uncle, William Watkins, who further schooled her in Garrison's values. The early reform activities of William J. Watkins provided a model for her to follow, but as his reform turned toward a blend of revolution and electoral politics, the model failed her, and she had to work out a feminine role for herself. Her considerable popularity as a speaker, or "doer of the word," was largely owing to a style no less devoted than her cousin's but more conciliatory, sentimental, and poetic. Still, the revolutionary turn that things were taking in 1854 provided the energy necessary to move her across the difficult boundary from private life to public.[33]

BENJAMIN ROBBINS CURTIS

Theodore Parker's great antagonist, Judge Benjamin R. Curtis, outlived him by fourteen years. When he died in 1874, his brother, George Ticknor Curtis, wrote of him that his "moral sentiments and convictions were very strong; but they lay deep beneath the surface, forming, like conscience, the unseen and silent guide of life." At whatever inaccessible depths they may have lurked invisible to others, it was said that his moral sentiments came out once, in 1857, when he wrote his dissenting opinion in the case of Dred Scott.[34]

Scott, slave of Irene Sanford Emerson and John Sanford, her brother, had been suing for his freedom in Missouri courts since before the Mexican War. The case arose because his owner at the time, army surgeon Dr. John Emerson, had taken him from Missouri to Illinois, a free state, and then to Fort Snelling in Wisconsin Territory, where slavery had been banned by the Missouri Compromise. Long after his return to Missouri, Scott decided that his temporary residence in the North had legally effected his liberation, and that he and his family had been held illegally ever since. The suits that he brought had been kept alive by a lawyer, Roswell Field, who saw that if a slave who had resided in free territory could sue his master in federal court, then trial by jury could not be denied to escaped and recaptured slaves. Such a result would effectively cripple the 1850 Fugitive Slave Law.[35]

When this complex case was argued for a second time before the Supreme Court in December 1856, two fundamental issues emerged. First was the jurisdictional question of Scott's right to sue in federal court. This involved determining whether Scott was a citizen of Missouri and thus entitled to the privileges and immunities conferred by the Constitution on citizens of the United States. If he were a citizen and not a slave, it could only have been because his residence in the North had altered his status, so the second issue was whether that transformation had legally occurred. The implications of this second issue were explosive: they involved testing for the first time the constitutionality of the Missouri Compromise, which, though it had been repealed in 1854, stood as the prime instance of the power of Congress to regulate slavery in the territories, still a live issue and indeed a main plank in the Republican platform, Frémont's recent defeat notwithstanding.

Scott's lead attorney, Montgomery Blair, an old Freesoiler and now a Republican, persuaded George Ticknor Curtis to assist him by arguing, before his brother and the eight other justices, the constitutionality of the Missouri Compromise and the power of Congress to determine questions of slavery and freedom in the territories. Blair himself would pursue the argument that free Negroes were citizens because they possessed civil rights if not the full panoply of political rights. Opposing counsel argued that Scott was not a citizen by birth and that he had not been (and could not be) naturalized, the only two means by which any person can become a citizen. Since he was not a citizen of Missouri, he could not be a citizen of the United States; consequently the lower federal court had erred in assuming jurisdiction on the basis that plaintiff and defendant were citizens of different states.[36]

Roger B. Taney's opinion for the Court stressed Scott's lack of standing in the federal court system. He was a slave. If he had been free, he would still have no standing because free blacks were not made citizens by the Constitution. He was not freed by virtue of his residence at Fort Snelling, because the Missouri Compromise was an unconstitutional interference with the right of property in slaves. He was also not free because it was up to Missouri to say whether it recognized, in a spirit of comity, the emancipatory effect of Illinois law in regard to Scott's temporary residence in that state.[37]

George T. Curtis was among the many who came to believe that this decision made the Civil War inevitable. The revolution in Northern sentiment at the time of the Burns case and the Kansas-Nebraska Act had, at least to outward appearances, seemed to cool in three years' time, and the election of a conservative Democratic administration was looked upon, by the Curtis circle, as a rebuke to the Republican movement and to the whole idea of sectional parties. Had it not been for this decision, as George Curtis later wrote, "we could have gained ten years more in the growth of the North and in the peaceful development of the power of the Federal government," in which case "Southern secession would never have been attempted."[38]

At the time, his brother shared this view and was likewise scandalized that Taney should corrupt the judicial process and impair the public's faith in the Supreme Court by pandering so flagrantly to the political interests of his section. Justice Curtis wrote a blistering dissent, embracing his brother's argument that the Missouri Compromise was constitutional and affirming that free blacks were indeed citizens, so recognized by five states (including North Carolina) at the time of the adoption of the Constitution. Since the majority held that Scott was not entitled to sue in federal court, Taney's ruling on the merits of the case, including his ruling against the Missouri Compromise, was unwarranted and out of order. If such a momentous step were to be taken, Curtis implied, it ought not to be accomplished by *obiter dicta,* which could only incite a public already convinced that the Court, with its Southern majority, was little more than a tool of the slave power.[39]

This was Curtis' last decision as a member of the Court, from which he now resigned, saying only—as he had said for years—that it was impossible to support himself on the salary it afforded. Many felt, then and later, that the antislavery character of his opinion in *Scott v. Sandford* belonged to a cynical design of public rehabilitation in advance of his return to private practice in Boston. But while it was clear by this time what Massachusetts expected of its public figures, the ungenerous inference is neither necessary nor wholly credible. Clearly, the dissent was popular in the North. When Herndon read it, he wrote to Parker to ask if it didn't seem that the leopard had changed his spots. But in fact there was no essential conversion. In theory at least, Webster's Union-saving compromise politics could be brought to bear against excesses on either side. If one chose not to take positions out of a sense of moral righteousness, one might, as Curtis seems to have done, take stands on the basis of what would generate the least amount of heat when the nation seemed a tinderbox.[40]

His consistent conservatism amounted in the end to a belief—which he seems to have shared with his father—that moral questions could be kept from resolving themselves. In 1860 he joined other Massachusetts conservatives, nominally led by the now retired Lemuel

Shaw (and including Emily Dickinson's father and the entire Harvard Law School faculty), in seeking the repeal of the 1855 Personal Liberty Law—a last-ditch effort to show the South the good faith of the Commonwealth. Curtis' last contribution to the debate came in 1862, when he published a pamphlet arguing that Lincoln had no legal authority to issue an Emancipation Proclamation. Parker, who died of tuberculosis and overwork in 1860, was no longer around to reply, but Curtis was confuted in a pamphlet issued by another old opponent, Charles M. Ellis.[41]

EDWARD GREELY LORING

When Curtis' step-brother, Judge Loring, declared Burns a slave, Charles Sumner, watching with intense interest from Washington, wrote, "I mourn the fate of that poor fugitive. But I mourn for the wretched commissioner still more." He had said the same thing in a speech in the Senate, and then repeated the observation in several private letters, as though conscious of having said something especially acute and noteworthy. It allowed the superficial inference that he had, of course, greater sympathy for the one to whom he was tied by racial, social, cultural, and professional affinities. There is more than a hint in Sumner's judgment that Loring had greater intrinsic capacities for suffering than Burns, whose slave history might be supposed to have included a sort of cauterizing of the sensibilities. To the extent that Sumner may actually have believed that, his judgment becomes further evidence of Burns's invisibility to the curious circle of white onlookers. But there are deeper levels of policy in Sumner's sentence, for he is proposing that the man who incurs moral guilt is in the nature of things more damaged and more to be pitied than any man he sins against. If the Burns case was Greek tragedy, as Sumner was inclined to suppose, then Loring, not Burns, was the self-destroying protagonist.[42]

In fact Loring was frequently subject to public humiliation in the years that followed, as he tried to go quietly about his double business as probate judge and slave law commissioner. The community quickly left off hanging him in effigy, and there were no more placards about "the memory of the wicked shall rot," but the people regarded him—and behaved toward him—as a public sinner, as guilty as Burns was innocent. While he became the darling of the dwindling set of proslavery Bostonians (Nehemiah Adams presented him with an inscribed copy of *A South-Side View of Slavery*), he was vastly more punished than rewarded. He lost his teaching job at Harvard, for example, which went to the cast-off Whig governor, Emory Washburn, an eminent Worcester lawyer. The antislavery legislature, at the urging of prominent abolitionists, kept recommending to Washburn's gubernatorial successor, Henry J. Gardner, that Loring be removed from his probate judgeship, but twice he declined to do it. Finally, in 1858, a new governor, Nathaniel P. Banks, acceded, and Loring was ousted.[43]

When the 1855 Personal Liberty Law went into effect, creating an incompatibility between state judicial offices and the position of federal slave law commissioner, Loring had persisted in holding both, convinced that the provision was unconstitutional. When he was at last removed by address, he argued that he ought to have been impeached, a proceeding that, he felt, would have tested the 1855 law and revealed not only its unconstitutionality, but its insidious threat to the independence of the state judiciary. "The probability and the peril of all this," he said, "will be the greatest, when the action of the Legislature of Massachusetts shall be controlled by a party, and her Executive shall be the prostitute of a party." By 1858 his own party had ceased to exist, so there was little to prevent the popular will from working.[44]

Still there were plums for loyal compromisers, and within weeks of his removal President Buchanan placed the rejected judge on the bench of the Court of Claims in Washington, where he presided noiselessly until his retirement in 1877. He was remembered by his friends as "a man of charming personality, a raconteur of the very highest order. He, with his wife and daughters, each brilliant and witty, rendered the Loring home, on K Street, a centre of social delight, unsurpassed elsewhere at the Capital."[45]

CHARLES F. SUTTLE

Colonel Suttle's later life was uneventful. He operated his general store in Alexandria—Green, Suttle & Company—for two decades, apparently without significant interruption from the war. In 1866 at the age of fifty-one he ended his long bachelorhood by marrying Emily Taliaferro Claiborne, a war widow from Baltimore. At home in Alexandria, Suttle enjoyed a middling prosperity, served on the city council, and held directorships in the Farmers' Bank of Virginia and the Orange, Alexandria & Manassas Railroad.

His health declining, he retired in 1879 to Rocky Mount, Virginia, in the Blue Ridge country, just a few miles from the cabin where Booker T. Washington had grown up in slavery. Here Suttle looked after the local interests of the Virginia Midland Railroad. His death, after a lingering illness, was reported to have occurred on December 19, 1880.

But this turned out to be an error. On February 11, 1881, the Alexandria *Gazette* issued a correction, saying that Suttle had in fact clung to life until February 9. Instead of repeating the obituary, the paper referred its readers to the earlier-published notice. "There is no doubt, however, of the death of the colonel this time, for official information has been received by the railroad authorities to that effect."[46]

🌿 An Emersonian Epilogue

A vast republic of escaped slaves. When you consider the hordes from eastern Europe, you might well say it: a vast republic of escaped slaves. But one dare not say this of the Pilgrim Fathers, and the great old body of idealist Americans, the modern Americans tortured with thought. A vast republic of escaped slaves. Look out, America! And a minority of earnest, self-tortured people.

D. H. Lawrence

Antislavery activity in Massachusetts commanded the attention of the whole country because of the energy, talent, and resources of the movement and its leaders there, but also because of the Commonwealth's unique place in a national mythology of protest and freedom reaching back through Hancock and Adams to Bradford and Winthrop. The response in Massachusetts to the enforcement of the Fugitive Slave Law and to the passage of the Kansas-Nebraska Act emboldened antislavery workers throughout the North, while at the same time blowing the dust off the tradition of Puritan dissent. As slavery was, without a near competitor, the dominant political issue in the 1850s, so it became for a time—at a critical time—the dominant trope through which Americans were encouraged to understand their private situation and national destiny. Slavery had slipped its bounds. It could no longer be regarded simply as the condition of some millions of black folk far removed in the South: it had become a belligerent philosophy of government predicated on the elimination of freedom. It was now evidently an aggressive, expansionist culture that proposed to remake by force the lives of all Americans.

To respond at all to a threat thus defined involved thinking in new ways about the meaning and value of freedom. It set more than a few white people in the North to planning how *they* might escape slavery. The Fugitive Slave Law had abolished slavery as a foreign concern and installed it for the first time, legally and psychologically, in Northern homes. What had been absent was now present; the crippling abolitionist requirement that one must care deeply and humanely about quite invisible, nearly fictitious sufferers was largely abrogated. The slave's freedom, becoming more familiar, got bound up with the free man's freedom, so that whites who now felt jeopardized, who were feeling a new sort of regard for their own liberties, were beginning to act rather like fugitive slaves themselves. Like the runaway (sometimes archly called the "self-emancipator"), the white Northern sympathizer was struggling to affirm a free identity. Both, after their fashion, believed that America was intrinsically a place where one either lived free or died (as they still say in New Hampshire), though all the real drama of that proposition had been centering for some time exclusively on the literal slave. Thus a despised and rejected race, an unassimilated fragment of the national community, had come into immediate and intimate possession of the identity of the whole—if that identity consisted, as had been steadily affirmed, in pressing toward freedom. Whether America was about freedom or about oppression (and whether it *could* be about one and not the other), whether its mission was a material or a spiritual and ideal one, whether it would survive as a unit, had come to be specialized implications of the slavery question.

Slavery redefined the Pilgrim and Puritan heritage and redefined the American Revolution. Slavery found new uses for such civil rights as trial by jury and the writ of habeas corpus and so redefined the law. Slavery precipitated the question of what constitutes American citizenship, and thus, in the Civil War and in the Civil War amendments to the Constitution, it redefined the country. It split denominations into Northern and Southern wings and set Protestant Christianity against Catholic, and so redefined American religion by the new test it set. One sees these new definitions clearly arising in the Revolution of 1854, but above all one sees how slavery redefined liberty itself— how in the famous icon of the fettered slave all the culture's serious thinking about freedom and revolution came to be concentered.

No one could resist this pressure, least of all the country's central thinkers. Emerson tried to hold out against it. Preferring to discuss freedom in the terms of his own proper culture, he explicitly resisted the call to drop what looked like an abstract and "philosophical" valuation of freedom in favor of the hot contentions of the antislavery platform. He excused himself, saying he had other souls to liberate than black ones, "spirits in deeper prisons, whom no man visits, if I do not." A long while he held out, supposing that he was attacking root causes where others addressed symptoms. But when Webster endorsed the Compromise of 1850 and the included Fugitive Slave Law, he found that discussing freedom in his own culture's terms now meant something different. Chattel slavery was no longer a single instance among others of the loss of freedom: it had become the commanding, present literal that organized and conferred meaning on those other forms by which the human spirit was coerced and curtailed—forms that now seemed to reappear as tropes of *it*. Slavery had centered itself, and, as Whittier testified in his poem, the landscape looked different in consequence.[1]

The country had talked itself out on the subject of freedom through two generations of Fourth of July speeches, mostly from party hacks like B. F. Hallett, who had made a specialty of such talk. Memorials of independence had become debased as rhetoric and needed to be recharged by renewed revolution. "Certainly the social state, patriotism, law, government, all did cover ideas," said Emerson, "though the words have wandered from the things." Over the revolution that would renovate the language the figure of the fugitive slave was bound to preside (as he did for Whitman) with the power of his defiance and the power of his jeopardy, his narratives of escape and self-determination. There were moments when Mrs. Stowe understood this, as when in *Uncle Tom's Cabin* she had George Harris turn and confront the slave-catchers who were pursuing his family, his friends, and himself. "I know very well that you've got the law on your side, and the power," he said to them from behind a gun. But "we don't own your laws; we don't own your country; we stand here as free, under God's sky, as you are; and by the great God that made us, we'll fight for our liberty till we die." Stowe called this "his declaration of independence" and compared his militant defiance to that of a Hungarian revolutionary. As evidenced also in Frederick Douglass' *Narrative* or its 1855 expansion, *My Bondage, My Freedom,* in James

Pennington's *Fugitive Blacksmith,* or William Craft's *Running a Thousand Miles for Freedom,* escaped slaves were the only certifiable revolutionaries in America at this time, though their white allies, now for the first time similarly armed and determined, were potential tropes of them, proxies in spirit. Higginson, Parker, Phillips, Dana, Conway, Thoreau—none of these could do much for freedom if not called out by an emergency, by the supplied peril of the trapped man who assigned to them their actions.[2]

But what, then, if not a revolutionary, was Emerson, whose force or influence was held in common by virtually all of those who *could* be thus called out? On the eve of the Burns case it was Emerson who was announcing that "Liberty is aggressive, Liberty is the Crusade of all brave and conscientious men. It is the epic poetry, the new religion, the chivalry of all gentlemen." More than most and as much as anyone, Emerson was now identifying the antislavery cause with "manhood and culture"; such language was meant to recruit soldiers and shame the enemy. In the immediate aftermath of the Burns case, as Emerson was inaugurating a series of Sunday evening talks on slavery at Concord, he simultaneously began his topical notebook, WO Liberty, purposing to make a regular study of the subject and to write a comprehensive treatise. It was, he thought, a consolation "that in the glare of passion the foundations of law are searched, and men become masters of the science of liberty." He may have been thinking, as well, of Theodore Parker's concurrent literary project or of how much more simply everyone knew about law these days.[3]

The immediate outcome of Emerson's self-imposed course of study was his lecture "American Slavery," which he was invited to give in a series organized for Boston by Vigilance Committee members Samuel Gridley Howe and Dr. James W. Stone. Wishing to avoid the usual speakers, they pointedly did not invite Garrison, Phillips, or Parker (all of whom felt slighted) but scheduled instead Emerson, Frederick Douglass, and Whig Congressman Charles Wentworth Upham (Hawthorne's political opponent from Salem and the model for Judge Pyncheon in *The House of the Seven Gables*). Scheduled to speak on behalf of slavery were two moderate Southerners, Texas Senator Sam Houston and Missouri Congressman (and former Senator) Thomas Hart Benton (both of whom had opposed the Kansas-Nebraska Act), and Georgia Senator Robert Toombs, who had spoken of sitting with his slaves in the shadow of Bunker Hill monument and who, in 1865, was one of only five Confederate leaders pursued by the government as war criminals.[4]

In his lecture, delivered on January 25, 1855, Emerson asserted that the great and overruling power in the universe called "Divine justice" underwrites human progress. All attempts to run against this force are doomed to failure, however much they may seem for a time to be controlling. Thus, for example, "in 1850, the American Congress passed a statute which ordained that justice and mercy should be subject to fine and imprisonment, and that there existed no higher law in the universe than the Constitution and this paper statute which uprooted the foundations of rectitude and denied the existence of God." Just as the government cannot repeal the law of gravity, such a monstrous attempt to revise the permanent moral nature of things has to be sustained, if at all, against the whole active force by which the universe is kept together. A state militia cannot do the job, nor can it be done by all the resources at the command of Franklin Pierce. The Fugitive Slave Law, opposed by all that is good, natural, and progressive, has been failing from its inception, and will, with complete certainty, give way sooner or later before the justice and mercy it artificially denies. "Secret retributions are always restoring the level, when disturbed, of the Divine justice. It is impossible to tilt the beam."[5]

Emerson's metaphor suggests that evil is an unsustainable violation of nature, an effort to make an ounce balance a pound. Men keep trying to win these unearned advantages, and the inevitable recoil has the character of a revolution. Emerson instanced the recent Know-Nothing landslide: "The late revolution in Massachusetts no man will wonder at who sees how far our politics had departed from the path of simple right." The farthest advance of unrighteousness marks a crisis, an edge, beyond which the restorative powers gain, as they must, the upper hand. "The laws of nature," Emerson had earlier said, "execute themselves"; yet if the process has this inevitable character, it is not accomplished without human agency. Men have a responsibility to act and must range themselves according to their character either for or against the triumph of right. In the opening of the address, Emerson acknowledged that "heaven too has a hand" in the antislavery struggle, "and will surely give the last shape to these ends which we hew very roughly, yet I remember that our will and obedience is one of its means." Nothing important, lasting, progressive, or liberating is ever done by human beings except in obedience to permanent laws, that "higher law" whose realization in action is equivalent to growth and progress. The greater the fidelity the actions bespeak, the larger and more worthy the actor. Conversely, acts of "skepticism" or "non-credence," antagonized by the nature of things, diminish the actor: Emerson implies this devolution by referring consistently to proslavery men as "quadrupeds" and by registering his dismay at finding such unevolved creatures in positions of power and respectability in Boston.[6]

Emerson's 1855 lecture on slavery is a remarkable instance of his ability to address the topic without retreating from his characteristic idealism, which is just the challenge that slavery is supposed to have set for him. How could this dealer in abstractions, with his reputation for keeping aloof from the real world, confront effectively (or at all) a problem so manifestly human and social? The assumption has generally been that in order to do so he would have somehow to forget that he was a Transcendentalist and repudiate or retreat from the principles that won him his first audience. There is a notable lack of consensus among historians and students of Emerson in regard to his handling of this alleged dilemma: a great many hold that Emerson simply could not suspend his idealism before the vulgar dispute between slave and master and so made himself and his followers irrelevant to the struggle; others suppose that his career in the 1850s was a more or less steady retreat from important early beliefs, and that while he indeed spoke forcefully and influentially on slavery, he did so at the cost of consistency and because the material circumstance now bulked larger in his thought.[7]

While there is some misleading grain of truth in both these views, neither does the slightest justice to the critically important fact that Emerson was a force in antislavery because of his idealism, not in spite of it. No one knew this better than Emerson himself. In fact his 1855 lecture may be seen as an effort to make explicit just those implications of his Transcendentalism that so influenced younger men such as Higginson, Alcott, Parker, Conway, and Thoreau, whom Emerson regarded as among the heroes of the Burns case.

Emerson was never more the Transcendental idealist than when he said, in this lecture: "Truth exists, though all men should deny it." Truth is not transactional, instrumental, or contingent; it is not an agreement of convenience among men, as the great political compromises, including the Constitution of the United States, had been.

Truth, Emerson believed, permanently overlooks the affairs of men, ratifies what is consistent with it, and makes untenable that which is inconsistent with it.

> There is a sound and healthy universe whatever fires or plagues or desolation transpire in diseased corners. The sky has not lost its azure because your eyes are inflamed. Seas and waters, lime and oxygen, magnesia and iron, salts and metals, are not wasted, their virtues are safe, if an individual or a species sicken. And there's a healthy interior universe as well, and men are great and powerful as they conform to, or become recipient of, the great equal general laws.

Men may be kidnapped by the government out of Brattle Street in the twilight of the day, the president may approve, the courts concur, and slaveowners rejoice, but the truth that declares it an act of injustice is exactly as pristine after the event as ever it was before. The "healthy interior universe" where no man is a slave is surely an abstraction, but it is also, amid the defections of law and government, the only practical reliance that justice and social progress permanently have.[8]

The way to become "great and powerful" is to work with, not against, the moral structure of the universe, to seek out and rely on that rather than on anything less, such as, in particular, a government of compacts and conscious compromises. Emerson goes on to ask: "what is the effect of this evil government?" It is not, ironically, to spawn unmitigated evil consequences, but, instead, "to discredit government."

> When the public fails in its duty, private men take its place . . . When the American government and courts are false to their trust, men disobey the government, put it in the wrong; the government is forced into all manner of false and ridiculous attitudes. Men hear reason and truth from private men who have brave hearts and great minds. This is the compensation of bad governments,—the field it affords for illustrious men.

Revolution is the privatization of government or an acknowledgment that authority, which effectively follows truth, has been recalled from the forms in which it had been vested back to its primitive sources. The implication is that the act of vesting authority in institutional forms (such as a particular government) is always a sort of makeshift, subject to dissolution and recall as soon as its corruption or variance from truth becomes practically intolerable. And how does one know when a revolution is in order? The answer seems to be that one doesn't know until it has already happened: that is, it occurs or has occurred when the critics of the government speak with profounder authority or with greater adherence to truth than the government does.[9]

Of course Emerson's real program is not revolution now, but revolution continually. The advantage of the present crisis lay in its showing that only those were duped by Webster and Pierce who took what amounted to a moral holiday, placing their faith in the government on the compromise supposition that it is going to be a good-enough practical expedient. The "brave hearts and great minds," on the other hand, constituted themselves as such by leaning all along on a better staff: the "right of private judgment."

Those who stress Emerson's irrelevance to the antislavery struggle of the 1850s have ignored or overlooked much evidence to the contrary; nevertheless, the fact remains that he spoke out more rarely and more selectively than such contemporaries as Phillips, Garrison, Douglass, or Parker—though often, for that very reason, to greater effect. It is also true that many of his actions on behalf of the cause were either ineffectual or unpublicized. That he did not come the twenty miles into Boston during the Burns trial is altogether characteristic. He knew and repeatedly said that others were better situated than he to advance the revolution, which he supposed—rightly enough—was a young man's crusade. Emerson turned fifty-one on the day that Burns was arrested, and he could be well content to make out his "relevance" on the ground he had always occupied, as an influence on others, a granter of permission, an encourager of righteousness.

Convinced that public affairs had reached a critical juncture, Emerson began in June 1854 to involve himself in such unaccustomed activities as political organization, local committee work, petitioning the governor, and raising funds for Kansas emigrants as also, a short while later, for John Brown and Harriet Tubman. The altered public climate transfigured the circle of Emerson's private acquaintance, which expanded to include powerful antislavery figures such as Sumner, George Stearns, and John Murray Forbes, as well as younger men like Conway and Frank Sanborn. This social transformation was reflected in the establishment, toward the end of 1854, of the Saturday Club, the first meeting of which was held at the Albion Hotel, General Edmands' erstwhile headquarters. The Transcendentalists were well represented, Emerson attending along with Alcott, Sanborn, John S. Dwight, and Thoreau's English friend

Thomas Cholmondeley. Discussion turned largely on the political situation and was dominated at the end of the evening by Dana's anecdotal review of the Burns case and by discussions of the upcoming trials of Phillips and Parker. The club, which quickly expanded to include a significant portion of Boston's intelligentsia, was the nucleus of a coalescing antislavery culture, out of which developed, within three years, its official organ, the *Atlantic Monthly*.[10]

These external developments, called out by events, were important enough in themselves, but Emerson never ceased to regard his own role in rather different terms. Few, he felt, could see quite as clearly as he the relation of America's political dilemma to the workings of the moral law or indeed the radical dependence of events on ideas. Annoyed at the scoffing which the "higher law" had received from public men, he insisted that the country was now paying the price of its disbelief, as in Judge Loring's courtroom:

> This skepticism assails a vital part when it climbs into the Courts, which are the brain of the state. The idea of abstract right exists in the human mind, and lays itself out in the equilibrium of nature, in the equalities and periods of our system, in the level of seas, in the action and reaction of forces, that nothing is allowed to exceed or absorb the rest; if it do, it is disease, and is quickly destroyed.

The idea of equal justice, in other words, is as intrinsic to the structure of the universe and as hard to be overborne, even temporarily, as the principle of physical equilibrium in nature. Emerson's explanation is that both are one idea, permanent and therefore preexistent, but differently manifested in the phenomenal world.[11]

Loring's decision is an instance of disbelief in the higher law; it therefore shows as disease and will be quickly destroyed. But slavery, the currently raging pandemic, invades and infects all aspects of the healthy culture, warring even against that "healthy interior universe" which it is the duty of each to explore and defend.

> Thus in society, in education, in political parties, in trade, and in labor, in expenditure, or the direction of surplus capital, you may see the credence of men; how deeply they live, how much water the ship draws. In all these, it is the thought of men, what they think, which is the helm that turns them all about. When thus explored, instead of rich belief, of minds great and wise sounding the secrets of nature, announcing the laws of science, and glowing with zeal to act and serve,

and life too short to read the revelations inscribed on earth and heaven, I fear you will find non-credence, which produces nothing, but leaves sterility and littleness.

The advancing negation represented by slavery can exercise its corrupting influence in the North because the slave power projects it "through their systematic devotion to politics, [having] the art so to league itself with the government, as to check and pervert the natural sentiment of the people by their respect for law and statute." So, it is the unself-reliant respect for forms and institutions that seduces the North from righteousness, with the result that while we have the forms, "we are swindled out of the liberty."[12]

The "natural sentiment" of the people exalts freedom. It takes a good deal of force and custom to sterilize and weaken this popular faith and to superinduce at last a preference for slavery. And yet that is just the course of the current disease. The health of the country (as of anything) consists in the fullest possession of its informing idea, and it was Emerson's belief that the United States had come into existence, however crossed, crippled, and ill-equipped, in order to give expression and practical development to the idea of liberty. "All the mind in America," he said, "was possessed by that idea. The Declaration of Independence, the Constitution of the States, the Parties, the newspapers, the songs, star-spangled banner, land of the brave and home of the free, the very manners of the Americans, all showed them as the receivers and propagandists of this lesson to the world. For this cause were they born and for this cause came they into the world."[13]

Our concern here should not be with the accuracy of this statement as an objective historical assessment, even though Emerson appears to offer it as such. Its whole importance is as an idea thrown into circulation and operative in 1855, one that helped to shape belief at that moment and that helps us now to understand how in the middle of the nineteenth century slavery lost its prestige in white America. It is a complex, deeply conditioned statement, yet at the same time easily appealing enough to win friends and impel heroes. The idea that America is "about" freedom has more than an appearance of plausibility, which is to say that Emerson's approach to the slavery question is demonstrably not founded on a lie. If there were different opinions on the question, for example, of whether the Constitution was a proslavery document; if the "manners of the Americans" included selfishness, intolerance, and racism as well as the egalitarian comradeship expressed by Melville and Whitman; if the star-spangled banner was planted on Indian land; and if the freedom which Americans sought was as yet bounded and incomplete, still what else but some idea of liberty, to be made perfect in progress, could be indicated by Emerson's list of cultural signs? Nor does it matter that professions of a love of liberty may be formal or hypocritical, jingoistic or insincere, since it is the reception of these signs and their "sure-fire" popularity that signify more than their authors' intent—more even than their reflection of conditions. Emerson's contention is certainly not that America is "a free country," but that it is historically and geographically consecrated to the purpose of installing freedom, and that it gets sick when it forgets what it means to do.

Emerson is associated quite properly with a certain idealistic moral style that has (with what propriety everyone may judge) fallen out of fashion. The main argument against it at the time was that it was either too "mystical" or too intellectually abstract to be brought to bear on the affairs of real life. More recent versions of the argument hold that it performed no useful "cultural work" or that because it honored and empowered the private self it was as apt to license oppressors as revolutionaries. None of these objections, however, prevented Emerson's idealism from putting Higginson in front of the Court House door, Thoreau on the platform at Framingham, or Whitman at his desk in Brooklyn. Not one of all his disciples could make his ethics square with slavery; indeed, the uniform effect he had on his followers was to make them take substantial risks for the antislavery cause.

To say that Emerson's moral style is out of fashion implies at a minimum that it is different from current styles. Bracketing any final judgment about its practical effectiveness in engaging the issues of those years before the Civil War, it will be useful to take a brief concluding look at some ways in which it truly is different.

Emerson's position seems to a modern reader even more abstract and disengaged than perhaps it really is because of the notable absence from it of any direct sympathy or fellow-feeling for the slave. Its central proposition has to do with the general benefit that obtains when freedom is conscientiously served. What is threatened, in Emerson's view, is not Anthony Burns or any particular slave or even slaves in general, but the regime of freedom, to realize which ensures the prosperity, moral and physical, of the country as a whole. Admittedly, this looks cold. To a great extent, this view of things appealed to male heroism but failed to move women, whose sympathies were more easily engaged with the victim. The words of Hebrews 13:3 were on many lips at this time ("Remember them that are in bonds, as bound with them; and them which suffer adversity, as being yourselves also in the body"), but it was the women, trained in sentiment, not the men, who found them directly useful.

Yet as a practical matter, it was not the women who needed convincing. If something were to be done about slavery, it was men's minds, not women's hearts, that had to be renovated, because power lay with the former. In that sense, it may have been fortunate that an effective and compelling argument could be made *without* invoking sympathy for the suffering other. If a racist society is to abolish slavery (and what other kind of society has that need?), it must either drop its racism or somehow come to regard itself as threatened by slavery. Women tended toward the first option, men toward the second. The latter was effectual. As women's power and freedom advanced over the next century, the two moral styles came to seem more complementary and less incompatible, so that eventually either one alone assumed an objectionably old-fashioned look, stigmatized as aloof and selfish on the one hand, as effusive and sentimental on the other.

But such a polarity is of course too simple. To recognize that is to see to an important secret at the bottom of Emerson's lecture. Having been invited to speak on slavery, Emerson might well have addressed himself to the troubles in Kansas. The reaction to the Kansas-Nebraska Act had by no means receded; indeed the Republican party was even then putting itself together on the strength of that reaction. Historians have long since agreed that Stephen Douglas' measure was the paramount incitement at this time to sectional politics. Then too, the question of slavery in the territories in some ways lent itself more obviously to a dispassionate defense of freedom than did cases of recaptured fugitive slaves. Yet in the address Emerson barely mentions Kansas. The context of his remarks is almost entirely a sustained, deeply probed outrage over the Fugitive Slave Law, that measure which had called out his denunciation in two previous lectures.

If the black man is again invisible in this idealistic and often abstract address of Emerson's, and if a personal sympathy is thereby ruled out, still Anthony Burns is not suppressed. His identity, his meaning for America, is borne out in every word.

NOTES

Dates are from 1854 unless otherwise indicated. For full citations of the short titles given here, see the Bibliography.

PREFACE

Epigraph: Hannah Arendt, *On Revolution,* 242. Quotations from this work in the following paragraphs are from 28, 114, 118–121, and 21.

THURSDAY, MAY 25, 1854

Epigraph: Boston Slave Riot (hereafter cited as *BSR*), 5.

1. Testimony of Rev. L. A. Grimes, Mass. House Doc. 205, 14–15.
2. Dana, *Journal,* 625. A substantially similar account is in Dana, *Remarks,* 15.
3. Dana, *Journal,* 625.
4. Testimony of Theodore Parker, Mass. House Doc. 205, 33.
5. Mass. House Doc. 93, 25; Phillips, *Argument,* 25; "The Case of Anthony Burns," 181. Ellis had been notified by Theodore Parker, who encountered him in Washington Street on the way to Dana's office; Mass. House Doc. 205, 28.
6. Dana, *Remarks,* 15; Phillips, *Argument,* 25–26; Mass. House Doc. 205, 28–29, 33–35.
7. Mass. House Doc. 205, 28–29, 35.
8. *BSR,* 6; Phillips, *Argument,* 25.
9. Dana, *Remarks,* 15–16; Mass. House Doc. 205, 19–21, 34. Ellis and Phillips supported Parker's recollections; Mass. House Doc. 205, 28–29, 36.
10. *BSR,* 6; "The Case of Anthony Burns," 182–183.

11. *BSR,* 6; "The Case of Anthony Burns," 182–183.
12. Dana, *Journal,* 626; Mass. House Doc. 93, 23; Dana, *Remarks,* 16–17; *BSR,* 14.

GRAPPLING

Epigraph: Weiss, *Life and Correspondence of Parker,* 2: 125.
1. Stevens, *Anthony Burns,* 26; Parker, "New Crime," 261; Mass. House Doc. 93, 29–30.
2. Bowditch, *Life and Correspondence,* 1: 264; Tiffany, *Samuel E. Sewall,* 77–78. The Boston Vigilance Committee (BVC) Executive Committee consisted of Theodore Parker (president), Charles M. Ellis, Lewis Hayden, Samuel Gridley Howe, Edmund Jackson, Francis Jackson, Wendell Phillips, Joshua B. Smith, and Charles K. Whipple. Of these men all but Phillips and Smith were members of Parker's Twenty-eighth Congregational Society.
3. Bronson Alcott, MS diary for 1854, 34, 37, Houghton Library, Harvard University (hereafter cited as Houghton Library), *59M-308(24); May to Higginson, May 25, in Ford, "Trial of Anthony Burns," 323; Mary Higginson, *Thomas Wentworth Higginson,* 142.
4. Boston *Post,* May 26; *Boston Daily Advertiser,* May 26. Wendell Phillips, son of a previous mayor, seems to have spoken directly with Smith and received assurances of his sympathy, though he would prove to be an unreliable ally. "The word 'dough-faces' was invented to describe those . . . who were ready to sacrifice everything to the South to help their party"; Clarke, *Anti-Slavery Days,* 112.
5. Phillips, *Speeches, Lectures, and Letters,* 1; Clarke, *Anti-Slavery Days,* 106; Wilson, *Rise and Fall,* 1: 383–387.
6. Broadside, Boston Public Library (hereafter cited as BPL), reproduced in Ripley, *Black Abolitionist Papers,* 4: 228. Weiss, *Life and Correspondence of Parker,* 2: 132, plausibly identifies Theodore Parker as the author.
7. Weiss, *Life and Correspondence of Parker,* 2: 134.
8. Howe, *Letters and Journals,* 2: 237–245, 269.
9. Wilson, *Rise and Fall,* 2: 436; Stevens, *Anthony Burns,* 31–33.
10. *Liberator,* June 2; Blackett, *Beating Against the Barriers,* 57–59; Stevens, *Anthony Burns,* 32–33.
11. Wilson, *Crusader in Crinoline,* 401; Hedrick, *Harriet Beecher Stowe,* 256–257; Donald, *Charles Sumner,* 259–260. Stowe's "Appeal" was reprinted in *Liberator,* March 3. She had also sponsored a series of antislavery lectures in Boston that winter, but they roused little public interest (Hedrick, 252).
12. *Right of Petition,* 1–2.
13. Frothingham, *Edward Everett,* 356–358; Appleton, *Selections from Diaries,* 168. Douglas' comments created a strong backlash among the New

England clergy, which conditioned their reaction to the Burns case. For typical responses to the congressional treatment of the petition, see Harris, "Politics and the Pulpit"; Eddy, *The Commonwealth;* and Foster, *Rights of the Pulpit.*

14. Frothingham, *Edward Everett,* 343–356; Boston *Post,* May 25; Dana, *Journal,* 624–625; Emerson, *Journals,* 11: 380.

15. Edward Everett, MS diary, May 25, Massachusetts Historical Society (hereafter cited as MHS). The *Commonwealth,* May 25, reported that Webster loyalist Rufus Choate had declined the nomination and that Otis P. Lord of Salem was Everett's likely successor. Antislavery men generally favored Samuel Hoar of Concord, though in the end Governor Emory Washburn chose moderate Whig Julius Rockwell.

16. Donald, *Charles Sumner,* 260–261; Sumner, *Final Protest,* 6.

FRIDAY, MAY 26

1. *BSR,* 25; *Liberator,* June 2 (speech of Wendell Phillips); Dana, *Journal,* 626–627. The office of commissioner had been created by the Judiciary Act of 1789, occupants to be appointed by the circuit courts and to have no more power than a justice of the peace: they could take affidavits, issue warrants, grant bail, etc.; in 1850 they were entrusted with administration of the Fugitive Slave Law, though the pretense was that this new duty did not require them to act in a judicial capacity at all. As we shall see, antislavery men argued that the office of the commissioner was itself unconstitutional.

2. Bradford, "Vindication," 389–390; Pope, *Loring Genealogy,* 112–113.

3. Warren, *History of Harvard Law School,* 2: 205–206; Bradford, "Vindication," 389–393; Parker, "New Crime," 291.

4. *Commonwealth,* May 27.

5. Phillips, *Argument,* 29; Parker, "New Crime," 302.

6. Mass. House Doc. 93, 28–29.

7. Stevens, *Anthony Burns,* 26–27; Mass. House Doc. 205, 16.

8. *Liberator,* June 2; Dana, *Journal,* 627.

9. The best account of the Boston Vigilance Committee is found in Bearse, *Reminiscences,* which provides a membership list. The Committee's account book, kept by Francis Jackson, was published in facsimile by the Bostonian Society in 1924. The most extensive study of the group was conducted by Wilbur H. Siebert, but see also Collison, "The Boston Vigilance Committee." Between the Sims case in 1851 and the Burns case in 1854, the Committee raised no money, and its functions were assumed by a core of five or six committed activists. For example, as Bearse explains, "People used to write to Mr. Phillips from the South . . . just before slaves were about to start. Mr. Phillips got the letters, and so was on the lookout when the vessels got into Boston harbor. He would know the name of the vessel, and who was on board, and be all ready to help them"; *Reminiscences,* 33.

From 1850 to mid-1854, the Committee assisted 230 fugitives to Canada or other destinations; Francis Jackson to Theodore Parker, June 11, 1854, quoted in Levesque, "Inherent Reformers," 510n.

10. Higginson, *Cheerful Yesterdays,* 147 (hereafter cited as *CY*); Bronson Alcott, MS diary for 1854, 47, Houghton Library.

THE JERRY RESCUE

Epigraph: Quoted in Galpin, "The Jerry Rescue," 20, from the Syracuse *Star,* May 28, 1851.

1. Sperry, *The Jerry Rescue,* 19.
2. Syracuse *Star,* May 28, 1851, quoted in ibid., 21.
3. Details of the Jerry case are drawn from May, *Some Recollections,* 373–384; Weiss, *Life and Correspondence of Parker,* 1: 321 and 2: 116–123; Ward, *Autobiography,* 117–118; Loguen, *The Rev. J. W. Loguen,* 442; Quarles, *Black Abolitionists,* 209–211; Campbell, *The Slave Catchers,* 154–157; Frothingham, *Gerrit Smith,* 117–122; Yacovone, *Samuel Joseph May,* 143–154; Galpin, "The Jerry Rescue"; and Sperry, *The Jerry Rescue.*
4. Sperry, *The Jerry Rescue,* 24.
5. May, *Some Recollections,* 377; Galpin, "The Jerry Rescue," 27, 31.
6. Campbell, *The Slave Catchers,* 156; Ripley, *Black Abolitionist Papers,* 4: 100–101n.

MARTIN STOWELL

Epigraph: Emerson, *Collected Works,* 2: 38.

1. Stowell, *Stowell Genealogy,* 410. The connection between shoemaking and radicalism was much commented on at the time. The despairing question of Hunker Democrat Caleb Cushing, "whether this State is to be 'shoe-makerized,'" was explained by Governor George Boutwell in the remark that "The 'shoe towns' generally supported the Free-soil Party" (Boutwell, *Reminiscences,* 119–120). Higginson noted that "Radicalism went with the smell of leather, and was especially active in such towns as Lynn and Abington, the centers of that trade" (*CY,* 115). John G. Whittier, Henry Wilson, Amasa Walker, and John B. Alley, among others, had been shoemakers. BVC member William Spooner was president of the New England Shoe and Leather Association (Abbott, *Cotton and Capital,* 27).
2. Stowell to Editor, *Liberator,* November 12, 1847, 181.
3. Ibid.; Stowell, *Stowell Genealogy,* 410; Stowell to W. L. Garrison, *Liberator,* June 2, 1848, 87.
4. Stowell to W. L. Garrison, *Liberator,* February 16, 1849, 27. The term "come-outism" (or "come-outer") derives from II Corinthians 6:17: "Wherefore come out from among them, and be ye separate, said the Lord, and touch not the unclean thing; and I will receive you."

5. Edelstein, *Strange Enthusiasm,* 135; Wilson, *Rise and Fall,* 2: 145; Nutt, *History of Worcester,* 1: 494–497. Foner, *Free Soil,* 124–125, points to earlier discussions in which a new party was talked of, but the Worcester convention of June 21, 1848, in the immediate aftermath of the Whig and Democratic nominating conventions, appears to be the earliest positive step in the formation of the national Freesoil party; the meeting was organized by Charles and George Allen of Worcester, together with Henry Wilson of Natick and Samuel Hoar of Concord.

6. Stowell to W. L. Garrison, *Liberator,* October 24, 1851, 171. The belief that Jerry's arrest had been staged came about because Webster, the previous May, had said that the law "will be executed in all the great cities, here in Syracuse—in the midst of the next antislavery convention, if the occasion shall arise." See Galpin, "The Jerry Rescue," 20–22, 25; and Campbell, *The Slave Catchers,* 154.

7. Edelstein, *Strange Enthusiasm,* 129–130.

8. Ibid., 85, 105–106; Weiss, *Life and Correspondence of Parker,* 2: 98. On the Crafts' case, see Blackett, *Beating Against the Barriers,* 87–137; Weiss, *Life and Correspondence of Parker,* 2: 92–98; Dana, *Journal,* 413n.; Commager, *Theodore Parker,* 214–216; Horton and Horton, *Black Bostonians,* 103–104; and [Craft,] *Running a Thousand Miles for Freedom.*

9. Edelstein, *Strange Enthusiasm,* 107, 110–113. On Shadrach, see *Report of the Proceedings . . . ;* Bearse, *Reminiscences,* 16–22; Wilson, *Rise and Fall,* 2: 329–333; and Collison, *Shadrach Minkins.* On Sims, see *Trial of Thomas Sims;* Parker, *The Boston Kidnapping;* Dana, *Journal,* 419–425; Wilson, *Rise and Fall,* 2: 333–336; Higginson, *CY,* 139–146; Greenough, "Thomas Sims Papers"; Catterall, *Judicial Cases,* 4: 514–516; Campbell, *The Slave Catchers,* 117–121; Levy, "Sims' Case" and *Law of the Commonwealth,* 92–104.

10. Maginnes, "Point of Honor," 70; Edelstein, *Strange Enthusiasm,* 112; Siebert, "Underground Railroad," 70; Higginson, *CY,* 140.

11. Levy, "Sims' Case," 51–52.

12. Dana, *Journal,* 419–425; Levy, "Sims' Case," 46–51; Levy, *Law of the Commonwealth,* 92–104; Wilson, *Rise and Fall,* 2: 333–336; Emerson, *Journals,* 11: 361.

13. Higginson, *CY,* 142–143; Wilson, *Rise and Fall,* 2: 335–336; Dana, *Journal,* 424; Levy, "Sims' Case," 63. This meeting was originally called by the Freesoilers before Sims was arrested in order to protest the Fugitive Slave Law. Nathaniel Hawthorne, who had little sympathy for the slaves but detested the law, was among those who signed the call, and while some signers withdrew their names when the radical nature of the meeting became evident, Hawthorne was unrepentant. See Levy, "Sims' Case," 63; Whittier, *Letters,* 2: 173; and Mellow, *Nathaniel Hawthorne in His Times,* 409–410.

14. Quoted in Edelstein, *Strange Enthusiasm,* 118.

STRATEGIES

Epigraph: This handbill was posted around the city and reproduced in several newspapers; see *BSR,* 7.

1. G. F. Hoar, *Autobiography,* 1: 290.
2. *Commonwealth,* May 26.
3. Whittier, *Letters,* 2: 257–258; Bowditch, *Life and Correspondence,* 1: 265. Whittier wrote "Moloch in State Street" in response to the Sims case in 1851.
4. Higginson, *CY,* 147; Edelstein, *Strange Enthusiasm,* 115–116.
5. Higginson, *CY,* 148. Bearse's association with the Transcendentalists went back to 1840, when he, his wife, Olive, and several other "Cape Cod Come-Outers" met with Parker, Alcott, George Ripley, and C. P. Cranch at the Groton Convention (see Weiss, *Life and Correspondence of Parker,* 1: 126–128).
6. Bowditch, *Life and Correspondence,* 1: 265; Wilson, *Rise and Fall,* 2: 436.
7. Higginson, *CY,* 149. Anne Warren Weston, who was visiting with Ann and Wendell Phillips, reported that a rescue "had been agreed on" at the BVC meeting; Ford, "Trial of Anthony Burns," 326.
8. Worcester *Daily Spy,* May 27; Horton and Horton, *Black Bostonians,* 55; Campbell, *The Slave Catchers,* 125. Hayden had been a slave in Kentucky, whose first wife was owned (and sold) by Henry Clay. For assisting in Hayden's escape, two abolitionists, Delia Webster and Calvin Fairbank, spent time in jail. In Boston Hayden conducted a flourishing clothing business on Cambridge Street and soon became wealthy, eventually endowing scholarships for black students at Harvard Medical School. When he sheltered William Craft at his home on Southac Street in 1850, he had two kegs of powder in the cellar ready to be touched off in the event of an attempt at recapture. Later Harriet Beecher Stowe visited Hayden's home while researching her *Key to Uncle Tom's Cabin* and found thirteen fugitive slaves being sheltered there. He later assisted John Brown. See Robboy and Robboy, "Lewis Hayden"; Runyon, *Delia Webster and Underground Railroad,* 11–21, 34–39, 91–94, 108–122, 140–146, 207–212; Siebert, "Vigilance Committee," 26; Clarke, "John Albion Andrew," 16; Bearse, "Memorial and Biographical Sketches," 8; Stowe, *Key,* 303–305.
9. See the *Essay on the Trial by Jury* (1852) by BVC member Lysander Spooner. The preference for democratic juries over aristocratic judges holds some irony for the many Boston abolitionists who were from old, well-to-do families: some, like Phillips, had consciously "de-classed" themselves by sacrificing social and professional position for the cause, but in all of them was an element of noblesse oblige.
10. Mass. Statutes 1837, chap. 11, sec. 1. On the writ of replevin, see Stevens, *Anthony Burns,* 48–60; Hurd, *The Law of Freedom and Bondage,* esp. 2: 32n.; and Morris, *Free Men All,* 11–12, 76–79, and passim.

11. Story regarded *Prigg* as a "triumph of Freedom" because it denied legal standing to slavery wherever it was not supported by positive state law—and in the case of fugitive slaves. See Story, *Life and Letters,* 2: 381–398; Sumner, *Selected Letters,* 1: 375; and Nogee, "The Prigg Case," 185–205. On Latimer see Levy, *The Law of the Commonwealth,* 78–85; Wilson, *Rise and Fall,* 1: 477–487; Campbell, *The Slave Catchers,* 13–14; Rosenberg, "Personal Liberty Laws," 28. Latimer's freedom was purchased by the Rev. Nathaniel Colver, and he remained in Boston; in 1851 he was paid by the BVC to maintain surveillance on Shadrach's pursuer, John Caphart (Jackson, *Account Book,* 18).

12. Dana, *Journal,* 421. On Sims see "Thomas Sims' Case," 7 Cushing (1851): 285–300; *Trial of Thomas Sims;* Greenough, "Thomas Sims Papers"; Levy, "Sims' Case." Devens, a schoolmate of Higginson's, later distinguished himself as a general in the Civil War.

13. Dana, *Journal,* 627; Parker, "New Crime," 306; *BSR,* 15; Parker, *Trial,* 154. The filled-out writ of replevin survives in the Dana Papers, box 40, MHS.

14. *Commonwealth,* May 27; *BSR,* 15; Stevens, *Anthony Burns,* 50.

BLACK BOSTON

Epigraph: From a broadside reproduced in Jacobs, *Courage and Conscience,* 219.

1. Quarles, *Black Abolitionists,* 199–200; Campbell, *The Slave Catchers,* 6; Nevins, *Ordeal: A House Dividing,* 243; Blackett, *Beating Against the Barriers,* 91; Horton and Horton, *Black Bostonians,* 103; Lankevitch, *Boston,* 43; Handlin, *Boston's Immigrants,* 250–251; Higginson, *CY,* 140; Landon, "The Negro Migration," 22–26; Levesque, "Black Boston," 516.

2. Lankevich, *Boston,* 36, 43; Horton and Horton, *Black Bostonians,* 2, 77.

3. Horton and Horton, *Black Bostonians,* 77–79; Douglass, "Learn Trades or Starve," in *Life and Writings,* 2: 223–225; Foner and Walker, *Proceedings of Black State Conventions,* 2: 87; William J. Watkins, "Destiny of the Colored Race," 195.

4. Stowe, *Uncle Tom's Cabin,* 515; Garrison, quoted in Merrill, *Against Wind and Tide,* 261.

5. *Proceedings of Colored National Convention . . . 1855,* 4.

6. See Pease and Pease, "Boston Garrisonians."

7. Jacobs, "The Nineteenth-Century Struggle"; Levy and Phillips, "The Roberts Case"; Litwack, *North of Slavery,* 143–144; Levy, *The Law of the Commonwealth,* 109–117; Horton and Horton, *Black Bostonians,* 70–75; Wilson, *Rise and Fall,* 1: 495–498.

8. Hall, "Massachusetts Abolitionists," 85; Maginnes, "Point of Honor," 58, 62; Karcher, *First Woman in the Republic,* 736 n. 114; Horton and Horton, *Black Bostonians,* 55–57, 125–127; Pauline Hopkins, "Famous Men," 337–342. In the trial of Charles G. Davis, charged in the Shadrach rescue,

Morris was identified in the testimony of a deputy U.S. marshal as "the little darkey lawyer"; *Report of Proceedings at Examination of Charles G. Davis,* 11.

9. Horton and Horton, *Black Bostonians,* 57, 100, 147n.; Ripley, *Black Abolitionist Papers,* 3: 448–449; Brown, *The Black Man,* 229.

10. U.S. Constitution, Art. 1, sec. 8, para. 15; Quarles, *Black Abolitionists,* 229; Frothingham, *Edward Everett,* 104–106.

11. Nell, *Colored Patriots,* 102. Morris and Charles Lenox Remond of Salem had petitioned the legislature on this subject a year earlier; see Quarles, *Black Abolitionists,* 230.

12. William J. Watkins, "Hints to the Free People of Color," *Liberator,* January 9, 1852, quoted in Finkenbine, "Boston's Black Churches," 170; and Levesque, "Black Boston," 492. Information on Watkins is drawn from Ripley, *Black Abolitionist Papers,* 4: 153–156; Quarles, *Black Abolitionists;* and Curry, *The Free Black,* 159. Watkins probably attended Parker's church; William Cooper Nell was a sexton there at the time of the Burns trial.

13. Watkins, *Our Rights as Men,* 4.

14. Ibid., 6. The term "Hunker" identified conservative Unionist supporters of the Compromise of 1850, whether Whig or Democrat. Its derivation is discussed in Douglass, *Papers,* 2: 363.

15. Nell also petitioned the legislature in 1851 for a monument to Attucks. He was unsuccessful. See Wesley, "Integration versus Separatism," 220.

16. Watkins to editor, Boston *Herald,* April 22, 1853, reprinted in Ripley, *Black Abolitionist Papers,* 4: 153–155; Nell, *Colored Patriots,* 101–111 (quotations from Choate and Hallett on 108, from Nell on 110–111). The Constitutional Convention of 1853 was an effort to weaken the control of conservative Boston over state affairs and was mainly the project of radical Freesoilers, including Wilson, Sumner, and Frank Bird, supported by Coalition Democrats who wanted to make headway against the Whigs. The defeat of the revised Constitution at the polls was blamed on key defections from the Freesoil ranks (J. G. Palfrey, C. F. Adams, and R. H. Dana), but more on the opposition of Catholics, who were concerned about school issues and about the reduced political representation of urban Boston.

17. Watkins, *Our Rights as Men,* 2.

ECLIPSE

1. Elizabeth Rogers Mason Cabot, MS diary, May 26, Rogers-Mason-Cabot Family Papers, MHS. Miss Mason later married Walter Cabot, son of Dr. Samuel Cabot (an organizer of the New England Emigrant Aid Company) and brother of Emerson's biographer, James Elliot Cabot. Her daughter, Elise, married Emerson's grandson, Ralph Emerson Forbes. See E. R. M. Cabot, *More than Common Powers of Perception.*

2. Edward Everett, MS diary, May 26, MHS; Frothingham, *Edward Everett,* 342, 365.

3. Caroline B. White, MS diary, May 26, American Antiquarian Society, Worcester, Mass. (hereafter cited as AAS). Mrs. White, twenty-six years old, was married to Francis Adams White, partner in a Boston leather-tanning firm.

4. Longfellow, *Letters,* 3: 434; *The Complete Poetical Works,* 191–192; Fanny A. Longfellow, *Mrs. Longfellow,* 199; Samuel Longfellow, *Life,* 2: 271. The quotation is the opening line of Shakespeare's *I King Henry VI.*

5. Francis Bennett Jr., MS diary, May 26 and May 3, AAS.

6. Forten, *Journal,* 35.

7. Higginson to Mary Higginson, May 26, quoted in Ford, "Trial of Anthony Burns," 323; and, partially, in Mary Higginson, *Thomas Wentworth Higginson,* 144; Higginson, *CY,* 149.

FANEUIL HALL

Epigraphs: Weston to "Dear Folks," May 30, in Ford, "Trial of Anthony Burns," 327; Parker, "New Crime," 290.

1. Dana, *Journal,* 2: 627–628.

2. Ibid.; O'Connor, *Lords of the Loom,* 97; Abbott, *Cotton and Capital,* 26.

3. Dana, *Journal,* 2: 628; Levy, *The Law of the Commonwealth,* 113n.

4. Swift, *Speech,* 9; Weston, quoted in Ford, "Trial of Anthony Burns," 327; Webster, "Another Interesting Letter"; Higginson, *CY,* 150–151.

5. *Liberator,* June 2; *BSR,* 7; Tiffany, *Samuel E. Sewall,* 80, 93; Levy, "Sims' Case," 50.

7. Lyman, "Memoir of George Robert Russell," 280–281; Ripley, *Black Abolitionist Papers,* 4: 301; Jackson, *Account Book;* Ford, "Trial of Anthony Burns," 327–328. Russell was Theodore Parker's friend and parishioner in West Roxbury, beginning in 1837. He was sympathetic to Transcendentalism, admired Alcott and Margaret Fuller, and subscribed to *The Dial.* Russell's mother and Dana's mother were cousins. S. G. Howe was Russell's classmate at Brown. Russell's wife, Sarah Shaw Russell, had belonged to Margaret Fuller's circle and attended her "Conversations." Higginson pointed out (*Margaret Fuller Ossoli,* 126–129) that the women in Margaret Fuller's classes were staunch abolitionists.

7. *BSR,* 8. See Bearse, *Reminiscences,* 3–5, for a list of BVC members.

8. Speeches at the meeting were stenographically reported by BVC member J. M. W. Yerrinton at the request of Thomas Drew, who published extracts in the Worcester *Spy* (see "Anthony Burns' Case"). Much of this material was reprinted in the *Liberator* and collected in *BSR,* 8–10. See Foner, *Free Soil,* 126, on Northern reaction to Kansas-Nebraska.

9. *BSR,* 8.

10. Ibid., 9; Stevens, *Anthony Burns,* 38–39.

11. Worcester *Spy,* May 24; Bennett, MS diary, June 1, AAS.
12. Parker's speech is given in Stevens, *Anthony Burns,* 289–295.

THE BATTLE AT THE COURT HOUSE DOOR

Epigraphs: Inaugural Address of J. V. C. Smith, in Whitmore, *Inaugural Addresses,* 68; Browne to Higginson, Higginson Papers, BPL.

1. Dana, *Journal,* 632. On Smith, see Holli and Jones, *Biographical Dictionary of American Mayors,* 333–334; Maginnes, "Point of Honor," 38–39; Parker, "Rights," 389; Handlin, *Boston's Immigrants,* 202; and Garland, "Jerome Van Crowninshield Smith," 303–304.
2. Whitmore, *Inaugural Addresses,* 65.
3. Savage, *Police Records,* 90–97; cf. Lane, *Policing the City,* 100.
4. Higginson, *CY,* 149–150.
5. Mary Higginson, *Thomas Wentworth Higginson,* 143; Higginson, *CY,* 150–151.
6. Boston *Post,* May 27; Clifford to Dana, June 10, Dana Papers, MHS. Frederick Douglass, who worked for Clifford as a servant in New Bedford in 1838, just after his escape from slavery, called him "the most aristocratic gentleman in Bristol county" (*My Bondage,* 313). In 1852 Clifford supplied Herman Melville with the "Agatha story," on which he tried to collaborate with Hawthorne (Mellow, *Nathaniel Hawthorne in His Times,* 417).
7. Ela, *Ela vs. J. V. C. Smith,* 17; Dana, *Journal,* 630.
8. Higginson, *CY,* 152–153.
9. Quoted in Mary Higginson, *Thomas Wentworth Higginson,* 144.
10. Newspaper accounts of the riot give few details not in Stevens, *Anthony Burns,* 29–47; and *BSR,* 10–12.
11. Testimony of Robert Taylor, *Commonwealth,* June 6; of Daniel M. Hill, *Commonwealth,* June 7; of Isaac Bullard, Boston *Post,* June 3; of Alonzo Coburn, Boston *Post,* June 7.
12. *Commonwealth,* June 6.
13. Higginson (*CY,* 157) and James Freeman Clarke ("Antislavery Movement," 398) identify Hayden and Webb as belonging to the party with the battering ram. See also Higginson, *CY,* 153–154.
14. Testimony of Isaac Jones and Sullivan W. Cutting, *Commonwealth,* June 5; "Anthony Burns' Case"; Webster, "Another Interesting Letter."
15. *Liberator,* June 2; Stevens, *Anthony Burns,* 44; Julia Ward Howe to Annie Ward Mailliard, May 27, Howe Papers, Houghton Library, *44M-314(557); Higginson, *CY,* 157, 159.
16. Bowditch, *Life and Correspondence,* 1: 265–266.
17. Phillips was chagrined that he had not been informed of Higginson's plan (Sherwin, *Prophet of Liberty,* 756). The women he escorted home—Anne Weston and Phoebe Garnault—were likewise sorry that a more concerted use of the meeting had not been made (Ford, "Trial of Anthony Burns,"

328–329). The abolitionist Lydia Maria Child was of the same opinion: "If they had only struck when the iron was hot, and used very slight precautions, I think the poor slave might have been rescued without shedding blood" (quoted in Karcher, *First Woman in the Republic,* 388–389).

18. Tiffany, *Samuel E. Sewall,* 80.
19. Higginson, *CY,* 158; cf. Willis, *Alcott Memoirs,* 74; and "Anthony Burns' Case."

AFTERMATH

Epigraph: BSR, 13.

1. Higginson, *CY,* 158–159; Stevens, *Anthony Burns,* 44–46; testimony of Watson Freeman and Sullivan Cutting, *Commonwealth,* June 5. According to the testimony of Silas Carlton and Isaac Bullard (Boston *Post,* June 3), swords and pistols were handed out only after Batchelder fell. Howe, *Letters and Journals,* 2: 270.
2. Stevens, *Anthony Burns,* 42n.
3. Clifford to Dana, June 10, Dana Papers, MHS; Boston *Post,* May 27.
4. The confrontation was not reported in the papers but was the subject of much gossip: see Deborah Weston to "Caroline," June 6, BPL; Clifford gives his account of it in his letter to Dana, June 10, Dana Papers, MHS.
5. *BSR,* 11–12, 27.
6. Ibid.; Stevens, *Anthony Burns,* 46–47; Ela, *Ela vs. J. V. C. Smith,* 17.
7. *Liberator,* June 9; *BSR,* 28.
8. Higginson, *CY,* 159–160; Ford, "Trial of Anthony Burns," 323.
9. Conway, *Autobiography,* 1: 62, 91, 171–172; d'Entremont, *Southern Emancipator,* 35–37, 44–45, 71–72.
10. Conway, *Autobiography,* 1: 176. Conway's recollection is clear, but he confused the order of events, placing this meeting on Monday. On the shawl, see Boston *Post,* June 7 (testimony of Alonzo J. Coburn); and Emerson's account of Lawrence's invention, *Journals,* 13: 119–120.
11. Conway, *Autobiography,* 1: 176.
12. Dana, *Remarks,* 18–19.
13. Mass. House Doc. 205, 31. Like Conway, Ellis had been deeply affected by Emerson: in 1842 he published, anonymously, *An Essay on Transcendentalism,* an earnest if early and awkward defense of Emerson's thought.
14. Higginson, *CY,* 160; Mass. House Doc. 205, 31, 35; Weiss, *Life and Correspondence of Parker,* 2: 125; *Liberator,* June 2; Richard Henry Dana Sr. to Mrs. Arnold, June 22, Dana Papers, MHS; Edward Griffin Parker to C. J. Lanman, [May 30], Miscellaneous Bound, MHS, in *Proceedings of the Massachusetts Historical Society* 50 (May 1917): 411–412; Myers, *Children of Pride,* 37.
15. Boston *Journal,* May 30; Dana, *Journal,* 631.

16. Arguments in court are given in "The Case of Anthony Burns" and in *BSR;* hereafter only direct quotations will be annotated.
17. *BSR,* 25.
18. "The Case of Anthony Burns," 184.
19. Boston *Post,* September 11, 1886. This account, presumably by Drew, is largely corroborated by Webster in "Another Interesting Letter." An anonymous article in the Boston *Daily Advertiser,* April 2, 1888, citing Drew among its sources, adds the detail that the gun was stashed with BVC member John Curtis, described as a "liberty loving tailor on North Street." The *Boston Almanac* lists "Curtis & Atkins," tailors, at 6 North Street.
20. *Liberator,* June 2; *BSR,* 16.

FOR SALE

Epigraph: Emerson, *Collected Works,* 2: 49.
1. Dana, *Journal,* 629.
2. Parker's account of his discussion with Grimes is in *BSR,* 86, a note added to the second printing; Parker, subscription paper, May 27, Miscellaneous Bound, MHS; Stevens, *Anthony Burns,* 61–62, attributes this offer of a sale to Suttle's fear of violence against himself.
3. Simmons, *Men of Mark,* 663. On Grimes see Brown, *The Rising Sun,* 218–220; Simmons, 662–665; Williams, *History of the Negro Race,* 2: 504–515; Ripley, *Black Abolitionist Papers,* 4: 184–185; Horton and Horton, *Black Bostonians,* 47–48; Bearse, *Reminiscences,* 12; Stevens, *Anthony Burns,* 203–209; Hayden, *Faith, Culture, and Leadership,* 28–30.
4. For Willis, see Garrison, *Letters,* 4: 608–609; *New England Genealogical and Historical Register,* 27: 118 and 33: 132.
5. Parker, "New Crime," 330; *BSR,* 19; *Liberator,* June 2; Mass. House Doc. 205, 10. The subscription paper survives in the Parker MSS, MHS: 21 persons pledged a total of $690 (see Maginnes, "Point of Honor," 120–122). Grimes was refused a donation by Abbott Lawrence but got $50 from Samuel A. Eliot, the only Massachusetts congressman who had voted for the Fugitive Slave Law; see Stevens, *Anthony Burns,* 64–65.
6. Dana, *Journal,* 630; Howe, *Letters and Journals,* 2: 268; Stevens, *Anthony Burns,* 66–67. John M. S. Williams, commission merchant and partner in the importing firm of Glidden & Williams, was, like Grimes, from Virginia; at this time he was working with Eli Thayer of Worcester in organizing and securing funding for the New England Emigrant Aid Company, which proposed to send Freesoilers to settle Kansas (Johnson, *Battle Cry of Freedom,* 11–12).
7. Elizabeth R. M. Cabot, MS diary, May 27, Rogers-Mason-Cabot Family Papers, MHS.
8. Mass. House Doc. 93, 31; House Doc. 205, 10–11; Parker, "New Crime," 303, 330; Stevens, *Anthony Burns,* 68–71. The manuscript bill of sale sur-

vives in the Theodore Parker Papers, Andover-Harvard Library.
9. Mass. House Doc. 205, 11.

ANTHONY BURNS

Epigraph: Doc Watson, *On Praying Ground,* Sugar Hill Music, 1990.
1. The record of the Virginia court, dated May 16, is given in Stevens, *Anthony Burns,* 252–253; and "The Case of Anthony Burns," 181–182; Conway, *Autobiography,* 1: 175; Landon, "Anthony Burns," 165.
2. Dickens, *American Notes,* chap. 9; Coppage and Tackitt, *Stafford County, Virginia,* 15; Jackson, *Free Negro Labor,* 203. Most of the information about Burns's early life comes from Stevens, *Anthony Burns,* 151–180, which is based on personal interviews with the subject.
3. Conway, *Autobiography,* 1: 91; Goolrick, *The Story of Stafford,* 5–15, 72–79.
4. Census records shed some light on Suttle and his family, but the principal sources of information, in addition to Stevens, are Myers, *Children of Pride,* 1696, and *Report . . . Relative to the Stafford Contested Election.*
5. Stevens, *Anthony Burns,* 157.
6. Moncure Conway's uncle, John Moncure, was among several Falmouth residents fined in October 1852 for allowing slaves to "go at large" and hire themselves: see Fitzgerald, *A Different Story,* 62.
7. Stevens, *Anthony Burns,* 164–165; *Liberator,* July 7.
8. Conway, *Autobiography,* 1: 101–124; d'Entremont, *Southern Emancipator,* 3–67.
9. Conway, *Autobiography,* 1: 109, 114.
10. D'Entremont, *Southern Emancipator,* 17.

SATURDAY, MAY 27

Epigraph: Bronson Alcott, MS journal for 1854, 55, Houghton Library.
1. Stevens, *Anthony Burns,* 27; *BSR,* 62. Subsequently Marshal Devens, Leonard Grimes, and Lydia Maria Child all tried, without success, to purchase Sims's freedom. He was liberated by Union troops during the Civil War. See Wilson, *Rise and Fall,* 2: 335; and Maginnes, "Point of Honor," 74–75n.
2. Alexandria *Gazette,* June 1, 1854, quoting an unidentified Northern newspaper.
3. *Liberator,* June 9; *BSR,* 16; Deveney, *Paschal Beverly Randolph,* 15–21. Hinckley, a radical feminist, was at this time a frequent attender at Bronson Alcott's "Conversations"; see *Liberator,* December 7, 1860. Spear was a co-worker with John Augustus, another BVC member, in temperance and prison reform. He published an autobiography in 1873 titled *Twenty Years on the Wing: Brief Narrative of My Travels and Labors as a Missionary Sent Forth and Sustained by the Association of Beneficents in Spirit Land.* See Perry, *Radical Abolitionism,* 218–222.

AUTOPSY

Epigraphs: Longfellow, journal, quoted in Samuel Longfellow, *Life,* 2: 271; Whitman, quoted in Traubell, *With Walt Whitman in Camden,* 3: 24.

1. *BSR,* 12, 16–17; Higginson, *CY,* 155n.
2. Higginson, *CY,* 157. The examining physician, Dr. Charles H. Stedman, was a relative of Dana's and the Dana family doctor. He was elected to the state legislature that fall as a Know-Nothing. The foreman of the coroner's jury, Francis D. Stedman, an insurance salesman from Roxbury, was Dr. Stedman's older brother. Both are mentioned frequently in Dana's journal. Juror George H. Munroe, a reporter for the Boston *Herald,* was Higginson's source of information (*CY,* 156). William F. Channing, a nonpracticing physician and a cousin of Higginson's, tried to attend the inquest but was barred; he was told—or surmised—that the private nature of the inquest meant that additional arrests were contemplated (Channing to Higginson, May 30, Higginson Papers, BPL).
3. "Anthony Burns' Case." On May 31 Charles G. Davis, lawyer and BVC member, wrote to Higginson: "The coroner and his jury are favourable to us, and I think we can get from them a verdict of accidental homicide by the police"; Higginson Papers, BPL.
4. Testimony of Asaph A. Smith and William Cheswell, *Commonwealth,* June 7; *Liberator,* June 2; *BSR,* 16, 36.
5. Massachusetts averaged less than one homicide per year during the first half of the nineteenth century, and although the murder rate was up sharply in the 1850s (to 5.9 per year), no doctors had much experience with fatal knife or gunshot wounds; Lane, *Policing the City,* 199. The case against Hopewell, which seemed strong at the arraignment, subsequently collapsed, and the charges against him were dismissed, without explanation, on June 6 (*Commonwealth,* June 7).

LAW

Epigraph: Emerson, *Journals,* 14: 375.

1. Phillips, *The Constitution* and *Can Abolitionists Vote?;* Cover, *Justice Accused,* 149–154. The "covenant with death" slogan derives from Isaiah 28:18; as Allan Nevins points out, the Shakers' Mother Ann Lee had earlier applied it to the marital relation; *Ordeal: Fruits of Manifest Destiny,* 146.
2. Emerson, *Collected Works,* 2: 63, 188.
3. Ibid., 27; *Emerson's Antislavery Writings,* 7, 53, 73, 91. On Emerson and antislavery in general, see Gougeon, *Virtue's Hero.*
4. *Emerson's Antislavery Writings,* 57; *Journals,* 11: 412.
5. Webster, *Papers,* 7: 94. For Emerson's reaction see *Journals,* 11: 358–359. For Furness' appeal see Conway, *Autobiography,* 1: 226–228; and Webster, *Papers,* 7: 6–7, 11–12. Nevins (*Ordeal: A House Dividing,* 287) claims that

Furness was "one of many" to urge this course on Webster, but the evidence does not appear. Until March 7 Webster was known as a friend of the Wilmot Proviso; he was also reassuring his correspondents that the Union was in no imminent danger. For Furness' career see Geffen, "W. H. Furness"; and Still, *Underground Railroad,* 684–691. Furness' response to the Burns case is given in *Christian Duty.*

6. Seward, *Works,* 1: 51–93; *Emerson's Antislavery Writings,* 59. Elizabeth Cady Stanton had made precisely the same point in the preamble to the resolutions adopted at the 1848 Seneca Falls Women's Rights conference. See Corwin, *"Higher Law" Background,* for a sketch of natural law theory from Cicero to the U.S. Constitution.

7. *Emerson's Antislavery Writings,* 53; *Collected Works,* 1: 234, 199.

8. Emerson, *Collected Works,* 3: 117.

9. Emerson's position is not discontinuous from American Revolutionary thought: in 1777 Benjamin Hichborn of Boston said: "I define civil liberty to be not a 'government by laws,' made agreeable to charters, bills of rights or compacts, but a power existing in the people at large, at any time, for any cause, or for no cause, but their own sovereign pleasure, to alter or annihilate both the mode and essence to any former government, and adopt a new one in its stead"; quoted in Corwin, *"Higher Law" Background,* 88.

10. Thoreau, "Resistance to Civil Government," in *Reform Papers,* 63.

11. Emerson, *Collected Works,* 2: 155. Emerson often uses the word "edge" to imply the defining boundary of some state or quality: crises define (create or constitute) a hero by discovering the point beyond which the individual cannot be driven or will not go. Compare Emerson's comment in "Self-Reliance" on indiscriminate charity: "Your goodness must have some edge to it—else it is none"; *Collected Works,* 2: 30.

12. Thoreau likewise admired Higginson, but each was at first inclined to think the other an imitator of Emerson; see Edelstein, *Strange Enthusiasm,* 95–98.

13. Lebeaux, *Thoreau's Seasons,* 74.

14. Thoreau, "Resistance to Civil Government," 76.

15. Ibid., 73–74.

16. Thoreau, *Journal,* 6: 305, 315.

EXTEMPORIZED SCRIPTURE

Epigraph: Weiss, *Life and Correspondence of Parker,* 2: 137.

1. *Liberator,* June 2; *BSR,* 29; Weiss, *Life and Correspondence of Parker,* 2: 135.

2. Stevens, *Anthony Burns,* 61–62n.; Myers, *Children of Pride,* 37; Conway, *Autobiography,* 1: 175.

3. *BSR,* 37, 40; Ford, "Trial of Anthony Burns," 327; Horton and Horton, *Black Bostonians,* 110. For Smith, a member of the Vigilance Committee, see Daniels, *In Freedom's Birthplace,* 449.

4. *BSR,* 17, 28, 37; Ford, "Trial of Anthony Burns," 331–332; *Liberator,* June 2; Willis, *Alcott Memoirs,* 75.

5. Edward Everett, diary, May 28, MHS; Conway, *Autobiography,* 1: 177; Howard, *Conscience and Slavery,* 19. Although Adams signed Stowe's clerical petition against the Nebraska Bill, he was consistently proslavery, as he showed, for example, in his direction of the American Tract Society, which refused for years to publish anything of an antislavery character (Ripley, *Black Abolitionist Papers,* 4: 344n.; cf. Clarke, *Anti-Slavery Days,* 107–108; and Parker, "The Rights of Man," 380). George Washington Blagden, Phillips' neighbor and brother-in-law, offered no help on Saturday night when apprised of the mob threats on the Phillips home (Ford, "Trial of Anthony Burns," 332); for his proslavery views, see his *Remarks and Discourse on Slavery.*

6. All quotations from Parker in this chapter are from "New Crime," 250–256, which includes his remarks on Sunday, May 28. This "Lesson for the Day" is also given in *BSR,* 30–33. The manuscript is with Parker's sermon 746, "Another Sermon on War" (May 28), Parker Papers, Andover-Harvard Library.

THE CURTII

Epigraph: Curtis, *Memoir,* 1: 136; also quoted in Parker, *Trial,* 165.

1. Commager, *Theodore Parker,* 291–292.

2. Bearse, *Reminiscences,* 19; Ticknor, *Life,* 2: 287; Worcester *Daily Spy,* May 24. For Curtis' decision in *Sims,* see *Trial of Thomas Sims,* 39–47. It was Webster's dying wish that Curtis write the *History,* which he had hoped to write himself. G. T. Curtis was named for his uncle, the Harvard scholar and linguist George Ticknor, another member of Webster's inner circle and a major influence on both Curtis brothers. Of Ticknor, Dana said that he was "a bitter man, with no knowledge of human nature, and being out of politics, no knowledge of the man on the stage, and yet he directs [George Stillman] Hillard [another member of the Curtis clique], who has to bear the consequences" (*Journal,* 558). Hillard, Nathaniel Hawthorne's friend and attorney, was a prominent Whig leader and yet another fugitive slave commissioner. Because his wife was active in the Underground Railroad, however, he was unusually conflicted about his duties in this office (Clarke, *Anti-Slavery Days,* 83). See also Tyack, *George Ticknor.*

3. For B. R. Curtis, see Curtis, *Memoir,* vol. 1; Gillette, "Benjamin R. Curtis"; and Leach, "Benjamin Robbins Curtis." His approach to the law was precisely the reverse of Emerson's: "a good system of law," Curtis wrote in 1836, "must be at the same time so extensive as to apply to and govern all the existing relations between men in society; so stable and fixed, in all important principles, as to furnish *a certain* guide; and so flexible as to be capable of adaptation to the ever-changing forms into which property is

thrown by the unwearied enterprise and all-absorbing love of gain which distinguish our people" (*Memoir*, 1: 75). His legal concern for property affected his response to the Second Seminole War of the same year, which conflict he lamented because "[m]any towns have been burnt: men, women, and children murdered, negroes and plantations destroyed and robbed" (ibid., 73). For the Morris case, see ibid., 161–163 and 2: 172–190. One bar to the more severe charge in this case was the argument that free blacks were not citizens and so by definition could not commit treason.

4. Webster, *Papers*, 7: 83; *Proceedings of the Constitutional Meeting;* Parker, *Trial*, 165–166.
5. For "Med" (*Commonwealth v. Aves*), see Curtis, *Memoir*, 1: 85–89, 2: 69–92; Levy, *Law of the Commonwealth*, 62–68. See also Parker, *Trial;* and the chapter "Endings" in this volume.

Lewis Hayden

Epigraph: Whittier, letter to the editor, Boston *Daily Times*, May 30, reprinted in *Letters*, 2: 259.
1. Higginson, *CY*, 155; Maginnes, "Point of Honor," 129; Horton and Horton, *Black Bostonians*, 60. See Fellman, "Theodore Parker," 668–669, 674–675, for Parker's tolerant views on violence.
2. Boston *Daily Times*, May 29; Whittier, *Letters*, 2: 260.

Not for Sale

1. Mass. House Doc. 205. 11; Dana, *Remarks*, 20; statement of Hamilton Willis, in Parker, "New Crime," 329–331; E. G. Parker to Charles J. Lanman, May 30, Miscellaneous Bound, MHS.
2. Stevens, *Anthony Burns*, 69–71; *BSR*, 17, 19. Allen published a series of letters in the Boston *Post* on June 3, 7, and 10, purporting to speak for his "friends" Suttle and Brent; see also rejoinders in the *Daily Advertiser* and *Commonwealth* (June 8) and in *Liberator* (June 9). Allen enrolled in the Law School on June 2 (Cassidy and Simpson, *Henry Watkins Allen*, 40–43, 172). He later distinguished himself as the very capable Confederate governor of Louisiana.
3. See Parker's statement in the *Daily Advertiser*, May 30, and his "Note" appended to the second issue of *BSR*, 86.
4. Testimony of Leonard Grimes, Mass. House Doc. 205, 10–12.
5. J. G. Palfrey to E. G. Loring, May 28, Palfrey Papers, Houghton Library. Palfrey had been helpful in getting Loring appointed to the Law School; see Gatell, *John Gorham Palfrey*, 219–220.
6. Worcester *Daily Spy*, reprinted in *Liberator*, June 2; Higginson to S. May Jr., May 28, quoted in Ford, "Trial of Anthony Burns," 324–325.

7. Higginson to S. May Jr., May 28, in Ford, "Trial of Anthony Burns," 325.
8. Ibid.

MONDAY, MAY 29

Epigraph: Emerson, "Freedom" (1853), in *Complete Works,* 9: 198.

1. Mass. House Doc. 205, 12–13; Stevens, *Anthony Burns,* 153. Later that day, Grimes officiated at the delayed dedication of his new church; Levesque, "Black Boston," 516.
2. Whittier, *Letters,* 2: 258–259.
3. Ibid., 259–260. In publishing the letter, the *Times* editor simply noted that it was from Whittier, adding optimistically: "It explains itself"; Boston *Post,* May 31.

MONDAY SESSION

Epigraph: Alcott, MS journal for 1854, 55, Houghton Library.

1. *BSR,* 38–39, 43–44; Stevens, *Anthony Burns,* 80–83; Charles C. Jones Jr. to Rev. C. C. Jones, May 30, in Myers, *Children of Pride,* 37.
2. *BSR,* 39, 44–45; Stevens, *Anthony Burns,* 83–85; Mass. House Doc. 205, 26.
3. For biographical information on Hallett, see the entry in the *Dictionary of American Biography;* Clarke, *Anti-Slavery Days,* 106; Wilson, *Rise and Fall,* 2: 132–133, 338–339; Boutwell, *Reminiscences,* 1: 114–115, 124; Sumner, *Selected Letters,* 1: 187n.; and Harrington, "Nathaniel Prentice Banks," 630, 633. Hallett had been a federal slave commissioner in 1850 but reportedly refused to act in the Craft case (Parker, "New Crime," 292–293).

    In *Luther v. Borden* (7 Howard, 1), Hallett argued for an extreme version of popular sovereignty and the right of revolution; in conjunction with this case, he published a treatise, *The Right of the People to Establish Forms of Government* (1848). As defense attorney for the Dorrites, he had argued that martial law was unknown to the Constitution, yet as district attorney during the Boston slave cases, he had constantly pestered Secretary of War Jefferson Davis to call out the military (Davis, *Papers,* 5: 26–27; Mowry, *The Dorr War,* 90–93, 232–237; Dennison, *The Dorr War,* 141–170). In other words, Hallett's opinions were determined less by ideology than by political ambition. As Dana put it, "Hallett, the Dorr-ite, the slang-whanging radical, turned into the fiercest, and most despotic engine of power. But the higher you put him, the more he shows his tail"; *Journal,* 414.
4. "Case of Anthony Burns," 185; *BSR,* 45.
5. "Case of Anthony Burns," 185; *BSR,* 45. In American courts at this time the primary parties to a suit did not testify, on the grounds that their statements would be self-serving and of diminished probative value. The par-

ties were also being spared the temptation to lie. See Friedman, *A History of American Law,* 136.

6. "Case of Anthony Burns," 186; *BSR,* 45–46.
7. Burns's version of this interview is given in Stevens, *Anthony Burns,* 18–19; cf. 88n.
8. Suttle had learned of Burns's whereabouts by means of a letter Burns had sent to an unnamed brother in Alexandria, a letter carefully mailed by way of Canada, but including reference to his working for Coffin Pitts in Brattle Street (*BSR,* 15; cf. Stevens, *Anthony Burns,* 180n.). Hallett claimed to have knowledge of a letter written by Burns to his brother Joshua, dated March 24, from Richmond. Although this letter was never introduced into evidence (and may never have existed), it seems to have been the basis for the claimant's erroneous contention that the escape occurred on or after that date; see Hallett to L. A. Grimes, April 6, 1855, Miscellaneous Bound, MHS.
9. "Case of Anthony Burns," 186; *BSR,* 46; Stevens, *Anthony Burns,* 88–89.
10. Dana Papers, box 40, MHS.

CLAIMANT RESTS

Epigraph: Samuel Longfellow, *Life,* 2: 271.

1. "Case of Anthony Burns," 186–187; *BSR,* 45–46.
2. Atkinson to Dana, May 30, Dana Papers, MHS. According to Page's testimony, Butman had deputized him after declaring, "You are just the man I want." When Ellis asked for an explanation of the remark, E. G. Parker objected, and the witness did not reply (*BSR,* 47). Perhaps the qualification was that Page at that time served as second lieutenant in a militia company of light artillery (*Boston Almanac,* 154). Both Ellis and Atkinson seemed concerned about the legality of the arrest itself, which, in the "lying charge" of robbing a jewelry store, may have involved Butman and his men in the impersonation of Boston policemen. This point, however, was not pressed.
3. "Case of Anthony Burns," 187–188; *BSR,* 47.
4. Conway, *Autobiography,* 1: 176.
5. Ibid., 175; Morse, *Life and Letters of Holmes,* 1: 303.
6. Emerson, *Journals,* 11: 249; Morse, *Life and Letters of Holmes,* 1: 300–302; Holmes, "Oration," 77, 80. Emerson, Theodore Parker, Wendell Phillips, and Horace Greeley were among those who rebuked Holmes for this speech, delivered to the New England Society of New York in 1855: see Tilton, *Amiable Autocrat,* 224; and Gougeon, *Virtue's Hero,* 219–220.
7. Reprinted in *Liberator,* June 16 (the spelling of "Clure" has been corrected). Cluer had tried to gain access to the Court House in the immediate aftermath of the riot but was turned away by the police (*BSR,* 12, 16, 36). Coincidentally, he had testified in the Wilson murder case the day before (Boston *Post,* May 27). For Cluer's connection to Higginson, see Edelstein,

Strange Enthusiasm, 157; Jackson, *Account Book;* and *Liberator,* August 4. Ten years later, Cluer's temperance work led him into an official position with the Boston Police Department as a probation officer for dipsomaniacs. Along with fellow BVC members John Augustus and John M. Spear, he pioneered in the belief that alcoholism was better treated medically than penally (see Lane, *Policing the City,* 135–136).

8. Statement by Willis in Parker, "New Crime," 330–331; Ford, "Trial of Anthony Burns," 333.
9. *Commonwealth,* May 31.
10. Boston *Post,* May 30; *Commonwealth,* May 30; *Liberator,* June 2; Parker, "New Crime, 306. Emory Washburn, a prominent Worcester attorney, was a major disappointment to the reformers. He spent most of Monday closeted in the annual meeting of the Bible Society and never did act in the case except to commend the military; when Bowditch finally spoke to him about the writ, he found the governor "cold as an icicle"; Bowditch, *Life and Correspondence,* 1: 267.
11. *BSR,* 43.
12. "A friend of the slave" to Wendell Phillips, May 28, Phillips Papers, Houghton Library.
13. *Boston Evening Transcript,* May 29; Horton and Horton, *Black Bostonians,* 110. There were numerous gunshops in Dock Square in the North End, which was the scene, less than ten years later, of the next calling out of the state militia: to quell the draft riots of 1863 (see Lane, *Policing the City,* 133).

THE DEFENSE OPENS

Epigraph: BSR, 49.
1. Ellis' opening statement is given most fully in *BSR,* 48–56.
2. This insistence on the presumption of freedom certainly reflects Ellis' belief that Loring had prejudged the case. He knew of the judge's remarks to Phillips in Cambridge on Friday, and knew as well that he had written out a bill of sale on Saturday, which he could have done only in the belief that Suttle owned what he was selling.
3. *Emerson's Antislavery Writings,* 73, 87; Samuel Longfellow, *Life,* 2: 266; Sumner, *Selected Letters,* 1: 404.
4. Details in this and the following paragraphs are from Jones's testimony, *BSR,* 56–58; and "Case of Anthony Burns," 188–191.

RICHARD HILDRETH

Epigraph: Hildreth, *Despotism in America,* 9.
1. *Emerson's Antislavery Writings,* 74.
2. Stowe, *Uncle Tom's Cabin,* 515; Dickens, *Bleak House,* 77; Emerson, *Journals,* 8: 134.

3. Emerson, *Collected Works*, 2: 42; *Complete Works*, 10: 329.

4. Conway, *Autobiography*, 1: 219; Willis, *Alcott Memoirs*, 69.

5. Foner, *Free Soil*, 40–72. Hildreth, a lawyer and historian, was the author of *The Slave; or, Memoirs of Archy Moore* (1836), the first antislavery novel. At the time of the Burns trial he seems to have been employed as a reporter for Horace Greeley's New York *Tribune*; see Wilson, *Rise and Fall*, 2: 407.

6. Hildreth, *Despotism in America*, 29.

7. Ibid., 93.

8. Ibid., 35, 49.

9. Ibid., 56, 81, 82, 63.

10. Ibid., 99, 102–103; Herndon to Parker, February 16, 1856, in Newton, *Lincoln and Herndon*, 86.

11. O'Connor, *Lords of the Loom*, 106; Cody, *Life*, 40–42.

12. Hildreth, *Despotism in America*, 97, 7.

13. Thoreau, "Resistance to Civil Government," in *Reform Papers*, 89; Hildreth, *Despotism in America*, 8.

14. Stowell alludes to Steward's presence in his letter to Thomas Drew, June 4, Higginson Papers, BPL. On Steward, see the entry in the *Dictionary of American Biography*; and Roediger, "Ira Steward," who infers the influence of the antislavery movement on Steward's thought despite the absence of a clear biographical connection.

15. Hildreth, *Despotism in America*, 97–98; Edelstein, *Strange Enthusiasm*, 157, plausibly links Steward and Cluer, both of whom were concerned with the issue of "wage slavery."

17. Hildreth, *Despotism in America*, 170–171.

18. Ibid., 171. Hildreth's theory is in counterpoint to a very active movement at this time among Whig jurists to emphasize the stability of contracts. See, e.g., the popular treatise *The Law of Contracts* (1853) by E. G. Loring's Harvard colleague Theophilus Parsons.

MONEY

1. Hamilton Willis to the editors of the Boston *Atlas*, June 5, reprinted in Parker, "New Crime," 331; Howe, *Letters and Journals*, 2: 268; *Commonwealth*, June 8.

2. Cheever diary, May 30, MHS.

3. Ibid., May 26; Barnes, *Lady of Fashion*, 254–263; Richmond *Enquirer*, June 2.

TUESDAY, MAY 30

Epigraph: Anthony Burns, 95–96.

1. Ford, "Trial of Anthony Burns," 332.

2. Ibid.; *BSR*, 56–58; and "Case of Anthony Burns," 188–91. Hannah

Stevenson was Charles P. Curtis' sister-in-law; at the time of the Civil War she supported Walt Whitman's work in the army hospitals.

3. *BSR,* 58; "Case of Anthony Burns," 191; Stevens, *Anthony Burns,* 93–94.
4. *BSR,* 58–60; "Case of Anthony Burns," 191–194; Stevens, *Anthony Burns,* 94–95.
5. May to Higginson, May 30, Higginson Papers, BPL.
6. Myers, *Children of Pride,* 37–38.
7. Phillips, *Argument,* 34.
8. Richmond *Enquirer,* June 2.

TREASON

Epigraph: "Experiences During Many Years," 9: 627. Shillaber, author of the 1854 best-seller *The Sayings of Mrs. Partington,* was at this time the city reporter for the Boston *Post,* having succeeded Simon P. Hanscom, the agitator, who now worked for the *Commonwealth.* Shillaber was the leading spirit in a group of Boston writers including John T. Trowbridge, Benjamin Drew, and William D. O'Connor, each of whom wrote a book inspired by the Burns case. Trowbridge's *Neighbor Jackwood* (1856) and O'Connor's *Harrington* (1860) were novels; Drew's *The Refugee: A Northside View of Slavery* (1855) was an important documentary record of the lives of fugitive slaves in Canada. Drew was the cousin of the flamboyant Thomas Drew of the Worcester *Spy;* Trowbridge and O'Connor later had important connections with Walt Whitman.

1. S. Higginson, W. F. Channing, S. May Jr., Louisa Higginson—all May 30 to T. W. Higginson, Higginson Papers, BPL. The admonitions of Dana and Andrew are contained in Channing's letter.
2. Higginson to Maria Weston Chapman, November 30, December 7, 1854, Higginson Papers, BPL.
3. Forten, *Journal,* 35–36; Browning, *Complete Works,* 3: 160–170.
4. Browning, *Complete Works,* 3: 385. Cf. idem, "A Curse for a Nation," 3: 354–358.

POLITICS AND FORCE

1. Ela, *Ela vs. J. V. C. Smith,* 11, 13–14; *Liberator,* June 9.
2. Davis, *Jefferson Davis,* 2: 360–361; *Liberator,* June 9; Mason, 43, 105. Cooper, born in New Jersey and a graduate of West Point, held his position until the Civil War, at which time he took up the same rank and responsibilities in the Confederate Army.
3. Forten, *Journal,* 36. Parker wrote an important address, which he had hoped to deliver at the antislavery convention; it was later published in expanded form as "The Progress of America" and collected in *Rights of Man,* 196–249.

4. Ford, "Trial of Anthony Burns," 333; *Liberator,* June 9.
5. *Liberator,* June 9.

DANA'S ARGUMENT

Epigraph: Adams, *Richard Henry Dana,* 2: 138.
1. *BSR,* 61–62, 71; "Case of Anthony Burns," 194–195.
2. Dana's outline is in Dana Papers, MHS. For the text of Dana's summation, see *BSR,* 62–72; or Dana, *Speeches in Stirring Times,* 210–233.

THOMAS' ARGUMENT

Epigraph: The remark was offered in the Massachusetts legislature during the debate over the repeal of the antimiscegenation law. Thomas, described as a "leader of the Democratic party," was, in 1842, still a radical Jacksonian; Wilson, *Rise and Fall,* 1: 491.
1. Thomas' summation is given in *BSR,* 72–76.
2. Dana, *Journal,* 632.

CONSPIRACY

Epigraphs: Higginson Papers, BPL.
1. Parker, "New Crime," 291. For the Loring-Mann friendship, see Messerli, *Horace Mann,* who also gives the story of an 1848 visit of Loring and his wife to the Manns' home in West Newton, which suggests that the judge's affability had its limits: they left early to avoid taking tea with Miss Chloe Lee, a black student who was there as a boarder. Mrs. Mann's sister, Sophia Hawthorne, was shocked that she would *"oblige* your *guests* to tolerate her presence" (447).
2. Channing to Higginson, May 31, Higginson Papers, BPL. Channing added: "Loring can discharge the man if he wants to & I think he will."
3. Conway, *Autobiography,* 1: 176.
4. The episode is described in Mass. House Doc. 205, 32, and in Stevens, *Anthony Burns,* 60n. The assasination plot against Parker, omitted from these accounts, is given in an undated but contemporaneous note from C. M. Ellis to Parker, preserved at the Andover-Harvard Library in a bound volume of Parker's manuscript sermons for 1854. I thank Dean Grodzins for calling my attention to this item.
5. Weiss, *Life and Correspondence of Parker,* 2: 134.
6. See the *Commonwealth,* June 1, for an account of the Freesoil convention and the quotations from Hale, Bird, and Giddings, below.
7. *Liberator,* June 9; *Post,* June 2.
8. Ford, "Trial of Anthony Burns," 333–334.
9. *Liberator,* June 9 and 16; Myerson, *New England Transcendentalists,* 79–80;

Emerson, *Complete Works,* 10: 584. Emerson's attention may have come to rest on Whiting because he spoke in support of Alcott's position on the Bible.

10. *Liberator,* June 9; Emerson, *Letters,* 3: 306–307, 394; Wilson, *Rise and Fall,* 1: 640, 643. Stetson was not a member of the Vigilance Committee, but made donations to it (Jackson, *Account Book,* 23). Many of the men most active in the Burns case first made their commitment to antislavery during the Texas annexation issue, including Samuel Gridley Howe and Theodore Parker.

11. For the meetings, see the *Commonwealth* and the *Post,* June 1; for Freeman's visit to Loring, see Dana, *Remarks,* 24.

12. Dana, *Remarks,* 24; Phillips, *Argument,* 32; Parker, "New Crime," 303–304; Mass. House Doc. 205, 32.

13. Ela, *Ela vs. J. V. C. Smith,* 5–6; Bearse, *Reminiscences,* 4; Bowditch, *Life and Correspondence,* 1: 267. Hayes's connection to the BVC ought not to have been the profound secret it seems to have been: in 1851 he was indicted for his part in the Shadrach rescue (Collison, *Shadrach Minkins,* 146). Another police officer, John T. Lawton, was also a member of the BVC; see Bearse, *Reminiscences,* 4; Campbell, *The Slave Catchers,* 120; and *Boston Almanac,* 170.

14. Ela, *Ela vs. J. V. C. Smith,* 5–6, 15; Mass. House Doc. 205, 33.

15. Forten, *Journal,* 36–37.

"BAD FRIDAY": JUNE 2

Epigraph: Parker, "New Crime," 319.

1. Boston *Transcript,* June 3.
2. *BSR,* 76.
3. Ela, *Ela vs. J. V. C. Smith,* 14; *Liberator,* June 9.
4. *BSR,* 76; *Liberator,* June 9; Ela, *Ela vs. J. V. C. Smith,* 17; Parker, "New Crime," 283.
5. Ela, *Ela vs. J. V. C. Smith,* 6, 13.
6. Dana, *Journal,* 632–633; Dana, *Remarks,* 23; *BSR,* 76.
7. *BSR,* 77; *Liberator,* June 9.
8. *Liberator,* June 9; cf. Stevens, *Anthony Burns,* 114.
9. Ela, *Ela vs. J. V. C. Smith,* 3; *Boston Almanac,* 154.
10. Loring's decision is given in *BSR,* 80–84; and in Stevens, *Anthony Burns,* 114–123.

THE CORTÈGE

Epigraph: Dana, *Journal,* 633.

1. Swift, *Speech,* 9–10.
2. Dana, *Journal,* 633.

3. Ibid., 414, 633; Dana, MS journal of the Burns Case, Dana Papers, MHS, p. 13; Mass. House Doc. 205, 25.

4. Bearse, *Reminiscences,* 12–13.

5. Stevens, *Anthony Burns,* 274.

6. Ibid., 138; Dana, *Journal,* 635; Ela, *Ela vs. J. V. C. Smith,* 6, 13.

7. Stevens, *Anthony Burns,* 137–139.

8. *Liberator,* June 30; Stevens, *Anthony Burns,* 277–278. See Ela, *Ela vs. J. V. C. Smith,* 5–6, for his subsequent employment. In December 1860 Hayes was involved in the Tremont Temple riot; on that occasion the Constitutional Unionists, desperate to make peace with the South, tauntingly called him out as "nigger Hayes"; McFeely, *Frederick Douglass,* 210.

9. Stevens, *Anthony Burns,* 267.

10. For Pearson, who was also involved in the return of a slave in the 1846 "Ottoman" case, see Wilson, *Rise and Fall,* 2: 54, 57, 335; Bearse, *Reminiscences,* 26–28; and Bowditch, *Life and Correspondence,* 1: 219–224 (which contains some errors). William F. Channing to Higginson, May 31, Higginson Papers, BPL: "John H. Pierson [*sic*] heads the petition in the Merchants Exchange for the repeal of the fugitive slave law!" Nineteen hundred men signed the petition, "most of the men who supported [the Fugitive Slave Law] before," according to Parker (see Gara, *The Presidency of Franklin Pierce,* 108). The government got permission to use T Wharf from the wharfinger, Joseph Sampson, a Hunker Democrat, who was fired by the owners that evening; he was immediately rewarded for his cooperation, however, by an appointment to the Custom House. Lawrence is quoted in Pease and Pease, *The Fugitive Slave Law,* 43. Another conservative defector at this time was Samuel A. Eliot, the only Massachusetts congressman to vote for the 1850 Compromise: see S. G. Howe to Horace Mann, June 18, in *Letters and Journals,* 2: 270; and Stange, "From Treason to Antislavery Patriotism," 466–469, 482. The *Liberator,* June 9, opined: "It was everywhere apparent that an entire revolution in public sentiment had taken place since the rendition of Thomas Simms; and the most conservative men in the city at that time, appeared . . . to be foremost in denunciation of the inhuman fugitive slave law, and all the proceedings under it."

11. *BSR,* 77; Stevens, *Anthony Burns,* 146; Wilson, *Rise and Fall,* 2: 440; Ford, "Trial of Anthony Burns," 334; Sterling, *Ahead of Her Time,* 292–293; Bowditch, *Life and Correspondence,* 1: 268.

12. Unidentified newspaper clipping in A. B. Alcott, MS diary for 1854, June 2, Houghton Library. Hannah Stevenson was also present at this incident; see Cheney, *Reminiscences,* 105–106.

13. *Liberator,* June 9; *BSR,* 77.

14. Whittier, *Letters,* 2: 165–166, 262–263; Freedman, *William Douglas O'Connor,* 38. Signers of the Faneuil Hall petition are identified in an undated *Boston Daily Advertiser* clipping in Parker Scrapbook, BPL. The death

of Forester, wife of the celebrated missionary Adoniram Judson, is noticed in the *Post,* June 3.

15. *Liberator,* June 23. On Thomas Knox see *Liberator,* January 29, 1864, and March 10, 1865.

16. Letter of Ann W. Weston, June 5, from Weymouth, BPL.

17. Deborah Weston to "Caroline," June 6, from Weymouth, BPL.

18. Conway, "Mayflowerings," 556–557; Clarke, *Memorial and Biographical Sketches,* 38–39; *Post,* June 3.

19. *Liberator,* June 9; Stevens, *Anthony Burns,* 146–147.

20. Phillips, *Argument,* 31; Dana, *Remarks,* 24. The deputies, in addition to Butman, were John H. Riley, George T. Coolidge, Charles Godfrey, and William Black; *BSR,* 78.

21. Letter of Hamilton Willis in Parker, "New Crime," 331–332; Adams, *Richard Henry Dana,* 1: 306. Bowditch, *Life and Correspondence,* 1: 264; Boston *Post,* September 11, 1886.

22. Ela, *Ela vs. J. V. C. Smith,* 15.

23. *BSR,* 77, 85; Stevens, *Anthony Burns,* 146; Dana, *Journal,* 635.

24. *Liberator,* June 9.

25. Dana, *Journal,* 636.

26. L. M. D., "An Old Letter."

27. *BSR,* 79, 85; *Liberator,* June 9 and 16.

28. S. May Jr. to T. W. Higginson, June 2, Higginson Papers, BPL; Deborah Weston to Caroline, June 6, BPL.

29. Bowditch, *Life and Correspondence,* 1: 268; Boston *Post* and *Commonwealth,* June 3. The League was actually formed as a secret society complete with grips and passwords. Among its membership of more than 100 men were Henry Bowditch, the elder Samuel May, John L. Swift, John Andrew, and the brothers Albert G. and John W. Browne. They met and practiced abduction techniques every two weeks for some eighteen months and took lessons from pugilists and wrestlers, though they never actually had occasion to snatch a slave hunter. See Bowditch, *Life and Correspondence,* 1: 272–278; and Wilson, *Rise and Fall,* 2: 441–443.

30. *BSR,* 79.

31. Howe, *Letters and Journals,* 2: 270.

32. Forten, *Journal,* 1, 37.

33. A. B. Alcott, MS diary for 1854, June 2, Houghton Library.

34. For the singing of "Carry Me Back," see *Liberator,* June 9; and Parker, "New Crime," 308; this is evidently not the more familiar version credited to James A. Bland, the black songwriter (b. 1854), which was adopted in 1940 as Virginia's state song. Stevens, *Anthony Burns,* 135–136, 140–141; Davis, *Papers,* 5: 347.

35. Ela, *Ela vs. J. V. C. Smith,* 3–4 and passim; *Liberator,* June 16; Stevens, *Anthony Burns,* 149n.; Dana, *Journal,* 635 (where Boyd is misidentified); Elizabeth R. M. Cabot, diary, June 2, Rogers-Mason-Cabot Family Papers, MHS.

36. *BSR,* 79, 84–86; *Liberator,* June 9. The cannon was at last fired around 4:00, when the *Morris* sailed out of the harbor.

GOING HOME

Epigraphs: *Liberator*, June 23, and Hoar, *Autobiography,* 1: 180.
  1. G. Osgood to T. W. Higginson, June 6, Higginson Papers, BPL.
  2. Whittier, "The Rendition," in *Writings,* 3: 170–171.
  3. The major source for this episode is Adams, *Richard Henry Dana,* 1: 298–330, which relies on Dana's manuscript account, prepared in 1876 as a lecture, Dana Papers, MHS. See also Dana, *Journal,* 636–638; and R. H. Dana Sr. to Caleb S. Henry, June 5, Dana Papers, MHS.
  4. Benjamin "Cocky" Heath later worked as a Boston policeman. In 1860 Anson Burlingame supported his application to Annapolis; Burlingame to Navy Secretary Isaac Toucey, April 9, 1860, BPL.
  5. William Watson to R. H. Dana, June 9, Dana Papers, MHS.
  6. Barnes, *The Lady of Fashion,* 257, 260–261; Cheever diary, June 2, MHS; Horton and Horton, *Black Bostonians,* 65, 68.
  7. Boston *Post,* June 2 and 3; Lankevitch, *Boston,* 41. Ex-Mayor Quincy left the city this day "as early as possible to avoid the painful scene of a human creature restored to bondage by the arm of the law . . . Events indicative of discontents, which are at no distant period, if not removed, to be the source of irretrievable discords and dangers to the continuance of the Union"; diary entry quoted in Warren, *History of Harvard Law School,* 2: 195.
  8. Barnes, *Lady of Fashion,* 262–289; cf. Frothingham, *Edward Everett,* 373–380.

REPUBLICANS

Epigraph: Sumner, *Selected Letters,* 1: 307. Sumner is vulnerable to the same charge of anti-institutionalism brought by Stanley Elkins and others against the Transcendentalists. Put into the Senate in 1851 by a coalition of Freesoilers and Democrats (which fell apart soon afterward), he did not have a true party affiliation until he embraced the Republicans in 1855. In principle he advocated the formation of a Northern party of freedom as early as 1851 (ibid., 331), but the lack of interest in the slavery question between the Sims and Burns cases made that course impractical. When Sumner and Salmon P. Chase (another partyless man) reacted to the Nebraska Bill with the "Appeal of the Independent Democrats" in January 1854, antislavery politics were further radicalized and isolated from party machinery. The political response to the Burns case in Massachusetts was thus affected, if never very explicitly, by the need to provide Charles Sumner with some organized political base.

1. Whittier, *Letters,* 2: 261.
2. Whittier to Higginson, June 4, Higginson Papers, BPL.
3. Emerson, *Journals,* 14: 385 and 13: 327.
4. *Commonwealth,* June 9; Whittier to Robert C. Winthrop, June 10: "Nothing but the assurance from myself and other friends of peace that a great Northern movement was on foot prevented a fearful outbreak in your city in the case of Burns"; *Letters,* 2: 264.
5. Dana to E. Quincy in *Liberator,* June 16; R. H. Dana Sr. to Caleb S. Henry, June 5, Dana Papers, MHS; C. M. Ellis to E. Quincy in *Liberator,* June 16.
6. Emerson, *Letters,* 4: 449; *Emerson's Antislavery Writings,* xliii; Bronson Alcott, MS diary for 1854, June 5, Houghton Library.
7. Emerson, *Letters,* 4: 444–445, 447–449. Sumner had written to Emerson in 1851, but evidently got no response; Sumner, *Selected Letters,* 1: 333–334.
8. Emerson, *Letters,* 4: 451 and 8: 404–405; *Liberator,* June 30.
9. Whittier, *Letters,* 2: 266–267; Harrington, "Nathaniel Prentice Banks," 636; Emerson, *Letters,* 4: 451 and 8: 404n.; Nutt, *History of Worcester,* 1: 499; Nason and Russell, *Life and Public Services of Henry Wilson,* 116–119; Wilson, *Rise and Fall,* 2: 414–415. Wilson struck a nativist note in accepting the nomination, praising "the descendants of that sturdy Puritan race, which from the beginning of our history has ever been prompt and resolute in defense of liberty"; Abbott, *Cobbler in Congress,* 58.
10. G. F. Hoar, *Autobiography,* 1: 152; Wilson, *Rise and Fall,* 2: 415.

CARRIED BACK

Epigraphs: Anthony Burns, 184; Richmond *Enquirer,* quoted in Sherwin, *Prophet of Liberty,* 333. In the wake of the Burns case the *Enquirer* advocated economic retaliation in preparation for Southern independence; see Gara, *The Liberty Line,* 158–159.

1. Norfolk *Herald,* June 11, reprinted in the Alexandria *Gazette,* June 15. The deputies were also given a tour of the tobacco warehouses, where they were shown happy slaves, earning from two to four dollars a week "over work"— money they could apply to buying their own freedom, which, however, they didn't want; *Commonwealth,* June 12 and 19.
2. Alexandria *Gazette,* June 14; Stevens, *Anthony Burns,* 187–190. Stevens asserts that Lumpkin was present when Burns arrived, but Dana's journal makes it clear that he was actually in Boston at that time, hunting a slave he used to own, named Robinson, who had escaped in 1840 and was now working for Joshua B. Smith, the caterer; Dana, *Journal,* 639–641.
3. Suttle to Willis, June 27, Miscellaneous Bound, MHS; also in Stevens, *Anthony Burns,* 76–78.

4. H. W. Allen to L. A. Grimes, July 1, Miscellaneous Bound, MHS; Stevens, *Anthony Burns*, 78–79.

KNOW-NOTHINGS

Epigraph: Mayer, *The Republican Party*, 27.

1. Nason and Russell, *Life and Public Services of Henry Wilson*, 118–119, 139. Anbinder, *Nativism and Slavery*, 41–42, points out that before October 1854 the lodges were ostensibly a sort of fraternal order and only then took on the form of a political party.

2. Mulkern, *The Know-Nothing Party*, 75, 105; Purdy, "Portrait of a Know-Nothing Legislature," 88; Anbinder, *Nativism and Slavery*, 90–91; Congdon, *Reminiscences of a Journalist*, 146.

3. Anbinder, *Nativism and Slavery*, 91; Abbott, *Cobbler in Congress*, 59–60.

4. Quincy, *Speech Before State Whig Convention*, 4–8. The Whigs based their hopes in 1854 on the chance that the voters would regard them as the main institutional alternative to the Democrats, and tried to present themselves as opposed to the Kansas-Nebraska Act.

5. G. F. Hoar, *Autobiography*, 1: 189; Mulkern, *The Know-Nothing Party*, 76; Anbinder, *Nativism and Slavery*, 92–95.

6. *Liberator,* quoted in Anbinder, *Nativism and Slavery*, 92; Wilson, *Rise and Fall,* 2: 441. Charles Francis Adams added, "There has been no revolution so complete since the organization of government"; quoted in Mulkern, *The Know-Nothing Party*, 76.

7. Anbinder, *Nativism and Slavery*, 136; Nell, *Colored Patriots*, 11 (quotation); Horton and Horton, "Affirmation of Manhood," 148; Ripley, *Black Abolitionist Papers*, 3: 308–309. Their petition was denied when Attorney General John H. Clifford pointed out that the U.S. Constitution restricted the militia to "free, able-bodied, white male citizens"; *Liberator,* September 14, 1855.

8. *Dictionary of American Biography,* s.v. "Eddy"; Eddy, *The Commonwealth*, 65. One measure adopted by the Know-Nothing legislature made daily readings in the King James Version of the Bible mandatory in the state schools; Anbinder, *Nativism and Slavery*, 135–136.

9. Haynes, "A Know-Nothing Legislature," 175–187; Anbinder, *Nativism and Slavery*, 137. Mulkern, *The Know-Nothing Party*, 117–118, suggests, rightly, that the scandal emboldened the already formidable Freesoil wing of the party and strengthened Henry Wilson's efforts to divert attention from nativism to antislavery. See also Mulkern, "Scandal." For the Wilson quotation, see Nason and Russell, *Life of Henry Wilson*, 119; Theodore Parker agreed, calling this "the strongest antislavery legislative body that had ever been assembled in the country" (quoted in Wilson, *Rise and Fall*, 2: 415). For Stone, see Anbinder, 154. Seven members of the BVC were elected to the State House in the fall of 1854: David Bryant, Jonas Fitch, Charles W. Slack,

James W. Stone, John L. Swift, David Thayer, and Albert J. Wright; Anson Burlingame, another member, was elected to the U.S. House of Representatives, defeating Cotton Whig William Appleton.

10. Morris, *Free Men All,* 168–173; Siebert, "Underground Railroad," 40; Stevens, *Anthony Burns,* 49n. This measure helped to bring the Know-Nothing movement into disrepute in the South; see Rosenberg, "Personal Liberty Laws," 34. Samuel Sewall and George F. Hoar had sponsored similar bills in 1852 and 1853 but were blocked by Henry J. Gardner; Dana, *Remarks,* 25–26; cf. Robinson, *"Warrington" Pen-Portraits,* 55.

11. Mass. House Doc. 93, 1; Gardner, "To the Speaker," 2; Stevens, *Anthony Burns,* 218, 224.

12. See *Remarks; Journal,* 671–674; and "The Decision," all by Dana, and "The Removal of Judge Loring." Testimony and rulings in the Loring case (1854–1858) are conveniently gathered in Finkelman, *Fugitive Slaves and American Courts,* vol. 3. See also Cover, *Justice Accused,* 179–182.

13. "Recent Legislation in Massachusetts," 132; and "Right of the Jury." This act repudiated the reasoning of B. R. Curtis in *U.S. v. Robert Morris* (Curtis, *Memoir,* 2: 172–190). As might be expected, a number of lawyers opposed the measure, including such Freesoilers as E. R. Hoar (*Charge to the Grand Jury*) and G. F. Hoar (*Autobiography,* 1: 164).

14. Haynes, "A Know-Nothing Legislature"; Purdy, "Portrait of a Know-Nothing Legislature," 95–96; Baum, "Know-Nothingism," 963; Horton and Horton, *Black Bostonians,* 64, 75–76; *Liberator,* December 17, 1855.

CATHOLICS AND ANTI-CATHOLICS

Epigraphs: Savage, *Police Records,* 113; Patrick Donohoe, "The Election," Boston *Pilot,* November 25.

1. Boston *Post,* January 5, 1855.

2. Purdy, "Portrait of a Know-Nothing Legislature," 228–237; Anbinder, *Nativism and Slavery,* 37.

3. Handlin, *Boston's Immigrants,* 52, 124–150; Rice, *American Catholic Opinion,* 62–109; Osofsky, "Abolitionists, Irish Immigrants, and Dilemmas," 890–893, 908; Bean, "Puritan versus Celt"; Ryan, *Beyond the Ballot Box,* 130. Catholic opinion may be traced in the Boston *Pilot* ("the Irishman's Bible"), founded by Bishop Benedict J. Fenwick in 1829 and subsequently owned by Patrick Donohue, but after 1850 edited by a disciple of Orestes Brownson, Father John T. Roddan (Walsh, "Who Spoke for Boston's Irish?"; Handlin, *Boston's Immigrants,* 140; Ryan, 101). Many of Brownson's controversial writings are gathered in his *Works.* While individual Catholics responded to the slavery issue as they might, the position of the Church in America had been laid out in several conferences at Baltimore (including the First Plenary Council in 1852) by men much influenced by Bishop John England of the diocese including Georgia and the Carolinas.

His views, given in *Letters to the Hon. John Forsyth* (1840–41), were not materially different from those of John C. Calhoun, who was in his own right a major influence on Brownson.

4. Parker, "The Rights of Man," 341, 342, 363, 343, 356. Lincoln must have paid special attention to this sermon (which Parker certainly sent to Herndon), for in addition to the phrase "government of all, by all, for all" (given twice), it contains this passage: "There can be no national welfare without national unity of action. That cannot take place unless there is national unity of idea in fundamentals. Without this a nation is a 'house divided against itself'; of course it cannot stand" (362).

5. Ibid., 357–358. Parker's stand against the forces of exclusion and in favor of Catholic civil rights was genuine: he was alarmed, for example, by Wilson's connection with the Know-Nothings, and advised him to be, consistently, "a champion of justice to all men" and to remember that "Catholics are also men" (Weiss, *Life and Correspondence of Parker*, 2: 210; cf. Purdy, "Portrait of a Know-Nothing Legislature," 91–92; and Fellman, "Theodore Parker," 677–678, which overstates Parker's anti-Irish bigotry). For Parker's balanced view of the Know-Nothings, see his letter of February 22, 1855, to James Orton (Weiss, 2: 238) and *The Rights of Man*, 413–419.

6. In general, Brownson's critique of Parker (see, e.g., *Works*, 14: 541 and 17: 17–39) simply repeats the argument that signaled his own break with the Concord group: "Protestantism Ends in Transcendentalism," *Brownson's Quarterly Review*, 2 (July 1846): 369–399. On Brownson's standing in the Catholic community, see Connelly, *Visit of Gaetano Bedini to United States*, 47; the *Commonwealth*, May 30; and the Boston *Pilot*, November 5, 1853, which recounts the visit to Brownson's home in Chelsea of the papal nuncio Cardinal Gaetano Bedini.

7. Brownson, *Works*, 17: 14–15.

8. Fitzhugh, *Sociology for the South*, 60.

9. Parker, "The Rights of Man," 357; Burlingame, *Oration at Salem*, 16; cf. Anbinder, *Nativism and Slavery*, 45–46.

10. Suspicions about Catholic secrecy were, of course, essentially baseless, as the Know-Nothing Nunnery Committee found: Bishop Fitzpatrick openly and vigorously endorsed the condemnation by the Sixth Provincial Council in Baltimore of all secret societies; O'Connor, *The Boston Irish*, 67–68.

11. Emerson, *Complete Works*, 5: 47.

12. Native American Party, MS Records, AAS; Handlin, *Boston's Immigrants*, 199; Savage, *Police Records*, 113–116; *Commonwealth*, May 30; Mitchell, *The Paddy Camps*, 136–137; Anbinder, *Nativism and Slavery*, 28–29; Boston *Post*, January 1, 1855, quoted in Purdy, "Portrait of a Know-Nothing Legislature," 45. Purdy (46) points out that membership in the Worcester Know-Nothing Lodge went from 106 to 511 during the few days following Gabriel's appearance.

13. Foster, *The Rights of the Pulpit*, 5, 25. In the preface to *Leaves of Grass* (1855),

Walt Whitman said: "There will soon be no more priests. Their work is done. They will wait a while . . . perhaps a generation or two . . . dropping off by degrees. A superior breed shall take their place . . . the gangs of kosmos and prophets en masse shall take their place. A new order shall arise and they shall be the priests of man, and every man shall be his own priest" (xi). The influence of the Know-Nothings on the first two editions of *Leaves of Grass* is palpable: see Reynolds, *Walt Whitman's America,* 148–153.

14. Foster, *The Rights of the Pulpit,* 6.
15. Ibid., 6–7.
16. Ibid., 8, 9–10. Theodore Parker came to a similar conclusion, which, in its greater reach and canniness, helps to explain his condescension toward political parties; in 1859 he noted that, philosophically, the old Freesoil party or the Republican party "contemplates no direct benefit to the slave, only the defense of the white man in his national rights, or his conventional privileges"—yet men so motivated would eventually see that "they cannot defend the natural rights of freemen without destroying that Slavery which takes away the natural rights of a negro"; Weiss, *Life and Correspondence of Parker,* 2: 176.
17. Foster, *The Rights of the Pulpit,* 44–46.

WALT WHITMAN

Epigraph: Pennington, *The Fugitive Blacksmith,* xi.

1. Whitman quoted in Reynolds, *Walt Whitman's America,* 119–120, who notes that "beginning with the topic of slavery," the lines move on to "curses," closely paralleling, one might add, Elizabeth Barrett Browning's response.
2. Ibid., 120. In 1850 Whitman published four poems: two in March against the Compromise ("A Song for Certain Congressmen" and "Blood-Money," of which the second caught Garrison's attention: see Garrison, *Letters,* 4:19–20); one in April ("The House of Friends"), which attacked the Hunker supporters of the Compromise; and one in June ("Resurgemus"), which was subsequently included in *Leaves of Grass.* Rubin, *The Historic Whitman,* 247–252; Klammer, *Whitman, Slavery, and Leaves of Grass,* 75–82; Erkkila, *Whitman the Political Poet,* 53–59.
3. Whitman, quoted in Erkkila, *Whitman the Political Poet,* 46.
4. Zweig, *Walt Whitman,* 133; Erkkila, *Whitman the Political Poet,* 19.
5. Rubin, *The Historic Whitman,* 296–297; Zweig, *Walt Whitman,* 221–222.
6. On Pennington, see *Liberator,* June 2; Blackett, *Beating Against the Barriers,* 57–59; and Still, *The Underground Railroad,* 685–686. The close connection between Whitman's personal engagement with the topic of slavery and the discovery of his own powers as a poet is convincingly argued by Klammer in *Whitman, Slavery, and Leaves of Grass.*
7. Whitman, *Leaves of Grass,* 89–90.

8. While Whitman was writing his poem, Theodore Parker was reminding his audience that Benjamin R. Curtis had "declared the fugitive slaves 'a class of foreigners'"; Parker, "The Rights of Man," 384.

9. Both remarks appear in the *Spy,* June 13.

EMERSON'S PULPIT (WHITSUNDAY)

Epigraphs: Forten, *Journal,* 37–38; Parker, "New Crime," 321; and Clarke, *The Rendition of Anthony Burns,* 23.

1. Higginson, *Massachusetts in Mourning,* 3.
2. Ibid., 4–5.
3. Ibid., 8, 10.
4. Ibid., 12–13, 14.
5. Parker, "New Crime," 324, 318, 284, 322, 290–292, 318.
6. Ibid., 318.
7. Ibid., 319.
8. Ibid., 315.
9. Ibid., 301.
10. Newton, *Lincoln and Herndon,* 51–52, 72–73; Donald, *Lincoln's Herndon,* 54–55. The "New York speech" was "An Address on the Condition of America," delivered on May 12.

IF WE FEEL NOT

Epigraph: Frothingham, *Recollections,* 47.

1. Ibid., 49–50.
2. Emerson, *Collected Works,* 1: 7, 92; Frothingham, *Recollections,* 50.
3. Frothingham, *The New Commandment,* 7, 8, 14, 15.
4. Ibid., 16–17.
5. Ibid., 18.
6. A Layman, *The New Commandment,* 8. The sermon was attacked by others as well: see Boston *Post,* June 7: "We are anxiously waiting to see what sort of a church is to be built up here in Salem, upon the ruins of the Bible, the adoption of mob-law, abolitionism, and 'modern infidelity.'" Further rejoinders are in the Salem *Observer,* June 10; Salem *Gazette,* June 14; and Boston *Post,* June 16. For Frothingham's career, see Caruthers, *Octavius Brooks Frothingham.*
7. Clarke, *Memorial and Biographical Sketches,* 190–191; W. C. Gannett, *Ezra Stiles Gannett,* 299. For Gannett on the Fugitive Slave Law, see his *Thanksgiving for the Union* (1850); for Parker's rejoinder, see, Parker, "The Fugitive Slave Law," 143–152.
8. W. C. Gannett, *Ezra Stiles Gannett,* 288–290.
9. Ibid., 290.
10. Gannett, *Relation of the North to Slavery,* 6, 7, 9, 10.

11. Ibid., 12–15.
12. Ibid., 16–22.
13. Curtis, *Observations,* 3, 6.
14. Ibid., 7, 8–9.
15. Ibid., 10.
16. Ibid., 12.
17. Ibid., 12–13, 16.
18. Ibid., 17–18.
19. Ibid., 21–22. A reviewer of Gannett's sermon, writing in the *Liberator* (probably Garrison), was no less contemptuous of the minister's change of heart, calling the performance "morally as 'crooked as a Virginia fence'" (July 7). Yet it was effective with conservative Unitarians; see Stange, "From Treason to Antislavery Patriotism," 482.

FOURTH OF JULY

Epigraph: Douglass, *Papers,* 2: 192.
1. Thoreau, *Journal,* 6: 303–304, 314, 323.
2. Ibid., 325, 328; Mary Higginson, *Thomas Wentworth Higginson,* 147; Stone, quoted in Edelstein, *Strange Enthusiasm,* 171.
3. *Liberator,* June 16, 23; "Not with Idle Boasts of Freedom," written by "Carrie" for the Framingham gathering, in *Liberator,* July 7; "The Flaunting Lie," by Charles G. Halpine, published anonymously as "Hail to the Stars and Stripes" in the New York *Tribune,* June 13. Rubin (*The Historic Whitman,* 295) suggests this might have influenced Whitman's "Boston Ballad"; it certainly attracted much attention at the time and was often mistakenly attributed to Greeley himself. Halpine was a member of Benjamin Shillaber's circle. See Derby, *Fifty Years among Authors,* 426–430; and Robinson, *"Warrington" Pen-Portraits,* 530–531.
4. *Liberator,* July 7. The burning of the documents had been suggested to Garrison by Henry C. Wright; see *Liberator,* June 30.
5. Phillips, quoted in Bearse, *Reminiscences,* 13.
6. Ibid.; Conway, *Autobiography,* 1: 185; see also *Liberator,* July 14 and 28; *National Anti-Slavery Standard,* June 17 and August 12; Sterling, *Ahead of Her Time,* 293–294.
7. See Albrecht, "Conflict and Resolution," for a fine general reading of the speech and (179, 184–186) a more particular discussion of Thoreau's use of the Sims material.
8. Thoreau, "Slavery in Massachusetts," in *Reform Papers,* 104, 103.
9. Ibid., 91. Here and in the first three paragraphs of the speech, Thoreau refers elliptically to the Concord meeting on June 22, so that his slighting references to "politicians" must be taken to include Emerson.
10. Ibid., 96.
11. Ibid., 98. Boston attorney Peleg Chandler exposed a similar irony when he

published an explanation of the illegal conduct of the city government in establishing martial law. The Reverend Whittemore's *Trumpet and Universalist Magazine* commented: "It turns out, then, after all the cry about *law* and *order,* that the true law and order party of the 2d of June were the *citizens;* it turns out that the volunteer militia . . . were not only acting without law, but against law; it turns out that Gen. Edmands . . . either did not know what the law was, or else he willfully violated it"; quoted in *Liberator,* June 30.

12. Thoreau, "Slavery in Massachusetts," 108, 106, 108.
13. Ibid., 108–109.

LETTERS FROM HELL

Epigraph: Swift, *Speech,* 21.

1. Weiss, *Life and Correspondence of Parker,* 2: 142–143; Thoreau, *Journal,* 6: 387; Emerson, *Letters,* 4: 452–453.
2. Johnson, *Battle Cry of Freedom,* 52; Nutt, *History of Worcester,* 1: 499.
3. Mary Higginson, *Thomas Wentworth Higginson,* 68; *Liberator,* August 4; Edelstein, *Strange Enthusiasm,* 166; Forten, *Journal,* 45–46. Under the prohibitory law of 1852, warrants against "rumsellers" would be issued on the complaint—often the very vague complaint—of three citizens, whereupon the sheriff would search and seize, destroying any liquor found. At the time of his arrest, Stowell had personally instituted between 70 and 90 of the 115 such actions pending in the Worcester district (Stowell to Higginson, June 1, Higginson Papers, BPL). Lemuel Shaw in *Fisher v. McGirr* (1854) noted the lack of due process and compensation in these acts of confiscation and ruled portions of the statute unconstitutional. Property rights were to be protected; Shaw would not allow them to be overcome without trial by jury and rights of clear appeal. If radical reformers were suspicious of property rights, conservatives would acquiesce in extending these rights to property in human beings. See Lane, *Policing the City,* 88–90; Levy, *The Law of the Commonwealth,* 282–289.
4. Johnson, *Battle Cry of Freedom,* 53, 57.
5. Emerson, *Letters,* 4: 460, 461.
6. Dana, *The Bible in Schools,* 8; "Dastardly Outrage in Ellsworth, Me.," *Liberator,* October 27. Dana's references to "the old English Bible, the only Bible the English tongue recognizes" (3), points to an important nondoctrinal issue in the general controversy over the schools: that the Irish found the whole New England educational system oppresively English. As William Cardinal O'Connell, who grew up in Lowell, recalled, "The schools were to all intents and purposes organs of Protestant propaganda," and "English history, as taught to high-school pupils in those days, was pure British anti-Catholic propaganda" (*Recollections of Seventy Years,* 8, 9). There was considerable truth in the accusation. See also O'Connor, *The Boston Irish,* 80–81; and Anbinder, *Nativism and Slavery,* 25.

7. Burns to Dana, August 23, Dana Papers, MHS.

8. Stevens, *Anthony Burns,* 191, 193–194.

9. Ibid., 194–196, 198; *Liberator,* January 5, 1855. At auctions in Richmond in 1854 it was customary to display the slave for some time without any clothes at all: see, e.g., William Chambers, *Things As They Are in America* (1854), in Rose, *A Documentary History,* 148. Stevens, *Anthony Burns,* 191, also comments on this practice.

10. Stevens, *Anthony Burns,* 196–197.

11. Burns to Dana, ca. December 18, Houghton Library. The letter also appears in facsimile in Bartlett, *Wendell and Ann Phillips,* 110–111. "Brother Cole" is unidentified.

12. Stevens, *Anthony Burns,* 202; Stockwell to Grimes, February 11 and 17, 1855, Miscellaneous Bound, MHS.

13. Barry Papers, MHS.

14. Stevens, *Anthony Burns,* 209–214; quotation on 213.

15. Ibid., 214–215; New York *Tribune,* March 3, 1855, reprinted in *Liberator,* March 9, 1855; Maginnes, "Point of Honor," 20; Boston *Daily Advertiser,* March 8, 1855. The Reverend Edward Kirk, a Congregational minister, who had played no previous part in the Burns affair, monopolized this occasion to speak against Kansas-Nebraska. He approved of Burns's speech, however, and thought he had "the true oratorical ring in him, like that of some of the Indian orators"; Stevens, *Anthony Burns,* 215.

16. Dana, *Remarks;* Dana, *Journal,* 674.

17. Dana, *Journal,* 672–673; Stockwell (Brooklyn) to Grimes, March 15, 1855, Miscellaneous Bound, MHS; Boston *Post,* June 2; Stevens, *Anthony Burns,* 46n.

18. Dana, *Journal,* 673.

TRIALS

Epigraphs: Curtis, *Memoir,* 2: 211; Parker, *Trial,* 17.

1. The full text of the charge is in Curtis, *Memoir,* 2:205–212. Maginnes, in "Point of Honor," 247–272, and "The Case of the Court House Rioters," discusses the prosecutions in detail, drawing heavily on Hallett's contemporaneous correspondence with Caleb Cushing and Franklin Pierce.

2. Weiss, *Life and Correspondence of Parker,* 2: 147.

3. Parker, *Trial,* x–xi, 179–180; Parker, "The Rights of Man," 388; Curtis, *Memoir,* 1: 174; Higginson to Maria Weston Chapman, November 30, and Phillips to Higginson, June 14, Higginson Papers, BPL; also in Sherwin, *Prophet of Liberty,* 333–334; Stowell to Higginson, June 7 and undated, Higginson Papers, BPL; Edelstein, *Strange Enthusiasm,* 171–172; Weiss, *Life and Correspondence of Parker,* 2: 147.

4. Parker, *Trial,* xix–xx; Curtis, *Memoir,* 1: 177–178.

5. In MS Index to Journal O (Library of Congress), under the date October

24, Parker notes that he returned the last proof sheets and that "Little & Brown do not wish to put their name on the Title Page." The same document records publication on November 1; *Trial,* 2, 17, 18.

6. Parker, *Trial,* 29–30.
7. Ibid., 50, 112, 176–178, 213. "Every thing looks permanent until its secret is known"; Emerson, *Collected Works,* 2: 180.
8. Ibid., 68, 108–110.
9. Newton, *Lincoln and Herndon,* 77.
10. Weiss, *Life and Correspondence of Parker,* 2: 149.
11. Parker, *Trial,* 156–161.
12. Ibid., 168.
13. Ibid., 169–170.
14. In "New Crime" (268), Parker had said that "Office is transient nobility; money is permanent, heritable nobility." These were, in Parker's view of the America of his day, the direct and indirect dispensations of slavery. "Accordingly, slavery is the leading idea of America—the great American institution." This formulation helps us to see the political bearing of Transcendental anti-institutionalism and to appreciate the significance of Whitman's satire in linking monarchism and Boston commerce, in "A Boston Ballad."
15. Curtis, *Memoir,* 1: 5. The father, Benjamin Curtis, was the older half-brother of George Ticknor, uncle and adviser to B. R. and G. T. Curtis.
16. Catterall, *Judicial Cases,* 4: 484, 489–490.
17. Curtis, *Memoir,* 1: 25.
18. Ibid., 2: 86; also quoted by Parker in *Trial,* 159; Weiss, *Life and Correspondence of Parker,* 2: 385.

ENDINGS

1. Stevens, *Anthony Burns,* 216n.; cf. Edelstein, *Strange Enthusiasm,* 173; and Landon, "Anthony Burns," 165; Burns to Garrison, July 1858, in *Liberator,* August 13, 1858, reprinted in Ripley, *Black Abolitionist Papers,* 4: 395–396.
2. From 1856 through 1858, Burns sold 100 copies of Stevens' book per year: see Landon, "Anthony Burns," 165; and *Liberator,* September 17, 1858.
3. Stowe, *Uncle Tom's Cabin,* 516; Fletcher, *History of Oberlin College,* 533; Burns to Parker, January 13 and ca. February 1856, in Weiss, *Life and Correspondence of Parker,* 2: 151–152.
4. Oberlin *Evangelist,* July 18, 1855.
5. Notes by Don C. Seitz, Burns folder, Oberlin Archives. Burns to Phillips, [August 2, 1856], in Bartlett, *Wendell Phillips,* 115. Weiss, *Life and Correspondence of Parker,* 2: 151–152, reports the account of one who knew Burns at Oberlin: "The change that came over him in a short time was one of the most wonderful things I have ever witnessed. When it fairly dawned

on him that he *could* learn to read, his zeal to improve was unbounded. He was at his books the whole time."

6. Burns to Rev. John Clark, *Liberator,* May 9, 1856, reprinted in Stevens, *Anthony Burns,* 280–283.

7. Burns to R. H. Dana, July 9, 1859, Dana Papers, MHS; Landon, "Anthony Burns," 164; Burns to J. F. Clarke, [spring 1862], Houghton Library.

8. Undated news clipping in A. B. Alcott, MS diary for 1854, 67, Houghton Library; Landon, "Anthony Burns," 165.

9. Higginson to Maria Weston Chapman, November 30, Higginson Papers, BPL.

10. The principal descriptions of the Butman riot are Higginson, *CY,* 162–165; Edelstein, *Strange Enthusiasm,* 167–171; G. F. Hoar, *Autobiography,* 1: 182–185; Sterling, *Ahead of Her Time,* 294–296; and Mabee, *Black Freedom,* 311–313.

11. G. F. Hoar, *Autobiography,* 1: 183. The Burns affair and the Butman riot prompted Foster to write his first abolition tract: *Revolution the Only Remedy for Slavery* (1855).

12. Higginson, *CY,* 155–157; Maginnes, "Point of Honor," 249–250; Siebert, "Underground Railroad," 38.

13. Stowell, *Stowell Genealogy,* 410; Johnson, *Battle Cry of Freedom,* 174; Hinton, *John Brown and His Men,* 96–97; Minick, "Underground Railroad in Nebraska," 76; Connelley, "Col. Richard J. Hinton," 487–490 (quotation on 489).

14. Edelstein, *Strange Enthusiasm,* 192–194.

15. Ibid., 186, 237; Stowell, *Stowell Genealogy,* 410.

16. Higginson, *CY,* 204, 230; Edelstein, *Strange Enthusiasm,* 353, 181, 183–184, 187, 189, 196; Johnson, *Battle Cry of Freedom,* 166, 173–174.

17. Edelstein, *Strange Enthusiasm,* 199; Emerson, *Letters,* 5: 23. In September 1856 Emerson was "glad to see that the terror at disunion and anarchy is disappearing"; *Emerson's Antislavery Writings,* 115.

18. Higginson, *CY,* 229–234; Emerson, *Letters,* 8: 645, 647; *Journals,* 14: 334; E. T. Emerson, *Letters,* 1: 210–211.

19. Higginson, *CY,* 251; Edelstein, *Strange Enthusiasm,* 254–256; Forten, *Journal,* 154. General Saxton was an ardent abolitionist from Greenfield, Massachusetts. His father, Jonathan Ashley Saxton, contributed an article, "Prophecy—Transcendentalism—Progress" to the *Dial* in 1841 and sent a son, Rufus' brother, to Brook Farm. At the time of the Burns trial, Fowler was a classmate of Conway at the Divinity School, where his belief in spiritualism brought him into conflict with the authorities (Conway, *Autobiography,* 1: 182). His arrest for protesting the Burns trial is noted in the Boston *Post,* May 30; and *BSR,* 41. He was out of jail in time to address the Unitarian conference and the New England Anti-Slavery Convention and to advise Higginson on legal strategies (*Liberator,* June 9; Fowler to Higginson, June 30, Higginson Papers, BPL). Many active Burns

sympathizers were also active in the Port Royal movement during the Civil War. Dr. Thomas P. Knox, who had provided the coffin at the Burns demonstration on June 2, was hired at Fowler's suggestion as a contract surgeon and worked on Coosaw Island. He created a stir in 1865 when, impatient with the slow pace of change, he called General Saxton "head overseer of the slaves there"; *Liberator,* February 24, 1865. John Andrew was the chairman of the Educational Commission, to which his fellow BVC members Henry I. Bowditch and Edward Atkinson also belonged. The principal architect of the Port Royal movement was lawyer Edward L. Pierce, a Milton, Massachusetts, neighbor of Emerson's close friend John Murray Forbes, himself a crucial supporter of the movement. Pierce was the protégé and subsequently the biographer of Charles Sumner; in 1863 he was succeeded in his supervision of Port Royal by the Court House rioter A. G. Browne Jr., subsequently the biographer of Governor Andrew. Frank Bird and F. B. Sanborn successfully lobbied Andrew and Sumner to create the Freedman's Inquiry Commission, whose report, written in part by S. G. Howe, has been called a "Blueprint for Radical Reconstruction." For the history of the Port Royal movement, see Rose, *Rehearsal for Reconstruction;* and Abbott, *Cotton and Capital.*

20. Forten, *Journal,* 115–116, 119–120, 137, and passim.
21. Edelstein, *Strange Enthusiasm,* 270–279.
22. D'Entremont, *Southern Emancipator,* 87–88, 91–92; Conway, *Autobiography,* 1: 187–188, 190.
23. Conway, *Autobiography,* 1: 191–192.
24. Ibid., 234, 243.
25. Ibid., 340–343; d'Entremont, *Southern Emancipator,* 157–159.
26. Conway, *Autobiography,* 1: 344, 347–349; d'Entremont, *Southern Emancipator,* 161–163; Emerson, *Letters,* 9: 68–69. Emerson's lecture, with its endorsement of Conway's plan, was published in the *Atlantic Monthly* in April.
27. Whitman, *Prose Works,* 1: 32–33.
28. For Watkins, see the biographical sketches in Ripley, *Black Abolitionist Papers,* 4: 155–156; Douglass, *Papers,* 2: 442; Horton and Horton, *Black Bostonians,* 87; Watkins, "Hints," 7.
29. Ripley, *Black Abolitionist Papers,* 4: 227–229.
30. Douglass, *Life and Writings,* 2: 284–289.
31. Quarles, *Black Abolitionists,* 187, 189; see Higginson, *CY,* 217; and Weiss, *Life and Correspondence of Parker,* 2: 164, for evidence of his connection with Brown.
32. Harper, *A Brighter Coming Day,* 13, 44. A portion of what was evidently her first speech is given in Harper, 101, a commentary on the Burns case, castigating the North for being "base enough to do [the South's] shameful service."
33. Peterson, *"Doers of the Word,"* 17 and passim. See Watkins' "Essay on

Christianity," which was singled out for praise by William Wells Brown, *The Black Man,* 160, as early as 1863.

34. Curtis, *Memoir,* 1: 91; Clarke, *Antislavery Days,* 167–168.
35. Hopkins, *Dred Scott's Case,* 1–20, 27.
36. Ibid., 47–52.
37. Ibid., 61–76.
38. Curtis, *Memoir,* 1: 195.
39. Wilson, *Rise and Fall,* 2:523–533; Hopkins, *Dred Scott's Case,* 82–87. Characterizing one strand of Curtis' argument, Hopkins wrote: "If it were conceded that property rights in slaves were the same as other property rights, all sorts of legal anomalies would result" (87). For the text of the dissent, see Curtis, *Memoir,* 2: 213–305. Lincoln is supposed to have kept a copy of this document in his pocket during his debates with Stephen A. Douglas (ibid., 1: 354n.).
40. Curtis, *Memoir,* 1: 192–263, closely examines the reasoning in this dissent and the motives for his brother's resignation. For Herndon, see Newton, *Lincoln and Herndon,* 115. See also Sherwin, *Prophet of Liberty,* 367–377, esp. 371.
41. Curtis, *Memoir,* 1: 329–346, 350–366; Crouch, "Amos A. Lawrence," 46–58; Rosenberg, "Personal Liberty Laws," 41; Curtis, *Executive Power,* in *Memoir,* 2: 306–335; Ellis, *The Power of the Commander-in-Chief.*
42. Sumner to Dana, June 3, Dana Papers, MHS; Sumner to unidentified correspondent, June 3, Miscellaneous Bound, MHS; Sumner to T. Parker, June 7, in *Selected Letters,* 1: 411.
43. *Liberator,* June 9; Parker, "New Crime," 309n.; Bradford, "Vindication of Overseers," 389–397; Warren, *History of Harvard Law School,* 2: 196–200; R. Story, *The Forging of an Aristocracy,* 143; Gardner, "To the Speaker"; Mass. Senate Doc. 84; Hackett, *Life and Services of Richardson,* 48–52. Banks was the first Republican governor of Massachusetts.
44. Loring, "Remonstrance" and "To the Inhabitants."
45. Garrison, *Letters,* 4: 331n.; Hackett, *Life and Services of Richardson,* 47.
46. I have not been able to add much to the information given in Myers, *Children of Pride,* 1696.

AN EMERSONIAN EPILOGUE

Epigraph: Lawrence, *Studies in Classic American Literature,* in Wilson, *The Shock of Recognition,* 911.

1. *Emerson's Antislavery Writings,* 73.
2. Ibid., 103; Stowe, *Uncle Tom's Cabin,* 232.
3. *Emerson's Antislavery Writings,* 88; Emerson, *Journals,* 14: 385, 421; *Letters,* 5: 18.
4. Howe, *Letters and Journals,* 2: 404–405; Myers, *Children of Pride,* 1704.
5. *Emerson's Antislavery Writings,* 98–99.

6. Ibid., 96, 91.

7. Arthur M. Schlesinger Jr., Stanley Elkins, George Fredrickson, and Anne C. Rose in various ways fault Emerson and other Transcendentalists for not putting their shoulders to the antislavery wheel in a hearty and cooperative way; this "irresponsible" behavior in the face of political calamity is a consequence of their eccentric individualism on the one hand and of an apparently unwarranted suspicion of institutional remedies on the other. Len Gougeon and Joel Myerson identify some of the problems with this influential line of interpretation in their Introduction to *Emerson's Antislavery Writings* (liii–lvi). John Carlos Rowe, dissenting from Gougeon and Myerson, has recently given the old objection of the historians a surprising development: "More often than not, transcendentalism works to rationalize present wrongs than bring about actual social change"; *At Emerson's Tomb*, 40.

8. *Emerson's Antislavery Writings*, 102.

9. Ibid.

10. Sanborn, "Manuscript Diary," 214–215: "Mr. D[ana] thought government a divine institution—not resting on the consent of the governed." Dana, *Journal*, 666–667: "it is quite surprising to see these transcendentalists appearing well as men of the world."

11. *Emerson's Antislavery Writings*, 98.

12. Ibid., 98, 104.

13. Ibid., 104. Cf. "America is the idea of emancipation" (*Journals*, 11: 406). Parker: "Freedom is the great idea of politics; it is self-evident that 'all men are created equal'" ("New Crime," 267). Parker: "That is the idea of freedom. It appears in the Declaration of Independence; it reappears in the Preamble to the American Constitution, which aims 'to establish justice, insure domestic tranquility, provide for the common defense, promote the general welfare, and secure the blessings of liberty.' That is a religious idea; and when men pray for 'the reign of justice' and 'the kingdom of heaven,' to come on earth politically, I suppose they mean that there may be a commonwealth where every man has his natural rights of mind, body, and estate" ("The Rights of Man," 364).

BIBLIOGRAPHY

Abbott, Richard H. *Cobbler in Congress: The Life of Henry Wilson, 1812–1875.* Lexington: University Press of Kentucky, 1972.

——— *Cotton and Capital: Boston Businessmen and Antislavery Reform, 1854–1868.* Amherst: University of Massachusetts Press, 1991.

Adams, Charles Francis, Jr. *Richard Henry Dana: A Biography.* 2 vols. Boston: Houghton Mifflin, 1890.

Adams, Nehemiah. *A Southside View of Slavery.* Boston: T. R. Marvin, 1854.

Albrecht, Robert C. "Conflict and Resolution: 'Slavery in Massachusetts.'" *ESQ: A Journal of the American Renaissance* 19 (1973): 179–188.

Alcott, A. Bronson. *The Journals of Amos Bronson Alcott.* Edited by Odell Shepard. Boston: Little, Brown, 1938.

Anbinder, Tyler. *Nativism and Slavery: The Northern Know Nothings and the Politics of the 1850s.* New York: Oxford University Press, 1992.

Annual Report to the American Anti-Slavery Society by the Executive Committee, 1855. New York: American Antislavery Society, 1855.

"Anthony Burns' Case: Correcting Some Popular Errors of History." *Boston Daily Advertiser,* April 2, 1888.

Appleton, William. *Selections from the Diaries of William Appleton.* Boston: Privately printed, 1922.

Arendt, Hannah. *On Revolution.* New York: Viking, 1963.

Barnes, Eric Wollencott. *The Lady of Fashion: The Life and the Theatre of Anna Cora Mowatt.* New York: Charles Scribner's Sons, 1954.

Bartlett, Irving H. *Wendell Phillips: Brahmin Radical.* Boston: Beacon Press, 1961.

Baum, Dale. "Know-Nothingism and the Republican Majority in Massachusetts: The Political Realignment of the 1850s." *Journal of American History* 64 (1978): 959–986.

Bean, William Gleason. "Puritan versus Celt, 1850–1860." *New England Quarterly* 7 (1934): 70–89.

Bearse, Austin. *Reminiscences of Fugitive-Slave Days in Boston.* Boston: Warren Richardson, 1880.

Beecher, Edward. *The Papal Conspiracy Exposed and Protestantism Defended in the Light of Reason, History, and Scripture.* Boston: Stearns, 1855.

Bell, Howard H., ed. *Minutes of the Proceedings of the National Negro Conventions, 1830–1864.* New York: Arno, 1969.

Blackett, R. J. M. *Beating Against the Barriers: The Lives of Six Nineteenth-Century Afro-Americans.* Ithaca: Cornell University Press, 1986.

Blagden, G. W. *Remarks and Discourse on Slavery.* Boston: Ticknor, Reed, and Fields, 1854.

Blue, Frederick J. *The Free Soilers: Third Party Politics, 1848–54.* Urbana: University of Illinois Press, 1973.

The Boston Almanac for 1855. Boston: John P. Jewett for Damrell and Moore, 1854.

The Boston Slave Riot, and Trial of Anthony Burns. Containing the Report of the Faneuil Hall Meeting, the Murder of Batchelder; Theodore Parker's Lesson for the Day; Speeches of Counsel on Both Sides, Corrected by Themselves; Verbatim Report of Judge Loring's Decision; and a Detailed Account of the Embarkation. Boston: Fetridge, 1854; reprinted, Northbrook, Ill.: Metro Books, 1972. Second issue reprinted in Finkelman, *Fugitive Slaves,* 2: 343–428.

Boutwell, George S[ewall]. *Reminiscences of Sixty Years in Public Affairs.* 2 vols. New York: McClure, Phillips, 1902.

Bowditch, Vincent Y. *Life and Correspondence of Henry Ingersoll Bowditch.* 2 vols. Boston: Houghton Mifflin, 1902.

Bowditch, William I. *The Rendition of Anthony Burns.* Boston: Robert F. Wallcut, 1854. Reprinted in Finkelman, *Fugitive Slaves,* 2: 429–468.

Bradford, Samuel D. "Vindication of the Overseers of Harvard College." Pp. 389–397. In *Works of Samuel Dexter Bradford.* Boston: Phillips, Sampson, 1858.

Brown, William Wells. *The Black Man, His Antecedents, His Genius, and His Achievements.* 2nd ed. 1863; reprint, New York: Johnson Reprint, 1968.

——— *The Rising Sun; Or, The Antecedents and Advancement of the Colored Race.* Boston: A. G. Brown, 1874.

Browne, Albert Gallatin, Jr. *Sketch of the Official Life of John A. Andrew.* New York: Hurd and Houghton, 1868.

Browning, Elizabeth Barrett. "The Runaway Slave at Pilgrim's Point." In *The Complete Works of Elizabeth Barrett Browning.* New York: Thomas Y. Crowell, 1900. 3: 160–170.

Brownson, Orestes A. *The Works of Orestes A. Brownson.* Edited by Henry F. Brownson. 20 vols. New York: AMS Press, 1966.

Burlingame, Anson. *Oration by Hon. Anson Burlingame, Delivered at Salem, July 4, 1854.* Salem: Gazette Office, 1854.

Bush, Charles P. *The Fugitive Slave Law: A Sermon Preached in the Fourth Congregational Church, Norwich, Conn., June 25th 1854.* Norwich, Conn.: Woodworth & Perry, 1854.

Cabot, Elizabeth Rogers Mason. *More than Common Powers of Perception: The Diary of Elizabeth Rogers Mason Cabot.* Edited by P. A. M. Taylor. Boston: Beacon Press, 1991.

Campbell, Stanley W. *The Slave Catchers: Enforcement of the Fugitive Slave Law, 1850–1860.* Rev. ed. Chapel Hill: University of North Carolina, 1970.

Caruthers, J. Wade. *Octavius Brooks Frothingham: Gentle Radical.* University: University of Alabama Press, 1977.

"The Case of Anthony Burns." *Monthly Law Reporter* 17 (August 1854): 181–205.

Cassidy, Vincent H., and Amos E. Simpson. *Henry Watkins Allen of Louisiana.* Baton Rouge: Louisiana State University Press, 1964.

Catterall, Helen Tunnicliff, ed. *Judicial Cases Concerning American Slavery and the Negro.* 5 vols. Washington, D.C.: Carnegie Institution of Washington, 1932–1938.

Cheney, Ednah Dow. *Reminiscences of Ednah Dow Cheney.* Boston: Lee and Shepard, 1902.

Clarke, James Freeman. *Anti-Slavery Days.* 1883; reprint, Westport, Conn.: Negro Universities Press, 1970.

———— "The Antislavery Movement in Boston." In *The Memorial History of Boston.* Edited by Justin Winsor. 4 vols. Boston: James R. Osgood, 1882. 3: 369–400.

———— *Memorial and Biographical Sketches.* Boston: Houghton, Osgood, 1878.

———— *The Rendition of Anthony Burns. Its Causes and Consequences. A Discourse on Christian Politics . . . June 4, 1854.* Boston: Crosby, Nichols, 1854.

Cody, William F. *The Life of Hon. William F. Cody, Known as Buffalo Bill.* Lincoln: University of Nebraska Press, 1978.

Collison, Gary L. "The Boston Vigilance Committee: A Reconsideration." *Historical Journal of Massachusetts* 12 (1984): 104–16.

———— *Shadrach Minkins: From Fugitive Slave to Citizen.* Cambridge, Mass.: Harvard University Press, 1997.

Commager, Henry Steele. *Theodore Parker, Yankee Crusader.* 1936; reprint, Boston: Beacon Press, 1960.

Congdon, Charles T. *Reminiscences of a Journalist.* Boston: J. R. Osgood, 1880.

Connelley, William E. "Col. Richard J. Hinton." *Transactions of the Kansas State Historical Society* 7 (1901–02): 486–493.

Connelly, James F. *The Visit of Archbishop Gaetano Bedini to the United States of America (June 1853–February 1854).* Rome: Università Gregoriana, 1960.

Conway, Moncure Daniel. *Autobiography: Memories and Experiences.* 2 vols. Boston: Houghton Mifflin, 1904.

———— *The Golden Hour.* Boston: Ticknor and Fields, 1862.

———— "Mayflowerings." *Fraser's* 71 (May 1865): 556–557.

———— *The Rejected Stone; Or, Insurrection vs. Resurrection in America.* Boston: Walker, Wise, 1861.

Copp, Joseph A[ddison]. *American Liberty and Its Obligations: A Discourse for the Times, Delivered in the Broadway Church, Chelsea, Mass., Sabbath, July 2, 1854.* Boston: C. C. P. Moody, 1854.

Coppage, A. Maxim, and James W. Tackitt. *Stafford County, Virginia, 1800–1850.* Concord, Calif.: Privately printed, 1980.

Corwin, Edward S. *The "Higher Law" Background of American Constitutional Law.* Ithaca: Cornell University Press, 1955.

Cover, Robert M. *Justice Accused: Antislavery and the Judicial Process.* New Haven: Yale University Press, 1975.

[Craft, William.] *Running a Thousand Miles for Freedom; Or, The Escape of William and Ellen Craft from Slavery.* London: William Tweedie, 1860.

Crouch, Barry A. "Amos A. Lawrence and the Formation of the Constitutional Union Party: The Conservative Failure in 1860." *Historical Journal of Massachusetts* 8 (1980): 46–58.

Curry, Leonard P. *The Free Black in Urban America, 1800–1850: The Shadow of the Dream.* Chicago: University of Chicago Press, 1981.

Curtis, Benjamin R., Jr. *A Memoir of Benjamin Robbins Curtis with Some of His Professional and Miscellaneous Writings.* 2 vols. Boston: Little, Brown, 1879.

Curtis, George Ticknor. *Life of Daniel Webster.* New York: D. Appleton, 1870.

[————] *Observations on the Reverend Dr. Ezra Gannett's Sermon Entitled "Relation of the North to Slavery."* Boston: Redding, 1854.

———— *Two Letters to the Editor of the New Bedford Mercury.* Boston, 1854.

D., L. M. "An Old Letter [by Martha Russell]." *Boston Evening Transcript,* ca. January 10, 1900. Clipping in extra illustrated edition of Garrison and Garrison, *William Lloyd Garrison,* vol. 2 (MHS) between pp. 412–413.

Dana, Richard Henry, Jr. *The Bible in Schools. Argument of Richard H. Dana, Jr. . . .* Boston, [1854].

———— "The Decision Which Judge Loring Might Have Given." Boston *Daily Atlas,* June 22, 1854. Reprinted in Stevens, *Anthony Burns,* 254–261.

———— *The Journal of Richard Henry Dana, Jr.* Edited by Robert F. Lucid. 3 vols. Cambridge, Mass.: Harvard University Press, 1968.

———— *Remarks of Richard H. Dana, Jr., Esq., before the Committee on Federal Relations . . . March 5, 1855.* 1855; reprinted in Finkelman, *Fugitive Slaves,* 3: 45–72.

———— *Speeches in Stirring Times and Letters to a Son.* Edited by Richard Henry Dana III. Boston: Houghton Mifflin, 1910.

Daniels, John. *In Freedom's Birthplace: A Study of the Boston Negroes.* Boston: Houghton Mifflin, 1914.

Davis, Jefferson. *Jefferson Davis, Constitutionalist: His Letters, Papers and Speeches.* Edited by Dunbar Rowland. 4 vols. 1923; reprint, New York: AMS Press, 1973.

———— *The Papers of Jefferson Davis.* Vol. 5. Edited by Lynda Lasswell Crist and Mary Seaton Dix. Baton Rouge: Louisiana State University Press, 1985.

Dennison, George M. *The Dorr War: Republicanism on Trial, 1831–1861.* Lexington: University Press of Kentucky, 1976.

d'Entremont, John. *Southern Emancipator: Moncure Conway: The American Years, 1832–1865.* New York: Oxford University Press, 1987.

Derby, J. C. *Fifty Years among Authors—Books and Publishers.* New York: G. W. Carleton, 1884.

Deveney, John Patrick. *Paschal Beverly Randolph: A Nineteenth-Century Black American Spiritualist, Rosicrucian, and Sex Magician.* Albany: State University of New York Press, 1997.

Dickens, Charles. *American Notes.* 1842.

———. *Bleak House.* 1853; reprint, Boston: Houghton Mifflin, 1956.

Donald, David Herbert. *Charles Sumner and the Coming of the Civil War.* New York: Alfred A. Knopf, 1960.

——— *Lincoln's Herndon: A Biography.* Rev. ed. New York: Da Capo, 1989.

Douglass, Frederick. *The Frederick Douglass Papers.* Edited by John W. Blasingame. 5 vols. New Haven: Yale University Press, 1979–1992.

——— "Is It Right and Wise to Kill a Kidnapper?" *Frederick Douglass' Paper,* June 2, 1854; reprinted in *The Life and Writings,* 2: 284–289.

——— *The Life and Writings of Frederick Douglass.* Edited by Philip Foner. 4 vols. New York: International Publishers, 1950–1955.

——— *My Bondage and My Freedom.* 1855; reprint, Chicago: Johnson Publishing, 1970.

Drew, Benjamin. *The Refugee: A North-side View of Slavery.* 1855; reprint, Reading, Mass.: Addison-Wesley, 1969.

Eddy, Daniel C[larke]. *The Commonwealth: Political Rights of Ministers; A Sermon Preached on Fast Day, April 6, 1854. The Times, and The Men for the Times; Sermons Preached on Sabbath Days, June 11 & 18, 1854.* Boston: Dayton & Wentworth, 1854.

Edelstein, Tilden G. *Strange Enthusiasm: A Life of Thomas Wentworth Higginson.* New Haven: Yale University Press, 1968.

Ela, William H. *William H. Ela vs. J. V. C. Smith and als. Heard in Norfolk County Supreme Judicial Court, February Term, 1855.* 1855; reprinted in Finkelman, *Fugitive Slaves,* 3: 313–330.

[Ellis, Charles M.] *An Essay on Transcendentalism.* 1842. Edited by Walter Harding. Gainesville, Fla.: Scholars' Facsimiles & Reprints, 1954.

[———] *The Power of the Commander-in-Chief to Declare Martial Law, and Decree Emancipation: As Shown from B. R. Curtis. By Libertas.* Boston: A. Williams, 1862.

Emerson, Ellen Tucker. *The Letters of Ellen Tucker Emerson.* Edited by Edith E. W. Gregg. 2 vols. Kent, Ohio: Kent State University Press, 1982.

Emerson, Ralph Waldo. *The Collected Works of Ralph Waldo Emerson.* Edited by Joseph Slater and Douglas E. Wilson. 5 vols. to date. Cambridge, Mass.: Harvard University Press, 1971–.

——— *Complete Works of Ralph Waldo Emerson.* 12 vols. Boston: Houghton Mifflin, 1903–1904.

———— *Emerson's Antislavery Writings.* Edited by Len Gougeon and Joel Myerson. New Haven: Yale University Press, 1995.

———— *The Journals and Miscellaneous Notebooks of Ralph Waldo Emerson.* Edited by William H. Gilman, Ralph H. Orth, et al. 16 vols. Cambridge, Mass.: Harvard University Press, 1960–1982.

———— *The Letters of Ralph Waldo Emerson.* Edited by Ralph L. Rusk and Eleanor M. Tilton. 10 vols. New York: Columbia University Press, 1939–1995.

Erkkila, Betsy. *Whitman the Political Poet.* New York: Oxford University Press, 1989.

Fellman, Michael. "Theodore Parker and the Abolitionist Role in the 1850s." *Journal of American History* 61 (December 1974): 666–684.

Finkelman, Paul, ed. *Fugitive Slaves and American Courts: The Pamphlet Literature.* 4 vols. New York: Garland, 1988.

Finkenbine, Roy E. "Boston's Black Churches: Institutional Centers of the Antislavery Movement." In Jacobs, *Courage and Conscience,* 169–189.

Fitzgerald, Ruth Coder. *A Different Story: A Black History of Fredericksburg, Stafford and Spotsylvania, Virginia.* N.p.: Unicorn, 1979.

Fitzhugh, George. *Sociology for the South; Or, the Failure of Free Society.* 1854; reprinted in *Ante-Bellum Writings of George Fitzhugh and Hinton Rowan Helper on Slavery.* Edited by Harvey Wish. New York: Capricorn Books/G. P. Putnam's Sons, 1960.

Fletcher, Robert S. *A History of Oberlin College from Its Foundations through the Civil War.* 2 vols. Oberlin: Oberlin College Press, 1943.

Foner, Eric. *Free Soil, Free Labor, Free Men: The Ideology of the Republican Party before the Civil War.* New York: Oxford University Press, 1971.

Foner, Philip S., and George E. Walker, eds. *Proceedings of the Black State Conventions, 1840–1865.* 2 vols. Philadelphia: Temple University Press, 1980.

Ford, Worthington C. "Trial of Anthony Burns." *Proceedings of the Massachusetts Historical Society* 44 (January 1911): 322–334.

Forten, Charlotte. *The Journals of Charlotte L. Forten.* Edited by Ray Allen Billington. New York: Dryden Press, 1953.

Foster, Aaron. *Liberty, the Nation, the Occasion.* Greenfield, Mass.: C. J. J. Ingersoll, 1854.

Foster, Eden B. *The Rights of the Pulpit, and Perils of Freedom. Two Discourses Preached in Lowell, Sunday, June 25th, 1854.* Lowell: J. J. Judkins, 1854.

[Foster, Stephen S.] *Revolution the Only Remedy for Slavery.* New York: American Anti-Slavery Society, [1855].

Fredrickson, George. *The Inner Civil War: Northern Intellectuals and the Crisis of the Union.* New York: Harper & Row, 1965.

Freedman, Florence Bernstein. *William Douglas O'Connor: Walt Whitman's Chosen Knight.* Athens: Ohio State University Press, 1985.

Friedman, Lawrence J. *Gregarious Saints: Self and Community in American Abolitionism, 1830–1870.* Cambridge: Cambridge University Press, 1982.

Friedman, Lawrence M. *A History of American Law.* New York: Simon and Schuster, 1973.

Frothingham, O. B. *Gerrit Smith: A Biography.* New York: G. P. Putnam's Sons, 1878.

———— *The New Commandment: A Discourse Delivered in the North Church, Salem, on Sunday, June 4, 1854.* 2nd ed. Salem: Printed at the Observer Office, 1854.

———— *Recollections and Impressions, 1822–1890.* New York, 1891.

———— *Theodore Parker.* Boston: J. R. Osgood, 1874.

Frothingham, Paul Revere. *Edward Everett: Orator and Statesman.* 1925; reprint, Port Washington, N.Y.: Kennikat Press, 1971.

Furness, W. H. *Christian Duty. Three Discourses . . . With Reference to the Recent Execution of the Fugitive Slave Law in Boston and New York.* Philadelphia: Merrihew and Thompson, 1854.

———— *A Discourse Occasioned by the Boston Fugitive Slave Case: Delivered in the First Congregational Unitarian Church, Philadelphia, April 17, 1851.* Philadelphia: Merrihew and Thompson, 1851.

———— *The Moving Power: A Discourse Delivered in the First Congregational Unitarian Church in Philadelphia . . . Feb. 9, 1851, after the Occurrence of a Fugitive Slave Case.* Philadelphia: Merrihew and Thompson, 1851.

Galpin, W. Freeman. "The Jerry Rescue." *New York History* 26 (January 1945): 19–34.

Gannett, Ezra Stiles. *Relation of the North to Slavery: A Discourse Preached in the Federal Street Meetinghouse, in Boston, on Sunday, June 11, 1854.* Boston: Crosby, Nichols, 1854.

———— *Thanksgiving for the Union: A Discourse Delivered in the Federal Street Meeting House, November 28, 1850.* Boston: Crosby, Nichols, 1850.

Gannett, William C. *Ezra Stiles Gannett: Unitarian Minister in Boston, 1824–1871.* Boston: Roberts Brothers, 1875.

Gara, Larry. *The Liberty Line: The Legend of the Underground Railroad.* Rev. ed. Lexington: University Press of Kentucky, 1996.

———— *The Presidency of Franklin Pierce.* Lawrence: University Press of Kansas, 1991.

Gardner, Henry J. "To the Speaker of the House . . . on E. G. Loring." House Document 302, May 10, 1855. Reprinted in Finkelman, *Fugitive Slaves,* 3: 245–256.

Garland, Joseph. "Jerome Van Crowninshield Smith." *New England Journal of Medicine* 283 (1970): 303–304.

Garrison, Wendell Phillips, and Francis Jackson Garrison. *William Lloyd Garrison, 1805–1879. The Story of His Life Told by His Children.* 3 vols. Boston: Houghton Mifflin, 1885–1889.

Garrison, William Lloyd. *The Letters of William Lloyd Garrison.* Edited by Walter M. Merrill. 6 vols. Cambridge, Mass.: Harvard University Press, 1971–1981.

Gatell, Frank Otto. *John Gorham Palfrey and the New England Conscience.* Cambridge, Mass.: Harvard University Press, 1963.

Geffen, Elizabeth M. "W. H. Furness, Philadelphia Antislavery Preacher." *Pennsylvania Magazine of History and Biography* 82 (July 1958): 259–292.

Gienapp, William E. *The Origins of the Republican Party, 1852–1856.* New York: Oxford University Press, 1987.

Gillette, William. "Benjamin R. Curtis." In *The Justices of the United States Supreme Court, 1789–1969: Their Lives and Major Opinions.* Edited by Leon Friedman and Fred L. Israel. New York: Chelsea House and R. R. Bowker, 1969. 2: 446–461.

Goodell, William. *Come-outerism. The Duty of Secession from a Corrupt Church.* New York: American Anti-Slavery Society, 1845.

Goolrick, John T. *The Story of Stafford: A Narrative History of Stafford County, Virginia.* Stafford, Va., 1976.

Gougeon, Len. *Virtue's Hero: Emerson, Antislavery, and Reform.* Athens: University of Georgia Press, 1990.

Gray, E[dgar] H[arkness]. *Assaults upon Freedom! Or, Kidnapping an Outrage upon Humanity and Abhorrent to God. A Discourse, Occasioned by the Rendition of Anthony Burns.* Shelburne Falls, Mass.: D. B. Gunn, 1854.

Greenough, Charles P. "Thomas Sims Papers." *Proceedings of the Massachusetts Historical Society* 55 (June 1922): 340–344.

Hackett, Frank Warren. *A Sketch of the Life and Public Services of William Adams Richardson.* Washington, D.C.: Privately printed, 1896.

Hall, Robert L. "Massachusetts Abolitionists Document the Slave Experience." In Jacobs, *Courage and Conscience,* 75–99.

Handlin, Oscar. *Boston's Immigrants.* Rev. ed. Cambridge, Mass.: Harvard University Press, 1959.

Harper, Frances Ellen Watkins. *A Brighter Coming Day: A Frances Ellen Watkins Harper Reader.* Edited by Frances Smith Foster. New York: Feminist Press, 1990.

Harrington, Fred Harvey. "Nathaniel Prentice Banks: A Study in Anti-Slavery Politics." *New England Quarterly* 9 (December 1936): 626–654.

Harris, Rev. S[amuel]. "Politics and the Pulpit." *New Englander* 12 (May 1854): 254–275.

Hayden, Robert C. *Faith, Culture, and Leadership: A History of the Black Church in Boston.* Boston: Boston Branch NAACP, 1983.

Haynes, George H. "A Know-Nothing Legislature." Pp. 175–187. In *Annual Report of the American Historical Association, 1896.* Washington, D.C.: Government Printing Office, 1897.

Hedrick, Joan D. *Harriet Beecher Stowe: A Life.* New York: Oxford University Press, 1994.

Higginson, Mary Thacher. *Thomas Wentworth Higginson: The Story of His Life.* 1914; reprint, Port Washington, NY: Kennikat Press, n.d.

Higginson, T. W. "African Proverbial Philosophy." *Putnam's Monthly Magazine* 4 (October 1854): 362–371.

——— *Cheerful Yesterdays.* Boston: Houghton Mifflin, 1898.

———— *Letters and Journals of Thomas Wentworth Higginson, 1846–1906.* Edited by Mary Thacher Higginson. Boston: Houghton Mifflin, 1921.

———— *Margaret Fuller Ossoli.* 1884; reprint, New York: Chelsea House, 1981.

———— *Massachusetts in Mourning. A Sermon Preached in Worcester . . . June 4, 1854.* Boston: James Munroe, 1854.

Hildreth, Richard. *Despotism in America: An Inquiry into the Nature, Results, and Legal Basis of the Slave-holding System in the United States.* 1854; reprint, New York: Negro Universities Press, 1968.

Hinton, Richard J. *John Brown and His Men.* 1894; reprint, New York: Arno Press, 1968.

Hoar, E. R. *Charge to the Grand Jury, at the July Term of the Municipal Court, in Boston, 1854.* 1854; reprinted in Finkelman, *Fugitive Slaves*, 2: 469–490.

Hoar, George F. *Autobiography of Seventy Years.* 2 vols. New York: Scribner's, 1903.

Hodgman, E[dwin] R[uthven]. *The Present Position of Our Country, and The Duty of the Patriot and Christian. A Discourse Delivered June 11, 1854, in the Evangelical Congregational Church, Lunenburg, Mass.* Fitchburg, Mass.: E. & J. F. D. Garfield, 1854.

Holli, Melvin G., and Peter d'A. Jones, eds. *Biographical Dictionary of American Mayors, 1820–1980: Big City Mayors.* Westport, Conn.: Greenwood Press, 1981.

Holmes, Oliver Wendell. "Oration, Semi-Centennial Celebration of the New England Society in the City of New York [1855]." In *The Autocrat's Miscellanies.* Edited by Albert Mordell. Pp. 58–82. New York: Twayne, 1959.

Hopkins, Pauline. "Famous Men of the Negro Race: Robert Morris." *Colored American Magazine* 3 (September 1901): 337–342.

Hopkins, Vincent C. *Dred Scott's Case.* 1951; reprint, New York: Athenaeum, 1976.

Horton, James Oliver, and Lois E. Horton. *Black Bostonians: Family Life and Community Struggle in the Antebellum North.* New York: Holmes and Meier, 1979.

———— "The Affirmation of Manhood: Black Garrisonians in Antebellum Boston." In Jacobs, *Courage and Conscience,* 127–153.

Howard, Victor B. *Conscience and Slavery: The Evangelistic Calvinist Domestic Missions, 1837–1861.* Kent, Ohio: Kent State University Press, 1990.

Howe, Julia Ward. *Julia Ward Howe, 1819–1910.* Edited by Laura Richards and Maud Howe Elliot. 2 vols. Boston: Houghton Mifflin, 1916.

———— *Reminiscences, 1819–1899.* 1899; reprint, New York: Negro University Press, 1969.

Howe, Samuel Gridley. *The Letters and Journals of Samuel Gridley Howe.* Edited by Laura E. Richards. 2 vols. Boston: Dana, Estes, 1906.

———— *The Refugees from Slavery in Canada West: Report to the Freedman's Inquiry Commission.* Boston: Wright and Potter, 1864.

Hurd, J. C. *The Law of Freedom and Bondage in the United States.* 2 vols. New York: D. Van Nostrand, 1858, 1862.

[Jackson, Francis.] *Account Book of Francis Jackson, Treasurer, The Vigilance Committee of Boston.* Facsimile. Boston: Bostonian Society, [1924].

Jackson, Luther Porter. *Free Negro Labor and Property Holding in Virginia, 1830–1860.* New York: D. Appleton–Century, 1942.

Jacobs, Donald M., ed. *Courage and Conscience: Black & White Abolitionists in Boston.* Bloomington: Indiana University Press, for the Boston Athenaeum, 1993.

———— "The Nineteenth-Century Struggle over Segregated Education in the Boston Schools." *Journal of Negro Education* 39 (Winter 1970): 76–85.

Johnson, Allen. "The Constitutionality of the Fugitive Slave Acts." *Yale Law Journal* 31 (1921): 161–182.

Johnson, Samuel. *The Crisis of Freedom. A Sermon Preached at the Free Church, in Lynn, on Sunday, June 11, 1854.* Boston: Crosby, Nichols, 1854.

———— *Lectures, Essays and Sermons.* Boston: Houghton Mifflin, 1883.

———— *Theodore Parker.* Chicago: C. H. Kerr, 1890.

Johnson, Samuel A. *The Battle Cry of Freedom: The New England Emigrant Aid Company in the Kansas Crusade.* Lawrence: University Press of Kansas, 1954.

Karcher, Carolyn L. *The First Woman in the Republic: A Cultural Biography of Lydia Maria Child.* Durham, N.C.: Duke University Press, 1994.

Klammer, Martin. *Whitman, Slavery, and the Emergence of Leaves of Grass.* University Park: Pennsylvania State University Press, 1995.

Lader, Lawrence. *The Bold Brahmins: New England's War Against Slavery, 1831–1863.* New York: E. P. Dutton, 1961.

Landon, Fred. "Anthony Burns in Canada." *Ontario Historical Society Papers and Records* 22 (1925): 523–531.

———— "The Negro Migration to Canada after 1850." *Journal of Negro History* 5 (January 1920): 22–36.

Lane, Roger. *Policing the City: Boston, 1822–1885.* Cambridge, Mass.: Harvard University Press, 1967.

Lankevich, George J. *Boston: A Chronological & Documentary History, 1602–1970.* Dobbs Ferry, N.Y.: Oceana Publications, 1974.

Lawson, Ellen N., and Marlene Merrill. "The Antebellum 'Talented Thousandth': Black College Students at Oberlin before the Civil War." *Journal of Negro Education* 52 (1983): 142–155.

A Layman [pseud.]. *The New Commandment: A Review of a Discourse Delivered . . . by the Rev. O. B. Frothingham.* Salem: Henry Whipple & Son, 1854.

Leach, Richard H. "Benjamin Robbins Curtis: Judicial Misfit." *New England Quarterly* 25 (December 1952): 507–523.

Lebeaux, Richard. *Thoreau's Seasons.* Amherst: University of Massachusetts Press, 1984.

Levesque, George August. "Black Boston: Negro Life in Garrison's Boston, 1800–1860." Ph.D. diss., SUNY Binghamton, 1976.

———— "Inherent Reformers—Inherited Orthodoxy: Black Baptists in Boston, 1800–1873." *Journal of Negro History* 60 (1975): 491–525.

Levy, Leonard. *The Law of the Commonwealth and Chief Justice Shaw.* 1957; reprint, New York: Oxford University Press, 1987.

———— "Sims' Case: The Fugitive Slave Law in Boston in 1851." *Journal of Negro History* 35 (January 1950): 39–74.

Levy, Leonard, and Harlan B. Phillips. "The *Roberts* Case: Source of the 'Separate but Equal' Doctrine." *American Historical Review* 56 (April 1951): 510–518.

Litwack, Leon F. *North of Slavery: The Negro in the Free States, 1790–1860.* Chicago: University of Chicago Press, 1961.

Loguen, Jermain Wesley. *The Rev. J. W. Loguen: As a Slave and As a Freeman.* Syracuse: J. G. K. Truair, 1859.

Longfellow, Fanny Appleton. *Mrs. Longfellow: Selected Letters and Journals.* Edited by Edward Wagenknecht. New York: Longmans, Green, 1956.

Longfellow, Henry Wadsworth. *The Complete Poetical Works of Henry Wadsworth Longfellow.* Boston: Houghton Mifflin, 1915.

———— *The Letters of Henry Wadsworth Longfellow.* Edited by Andrew T. Hilen. 6 vols. Cambridge, Mass.: Harvard University Press, 1966–1982.

Longfellow, Samuel. *Life of Henry Wadsworth Longfellow.* 2 vols. Boston: Ticknor, 1886.

Lord, Nathan. *A Letter of Inquiry to Ministers of the Gospel of all Denominations, on Slavery.* Boston: Fetridge, 1854.

Loring, Edward Greely. "Remonstrance and Protest of Edward G. Loring." House Document 63, February 9, 1855. Reprinted in Finkelman, *Fugitive Slaves,* 3: 155–159.

———— "To the Inhabitants of the County of Suffolk." March 27, 1858. Newspaper clipping, reprinted in Finkelman, *Fugitive Slaves,* 3: 243.

Lyman, Theodore. "Memoir of George Robert Russell." *Publications of the Massachusetts Historical Society* 18 (December 1880): 280–281.

Mabee, Carleton. *Black Freedom: The Nonviolent Abolitionists from 1830 through the Civil War.* London: Macmillan, 1970.

Maginnes, David R[ussell]. "The Case of the Court House Rioters in the Rendition of the Fugitive Slave Anthony Burns, 1854." *Journal of Negro History* 56 (January 1971): 31–42.

———— "The Point of Honor: The Rendition of the Fugitive Slave Anthony Burns, Boston, 1854." Ph.D. diss., Columbia University, 1973.

Maizlish, Stephen E. "The Meaning of Nativism and the Crisis of the Union: The Know-Nothing Movement in the Antebellum North." In *Essays on American Antebellum Politics, 1840–1860.* Edited by Stephen E. Maizlish and John J. Kushma. College Station: Texas A & M University Press for University of Texas at Arlington, 1982.

March, Daniel. *The Crisis of Freedom: Remarks on the Duty which all Christian Men and Good Citizens Owe to their Country in the Present State of Public Affairs.* Nashua, N.H.: Dodge & Noyes, 1854.

Maro, P. Virgilius [pseud.]. *The Fugitive: An Epic Poem.* Boston: Fetridge, 1854.

Mason, Virginia. *The Public Life and Diplomatic Correspondence of James M. Mason.* New York and Washington, D.C.: Neale Publishing, 1906.

Massachusetts. House Document 93. "Committee on Federal Relations, Petitions for Removal of Loring," March 22, 1855. Reprinted in Finkelman, *Fugitive Slaves,* 3: 161–203.

———— House Document 205. "Joint Standing Committee on Federal Relations . . . on the Case of Loring," April 4, 1855. Reprinted in Finkelman, *Fugitive Slaves,* 3: 205–242.

———— Senate Document 84. "To Senate and House of Representatives. Statement of Gov. N. Banks," March 19, 1858. Reprinted in Finkelman, *Fugitive Slaves,* 3: 295–300.

May, Samuel J. *Some Recollections of Our Antislavery Conflict.* Boston: Fields, Osgood, 1869.

Mayer, George H. *The Republican Party, 1854–1964.* New York: Oxford University Press, 1964.

McFeely, William S. *Frederick Douglass.* New York: W. W. Norton, 1991.

Mellow, James R. *Nathaniel Hawthorne in His Times.* Boston: Houghton Mifflin, 1980.

Merrill, Walter M. *Against Wind and Tide: A Biography of Wm. Lloyd Garrison.* Cambridge, Mass.: Harvard University Press, 1963.

Messerli, Jonathan. *Horace Mann: A Biography.* New York: Alfred A. Knopf, 1972.

Minick, Alice A. "Underground Railroad in Nebraska." *Nebraska State Historical Society,* 2d ser., 2 (1898): 70–79.

Mitchell, Brian C. *The Paddy Camps: The Irish of Lowell, 1821–61.* Urbana: University of Illinois Press, 1988.

Morison, John H. *A Sermon Preached in the First Congregational Church . . . June 4, 1854.* Boston: Benjamin H. Greene, 1854.

Morris, Thomas. *Free Men All: The Personal Liberty Laws of the North, 1780–1861.* Baltimore: Johns Hopkins Press, 1974.

Morse, John T. *Life and Letters of Oliver Wendell Holmes.* 2 vols. 1896; reprint, New York: Chelsea House, 1980.

Mowry, Arthur May. *The Dorr War: The Constitutional Struggle in Rhode Island.* 1901; reprint, New York: Chelsea House, 1983.

Mulkern, John R. *The Know-Nothing Party in Massachusetts: The Rise and Fall of a People's Movement.* Boston: Northeastern University Press, 1990.

———— "Scandal behind the Convent Walls: The Know-Nothing Nunnery Committee of 1855." *Historical Journal of Massachusetts* 11 (1983): 22–34.

Myers, Robert M., ed. *The Children of Pride: A True Story of Georgia and the Civil War.* New Haven: Yale University Press, 1972.

Myerson, Joel. *The New England Transcendentalists and the Dial.* Rutherford, N.J.: Fairleigh Dickinson University Press, 1980.

Nason, Elias, and Thomas Russell. *The Life and Public Services of Henry Wilson.* Boston: B. B. Russell, 1876.

Nell, William C. *The Colored Patriots of the American Revolution.* Boston: R. F. Wallcut, 1855.

Nevins, Allen. *Ordeal of the Union: Fruits of Manifest Destiny, 1847–1852.* New York: Charles Scribner, 1947.

———— *Ordeal of the Union: A House Dividing, 1852–1857.* New York: Charles Scribner, 1947.

Newton, Joseph Fort. *Lincoln and Herndon.* Cedar Rapids, Iowa: Torch Press, 1910.

Nichols, Roy F. *Franklin Pierce: Young Hickory of the Granite Hills.* Rev. ed. Philadelphia: University of Pennsylvania Press, 1958.

Nogee, Joseph L. "The Prigg Case and Fugitive Slavery, 1842–1850." *Journal of Negro History* 39 (July 1954): 185–205.

Nutt, Charles. *History of Worcester and Its People.* 4 vols. New York: Lewis Historical Publishing, 1919.

O'Connell, Cardinal William. *Recollections of Seventy Years.* Boston: Houghton Mifflin, 1934.

O'Connor, Thomas H. *The Boston Irish: A Political History.* Boston: Northeastern University Press, 1995

———— *Lords of the Loom: The Cotton Whigs and the Coming of the Civil War.* New York: Scribner, 1968.

O'Connor, William Douglas. *Harrington: A Story of True Love.* 1860; reprint, New York: Johnson Reprint, 1970.

Official Report of the Debates and Proceedings in the State Convention. 3 vols. Boston: White and Potter, 1853.

Osofsky, Gilbert. "Abolitionists, Irish Immigrants, and the Dilemmas of Romantic Nationalism." *American Historical Review* 80 (1975): 889–912.

Parker, Edward G. *Reminiscences of Rufus Choate, the Great American Advocate.* New York: Mason Bros., 1860.

Parker, Theodore. *The Boston Kidnapping.* 1852; reprint, New York: Arno, 1969.

———— *The Collected Works of Theodore Parker.* 14 vols. Edited by Francis P. Cobbe. London: Trübner, 1863–1874.

———— "The Fugitive Slave Law." In Parker, *The Rights of Man in America,* 143–152.

———— "The New Crime against Humanity." In Parker, *The Rights of Man in America,* 250–332.

———— "The Rights of Man in America." In Parker, *The Rights of Man in America,* 333–396.

———— *The Rights of Man in America.* Edited by F. B. Sanborn. 1911; reprint, New York: Negro University Press, 1969.

———— *The Trial of Theodore Parker, for the "Misdemeanor" of a Speech in Faneuil Hall Against Kidnapping.* 1855; reprint, New York: Negro University Press, 1970.

Peabody, Andrew Preston. *Reform and Reformers. A Sermon Preached on Sunday Afternoon, June 11, 1854.* Portsmouth, N.H.: J. F. Shores, Jr., 1854.

Pease, Jane H., and William H. Pease. "Boston Garrisonians and the Problem of Frederick Douglass." *Canadian Journal of History* 2 (September 1967): 29–48.

———— *The Fugitive Slave Law and Anthony Burns: A Problem in Law Enforcement.* Philadelphia: J. B. Lippincott, 1975.

Pennington, James W. C. *The Fugitive Blacksmith.* 3rd ed. 1850; reprint, Westport, Conn.: Negro Universities Press, 1971.

Perry, Lewis. *Radical Abolitionism: Anarchy and the Government of God in Antislavery Thought.* Ithaca: Cornell University Press, 1973.

Peterson, Carla L. *"Doers of the Word": African-American Women Speakers and Writers in the North (1830–1880).* New York: Oxford University Press, 1995.

Phillips, Wendell. *Argument of Wendell Phillips, Esq., Against the Repeal of the Personal Liberty Law, before the Committee of the Legislature, Tuesday, January 29, 1861.* Boston: R. F. Wallcut, 1861.

———— *Argument of Wendell Phillips, Esq., Before the Committee on Federal Relations* . . . 1855; reprinted in Finkelman, *Fugitive Slaves*, 3: 1–43.

———— *Can Abolitionists Vote or Take Office Under the Constitution of the United States?* New York: American Antislavery Society, 1845.

———— *The Constitution a Pro-Slavery Compact* . . . 1844; reprint, New York: Negro Universities Press, 1969.

———— *Speeches, Lectures, and Letters.* 1863; reprint, New York: Negro University Press, 1968.

Pierce, Edward Lille. *Memoir and Letters of Charles Sumner.* 4 vols. Boston: Roberts Brothers, 1878–1893.

Pope, C. H. *Loring Genealogy.* Cambridge: Murray and Emery, 1917.

Porter, Dorothy B. "Sarah Parker Remond, Abolitionist and Physician." *Journal of Negro History* 20 (1935): 291–295.

Proceedings of the Colored National Convention, Held in . . . *Philadelphia, October 16th, 17th and 18th, 1855.* 1856; reprinted in Bell, *Minutes of the Proceedings of the National Negro Conventions, 1830–1864.*

Proceedings of the Constitutional Meeting at Faneuil Hall, November 26th, 1850. Boston: Beals and Greene, 1850.

Proceedings of the Worcester Disunion Convention, January 15–17, 1857. Boston: Privately printed, 1857.

Purdy, Virginia C. "Portrait of a Know-Nothing Legislature: The Massachusetts General Court of 1855." Ph.D. diss., George Washington University, 1970.

Quarles, Benjamin. *Black Abolitionists.* New York: Oxford University Press, 1969.

Quincy, Josiah, Sr. *Speech Delivered* . . . *Before the State Whig Convention, Assembled at the Music Hall, Boston, Aug. 16, 1854.* Boston: John Wilson & Son, 1854.

"Recent Legislation in Massachusetts." *Monthly Law Reporter*, n.s., 8 (July 1855): 121–143.

"The Removal of Judge Loring." *Monthly Law Reporter*, n.s., 8 (May 1855): 1–22.

Report of the Committee of Privileges and Elections Relative to the Stafford Contested Election. [Richmond, Va.,] 1850.

Report of the Proceedings at the Examination of Charles G. Davis, Esq., on a Charge of Aiding and Abetting in the Rescue of a Fugitive Slave. 1851; reprinted in Finkelman, *Fugitive Slaves,* 1: 573–616.

Reynolds, David S. *Walt Whitman's America: A Cultural Biography.* New York: Alfred A. Knopf, 1995.

Rice, Madeleine Hooke. *American Catholic Opinion in the Slavery Controversy.* New York: Columbia University Press, 1944.

"Right of the Jury to Judge of the Law." *Monthly Law Reporter,* n.s., 8 (July 1855): 176.

Right of Petition; New England Clergymen. Remarks of Messrs. Everett, Mason, Pettit, Douglas, Butler, Seward, Houston, Adams, Badger, on the Memorial from Some 3050 Clergymen of All Denominations and Sects in the Different States of New England, Remonstrating Against the Passage of the Nebraska Bill, Senate of the United States, March 14, 1854. Washington, D.C.: Buell & Blanchard, 1854.

Ripley, C. Peter., ed. *The Black Abolitionist Papers.* 4 vols. Chapel Hill: University of North Carolina Press, 1985–1991.

Robboy, Stanley J., and Anita W. Robboy. "Lewis Hayden: From Fugitive Slave to Statesman." *New England Quarterly* 46 (December 1973): 591–613.

Robinson, Mrs. William S. *"Warrington" Pen-Portraits.* Boston: Lee and Shepard, 1877.

Roediger, David. "Ira Steward and the Anti-Slavery Origins of American Eight-Hour Theory." *Labor History* 27 (1986): 410–426.

Rose, Anne C. *Transcendentalism as a Social Movement, 1830–1850.* New Haven: Yale University Press, 1981.

Rose, Willie Lee. *A Documentary History of Slavery in North America.* New York: Oxford University Press, 1976.

——— *Rehearsal for Reconstruction: The Port Royal Experiment.* Indianapolis: Bobbs-Merrill, 1964.

Rosenberg, Norman L. "Personal Liberty Laws and the Sectional Crisis: 1850–1861." *Civil War History* 17 (March 1971): 25–44.

Rowe, John Carlos. *At Emerson's Tomb: The Politics of Classic American Literature.* New York: Columbia University Press, 1997.

Rubin, Joseph Jay. *The Historic Whitman.* University Park: Pennsylvania State University Press, 1973.

Runyon, Randolph Paul. *Delia Webster and the Underground Railroad.* Lexington: University Press of Kentucky, 1996.

Russell, Martha. *Stories of New England Life.* 1854; reprint, Boston: John P. Jewett, 1857.

Ryan, Dennis P. *Beyond the Ballot Box: A Social History of the Boston Irish, 1845–1917.* Rutherford, N.J.: Fairleigh Dickinson University Press, 1983.

Sanborn, Franklin Benjamin. "Manuscript Diary of Franklin B. Sanborn." In *Transcendental Climate.* Edited by Kenneth W. Cameron. 3 vols. Hartford: Transcendental Books, 1963. 1: 205–243.

Savage, Edward H. *Police Records and Recollections; Or, Boston by Daylight and Gaslight for Two Hundred and Forty Years.* Boston: John P. Dale, 1873.

Schwartz, Harold. "Fugitive Slave Days in Boston." *New England Quarterly* 27 (June 1954): 191–212.

——— *Samuel Gridley Howe: Social Reformer, 1801–1876.* Cambridge, Mass.: Harvard University Press, 1956.

Seward, William H. *The Works of William H. Seward.* Edited by George E. Baker. 5 vols. Boston: Houghton Mifflin, 1887–1890.

Shapiro, Samuel. "Rendition of Anthony Burns." *Journal of Negro History* 44 (January 1959): 34–51.

——— *Richard Henry Dana, Jr., 1815–1882.* East Lansing: Michigan State University Press, 1961.

Sherwin, Oscar. *Prophet of Liberty: The Life and Times of Wendell Phillips.* New York: Bookman Associates, 1958.

Shillaber, Benjamin P. "Experiences During Many Years." *New England Magazine* 8 (June 1893): 511–525, (July 1893): 618–627, (August 1893): 719–724; 9 (September 1893): 88–95, (October 1893): 153–160, (December 1893): 529–533, (January 1894): 625–631; 10 (March 1894): 29–36, (April 1894): 247–256, (May 1894): 286–294.

Siebert, Wilbur H. "The Underground Railroad in Massachusetts." American Antiquarian Society *Proceedings,* n.s., 45 (April 1935): 25–100.

——— "The Vigilance Committee of Boston." *Proceedings of the Bostonian Society* 12 (1953): 23–45.

Simmons, Rev. William J., D.D. *Men of Mark: Eminent, Progressive and Rising.* 1887; reprint, New York: Arno, 1968.

Sperry, Earl E. *The Jerry Rescue.* Syracuse: Onondaga Historical Association, 1924.

Spooner, Lysander. *Collected Works.* Vol. 4: *Antislavery Writings.* Weston, Mass.: M & S Press, 1971.

——— *Essay on the Trial by Jury.* Boston: John P. Jewett, 1852.

Stange, Douglas. "Abolitionism as Treason: The Unitarian Elite Defends Law, Order, and the Union." *Harvard Library Bulletin* 28 (April 1980): 152–170.

——— "From Treason to Antislavery Patriotism: Unitarian Conservatives and the Fugitive Slave Law." *Harvard Library Bulletin* 25 (October 1977): 466–488.

——— *Patterns of Antislavery among American Unitarians, 1831–1860.* Rutherford, N.J.: Fairleigh Dickinson University Press, 1977.

Sterling, Dorothy. *Ahead of Her Time: Abby Kelley and the Politics of Anti-Slavery.* New York: W. W. Norton, 1991.

Stevens, Charles Emery. *Anthony Burns: A History.* Boston: John P. Jewett, 1856; reprints, New York: Negro University Press, 1969; Williamstown, Mass.: Corner House, 1973.

——— "The Anthony Burns Case." *Boston Daily Advertiser,* April 5, 1888.

Still, William. *The Underground Railroad.* 1871; reprint, Chicago: Johnson Publishing, 1970.

Stone, James W. *Removal of Judge Loring. Remarks of James W. Stone, of Boston, in* the *Massachusetts House of Representatives, April 13, 1855*. 1855; reprinted in Finkelman, *Fugitive Slaves*, 3: 73–86.

Story, Ronald. *The Forging of an Aristocracy: Harvard and the Boston Upper Class, 1800–1870*. Middletown: Wesleyan University Press, 1980.

Story, William Wetmore. *The Life and Letters of Joseph Story*. 2 vols. Boston: Little, Brown, 1851.

Stowe, Harriet Beecher. *The Key to Uncle Tom's Cabin*. 1853; reprint, New York: Arno, 1968.

——— *Uncle Tom's Cabin*. In *Harriet Beecher Stowe: Three Novels*. New York: Library of America, 1982.

Stowell, Martin. *An Exposition of the Secret Order of the Sons of Temperance, with facts in relation to secret societies generally*. West Brookfield, Mass.: Cooke and Chapin, 1848.

Stowell, William Henry Harrison. *Stowell Genealogy*. Rutland, Vt.: Tuttle, 1922.

Sumner, Charles. *Defense of Massachusetts: Speeches of Hon. Charles Sumner, on the Boston Memorial for the Repeal of the Fugitive Slave Bill . . . June 26 and 28, 1854*. Washington, D.C.: Buell & Blanchard, 1854.

——— *Final Protest for Himself and the Clergy of New England against Slavery in Kansas and Nebraska*. Washington, D.C.: Buell & Blanchard, 1854.

——— *The Selected Letters of Charles Sumner*. Edited by Beverly Wilson Palmer. 2 vols. Boston: Northeastern University Press, 1990.

Sweeney, Kevin. "Rum, Romanism, Representation, and Reform: Coalition Politics in Massachusetts, 1847–1853." *Civil War History* 22 (June 1976): 116–137.

Swift, John L. *Speech of John L. Swift, Esq., of Boston, on the Removal of E. G. Loring . . . Delivered in the Massachusetts House of Representatives, Tuesday, April 10, 1855*. 1855; reprinted in Finkelman, *Fugitive Slaves*, 3: 87–122.

Thomas, John L. *The Liberator: William Lloyd Garrison*. Boston: Little, Brown, 1963.

Thoreau, Henry David. *The Journal of Henry David Thoreau*. 14 vols. Boston: Houghton Mifflin, 1906.

——— *Reform Papers*. Edited by Wendell Glick. Princeton: Princeton University Press, 1973.

Ticknor, George. *Life, Letters, and Journals of George Ticknor*. [Edited by Anna Ticknor.] 2 vols. Boston: James R. Osgood, 1876.

Tiffany, Nina Moore. *Samuel E. Sewall: A Memoir*. Boston: Houghton Mifflin, 1898.

Tilton, Eleanor M. *Amiable Autocrat: A Biography of Dr. Oliver Wendell Holmes*. New York: Henry Schuman, 1947.

Traubell, Horace. *With Walt Whitman in Camden*. 3 vols. New York: Rowman and Littlefield, 1961.

Trial of Thomas Sims, on an Issue of Personal Liberty, on the Claim of James Potter, of Georgia, against Him, as an alleged Fugitive from Service. Arguments of Robert

Rantoul, Jr. and Charles G. Loring, With the Decision of George T. Curtis . . .
1851; reprinted in Finkelman, *Fugitive Slaves*, 1: 617–663.

Trowbridge, John Townsend. *My Own Story: With Recollections of Noted Persons.*
Boston: Houghton Mifflin, 1903.

———— *Neighbor Jackwood.* 1856; reprint, Upper Saddle River, N.J.: Gregg
Press, 1968.

Tyack, David B. *George Ticknor and the Boston Brahmins.* Cambridge, Mass.:
Harvard University Press, 1967.

Walsh, Francis R. "Who Spoke for Boston's Irish? The Boston *Pilot* in the
Nineteenth Century." *Journal of Ethnic Studies* 10 (1982): 21–36.

Ward, Samuel Ringgold. *Autobiography of a Fugitive Negro: His Anti-Slavery
Labors in the United States, Canada, & England.* 1855; reprint, Chicago:
Johnson Publishing, 1970.

Warren, Charles. *History of the Harvard Law School and of Early Legal Conditions
in America.* 3 vols. New York: Louis Publishing, 1908.

Watkins, Frances Ellen. *Poems on Miscellaneous Subjects.* Boston: J. B. Yerrinton,
1854.

Watkins, William J. "Destiny of the Colored Race." *Liberator,* December 5,
1851, p. 195.

———— "Hints to the Free People of Color." *Liberator,* January 9, 1852, p. 7.

———— *Our Rights as Men. An Address Delivered in Boston, before the Legislative
Committee on the Militia, February 24, 1853 . . . on behalf of Sixty-five Colored
Petitioners . . .* 1853; reprinted in *Negro Protest Pamphlets.* Edited by William
Loren Katz. New York: Arno, 1969.

Webster, Daniel. *The Papers of Daniel Webster: Correspondence.* Vol. 7:
1850–1852. Edited by Charles M. Wiltse and Michael J. Birkner. Hanover,
N.H.: University Press of New England, 1986.

Webster, William E. "Another Interesting Letter on the Anthony Burns
Meeting." *Boston Transcript,* June 3, 1911.

Weiss, John. *Life and Correspondence of Theodore Parker.* 2 vols. New York: D.
Appleton, 1864.

———— *Reform and Repeal . . . and Legal Anarchy . . .* Boston: Crosby, Nichols, 1854.

Wesley, Dorothy Porter. "Integration versus Separatism: William Cooper Nell's
Role in the Struggle for Equality." In Jacobs, *Courage and Conscience,*
207–224.

Whitman, Walt. *Leaves of Grass.* New York: Fowler & Wells, 1855.

———— *Prose Works.* Edited by Floyd Stovall. 2 vols. New York: New York
University Press, 1963.

Whitmore, William H., ed. *Inaugural Addresses of the Mayors of Boston.* Vol. 2:
From 1852 to 1867. Boston: Rockwell and Churchill, 1896.

Whittier, John Greenleaf. *The Letters of John Greenleaf Whittier.* Edited by John
B. Pickard. 3 vols. Cambridge, Mass.: Harvard University Press, 1975.

———— *The Writings of John Greenleaf Whittier.* 7 vols. Boston: Houghton
Mifflin, 1888.

Williams, George W. *A History of the Negro Race in America.* 2 vols. 1883; reprint, New York: Bergman, 1968.

Willis, Frederick L. H. *Alcott Memoirs.* Boston: Richard G. Badger, 1915.

Willson, E[dmund] B[urke]. *The Bad Friday: A Sermon Preached in the First Church, West Roxbury, June 4, 1854* . . . Boston: J. Wilson, 1854.

Wilson, Edmund, ed. *The Shock of Recognition.* New York: Modern Library, 1955.

Wilson, Forrest. *Crusader in Crinoline: The Life of Harriet Beecher Stowe.* Philadelphia: J. B. Lippincott, 1941.

Wilson, Henry. *History of the Rise and Fall of the Slave Power in America.* 3 vols. Boston: J. R. Osgood, 1872–1877.

Yacovone, Donald. *Samuel Joseph May and the Dilemmas of the Liberal Persuasion.* Philadelphia: Temple University Press, 1991.

York, Robert M. *George B. Cheever, Religious and Social Reformer, 1807–1890.* Orono: University of Maine Press, 1955.

Young, Joshua. *God Greater Than Man: A Sermon Preached June 11th After the Rendition of Anthony Burns.* Burlington: Samuel B. Nichols, 1854.

Zweig, Paul. *Walt Whitman: The Making of the Poet.* New York: Basic Books, 1984.

🔥 INDEX

Northwest Ordinance, 253
Nurse, Gilbert, 63

Oberlin College, 302–304
O'Connell, Daniel, 243
O'Connor, William Douglas, 356n
Olmsted, Frederick Law, 153
Onesimus, 89
Orr, John ("Gabriel"), 242, 248–249, 255
Osgood, George, 219–220
Otis, James, 11
Owen, Robert, 156

Page, Caleb, 134–135
Palfrey, John Gorham, 29, 120–122, 190
Palm, James, 108
Park, John C., 208
Parker, Edward Griffin, 4, 5–6, 75–76, 78, 79–80, 82, 83, 119–120, 130, 166, 183, 211–212, 235, 236
Parker, Isaac, 201, 299
Parker, Joel, 16
Parker, John, 109
Parker, Theodore, 1, 3–8, 10, 11, 16, 27, 30, 32, 46, 69, 74, 75, 83, 95, 118, 123, 128, 139, 146, 164, 175, 191, 196, 207, 208, 214, 240, 242, 267, 268, 270, 271, 286, 293, 304, 307, 309, 317, 320, 325, 327, 329, 330, 366n16; at Faneuil Hall, 54, 58–61, 64, 66; preaching of, 107–113, 244–245, 259, 261–265; on Loring, 113–115; on Curtis family, 115–117, 120, 297–298; and W. H. Herndon, 155–156, 265–266, 319; targeted by Hallett, 168–169; Brownson on, 245–246; writes to Burns, 303; *The New Crime Against Humanity*, 259, 261–265, 279; "The Progress of America," 356n3; *The Trial of Theodore Parker*, 294–298, 301

Parkman, John, 271
Parsons, Theophilus, 16, 355n18
Pearson, John H., 207, 211
Pennington, James W. C., 12, 253, 255; *Fugitive Blacksmith*, 325
Personal liberty laws, 34–35, 56, 240, 273, 305, 320. *See also* Latimer Law
Personal replevin, writ of, 28, 33–37, 59–60, 138, 193, 211
Phenix, Walter, 67, 93
Phillips, Ann, 70, 108
Phillips, Tom, 108
Phillips, Wendell, 8, 9–10, 18–19, 20, 28, 29, 32, 59, 63, 64, 66, 69–70, 73, 75, 108, 110, 129, 139, 167, 168, 173, 175, 196, 211, 243, 265, 279, 281, 293, 311, 325, 329, 330, 337n9, 340n9; attends hearings, 4, 7, 128, 164–165, 208; negotiates with Loring, 15–18; at Faneuil Hall, 54–58, 61; speaks to Burns, 205–206; agitates Loring's removal, 240, 280; at Framingham, 278, 280
Pierce, Edward L., 372n19
Pierce, Franklin, 16, 72, 106, 128, 129, 130, 168, 174–175, 177, 238, 293, 326, 329, 370n1
Pierce, T. J., 198
Pilot (Boston), 242, 364n3
Pindall, Edward, 43
Pine Street Antislavery Society, 290
Pitts, Coffin, 1, 16, 18, 20, 90, 205
Police, 62–63, 65–67, 71–72, 74, 77–78, 95, 108, 127, 138, 201, 212, 213, 216, 249, 358n13
Polk, James Knox, 129
Port Royal experiment, 310
Post (Boston), 92–93, 126, 129, 168–169, 171, 194, 216
Post (New York), 258
Price, E. Sewall, 94